HUMAN RELATIONS
Law Enforcement
in a Changing Community

Alan Coffey
Edward Eldefonso
Walter Hartinger

2nd EDITION
HUMAN RELATIONS
Law Enforcement
in a Changing Community

PRENTICE-HALL, INC., *Englewood Cliffs, New Jersey*

Library of Congress Cataloging in Publication Data

COFFEY, ALAN
   Human relations.

   Includes bibliographies and index.
   1. Public relations—Police. I. Eldefonso,
Edward, joint author. II. Hartinger, Walter, joint
author. III. Title.
HV7936.P8C62   1975   659.2'3632   75-17815
ISBN 0-13-445692-0

© 1976 by PRENTICE-HALL, INC.
Englewood Cliffs, New Jersey

Printed in the United States of America

10 9 8 7 6 5 4 3 2

PRENTICE-HALL INTERNATIONAL, INC., *London*
PRENTICE-HALL OF AUSTRALIA, PTY. LTD., *Sydney*
PRENTICE-HALL OF CANADA, LTD., *Toronto*
PRENTICE-HALL OF INDIA PRIVATE LIMITED, *New Delhi*
PRENTICE-HALL OF JAPAN, INC., *Tokyo*
PRENTICE-HALL OF SOUTHEAST ASIA (PTE.) LTD., *Singapore*

CONTENTS

v

3

SOCIAL PROBLEMS AND CONSTITUTIONAL GOVERNMENT:
Impact on Law Enforcement   71

4

THE PROBLEMS OF POLICE IMAGE IN A CHANGING COMMUNITY   96

2

EXPLORING RACIAL AND COMMUNITY TENSION
Minority Group Crime

5

SOME COMMENTS ON RACE AND PREJUDICE   135

6

EQUAL JUSTICE AND MINORITY GROUPS   158

7

THE ENFORCEMENT OF LAW DURING SOCIAL CHANGE AND COMMUNITY TENSION   182

8

SIGNIFICANCE OF ATTITUDE IN POLICE WORK   200

3

COMMUNITY RELATIONS: Programs for Prevention

9

SIGNS OF THE PROBLEMS 221

10

IMPLICATIONS OF GROUP BEHAVIOR FOR POLICE 243

11

LAW ENFORCEMENT IMPLICATIONS OF INTERGROUP AND INTERRACIAL RELATIONS 261

12

PREFACE

The question is often asked by many—including prospective law enforcement personnel as well as practitioners in the law enforcement field: "Why are policemen the 'recipients' of grievances ignored by those who control the lives of others"? The authors of this volume are of the opinion that such a query is proper. For it is true that when enough people with similar feelings assemble; when they share an awareness of being oppressed or blocked in their desire for a change in policy; when they feel depressed, deprived and frustrated; when they are unable to participate in the major decisions of a governing body that affects their whole lives; when they are exploited, suppressed, subjugated, and are aware of their subjugation, the conditions for striking out at the "enforcement arm" of the government, the *police*, are present. In this perspective, the police are *viewed*, unfortunately, as the ancillary aid to the status quo—to the "value"—maintaining processes operating as a "symbolic" agent of social control.

The *reaction* of police to mass demonstrations (disruptive or peaceful), group protests, campus unrest, or other "unattended grievances" (legitimate or "otherwise"), to a great extent, usually determines whether *predisposed beliefs* (i.e., perhaps beliefs about how "unfair" policemen "really" are—*unfairness* being defined as arrest, ect.), are *perceived as "valid."* For the individual citizens who are convinced that police are, say, unfair or brutal, will probably find it difficult to respect police goals—particularly if the unfairness or brutality is believed to be directed toward only certain minorities. As a practical matter, the *validity* of the belief may matter less than the *strength* of the belief. *The individual funcions on the basis of what is believed re-*

gardless of the validity of the belief. Situations however, may be created—such as provoking an arrest requiring physical restraint, thus solidifying a "belief." In other words, if police response to a situation is actually beyond the acceptable "boundaries" of professional police ethics or is *perceived* as such, the situation will rapidly polarize, resulting in antagonistic police-citizenry confrontation.

What does this all mean? It *appears* that police are, to use an old axiom, "damned if they do and damned if they don't." The point we are making here, and which we suggest throughout the volume, is simply that: *(1) The police must recognize that the capacity of a law enforcement agency to deal with crime depends to a large extent on its relationship with the citizenry, and, (2) The police understand and accept the fact that their constant visibility serves as reminders and symbols of societal expectations. In this role, they represent passive, potential and symbolic force.*

They are, therefore, regarded ambiguously by the people they serve and they may generate feelings of antipathy or both fear and awe.

The *first edition* of this volume truly reflected, we feel, the public's inconsistent expectations of the police role as well as the psychological environment of the policeman. The first edition also depicted the turmoil and strife of the 1960s, a condition which has declined (somewhat) in the middle 70s. The second edition of *Human Relations: Law Enforcement in a Changing Community* takes note of this salient change in our society as well as a change in the police role which reveals a concerted effort by police to anticipate and prevent disturbance of peace by being actively involved in programs to reduce general community tensions.

This second edition serves to suggest and define not only the problems from which police-community relations derive, but to develop appropriate avenues of solution for conflicts and tensions. It probes the emerging law enforcement concept of active involvement in community relations. It examines the historical and contemporary development of contributing community social forces and the problems presented to the implementation of effective enforcement of law. Dealing as it does with what is perhaps the most critical problem of law enforcement in the modern society, this study represents essential reading for all professionals in police work, as well as readers preparing to enter the field of law enforcement.

Although the second edition represents a *major* revision (i.e., material updated and expanded from 241 to more than 350 pages), we have retained the initial philosophical approach to the problem of police-community relations. *The initial interdisciplinary approach (i.e., psychological, sociological, and anthropological disciplines) to the subject continues to play a premoninant part in this volume.* An eclectic approach, we felt, will enable the reader to understand the many aspects of police relationship with the citizenry in different contexts.

Beginning with a portrait of traditional police practices and the community in transition, there is an historical discussion of the problem of riot and dissent. This is carried through to contemporary issues. The social problems and the reasons or contributing factors leading to a poor police image are examined, and possible solutions are developed in detail.

The second part of the work explores the subject of racial and community tension and minority group crime. It provides the law enforcement professional with a unique insight into minority-group problems relating to equal justice. It also offers incisive discussions of sociological change and community tension, and a valuable perspective of the psychology and significance of attitudes.

The third and concluding section of this book offers a development of programs for prevention of the tensions and dissent that arise in community relations. It details the warning signs of problems, outlines the implications of group behavior, traces intergroup and interracial human relations, and develops community relations programs, detailing their nature and purpose.

While retaining the law enforcement perspective, this book covers the entire range of social factors of importance to community relations.

Also included in the second edition are appendices germane to subjects discussed in the text. Although there will be detractors, we feel that the second edition of *Human Relations: Law Enforcement in a Changing Community* truly reflects police-community relations in the 1970s.

ACKNOWLEDGMENTS

With the usual proviso that they cannot be held accountable for either errors of omission or commission, the authors express their gratitude for the advice, counsel, and encouragement tendered by B. Earl Lewis, Professor, Department of Law Enforcement Education, DeAnza College and the Administration and Staff of the Santa Clara County Juvenile Probation Department, San Jose, California. Also, we wish to express our gratitude to the International Association Chiefs of Police, specifically Mr. Charles E. Higginbotham, Consultant, Professional Standards Division, for his generosity in permitting us to utilize some of the late N. A. Watson's excellent material on "Threats and Challenges in Police Work"; and the Los Angeles, San Francisco and Berkeley, California Police Departments for many of the photos used in this volume.

As far as the authors are concerned, acknowledgments are not complete without some mention of our wives and children. Actually, without their firm support and understanding, this volume, like the others we have written, would not have been possible, so to *Mildred Ann Eldefonso, Beverly May Coffey, and Patricia Hartinger, we express our gratitude and appreciation. We thank you.*

HUMAN RELATIONS
Law Enforcement
in a Changing Community

TRADITIONAL POLICE PRACTICES AND THE COMMUNITY IN TRANSITION:
Historical and Contemporary Aspects

PART 1

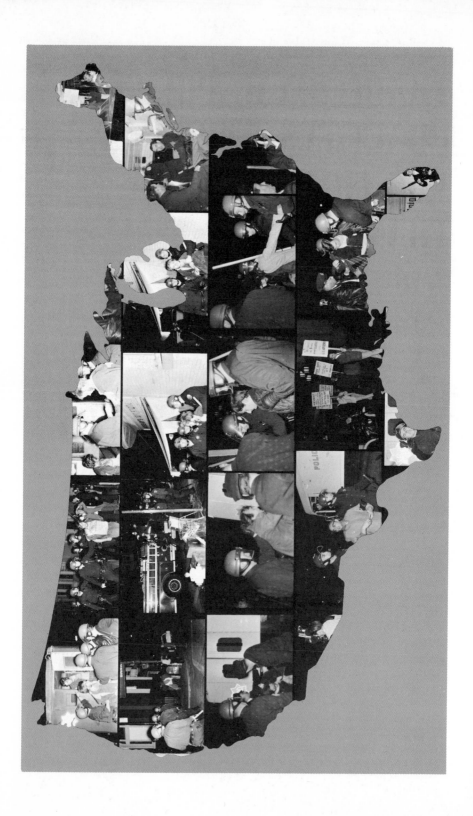

AN INTRODUCTION TO THE PROBLEM

1

One of the major social characteristics that appears to be descriptive of our society is the presence of groups in conflict with each other. Not only is there conflict between groups, but there are major divisive tensions within groups. Nowhere is this conflict more evident than between the police and the community. In these times of social upheaval and strife the law enforcement agencies come under much criticism from the community because of the way the police are perceived to be resolving problems not of the community's making. *The police, on the other hand, see the community as making their job much more difficult by lack of support and cooperation. Each group attempts to place the responsibility for social problems on the other. This antagonistic situation is particularly true between the minority-group person and the policeman.* This is vividly portrayed in a study by the late Joseph D. Lohman and Gordon E. Misner in a report prepared for the *President's Commission on Law Enforcement and Administration of Justice.* They describe the situation as "a basic police failure, i.e., the failure to communicate effectively with certain members of the minority community."

> The description of a rookie policeman . . . expecting to find a majority of inhabitants to have criminal tendencies and to be antagonistic to law and order is not an uncommon observation. . . . There is repeated reference to the lack of communication which might be initiated by the police officer on patrol. There is constant referral to his unwillingness to learn the language of the people . . . to appreciate their culture and motivations. According to this belief, a policeman sets himself up as

one who is not to be questioned, whose actions are not to be attacked; to question him means to attack him. There is a built-in barrier to communication which underlies distrust of him and what he represents. Thus, there is fashioned an image which may be predestined to give negative flavor to the contact that arises when a police officer confronts a citizen. . . . The police contact with the man in the community should be of primary importance in assuaging the tensions which may underlie the attitudes of community members; if this contact generates tension rather than assuaging it, then an essential aspect of the police purpose has been lost.[1]

Deterioration in the police–minority-group relationship is increasingly evident. During the last six years, we have seen a great deal of publicity relating to charges of police brutality and demands for greater assertion of civilian control over police actions.

POLICE–MINORITY-GROUP RELATIONS: A DISTORTED IMAGE

Relationships between the police and the ethnic minority groups appear to be conditioned by many factors, among which are *the police view and attitude toward ethnic minority groups, the customs and the traditions of the police service, and a built-in resistance to outside pressure.* Consequently, the relationships are almost inevitably negative. The policeman is provided with an automobile which gives him mobility but isolates him from basic contact with the public. His mission is to enforce the law, particularly in those locations where statistics prove that violations of the law occur with predictable regularity. Because of his workload, he has few opportunities to relate in any other fashion to the residents he is assigned to "police." His only long-term, persistent association with people in a community is the one that has been construed for him—that is, a negative enforcement relationship.

Consequently, bad stereotypes form which create filters in the perceptual screens of each group, distorting images and information about each other. At a time when clear communication is most important between groups it tends to decrease; neither group wants to listen to the other, hearing only information that supports its own position. Each group is focused only on the differences, obscuring the similarities or common goals they might share. When solutions are offered, each group feels committed to defend its own proposals rather than consider the merits of the other group's solutions. Mutual distrust and defensiveness prevent most attempts to get together to resolve differences and to work cooperatively on community

[1]*The Police and the Community: The Dynamics of Their Relationship in a Changing Community,* Vol. 1 (Washington, D.C.: U.S. Government Printing Office, 1966), p. 14.

problems. The police and the community conflict interferes seriously with public confidence in police and consequently with the ability of the police to deal effectively with the crime problem. Without doubt, the community's hostility toward and lack of confidence in the police interfere with police recruiting, morale, day-to-day operations, and safety of the individual officer. This obviously has an adverse effect on total community stability. Hostility toward the police is often so intense that even routine police procedures antagonize ordinarily law-abiding residents. Because for many members of minority groups the police symbolize all that is hated and feared in the dominant society, the policeman receives hostility which actually has very little to do with him. It is a hostility generated by social conditions such as inadequate housing and underemployment. Actual police misconduct, as documented by four authoritative national commissions,[2] further intensifies hostility toward the police.

Thus we have two groups in conflict, each perceiving the other as the

FIGURE 1.1 (a).   Police officers attempt to control sniper fire during a riot. Courtesy San Francisco Police Department, San Francisco, Cal.

[2]"Report on Lawlessness, 1931"; "To Secure The Rights, 1947"; "The Fifty State Report, 1961"; "Report of National Advisory Commission, 1968".

FIGURE 1.1 (b).   *Courtesy San Francisco Police Department, San Francisco, Cal.*

enemy and each feeling that it has to defend its own position. Bayley and Mendelsohn point out that, considering the expectations that most police-men have about the reception they will receive from members of a minority group,

> . . . it seems plausible to expect that they might build up an enormous amount of resentment against them. The middle-class and upper-class dominant community, constituting the majority of people in the city, are seen by policemen as being cooperative, making straight-forward demands involving little risk to the officer, and frequently requiring no enforcement at all. At the same time, these people are familiar with avenues of redress and not unwilling to challenge the officer who they believe presumes too far. Nevertheless, since their demands are gen-erally not exorbitant from the point of view of the officer, policemen may not mind becoming unassuming, informal, polite, and even deferential in their presence. Minorities, on the other hand, especially Negroes, in the eyes of police personnel, demand the most, raise the greatest amount of anxiety about personal safety, pose the greatest criminal threat, are the most hostile, and on top of it all are as likely to be truculant in their appeals against officers as prosperous Dom-inants. . . . One can understand why policemen often show a sense of being aggrieved, mistreated, and put-upon by minorities. Minorities

react in an exactly similar fashion against members of the majority community. *There seems to be a reciprocating engine of resentment at work in relations between police and minorities, an engine which is fueled with demands each side makes on the other and the expectations each entertains about the other.* If police-community relations are to be improved, the nature of this relationship—and especially of the structural basis for it—must be understood and studied in great detail.[3]

The situation confronting the law enforcement officer is undoubtedly far from ideal, but he is still responsible for the maintenance of an orderly society. The laws of the United States, of course, continue to include the minimum obligations imposed on any free society: to provide in an *impartial manner* both *personal safety* and *property security.*

In a fundamental context, all regulated behavior—from some family activities to vehicle speed—are law enforcement functions. And as the complexities of maintaining order through law enforcement multiply, there is an ever-increasing responsibility placed on those who enforce the law. This responsibility is to learn to *anticipate* and prevent the destruction (of any kind) of an orderly society.

THE RANGE OF PROBLEMS CONFRONTING THE POLICE[4]

Although everyone has a somewhat different impression of the nature of the police function, based primarily upon his personal experiences and contacts with police officers, there is a general popular conception of the police that is supported by news and entertainment media. Through these, the police have come to be viewed as a body of men continually engaged in the exciting, dangerous, and competitive enterprise of apprehending and prosecuting criminals. Emphasis upon this one aspect of police work has led to a tendency on the part of both the public and the police to underestimate the range and complexity of the total police task.

A police officer assigned to patrol duties in a large city is typically confronted with at most a few serious crimes in the course of a single tour of duty. He tends to view such involvement, particularly if there is some degree of danger, as constituting real police work. But it is apparent that he spends considerably more time keeping order, settling disputes, finding missing children, and helping drunks than he does in responding to criminal conduct that is serious enough to call for arrest, prosecution, and conviction.

---

[3]D. H. Bayley and H. Mendelsohn, *Minorities and The Police: Confrontation in America* (New York: The Free Press, 1971), pp. 107–108. (Italics added.)

[4]Adapted from the President's Commission on Law Enforcement and Administration of Justice, "Law Enforcement Policy: The Police Role," *Task Force Report: The Police* (Washington, D.C.: U.S. Government Printing Office, 1967), pp. 14–23.

This does not mean that serious crime is unimportant to the policeman. Quite the contrary is true. But it does mean that he performs a wide range of other functions which are of a highly complex nature and which often involve difficult social, behavioral, and political problems.

Individual misbehavior with which the police must deal, for example, ranges from that of a highly dangerous, assaultive offender to that of the petty thief or common drunk. Organized criminal activity varies from "numbers" rackets to the two-party agreement between a burglar and the person buying his stolen property. The peace-keeping function of the police requires that they deal with human conflicts ranging from large-scale rioting to disputes between husbands and wives. Laws enacted to preserve order within a community require the police to perform a variety of tasks, from enforcing traffic regulations to assuring that dogs, peddlers, and various businesses have proper licenses. In addition, the police are called upon to provide certain emergency services which their availability and skills qualify them to fulfill—services largely unrelated to crime or potential crime situations.

It is generally assumed that police have a preventive and protective role as well. Thus, for example, the police endeavor, through such activities as patrol, to lessen opportunities for the commission of crimes. They initiate programs to reduce the racial tensions that exist in the ghettos of large cities; they conduct educational programs to promote safe driving and prevent accidents. Police are expected to afford protection to individuals who are likely to be victimized or are in some other way prey to harm—the down-and-out drunk, the mentally ill, or the naive patrons of vice activity who may be subjecting themselves to the risk of robbery or worse. Moreover, they are expected to preserve the right of free speech—even when that speech is intensely antagonistic and likely to incite opposition.

To fulfill their obligations, the police are given formal authority to invoke the criminal process—to arrest, to prosecute, and to seek a conviction. But making use of this traditional process is much more complex than is commonly assumed, owing to the infinite complications that distinguish separate incidents. The police must make important judgments about what conduct is in fact criminal; about the allocation of scarce resources; and about the gravity of each individual incident and the proper steps that should be taken.

When the police are dealing with highly dangerous conduct, for example, they are expected to arrest the offender and participate in his prosecution in order to insure correctional treatment. But when the conduct is not considered particularly dangerous, as in the case of the common drunk, police may conclude—given the volume of cases—that it is not worth the effort to invoke the full criminal process. Often the police will simply pick up the drunk, detain him overnight, and release him when sober.

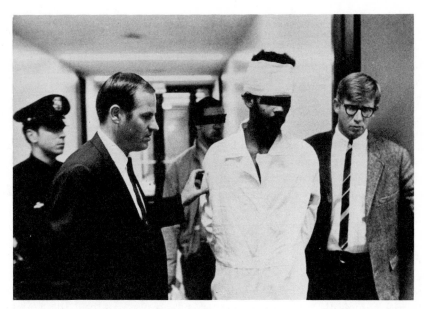

FIGURE 1.2.   *E. Thompson, young slayer of a San Jose policeman, was formally sentenced to life imprisonment on Dec. 2, 1971. It was brought out at the hearing that Thompson shot the policeman while under the influence of LSD. He is shown here almost immediately after he was apprehended. He was injured during the apprehension process (note gauze bandage). Courtesy of the San Jose Mercury-News newspaper, San Jose, Cal.*

Domestic disputes account for a high percentage of the total number of incidents to which the police are summoned. These generally occur late at night and result in a call for the police because an assault has taken place, because there is the potential for violence, because the neighbors are disturbed, or simply because there is no other source of help in arbitrating marital conflicts. The formal system of arrest, prosecution, and conviction is rarely an appropriate means for dealing with these disputes. In the absence of likely alternatives to police involvement, police officers are left with the responsibility for dealing with such situations without being adequately equipped to do so. (The use of crisis intervention as a useful method to deal with such problems is discussed in Chapter 12.)

When criminal activity involves a "willing buyer" and a "willing seller," a somewhat different problem is present. Widespread community support for some forms of gambling activity or an ambivalent community attitude toward some forms of sexual conduct require that a police agency decide what constitutes an appropriate level of enforcement. In the absence of a complainant, police must determine the amount of resources and the investigative procedures they should employ to discover criminal offenses.

Because a high percentage of crimes is committed by juveniles, police are frequently called upon to deal with a youthful offender. In spite of this, there remains uncertainty as to the proper role of the police in the juvenile process. In practice, most incidents involving juveniles are disposed of by the police without referral to a social worker or a judge, and consequently what police do is of great significance.

Finally, police must respond to the conflicts that arise out of what has been termed the "social revolution." It is difficult, in policing such situations, to distinguish between legitimate and illegitimate group behavior and to balance the value of free expression against the risk of public disorder. The lines that must be drawn are difficult to determine and call for policy decisions quite different from those made in traditional crimes like burglary.

It has been argued that many of the complex problems of the criminal process could be solved by more narrowly defining the police function. If drunkenness were dealt with by medically qualified people, for example, police would not have to contend with the habitual drunk. If family problems were handled by social agencies, police would not have to deal with the many domestic and juvenile matters which now confront them. If the substantive criminal law were revised, police would not be confronted with

FIGURE 1.3. The juvenile's best contact with authority is when he is taken into custody. The arresting officer has a great deal of discretion as to the final disposition of the juvenile's case. Therefore, the action taken by the arresting officer will be of great significance. Courtesy Campbell Police Department, Campbell, Cal.

the difficult decisions resulting from broad prohibitions against narcotics, gambling, prostitution, and homosexual activity. And if increased efforts were made to solve some of the social ills that give rise to criminality, the police could be relieved of many of their crime prevention functions.

But little effective action has been taken to develop the kind of resources required by the adoption of any of these alternatives. Some courts have recently held that it is unconstitutional to treat habitual drunkenness as a criminal offense. Presumably, this means that the police should no longer be concerned with public drunkenness, although it is possible that they might be involved through a process which is medically rather than criminally oriented. But the test of such decisions is in whether they result in a more adequate and humane method of dealing with drunks rather than in their conformity with principle. Because few efforts have been made to develop alternatives to police involvement, the consequence of police not taking action would be that drunks were left to lie where they fall.

Proposals to relieve the police of what are essentially social service duties have also been lacking in their consideration of the relationship of such services to the incidence of more serious crimes. A domestic disturbance, for example, often culminates in a serious assault or a homicide. The down-and-out drunk will almost certainly be a victim of a theft if he is left to lie on the street and has any article of value on him. The prostitute may, in one sense, be primarily a social problem, but many streetwalkers engage regularly in arranging the robbery of their patrons as a supplement to their incomes.

It might be desirable for agencies other than the police to provide community services that might help prevent some social problems. But the failure of such agencies to develop and the relationship between the social problems in question and the incidence of crime suggest that the police are likely to remain, for some time, as the only 24-hour-a-day, 7-day-a-week agency that is spread over an entire city in a way that makes it possible for them to respond quickly to incidents of this kind.

If, as seems apparent, continued reliance is to be placed upon law enforcement agencies for meeting the wide range of functions that now comprise their task, it is important that attention be turned to the manner in which they perform those functions.

The Police Response[5]

To urge recognition of the fact that the police task covers a wide range of activities and that it is highly complex is not to maintain that the police adequately fulfill all their functions. It is obviously difficult and often impossible for police officers to respond in an appropriate manner to the numerous incidents called to their attention. They are under constant pres-

[5]Ibid., pp. 14–18 (material adapted).

sure, especially in highly congested areas, to handle a volume of cases that is beyond their capacity. This forces them to develop short-cut responses to run-of-the-mill situations. They lack adequate training with respect to some of the more complex social problems. And there has been little effort to provide individual officers with the guidelines needed for making more effective and judicious decisions in disposing of the incidents which come to their attention. In the absence of adequate resources, training, and guidance, the tendency is for individual police officers to attempt to meet largely by improvisation the varied demands made upon them.

Some indication of the manner in which this is achieved can be gathered from the following account of an observer who accompanied two police officers functioning in a congested urban area during a tour of duty that began in the early evening hours:

> After receiving routine instructions at the roll call held at the precinct station, Officers Jones and Smith located the car to which they were assigned and started out for the area in which they would spend their tour of duty. While enroute, the officers received instructions from the dispatcher to handle a fight in an alley. Upon arrival, they found a group of young men surrounded by their parents, wives, and children. One of the young men, A, had a couple of knives in his hand. While the knives were within legal limits, Officer Smith took them (and later disposed of them in a refuse container). Another of the young men, B, stood by his mother. The third, C, stood by A, from whom the knives had been taken.
>
> The mother of B was the complainant. She claimed that C had attacked her son with a knife and she demanded that C be arrested and jailed. C readily admitted he had been fighting with B, but he claimed that he had just tried to protect A. C had been drinking and was very belligerent. He indicated a readiness to take on anyone and everyone, including the police. He kept shouting and was obviously antagonizing the officers.
>
> A attempted to explain the situation. He stated that he had been the one originally fighting B and that C had merely come to his aid. B concurred in this account of what had taken place, though he did not reflect very much concern as the supposed victim of the attack.
>
> A's mother-in-law interrupted at this time to claim that A was innocent; that the fight was B's fault. B's mother did not stand for his accusation and entered the fray.
>
> The confusion spread. Other police officers, in the meantime, had arrived at the scene and the number of observers had grown. Officers Jones and Smith decided to take the participants to the precinct station where conditions would make it possible to make a more orderly inquiry.
>
> At the station, the families and participants were separated and talked with individually. The mother of B insisted on signing a complaint

against C and A, but finally relented as to A when he promised not to allow C to come to his apartment.

C was then formally arrested and charged with disorderly conduct. A and B were sent home with their wives and mothers. By charging C with disorderly conduct rather than a more serious crime, the officers observed that they were saving themselves some paperwork. They felt that their action in letting the mother sign a complaint against the "loudmouthed" C had served to pacify her.

After filling out the arrest reports on C, Officers Jones and Smith notified the dispatcher that they were available and resumed patrolling. But in several minutes they were dispatched to another beat to handle a domestic situation.

A young Indian girl met them at the door. There obviously had been a fight; the place was a shambles. Furniture was broken, food was on the floor, and beer cans were scattered everywhere. The girl gave an explanation to which the police officers were very much accustomed— her husband had gotten drunk, had become angry, and had gone on the "warpath." When she told the officers that her husband had been behaving in this manner for 5 years, any sympathy which they had for the girl disappeared. They explained that they were not in a position to do anything for her since her husband was not there. They advised her to go to court to obtain either a warrant for his arrest or to arrange for the issuance of a peace bond.

Upon reporting back in service with the dispatcher, Smith and Jones were assigned a domestic problem involving a couple who had been married for 27 years. The couple had only recently begun to have trouble getting along. But when the difficulty started, it was serious. The wife had been attacked by the husband a week previously and had suffered a concussion. She was now back from the hospital and wanted her husband locked up. The woman led the officers to the apartment, but the husband had, in the interval, left. They then went through the ritual of telling the wife the procedure by which she could obtain a warrant or a peace bond. They also told her to call back if she had any more trouble.

After this call, there was a short lull in activity, during which the officers patrolled the southeast corner of their assigned area. They were then told to see a complainant at a designated address.

The complainant, it turned out, was a landlord. One of his tenants had a child who had been bothering other tenants. The mother had been told to quiet the child down, but she apparently had not done so. In addition, the mother was behind in the rent. The landlord had attempted to serve her with an eviction notice but had not been able to find her at home.

The mother was at work at a lounge and the landlord asked the officers to serve the eviction notice on her there. The officers explained that they would not be able to do so since the lounge was outside the district to which they were assigned. The landlord countered this by contending that he had been a friend of the police and that he had helped them in the past. He also stressed that he was a taxpayer. Officer Jones reacted by requesting the dispatcher to assign a police officer to meet the landlord at the lounge and help him in serving the notice. The officers, in this manner, disposed of the incident.

Smith and Jones were next dispatched to investigate a noisy party. When they arrived at the scene, they found the party was "full blast." They knocked and, when the door was answered, Officer Smith asked for the host. He told the person who then came to the door that someone had complained and that they would have to "hold the noise down." The host and others who were listening in readily agreed. When Officer Jones notified the dispatcher that the first party had been quieted, the men were dispatched to another.

The officers could not find the second party and could hear no loud noise at the address which had been given. Officer Jones requested the apartment number from the dispatcher. Both officers then went to the apartment. When the hostess came to the door, Officer Smith told her that someone had complained about a loud party. He told her that while the party seemed quiet enough at the moment, she should be careful because she evidently had some touchy neighbors.

Smith and Jones stopped for a coke before placing themselves back in service. While they were parked, Officer Jones spotted a "downer" in the doorway of the office occupied by the city council member representing the area. They called for a patrol wagon. They then went over to the drunk, awakened him, and asked him some questions. He had been sleeping and eating wherever he could, having slept the previous night in a "flophouse" downtown. When the wagon arrived the "downer" was placed in it and taken to jail.

When the officers reported back in service, they were immediately assigned to a juvenile disturbance at a hotdog stand. They did not rush to the scene, since they had been there numerous times in the past.

The owner of the hotdog stand would not force the youths to leave, letting them stand about until the whole parking area was congested. He would then call the police. Smith and Jones dispersed the crowd. One youth started to resist but moved on when Officer Jones threatened him with jail.

The officers informed the dispatcher that they had handled the problem at the hotdog stand and then resumed patrol. They had traveled several blocks from the hotdog stand when they observed a driver run a red light. The officers gave chase and pulled the vehicle over to the side of the street. The motorist, it was revealed, had just returned from Vietnam and Officer Smith felt that he deserved a break. He released him with a suggestion that he be more careful. While Officer Smith was talking to the veteran, Officer Jones spotted a fight between two youths. He ran over, broke it up, and talked to the combatants. He sent them on their way with a warning.

The officers requested permission from the dispatcher to take time out to eat, but he responded by sending them back to the first party that they had quieted.

A great deal of damage had been done by the time they arrived. The youths had gotten drunk and loud. They had created a disturbance when the party broke up and the manager of the building had called the police. The officers advised the manager to exercise more care in deciding upon the people to whom she rented her apartments. Since the persons causing the disturbance had already gone, there was nothing else that the officers could do; they departed.

They again asked permission to take time for food, but were instead dispatched to the scene of a stabbing. They hurried to the location, which turned out to be a new portable public swimming pool.

There were three persons present—two lifeguards and a watchman. One of the lifeguards had been knifed. He was placed in the police car and officers started off for the nearest hospital. Enroute, the victim told the officers that a man had tried to go swimming in the pool after it had been closed for the night. When the lifeguard attempted to stop the intruder, he was stabbed during the scuffle. The other lifeguard called the police. At the hospital, the officers made out their reports while the victim received medical care. They later returned to the scene but found no additional information or people who could assist in the identification of the assailant. The reports were turned in for attention by the detectives.

The officers then, without asking, took their meal break, after which they reported that they had completed their work on the stabbing. They were dispatched to a party disturbance. Upon arriving at the scene, they encountered a young fellow walking out of the building carrying a can of beer.

He was stopped and questioned about the party. Officer Smith told him that "this is not Kentucky" and drinking on the street is not allowed. The fellow agreed to take the officer up to the party. When he turned to lead the way, Officer Jones observed a knife in the youth's back pocket. He took the knife away. There was not much going on at the party. Those present were admonished to keep it quiet.

Back on patrol, the officers cruised for a short period. It was soon quitting time, so they headed in the direction of the precinct station. As they turned a corner, Officer Smith saw a couple of fellows drinking on the street, but rather than get involved at this time, nothing was done.[6]

This day in the life of Officers Jones and Smith reflects the broad and varied demands for police service, the pressures under which it is provided, and the informal and improvised responses which tend to develop. Though

[6]Ibid., pp. 15–16.

they are neither articulated nor officially recognized, common responses obviously tend to develop in frequently recurring situations.

A new police officers quickly learns these responses through his associations with more seasoned officers. The fact that a response is routine does not mean that it is satisfactory. To the contrary, many routine responses are applied on the basis of indefensible and improper criteria. But once developed, they are generally immune to critical reevaluation unless a crisis situation arises. Because of their informal character, such responses tend not to be influenced by developments in police training. And, because they consist of the accumulated experience of front-line officers, they tend to take on vitality that continues even without the active support of the higher echelon of police administration.

Unique situations do arise, usually where the frequency of a given kind of incident is small, for which there is no routine response. Unless time permits him to confer with his sergeant, the individual officer is left to respond without any form of guidance. Under such circumstances, the decision of the individual officer will reflect his own personal values and opinions about people and about group behavior.

Improvement in the capacity of law enforcement agencies to perform the essential and highly sensitive functions that comprise the total police task requires a willingness on the part of the public and the police to take several bold steps. There must, in the first place, be a more widespread recognition on the part of the citizenry and the police of both the range and the complexity of the problems which the police confront. Secondly, there must be a willingness on the part of the police to respond to these problems by the careful development and articulation of policies and practices which are subject to continuing reevaluation in the light of changing social conditions.

THE PROBLEMS IN POLICE–COMMUNITY RELATIONS

Undoubtedly, one of the major problems in law enforcement in the United States involves the question of community acceptance and support of law enforcement and its agents. Let it be noted at the outset, that this, like many issues in the area of police–community relations, is *not strictly* a racial problem; the poor public attitudes toward police work in general are common to all citizens.

Unlike the police force in Great Britain, which generally enjoys not only a considerable degree of public confidence but also a measure of real popularity, police officers in the United States have been accorded a second-class position in society. They are frequently the object of attack by press and pulpit, bench and bar, civic and commercial associations, labor leaders, professional politicians, ambitious office-seekers, reformers, and criminals. Police work by its very nature is not calculated to be highly successful; that is, it can never succeed in completely preventing the occurrence of crime or apprehending everyone who commits a criminal act. It is obvious, however, to all law-abiding citizens, that a healthy society owes its agents of law enforcement a profound respect, for a good police department is a bulwark against a sea of disorder. The general attitude in the community today, however, toward the agents of law enforcement is frequently one of apathetic indifference if not social antagonism—neither of which is beneficial in effecting vigorous enforcement of the law.

Also, the American law enforcement tradition appears to be influenced by the major differences in the backgrounds of those comprising the population of the cities; i.e., Black, Puerto Rican, Italian, Mexican, and White culture, Oriental influences, and so on. What these various peoples seek in terms of law and order no doubt varies, as do the methods of those providing the enforcement. To get an idea of the variation, consider a mythical western sheriff attempting to bring his anti-cow rustling skills to bear on the violence of San Francisco's early Chinatown or New York's 1844 immigration riots or interstate prostitution.[7]

The frustrations of this imaginary sheriff would probably be no greater than those experienced by many contemporary police officers confronted with civil disobedience, sit-ins, protest demonstrations, riots, and unfounded charges of brutality—all occurring in the most affluent society the world has ever known. Indeed, on a comparative basis, the sheriff might well be envied for his firm and uncomplicated belief that people were either good or bad—with the bad ones placed in jail, where they learned to be good. Uncomplicated beliefs of this nature would permit the ever-increasing forces of social change to be interpreted simply. But they are not simple; neither is the tremendous task of understanding and programming effective community relations.

Through evolution, society's enforcing of behavior regulation has moved beyond the point of uncomplicated answers for law enforcement agencies. Now police teams, chemicals, and noise generators are steadily supplementing police in the control of violent demonstrations. And the causes of these demonstrations—the various community tensions—have become a legitimate law enforcement concern.

In our grossly complicated, urbanized society the philosophy of enforcing law must continue to expand. In the matter of *personal safety* and *property security*, law enforcement must include positive efforts to anticipate and redirect those social forces which jeopardize the personal safety and

---

[7]E. Eldefonso, A. Coffey, and R. C. Grace, *Principles of Law Enforcement*, 2nd ed. (New York: Wiley & Sons, 1974), pp. 165–75.

property security of individuals. Discharge of this particular responsibility must necessarily become a matter of community relations.

Community and Human Relations

If society is to survive,[8] at least in a civilized manner, it is imperative that laws be enforced. Because the observance of law is so vital, society cannot depend on simple persuasion for its accomplishment; rather it must rely in part on force. The term *enforcement*—and indeed, the very nature of man —implies a possible use of force. This potential to wield force, then, is necessarily part of the police image. The manner in which the potential is viewed by the public often determines whether the police image is good or bad. And, because a good police image tends to affect favorably an individual's willingness to observe the law voluntarily, police retain a rightful interest in having a good image. The police officer embodies the law so visibly and directly that neither he nor the public finds it easy to differentiate between the law and the enforcement of such law. The public is confused and unable to recognize the broad concept of the police officer. As the late Bruce Smith pointed out,

> Relatively few citizens recall ever having seen a judge; fewer still, a prosecutor, coroner, sheriff, probation officer or prison warden. The patrolman is thoroughly familiar to all. His uniform picks him out from the crowd so distinctly that he becomes a living symbol of the law—not always of its majesty, but certainly of its power. Whether the police like it or not, they are forever marked men.[9]

Any officer of the law is partly a symbol, and law enforcement work consists to some extent in creating impressions based on symbolic attributes. Thus, an unoccupied police vehicle can slow down turnpike traffic or motivate drivers to stop at designated intersections, and the presence of half a dozen officers can control a large crowd.[10]

The uniform of the police officer is viewed as a symbolic license to judge and punish. It not only represents the right to arrest but also connotes the role of a disciplinarian. Unfortunately, it is for this reason that many parents may make small children behave by repeated pointed references to policemen. Needless to say, this "punishing role" does not lend itself to the promotion of any social role other than as an "enforcer."[11]

---

[8]See Ibid., pp. 35–49.

[9]"Municipal Police Administration," *Annals of the American Academy of Police and Social Science*, 40, No. 5 (Sept. 1971), p. 22.

[10]H. H. Toch, "Psychological Consequences of the Police Role," *Police*, 10, No. 1 (Sept.-Oct. 1965), p. 22.

[11]Ibid. See also T. J. Crawford, "Police Overperception of Ghetto Hostility," *Journal of Police Science and Administration*, 1, No. 2 (1973), pp. 168–74.

Police interest in a good image is vital for a number of reasons. One that is singularly practical is that the greater the voluntary law observance, the less the need for *forceful* enforcement. So the question becomes, What can be done to promote the standing of the police officer and of social influences to encourage voluntary law observance?

The various theories presented in numerous books make clear the lack of agreement concerning the causes of crime among biologists, anthropologists, criminologists, sociologists, and psychologists and psychiatrists. Yet these behavioral scientists generally agree that societal influences both encourage and discourage crime. As it relates to criminal behavior, influence is merely a power to affect human willingness to conform to law. And so the question of influence becomes a consideration of those forces having enough power to encourage voluntary law observance.

The manner in which the public views a police method of enforcement is considered as one such force. Another perhaps more fundamental force relates to the manner in which children are raised. The old saying, "As the twig is bent, so grows the tree," has particular significance in every society. The citizen who holds little respect for law enforcement goals may merely reflect the values he learned as a child. Racial tensions, economic conditions, and various physical and emotional deprivations have probably helped shape his attitude. But it is likely that the major contributing factor might have been early and unfortunate experiences with police. The detrimental and sometimes lasting effects of such unfortunate encounters will be discussed in later chapters. For now, mention of experiences of this nature serves to introduce the subject of *human relations*—a matter of increasing concern to police as evidenced, for example, by the great number of courses devoted to this subject at most police academies and colleges throughout the United States.

Human Relations Defined[12]

More and more, the literature reflects an implied definition of human relations in terms of "avoiding police brutality."[13] A further definition includes police discretion or decision in terms of "police attitudes."[14] Going beyond these rather narrow considerations, a definition of law enforcement human relations might be: *police participation in any activity that seeks*

---

[12]Eldefonso, et al., *Principles of Law Enforcement*, p. 36.

[13]See, for example, L. E. Berson, *Case Study of a Riot: The Philadelphia Story* (New York: Institute of Human Relations Press, 1966); C. Westley, "Violence and the Police," *American Journal of Sociology*, 59, No. 34 (1953); *The Economist*, December 31, 1955, p, 1159; E. H. Sutherland, and D. R. Cressy, *Principles of Criminology*, 6th ed. (Philadelphia: J. B. Lippincott Co., 1960), p. 341; D. R. Ralph, "Police Violence," *New Statesman*, 66, No. 102 (1963).

[14]J. H. Skolnick, *Justice Without Trial: Law Enforcement in Democratic Society* (New York: Wiley & Sons, 1966).

law observance through respect and acceptance of enforcement of laws in a positive manner. This definition will be further elaborated and clarified.

Regardless of how the term *human relations* is defined, however, police interest in the subject should be related in some way to the "causes" of crime. It has been noted already that behavioral scientists fail to agree on these. A cause or a group of causes can be isolated—such as alcoholism, poverty, broken homes, and parental neglect—which seem to turn one individual to crime but not another, although both may be subject to precisely the same influences. Even such an extensive catalog of human characteristics as the Yale University Human Relations File (originally the Cross-Cultural Survey) fails to clarify how cultural causes affect different people in different ways.

Regardless of the behavioral scientists' lack of agreement on crime causes, law enforcement practitioners tend to agree that there appears to be a relationship between at least some kinds of crime and certain community influences. These influences, more often than not, relate to combinations of problems such as poverty, racial tensions, and parental inadequacies. An additional influence that has already been indicated is the police image—which will be thoroughly discussed in another chapter—held by the community.

Because the community's attitude toward police (or the police image) is one of the primary influences with enough force to encourage voluntary law observance, it is of primary concern to law enforcement. The individual citizen who is convinced that police are brutal will probably find it difficult to respect police goals, particularly if the brutality is believed to be directed only toward certain minorities. And, as a practical matter, the *validity* of the belief matters less than the *strength* of the belief. An individual usually functions on the basis of what he believes, regardless of the validity of his beliefs.

LAW ENFORCEMENT—A PERIOD OF UNUSUAL UNCERTAINTY

Currently law enforcement agencies are caught in a period of unusual uncertainty. Primarily, this state can be attributed to two separate but relatively interdependent developments. The first, elaborated upon in Chapter 3, is directly related to the United States Supreme Court. The Court has made a series of decisions relative to the protection of personal liberties of those accused of crimes. In 1963, the Supreme Court ruled on the appeal case of *Gideon v. Wainwright.* The effect of the ruling was that new trials could be demanded by anyone convicted of crime who did not have legal counsel. Moving closer to the field of law enforcement, a 1964 decision was handed down in the case of *Escobedo v. Illinois.* This decision, based on a 5 to 4 majority, protected the constitutional right of an indigent to be provided with legal counsel at the time of interrogation. Then, in June 1966, a ruling was handed down in *Miranda v. Arizona* (again by 5 to 4 majority) that provides for legal counsel as soon as the interrogated person is considered a specific suspect in an investigation.

The mixed feelings regarding Supreme Court decisions was the subject of a Task Force study in San Diego, California.[15] The study showed that judges and lawyers in San Diego generally support the recent Supreme Court decisions regarding police interrogation. Most emphasize, however, that it is a complex issue and that the decisions have mixed benefits. The tone of many of the comments is that the decisions are necessary to counteract police abuses in the past. As one explained, the police departments "have no one to blame but themselves." He notes:

> Cases have been coming up to the Supreme Court for decades showing abuses by police forces and policemen across the country—third degree, prisoners being beaten, confessions that were extorted out of individuals. There was a wide variety of abuses of individuals' rights to due process. . . . The Supreme Court in all those years was reluctant to get involved in this squabble, except in a few minor areas . . .[16]

A lawyer states that he is very much in favor of the decisions, for they curb practices that have long needed control. Another lawyer expresses support but explains some of his reservations in this manner:

> The decisions indicate an imbalance. The problem is to give the accused full protection of his rights yet give society its protection against criminal elements. I take full cognizance of the fact that there is a good deal of crime on the streets. The difficulty is that police officers were abusing the rights of the accused and I would prefer to see some system by which it was possible to hit the police officer directly. I feel that the Supreme Court has taken really the only practical course available to it—namely that the evidence that the police obtained would have to be held inadmissible in court and thereby discourage officers from abusing the rights of the accused. I still resent the fact that this has to be done, for it impairs the right of society generally to be secure itself.[17]

Several judges comment that they do not think the decisions will hinder law enforcement. Federal agencies, for example, have high-caliber personnel and they have worked within these restrictions for a long time. Some judges do express the opinion that the decisions will "hamstring" local

[15]Reported in Lohman and Misner, *The Police and the Community*, p. 15.
[16]Ibid.
[17]Ibid.

police departments, but they do not elaborate further. Some say that not all police departments will be able to afford the competent policemen needed for effective conformance with the court rulings. Those who state that they are aware of investigative procedures of the San Diego Police Department do not believe that it will need to make any changes.

A number of judges and lawyers criticize police departments for "belly-aching" about the Supreme Court decisions, and they think police should stop complaining, accept the rulings, and do their job. "Some in the legal community support the need for the changes required by the Dorado decision but think that Miranda goes too far."[18]

These decisions have elicited a great deal of debate—hot debate—and have been attacked as placing a great deal of restraint on the police by "coddling" the law violator. Furthermore, according to the dissenters, the police are placed in a position where they must fight by "Marquis of Queensberry Rules," while criminals are not bound by such rules. On the other hand, these decisions have been received as evidence that the Supreme Court has finally become more concerned with human liberty than with the protection of property rights.

The second development, which is just as important, is that law enforcement is experiencing a series of civil disturbances associated with a wide range of efforts to upgrade minority groups to the full citizenship and socioeconomic privileges guaranteed by the U.S. Constitution. The strategies and nonviolent techniques of civil rights groups are creating unusual problems for law enforcement agencies because exploiting excessive use of police coercion is one of their major weapons. *This nonviolent method involves the explicit and knowing violation of a particular law by persons who are quite ready to accept, without resistance, the retribution attached to that specific law violation. By utilizing the nonviolent resistance method, minority groups dramatize certain laws as unjust.* Furthermore, the use of police coercion is invited (and welcomed) as an opportunity to identify peace officers as "the intimidators or aggressors" against "peaceful demonstrators." It is not unusual to use children, women, ministers, and other responsible persons who have a favorable public image as "victims" for police "aggression." Needless to say, the resulting arrests play havoc with the judiciary machinery. Nonviolent resistance has its ideological genesis in the values of Christian morality and humanitarianism through the premise that minority groups have a moral obligation *not* to cooperate with the forces of "evil."

> In essence, the nonviolent resistance is a form of passive aggression, in that it frustrates its opponents by enveloping them in a cloud of "Christian love" for one's enemies. The established power structure of

[18]Ibid.

the community is to be forced into the role of "bad guys," whereas the Negroes assume the mantle of Christian heroes. Noncompliance with carefully selected laws creates a community crisis, but, by refraining from violent resistance, the law violators make application of police coercion an opportunity to present social protest as consistent with the highly prized values of humanitarianism and concern for the underdog.[19]

As has been so explicitly pointed out by a noted author and professor in the fields of criminology and law enforcement,

Another area of current dispute is "control of conduct" or "maintenance of the peace." This nation is currently beseiged by acts of violence, civil disobedience and riot. On the other hand, there is a cry for "law and order," and on the other hand some espouse a policy of "absolute permissiveness." The police are presently the scapegoats of this dichotomy, therefore it is imperative that standards be established that will protect us from anarchy, and at the same time, allow for reasonable dissent.[20]

A SPECIFIC PROBLEM: THE BLACK REVOLT

Because of the nature of this chapter, it is appropriate at this time to introduce the rudimentary rationale pertaining to the black revolt.[21] (These factors will be elaborated upon in Chapter 2.) The issues are complex and interacting; they vary significantly in their effect from city to city and from year to year; and the consequences of one disorder that generates new grievances and demands become the causes of the next.

Despite these complexities, however, certain things are clear. Of these, the most fundamental is the racial prejudice displayed by some white Americans toward black Americans. Racial prejudice has shaped our history decisively; now, according to the *Report of the National Advisory Commission on Civil Disorders*, it threatens to affect our future.

White racism is essentially responsible for the explosive mixture that has been accumulating in our cities, particularly since the end of World War II. The government report states that among the ingredients of this mixture are

[19]E. H. Johnson, "A Sociological Interpretation of Police Reaction and Responsibility to Civil Disobediance," *Journal of Criminal Law, Criminology and Police Science*, 58, No. 3 (Sept. 1967), p. 407.

[20]H. W. More, Jr., *Critical Issues in Law Enforcement* (Cincinnati: W. H. Anderson Co., 1972), p. 7.

[21]For a competent analysis of the reasons racial unrest is sweeping America today, as well as the history behind freedom riders, sit-ins, prayer marches, refer to L. E. Lomax, *The Negro Revolt* (New York: Harper & Row, 1964).

Pervasive discrimination and segregation in employment, education and housing, which have resulted in the continuing exclusion of great numbers of Negroes from the benefits of economic progress.

Black in-migration and white exodus which have produced the massive and growing concentrations of impoverished Negroes in our major cities, creating a growing crisis of deteriorating facilities and services and un-met human needs.

The black ghettos where segregation and poverty converge on the young to destroy opportunity and enforce failure. Crime, drug addiction, dependency on welfare and bitterness and resentment against society in general, and white society in particular, are the results.[22]

At the same time, most whites and some blacks outside the ghetto have prospered to a degree unparalleled in the history of civilization. Unfortunately, through television and other media this affluence has been flaunted before the eyes of the black poor and jobless ghetto youth.

Yet these facts alone cannot be said to have caused the disorders. Recently, according to the Commission, other powerful ingredients have begun to catalyze the mixture.

Frustrated hopes are the residue of the unfulfilled expectations aroused by the great judicial and legislative victories of the Civil Rights Movement and the dramatic struggle for equal rights in the South.

A climate that tends toward approval and encouragement of violence as a form of protest has been created by white terrorism directed against nonviolent protest; by the open defiance of law and federal authority, by state and local officials resisting desegregation who turn their backs on nonviolence, go beyond the constitutionally protected rights of petition and free assembly, and resort to violence to attempt to compel alteration of laws and policies with which they disagree.

The frustrations of powerlessness have led some blacks to the conviction that there is no effective alternative to violence as a means of achieving redress, of grievances and of "moving the system." These *frustrations are reflected in alienation and hostility* toward the institutions of law and government and the white society which controls them, and the reach toward racial consciousness and solidarity reflected in the slogan, "Black Power."

A new mood has sprung up among blacks, particularly among the young, in which self-esteem and enhanced racial pride are replacing apathy and submission to "the system."[23]

In addressing ourselves to the question of why this has happened, we

[22]Report of the *National Advisory Commission on Civil Disorders* (Washington, D.C.: U.S. Government Printing Office, 1968), pp. 9–11.
[23]Ibid.

shall shift our focus to a situation that has created a hostile demeanor among many blacks in our society.

The most important fact about the relationship of the black to American society is his subordinate social status. In the South, social position has been so rigidly defined as to constitute a caste system, and even in the North and the West, in spite of a certain amount of equality with respect to civil rights, the black is generally subjected to social ostracism and economic discrimination.

> Of all the ethnic groups to have come to this country, the black is the only one to experience the degradation of slavery and a persistent status of subordination. Slavery in a sense dehumanized the blacks. It disrupted his native culture and taught him the rudiments of white civilization, but it did not permit him to develop as a whole man. It prevented the development of three things which are generally considered essential for normal group life: stable family relationships, stable economic organization, and stable community life. Furthermore, slavery nurtured a set of habits and attitudes which still afflict many thousands of blacks. Among these are lack of self-respect, lack of self-confidence, a distaste for hard work, a habit of dependence upon white friends, lack of regard for the property of others, a feeling that "the white folks owe us a living," a distrust of the white man's law and a tendency to "let tomorrow take care of itself."[24]

Opportunity for blacks was not given impetus by emancipation; the black is still unable to compete on even terms with other citizens in his attempts to obtain a moderate existence. His heritage—reinforced by a continuing vicious circle of caste barriers—has, to a large degree, caused cultural retardation and economic disabilities. The answer to the question, Why is it that other minority groups have managed to move ahead? can only be, then, that

> The difference between the experience of the black and the experience of other ethnic groups in American society is not merely one of degree but actually a difference in kind—a fact which certainly has some connection with the incidence of social conditions which are associated with crime.[25]

The points mentioned have attempted to identify the prime components of the "explosive mixture." In the chapters that follow, we seek to analyze them in the perspective of history and in a manner through which law enforcement personnel may find possible solutions applicable for use.

[24]Ibid.

[25]G. R. Johnson, "The Negro and Crime," *Annals of American Academy of Political and Social Services,* 4 (Sept. 1971), pp. 93–104.

Their meaning, however, is clear: *the holding down of the black (and other minorities) in American society—with all that this means in terms of subordination, frustration, economic insecurity, and incomplete participation—enters significantly into almost every possible aspect of racial strife and tension.* Indeed, it is so important as to constitute virtually a special, and major, set of sociological and psychological factors which can "explain" black protest, insofar as it needs special explanation. The *administration of justice* itself is from beginning to end so much a part of the whole system of black-white social relations that it must be viewed as a process that discriminates against blacks and thus acts as a direct and indirect causative factor in producing poor relations between blacks and police[26]. The administration of justice is beyond the scope of this chapter and will be analyzed in Chapter 6, "Equal Justice and Minority Groups."

DISSENT AND CIVIL DISOBEDIENCE

In the United States, the question is *not* "May I dissent?" because that *right* is guaranteed by both the Constitution and the courts; however, there is a question as to *how* the dissent shall be carried out. The First Amendment confers "the right of the people peaceably to assemble and to petition the Government for a redress of grievances"—but there are limitations to the right. And contrary to popular belief, freedom of speech does not guarantee the individual's right to offer a false statement about an individual (there is a possibility of a civil suit, or tort).[27] Nor does it permit him to state what is on his mind anytime, anywhere. No one, according to Justice Oliver Wendell Holmes, may shout "Fire!" in a crowded theater when he is fully aware that such a warning is untrue. Regardless of how positive one's motive may be,—e.g., dissatisfaction with inadequate fire regulations—actions that will injure others cannot be excused.

Policemen are being called "pigs" to their faces by both whites and blacks who resent them. Freedom of speech entitles these individuals to their own opinions and to the selection of their own description, but it does not entitle them to insult people to their faces. Should the community allow its law enforcement officers to be insulted with impunity? Should a policeman be required to permit others to call him a pig in public? The intent is certainly provocative, the purpose to reduce the authority of and respect for the law. Policemen, unlike judges, cannot punish people directly. Insults to an officer of the law in the performance of his duties are, however, every

[26]Ibid.

[27]For a concise definition of tort, refer to W. L. Marshall, and W. L. Clark, *A Treatise on the Law of Crimes* (Chicago: Callaghan, Callaghan & Co., 1952), pp. 102-105.

bit as detrimental to public order as are insults to a judge, and they should be treated as misdemeanors and be legally punished.

Abe Fortas, former justice of the Supreme Court, stated that the term *civil disobedience*, which has been utilized to apply to an individual's refusal to obey a law—a law believed to be immoral or unconstitutional—has in recent years been misapplied. Civil disobedience does not apply to attempts to overthrow or seize control of the government by force; nor does the term apply to the use of violence in order to compel the government to grant a measure of autonomy to a segment of its population. Such programs advocate revolution and the term *civil disobedience* is not appropriately used in this context.

Some propagandists seem to think that people who violate the laws of public order ought not to be punished if their violation has protest

FIGURE 1.4 (a).   *The black minorities vocal attack against police authority has reached a point whereby positive communication between groups is almost nonexistent. These pictures depict the antagonism displayed toward the San Francisco Police Department during a Black Panther Rally. Courtesy San Francisco Police Department, San Francisco, Cal.*

FIGURE 1.4 (b).   *Courtesy San Francisco Police Department, San Francisco, Cal.*

as its purpose. By calling criminal acts "civil disobedience," they seek to persuade us that offenses against public and private security should be immune from punishment and even commended. They seek to excuse physical attacks upon police; assaults upon recruiters for munitions firms and for the armed services; breaking windows in the Pentagon and in homes; robbing stores; trespassing on private premises; occupying academic offices, and even looting, burning and promiscuous violence.[28]

The First Amendment freedoms are not a sanction for riotous behavior; freedom of speech, freedom of the press and of assembly do not correlate with looting, burning, assault, and physical abuse. The United States Supreme Court has stated explicitly that the First Amendment protects the right to *assemble* and to *petition*, but it requires that the rights be peacefully executed.[29]

The police department is recognized as the strongest and most sensitive arm of the local government; therefore, as such, it is the normal agent

[28]A. Fortas, *Concerning Dissent and Disobedience* (New York: The New American Library, 1968), p. 10.
[29]Ibid.

for promoting a community relations problem. The identification is not founded in political essence, but is an offspring of social values as well. As mentioned in this chapter and elaborated in chapters to follow, the ills of a community are most apt to be directed toward the symbolic wielder of community's authority, and the police agency is the normal objective of the scorn of the oppressed.

In the final analysis, effective law enforcement depends upon the full participation of all members of our society in the legislative and administrative process. In this period of dynamic social change and the movement toward full integration of hitherto excluded minorities into the decision-making structure, there will continue to be difficulties, tensions, and crises that spring from the dissatisfaction and despair fostered by social, economic, and political patterns of discrimination against minority groups.

The deteriorating relationships of minorities and young citizens with law enforcement agencies offer perhaps the most poignant evidence of the need for closing the communication gap between police and these citizens. Much hostility of the violent crowds in Watts, Harlem, Philadelphia, Rochester, Newark, Chicago, Detroit, and other cities or communities mentioned in this volume was directed toward the most visible symbol of community restrictiveness, the police force. As minorities, civil rights organizations, and young students continue to use violent and nonviolent demonstrations to dramatize social problems and revoke the inequities of racial discrimination, inevitably there will be increasing confrontation of police and representatives of these groups, requiring special insights and attitudes on the part of both law enforcement officials and the leaders of these groups.

FIGURE 1.5.

SUMMARY

Chapter One introduces the problems relating to police-community relations. It also comments on the conflicts between minority groups and police agencies. Along these lines, it is pointed out that when clear communication is most important between minorities and policemen, it actually tends to decrease, thus obscuring the similarities or common goals they might share. This conflict interferes seriously with public confidence in police and consequently with the ability of the police to deal effectively with the crime problem.

American law enforcement tradition appears to have been influenced by major differences in the ethnic background of those comprising the city's population. Society's enforcement of behavior regulations has moved beyond the point of simple, uncomplicated answers, and law enforcement in urbanized societies increasingly needs positive efforts to anticipate and redirect these social forces tending to jeopardize the personal safety and property security of individuals. Discharge of this particular police responsibility therefore must become a matter of community relations.

Law enforcement human relations is defined in this chapter as "police participation in an activity that seeks law observance through respect rather than enforcement."

The absence of adequate resources, training, and guidance for policemen is discussed, as is the concurrent tendency for individual police officers to depend largely on improvisation. The latter part of the chapter focuses on the problems associated with enforcement of laws during the last decade. This situation relates to two developments: (1) recent decisions made by the United States Supreme Court and (2) the series of civil disturbances associated with efforts to upgrade the status of minority groups.

Finally civil disobedience is defined and described. Civil disobedience does not apply to violent and destructive behavior, but instead to peaceful demonstration against laws believed to be unjust or immoral.

DISCUSSION TOPICS

1. Discuss the problem of police-community relations.
2. Define human relations.
3. Why is law enforcement undergoing a period of uncertainty?
4. Discuss the "Black Revolt," a specific problem in police-community relations.
5. Discuss the misapplication of the term *civil disobedience*.

ANNOTATED REFERENCES

BAYLEY, D. H., AND H. MENDELSOHN, *Minorities and The Police: Confrontation in America.* New York: The Free Press, 1968. The authors explore the "texture of relations between the police and the community, especially minority groups." In this particular study, completed in Denver, Colorado, the authors show how police and minorities perceive their relationship and, furthermore, attempt to show what factors cause minorities and police to view one another in a particular way. An excellent study, relating quite significantly to the subject matter in Chapter One.

BOUMA, D., *Kids and Cops: A Study In Mutual Hostility.* Grand Rapids: William B. Erdmans, 1969. This volume concerns itself with police-community relations with the youth. It discusses the opinions held by young people relating to the police and vice versa. This particular study included 10,000 students in ten Michigan cities, and over 300 police officers in three cities. Along the same lines, ROBERT L. DERBYSHYRE's article on "Children's Perceptions of the Police" published in the *Journal of Criminal Law, Criminology and Police Science*, June 1968, covers the same topic, with emphasis on the younger child. See also: R. PORTUNE, *Changing Adolescent Attitudes Toward Police.* Cincinnati: W. H. Anderson Co., 1971. Portune's book covers the same subject but in a much more extensive manner.

CRAWFORD, T. J., "Police Overperception of Ghetto Hostility," *Journal of Police Science and Administration*, 1, No. 2 (June 1973), pp. 168–74. An excellent, concise study of the subject title. The authors suggest that police violent overreaction to relatively slight hostile acts changed what might have been minor incidents into major disorders. See also in the same journal, G. E. CARTE, "Changes in Public Attitudes Toward Police: A Comparison of 1938 and 1971 surveys," pp. 182–200.

KUYKENDALL, J. L., "Police and Minority Groups: Toward a Theory of Negative Contacts," in *Police.* Springfield, Ill.: Charles C. Thomas, Publisher, 1970. Kuykendall discusses the hostility, danger, anxiety, distrust, and hatred inherited in police–minority-group contacts. He also examines these relationships and the dynamics of the negative contact situations. The author gives a vivid picture of each minority group.

LOMAX, L. E., *The Negro Revolt.* New York: Harper & Row, 1964. Explains the history behind freedom riders, sit-ins, prayer marches, and the development and meaning of the racial protests of the last decade.

REASONS, C. E., AND J. L. KUYKENDALL, eds., *Race, Crime, and Justice*. Pacific Palisades, Goodyear Publishing Co., Inc., Cal.: 1972. This reader incorporates interdisciplinary writings which assess both historical and contemporary ramifications of a dual system of justice. It also probes the dense convoluted relationship between the American legal structure and racial minorities.

WATSON, N. A., *Issues in Human Relations*. Gaithersburg, Md.: International Association of Chiefs of Police, 1973. In reviewing the need for public support of police goals, this book deals with the attitude and procedures of police agencies in the context of community relations programming.

POLICE AND THE COMMUNITY:
Historical and Contemporary Perspectives

2

Law enforcement and the equal administration of justice have become of major concern in recent years. The rapid growth of our population—particularly in our urban areas—with attendant problems in housing, education, employment, and social welfare services has accentuated these concerns and has been highlighted by the increasing social change. The subject of social change has many facets, but its most popular concept is bound to involve the struggle of the minorities to gain equality in all aspects of everyday life. This struggle is moving forward rapidly on the American scene. Its effect on the administration of criminal justice, particularly the police segment, is more than merely incidental. The effect of ghetto life on crime and delinquency is substantial; crime rates have been generally higher in these areas where poverty, family disintegration, unemployment, lack of education, minority-group frustration, and resentment in the face of social and economic discrimination—the ghetto syndrome—are manifest. The expectations, excitements, and additional frustrations engendered by the failure of some to understand fully the aspirations and problems of minority groups have compounded the difficulties in law enforcement and administration of justice.

Foremost among these difficulties are the relationships among police, minority groups, and the general community. There is increasing evidence of deterioration in these relationships and they incorporate polarities between the police and the groups within the community they serve. There are widespread charges of "police brutality" and demand for greater assertion of civilian control over police actions. On the other hand, many police officials decry the growing disrespect for law, public apathy, mollycoddling of "criminals" by the courts, and political influence on the law enforcement process. Some police continue to view civil rights group members as trouble-makers, disruptive of the law and order the police have sworn to uphold. At the same time, some minority-group members hold a stereotyped image of the policeman. These misconceptions severely hamper cooperative relationships.

SOCIAL CHANGE: IMPLICATIONS FOR LAW ENFORCEMENT

According to population experts, America is undergoing dramatic changes in urban population. This means that reappraisals must be made of most governmental operations. Vast are the implications of these changes for the reorganization of law enforcement agencies and for the redefinition of their functions. Quantitatively, the displacement of booming populations to growing suburban areas and the emerging of the "metropolitan area" has introduced new problems of crime control in general, and police-community relations in particular. Even more elusive and perhaps even more difficult to resolve are the qualitative effects. Population growth has changed central-city concentration little, but the "flight to the suburbs" has drained the inner city of those groups in the population which traditionally were forces for social control and stability. Responsibilities for such control come to rest more and more in government—more specifically, in law enforcement agencies. While the city provides decreasing psychological security for its inhabitants, it is the crying need for some security that characterizes increasing proportions of the population, especially the rapidly growing numbers of minority-group members caught in the difficult transition from folk to urban values. With constant changes in composition in the population, unceasing reassessment is required. If the dialogue between the community and law enforcement agencies breaks down, reassessment becomes impossible and the potential for constructive action is sharply curtailed.

The People and the Police:
Potential Explosiveness in Continuing Conflict

A process has taken place in the United States that has afflicted many civilizations in the past and has usually been a prelude to their disintegration. It is that people who have traditionally made a living from agriculture were driven from the land by technological changes and poured into metropolitan cities that were not able to absorb them.

In the third century A.D., for example, there were drastic changes in the agriculture of the Roman world. Small farms gave way to the latifundia

—huge holdings engaged in mass production based on slave labor. The productivity of the land was increased by the use of technology, but when free farmers were no longer able to till the soil, their migration caused chaos in the cities. "The social consequence," wrote Arnold Toynbee in *A Study of History*, "was the depopulization of the countryside and the creation of a parasitic urban proletariat in the cities. . . ."

The parallel with the American dilemma is striking. Technological changes in agriculture—primarily the replacement of men by machines—have uprooted masses of farm workers and driven them to the cities to seek precarious refuge in the slums and ghettos. Thus far, American leaders seem as helpless before the problem as were the Romans.

State legislatures and the United States House of Representatives have failed to reapportion themselves sufficiently as a population has moved from farm to town. Still another problem to be analyzed in the future concerns the effects the energy crisis will have on city dwellers. The mobility of the urban dweller has been acknowledged as a barrier to complete disintegration in the *total* lack of respect and cooperation with agents of the administration of justice. If this mobility is removed, there may be some justification, at least for the activists in our cities, for striking out at the police—"a symbol of the injustices of our society." To some, police are symbolic of all that is wrong in our society.

We are witnessing a breakdown in dialogue. Rather than standing in a *relationship* to the people, the police are now in the unfortunate position of being in *confrontation* with racial and ethnic groups, social action and civil rights groups, the adolescent community, and the court. More than at any other time in our history, the police are estranged from other agencies and from groups within the community. This is the most urgent problem facing our police today.

If the emotions of fear and hate characterize the current relationship between the ethnic minority community and the police, there is both an immediate and a long-range effect of the continuation of these conflicts. An immediate effect is the fact that every contact between a policeman and a minority-group member is tinged with the possibility of violence. Of even greater concern, however, is the transmission of these attitudes to succeeding generations of young people.

The most serious problems are not with the general community; rather, they are found in the relationships the police have with *youth* and *ethnic minority groups*. In these two portions of the community, it is fair to say that the police have been unable to develop effective means of communication. It is doubtful that even the most imaginative public relation techniques would ever be successful, although they must continue to try to resolve differences, in the case of some ethnic minority groups. These techniques, unfortunately, are viewed by some as "self-serving" and "phony," and immediately become suspect. The "hard-to-reach" cannot effectively be engaged with anything less than genuine communication, and this involves a desire and a willingness to talk, to listen, to discuss, and to act. Genuine communication includes the willingness to adjust operating procedures (i.e., harassment, disrespect, discourteous demeanor, etc.) when they appear to be irritating already existing police-community relation problems. It also involves a continuous process of dealing effectively with personal problems in the community.

It is expected that the people deeply involved in confrontations or conflicting viewpoints (such as civil rights movements or civil disobedience campaigns) are not going to see things from the same point of view as the police. The diversity of viewpoints between demonstrators, minority-group members, civil rights participants, or civil disobedience campaigns (those who have been very critical of police actions in many places) and law enforcement personnel (who consider their actions necessary and proper for preserving public peace and order) are the things about which bitter complaints are often made. The complaints quite often concern the *attitudes* shown by the police as well as the *tactics* used. The following illustrates the conflicting viewpoints held by both parties involved. Let us first examine the *complaints against the police*.[1]

> *Police Brutality.*   The most frequently mentioned charge is that the police are brutal in their handling of demonstrators and others, even criminals. Police experience shows that these charges range from vague, nonspecific opinions to cases which do involve excessive use of force contrary to police rules and regulations. What is regarded as brutal depends, of course, on the situation and the individual. Thus, such police actions as restraining individuals in a crowd from proceeding with a march where officers do no more than block the way, especially if they have to shove people back, may be so characterized. Any use of the baton, firing over the heads of the crowd, and use of tear gas, fire hoses, or dogs are tactics often included under the term brutality. The extreme is illustrated in the comment of one Black leader who said Blacks are "fed up with what they consider unprovoked shooting and killing by police." There have been instances in which the use of language itself has been called brutal. Objection has been made to verbal abuse. Rough, harsh language, and especially the use of such derogatory terms as "nigger" and even "boy" is interpreted by many as indicative of a brutal attitude. As Bowen pointed out:
>
>> The Negro fight for civil rights has created a climate of mind in which any arrest or prosecution of a Negro takes on, for many Negroes and

[1]N. A. Watson, *Police-Community Relations* (Washington, D.C.: International Association of Chiefs of Police, 1966), pp. 28–37 (summarized). Courtesy of the publisher.

some whites too, an aspect of discrimination. And it has called down upon the police departments a "brutality" charge that has impaired the morale of policemen and hindered police recruitment.

To a great extent the "police brutality" cries are directed not against actual instances of brutality but against the police as symbols and agents of a white-dominated society. Over a three-year period ending in mid-1965, a total of 4,755 allegations of "police brutality" involving possible violations of Federal law, were referred to the FBI. Out of all these, indictments were returned in 41 cases and convictions were secured in ten. The smoke billows forth, apparently, out of all proportion to the fire.[2]

Differential Treatment of Negroes. Just about as frequent as complaints of police brutality are complaints of differential treatment. This is also at times a rather vague and nonspecific charge. It includes a variety of practices that are regarded as discriminatory. Complainants say, for example, that a black is far more likely to be arrested for a given act than a white man is. And, when arrested, he is more likely to be convicted and sent to jail. Blacks complain they are more frequently accosted and questioned by police—in other words, suspected—than are white citizens. Police are believed by blacks to be more officious with them, i.e., to order them around. Also, and very important, they feel that police do not pay as much attention to complaints by blacks, that they do not take as seriously offenses by blacks against blacks, as they would if a white person were the victim. In line with the brutality charges, they see the police as more likely to use physical force against them than against whites.

One of the problems here, as seen by blacks and others who are largely in working-class minorities, is policing on the basis of social class. Many lower-class people believe that they get different treatment at the hands of the police than do people of greater means. A black who is an official in a labor union drives a Thunderbird. He says he has been stopped by the police five times in two years merely for questioning. On the occasions when he was well-dressed he was courteously requested to show his driver's license and car registration and permitted to go on. On one occasion he was working around his house and, roughly dressed, went to a lumber yard for some supplies. That time he was ordered out of the car, spread-eagled against it and searched. Obviously the officers must have thought that a person dressed as he was must have stolen the car. The man was not charged with a traffic violation at any time.

Another example is that of a white-collar type businessman who drives a nice looking automobile that was involved in an accident. He did not stop in time at a traffic light and rammed the car in front. The car he hit was a rattletrap driven by a poorly dressed black. The police

[2]W. Bowen, "Crime in the Cities, An Unnecessary Crisis," *Fortune* (Dec. 1965), p. 141.

came to investigate. The businessman said, "They were 'sir-ing' me all over the place, but they were harsh and gruff with the man whose car I hit. I had to remind them that I was the one who was at fault."

Another aspect of this class-based treatment is the use of language or remarks which show disapproval or disparagement, which belittle or discredit the person being contacted. An officer stopped a black woman on the street late one night and asked her what she was doing there. She replied she had just finished work and was on her way home. He asked where she worked and what she did. She told him she worked at the Hotel _____ (a high-class place) and that she was a cook. The officer said, "You mean you're a dishwasher?" The woman really was a cook. This is one small example of downgrading by a thoughtless remark. It is a type of carelessness we must guard against in our contacts.

It is important for us to understand that when people think they are being treated differently, they are likely to react differently. Acts which to the officer seem entirely proper and justified may be regarded as highly discriminative. It is not unexpected, therefore, that blacks regard some arrests as maliciously intended. This is often the reaction, too, to actions taken by police when searching for logical suspects in a crime.

"Overpolicing" in Minority Districts. This complaint is actually another instance of differential treatment, but it bears special mention because of its relationship to one of the basic principles of police administration. The effective allocation of men and selective enforcement are administrative procedures which aim at economical and effective deployment of manpower. Police attempt to concentrate their enforcement resources at those times, places, and events where violations of law are more likely to occur. To do otherwise would result in inefficiency and waste as well as markedly reduced progress toward the objectives for which police are maintained.

It so happens, however, that the concentration of police in black districts is regarded by many as both insulting and threatening. The presence of police obviously does lead to arrests for violations of the law. Arrest statistics together with complaints and offenses otherwise known do tend to show higher crime rates in those districts where there are more officers. Some minority-group leaders have maintained that this concentration of police in itself helps produce comparatively higher crime rates because offenses in other districts are going unnoticed since the police are not there. The difference here is, in part, a controversy as to which is cause and which is effect.

Another aspect of this complaint is the charge by blacks that police harass them. Harassment, they maintain, involves unnecessary and unjustified questioning, frisking under questionable circumstances, traffic stops and car searches on flimsy suspicions, breaking up of small gatherings where no law is being violated, and other practices. They see as a special kind of harassment what they regard as the harsh and unsympathetic reception given a Negro who lodges a complaint against an officer. Arrests on trumped-up charges, false arrests, are also mentioned as a type of harassment.

An example of the kind of policing involved in this complaint was recounted by a member of a Human Relations Commission. In a certain city there was a honky-tonk district where rowdyism on New Year's Eve was common. This particular New Year's Eve was no exception. A fight broke out and officers on the scene called for help. Some of the persons involved were blacks; most were not. Squad cars were dispatched to the scene. But, curiously, squad cars were also dispatched "on the double" to the "downtown" area of the black section—where there was no trouble. The people there pointed to this circumstance as an indication of the readiness of the police to believe the worst about all blacks.

In contrast to the attitude of some blacks relative to the presence of police, is the widespread feeling among middle- and upper-class blacks that they want and need police protection. Police experience shows that these citizens are just as concerned about civil disorder and crime as white citizens in similar socioeconomic brackets. Instead of complaining about the presence of police, they request it.

Improper Policing of Demonstrations.   Complaints have been made that police are too strict in their supervision of legitimate demonstrations. The conditions laid down by the police, the ground rules, are sometimes regarded as unfairly restrictive. Some complainants allege suppression of legitimate demonstrations. This would involve such practices as refusal to grant parade permits and blocking access to the objective of the demonstration as, for example, city hall. Some demonstrators have complained about police taking their pictures during a demonstration, a procedure they regard as a threat.

Associated with this charge are additional complaints of police brutality. Demonstrators who refuse to move after proper warning and who have to be bodily carried to police vehicles complain of intentional rough handling. Occasionally, women have complained that officers have taken immoral advantage of this situation or have embarrassed them by careless, "undignified," or "ungraceful" handling.

It is unquestionably true that improper policing of demonstrations can divert the demonstrators from their original target and cause them to focus on the police. Militant leaders can take advantage of inept incorrect police action to escalate the demonstration and enlist sympathizers. The right to demonstrate peaceably, the right of peaceful protest, is basic to our form of government. The actions of demonstrators and protestors, no matter how peaceful, however, cannot be permitted to prohibit the free exercise of the rights of others. This is one of the reasons police control is required. In our democracy it is not the function of the police to prevent properly conducted demonstrations or protests no matter how distasteful they may be so long as they do not violate the law. It is the function of the police to protect peaceful demonstrators against interference by rowdies or counter-demonstrators. The police are not in business to maintain the old way of life by preventing social change. In these matters there is a fine line between proper and improper policing. This is one of the reasons a community cannot afford untrained police.

Use of Black Officers.   The confusion that exists is well illustrated in charges involving discriminatory assignment of black policemen. On the one hand, several instances were reported in which blacks had expressed displeasure when black officers were assigned to answer their calls; they wanted white policemen. So did some white persons. On the other hand, there are also complaints from blacks that not enough black officers are assigned to duty where they live. Then, too, there are complaints that not enough blacks are employed as policemen and that too few of them are employed in command positions. A few years ago, just seeing blacks as officers was enough, but we have moved on from there and now blacks want increasingly to see black officers move up the ladder. Blacks also sometimes object that black officers are assigned only to black districts, that they are not permitted to arrest white offenders, that they are discriminated against in promotions, and that when police work in pairs they are assigned only with other blacks. One chief reported he had been criticized for not seeking to recruit black officers in other cities when he pointed out the lack of qualified applicants at home.

Lack of Confidence in Police.   There have been well-publicized charges that police are "on the take," some of which are true. Some complaints have charged that police permit gambling, prostitution, illegal liquor and narcotic activities, fencing operations, and the like because they are being paid off by the criminals. Such beliefs produce a lack of confidence in law enforcement in general. The racial situation as it has developed in the past few years has resulted in increased sensitivity on the part of the populace and the police to those aspects of police operations that impinge on the civil rights question. Some police executives have noted that complaints about the police seem to relate more directly to bad attitudes, whether fancied or real, on the part of officers than they do to improper actions. This lack of confidence has produced demands for Citizens' Review Boards to review complaints concerning police actions.

A good indication of the problems as seen by *police officers* can be achieved by reviewing the complaints they made. Their complaints, which are self-explanatory, are as follows:

1.   Assaults on officers.
2.   Verbal abuse, provocation, and baiting of police.

3. Defiance and interference with lawful arrests and other police functions.

4. Lack of respect for police authority and the law. In this connection several respondents remarked that their men have noticed an increasing belligerence and arrogance.

5. Lack of manpower and fear of unwarranted attacks against lone officers by black groups when making routine traffic stops or other normal enforcement activities.

6. Black officers complain about abusive language from black demonstrators.

7. False accusations against police. In connection with these accusations, some have noted that the purpose behind them seems to be harassment of the police. Some have also complained that lack of prosecution for false accusations encourages more of the same. As a sidelight, some police officers have complained about the detailed reports that are required when such complaints are made even though the complaints are patently false. In this connection, a man engaged in police-community relations activities in a large city told the writer of his experience. This man is a black and is not a policeman. He said that in his police-community relations work he has talked with many blacks who complained about police behavior. Some of the cases, although minor in nature, appeared to be justified in that the officer probably could have handled himself with greater finesse. On the other side of the coin, he said he had been told by some complainants that they had made the complaint as defensive strategy. They felt that a complaint of brutality would give them some bargaining leverage. In other instances, they admitted that the complaint was made in order to "get back at" the officer for arresting them.

8. Lack of police power to take effective action *before* overt acts of violence occur.

9. Despite the fact that many police departments would gladly employ qualified blacks as police officers, they are sometimes unable to do so because blacks will not apply. Some respondents attribute this to the fact that police are looked upon with such disfavor by the black community that young men who would make good policemen are unwilling to face the disapproval they fear would result. Others say it is mainly because qualified blacks can command higher pay than police departments are able to offer. It should be said here that the reaction of many police chiefs to this situation is not one of complete resignation to a hopeless situation. Some have taken special steps to find qualified men. The general feeling is that qualifications should not be lowered. Nor should [black] applicants be hired simply for the sake of having some blacks in uniform. That would not be fair to the public, including blacks.

10. Growing resistance to overtures at friendly communication on police beats in minority areas. Some have complained that even though police officers have tried to establish friendly relationships in

FIGURE 2.1 (a). *Dramatic sequence photos depict the event that led to blow-off in yester-year's anti-war demonstration violence in Union Square. After a minibus has been ordered stopped by demonstrators and its passengers forced to leave, motorcycle policemen reach the scene. A policeman skids off safety isle and almost falls. Someone has thrown a small fire missile, which sends up a thin trail of smoke as it sizzles near the machine. The spark reaches the spilled fuel and the motorcycle erupts into flame. Courtesy San Francisco Examiner newspaper, San Francisco, Cal.*

FIGURE 2.1 (b).

FIGURE 2.1 (c).

FIGURE 2.1 (d).   Courtesy of San Francisco Examiner newspaper, San Francisco, Cal.

the interest of harmony and good police service, they have been unable to do so because the people react to them with coldness and remain aloof, if not actually hostile.

11.   Many officers have complained that the law is being applied unequally, with preferential treatment being given to minority groups. They feel that pressure groups have succeeded in preventing police from fully enforcing the law where minority individuals are concerned. Officers complain that they must assume a "kid gloves" attitude in order not to overstep their authority and to avoid criticism against which they have no adequate defense. Many officers feel that no amount of "bending over backwards to be fair" can satisfy what they regard as the unreasonable expectations of the more militant leaders and, at the same time, allow for effective enforcement of the law.

12.   Apathy of the public and lack of backing in enforcing the law. Police sometimes feel that they are being asked to do an impossible job. They are expected to maintain order and to arrest violators and, having done so, find that when the "heat is turned on" they are "left holding the bag." In this connection, they find particularly discouraging the support given by some public officials to acts of civil disobedience. They see in this a kind of encouragement for lawbreaking with the officials "feathering his political nest," at the expense of respect for law and order. On the other hand, the police are required by law to protect from interference and violence persons who are engaging in peaceful protest or demonstration. That is a right guaranteed to any citizen, but many people, sometimes the majority, will turn against the police when they offer that protection.

13.   Police often complain about the lenience of the courts and their hesitance to convict when the race issue is raised as a defense

14.   Officers remark that minority group members seem increasingly ready to complain about minor matters, routine matters, and police actions that are essential and unavoidable in the enforcement of the law. However, we must realize that even routine methods that are legally right and properly used may be regarded as objectionable by persons who dislike the police anyway.

15.   Some officers feel that undue emphasis is being placed on the racial aspects of many questions affecting police performance at the expense of successful enforcement against criminals.

16.   Unfair treatment by the news media. Police complain about the nature of the photographs that are printed in newspapers and the interpretation placed upon them. They often feel that the police are portrayed unfavorably and are being used as whipping boys.

17.   Complaints have been registered about inflammatory public statements by religious and other minority group leaders which stereotype police officers as prejudiced and insensitive.

18.   In a few instances officers have complained that incidents have

been set up or manuevered in such a way as to deliberately place the police in an unfavorable light.[3]

It can be seen from a study of these complaints that there remains a serious communication gap. The viewpoints as to the realities of situations growing out of racial tensions are certainly widely divergent. As one official remarked, "There appears to be a communications block between law enforcement administrators and police officers on the one hand and minority group leaders and the minority group 'man on the street' on the other." He expressed the opinion that this "block" appears to be growing. He said, "The minority group leaders seem to have an increasing fear of an Uncle Tom label which militant leaders place upon those who do communicate." He feels that the average minority-group citizen is being unduly influenced by what he calls the propaganda of the militant leaders, which labels law enforcement as a tool of the white power structure. The differences in viewpoint illustrated by the foregoing point out the difficulties involved in impartially and impersonally enforcing the law and the importance of reaching an effective medium of communication.

The urgent need for clear understanding of the problems as the people see them requires that we go to them. It is only by listening attentively to their ideas and suggestions—even when these are only implied in complaints—that we can arrive at a productive definition of the problems. Why should we not seek the help of our constituents? In their counsel we may find the answers to aggravating situations. One Negro leader who had been invited to speak to a police-community relations forum started off by saying, "I am a militant, I am a radical. But I am not a lunatic. My reaction to the invitation to speak to you was first one of amazement. This is the first time in all the years I have been active in this work that the police have ever shown any interest in hearing what I have to say. Second, my reaction is one of gratitude. I am pleased to discuss our problems with you. I don't expect you to like everything I have to say, but I do expect that we will all go away with a better understanding of each other." The rest of his talk and the dialogue that followed did promote better understanding. It is a certainty that the police officials in attendance went away enriched in their ability to cope with the kinds of problems that were brought out. It would seem wise to listen to the viewpoints, the gripes, the suggestions of many kinds of people— businessmen, the poor, youths, ethnic group representatives, civic leaders, and so on.

Although we will discuss attitudes more fully in Chapter 4, it is appropriate to point out here that the view law enforcement has of demonstrators,

---

[3]Watson, *Police-Community Relations*. By permission of the publisher.

civil disobedience participants, and certain members of the minority groups is often a result of the attitudes taken toward law enforcement. Attitudes on both sides must change. If law enforcement programs ignore the conditions that have motivated the behavior of these groups, then police officers will continue to act in ways that invite hostility, anger, and even outright violence.

Violence has been known to our society. It has been part of the history of the United States and other countries for many centuries. The historical content of such activities will be discussed in the following section as well as the tangle of issues and circumstances—social, economic, political, and psychological—which arise out of the historic pattern of police-community relations in America.

RIOTS AND CIVIL DISOBEDIENCE: HISTORICAL AND CONTEMPORARY ASPECTS

As we have seen, civil disobedience, racial violence, and riots have been part of the history of the United States. Citizen-police confrontations have, therefore, existed as a law enforcement problem in one form or another for a long time. Perhaps such confrontations are indigenous to our society, which was largely founded by dissenters and was from the beginning dedicated to the freedom of expression and conscience.

Curry and King state in their book, *Race, Tension and the Police*,[4] that violence has changed very little through the years. Some of the contemporary disturbances in the United States are similar in many respects to those that have occurred throughout history. Thus, the contemporary literature draws on established elements of both past and contemporary problems: persuasive insecurities, a mounting current of crime, prosperity existing side by side with poverty, and the ironic contrast between the positive aspects of our competitive society and the continued spread of crime.[5]

Historical Aspects

In this section, we trace the pattern and identify the recurrent themes of political and social unrest and, most importantly, provide a perspective for protest activities of the present era. This section, therefore, begins with an outline of citizen demonstrations and a brief account of their development. *The past has much to tell us about the present.* To comprehend the contemporary police-community relation problems in the United States, it is necessary to examine, evaluate, and derive some understanding of such historical problems.

[4]J. E. Curry and G. D. King, *Race, Tension and the Police* (New York: Wiley & Sons, 1970).

[5]D. J. Bordua, ed., *The Police: Six Sociological Essays* (New York: Wiley & Sons, 1967), p. 3.

The following are brief summaries of some of the most serious disturbances in the United States. (For an extensive examination of such historical disturbances, see Appendix A.) Selected from Thomas J. Fleming's article, *"Revolt in America,"*[6] they represent the varied types of problems which have led to violence over a broad period of time and in different geographical areas.

SHAYS' REBELLION: In 1786, Daniel Shays—captain of a regiment during the War of Independence—along with 1,500 farmers, prevented the state's court from convening for the purpose of foreclosure proceedings for debts resulting from a depression in the state of Massachusetts. They blocked all attempts on foreclosures of property for debt. The mob soon got out of control and proceeded to physically abuse officials, loot homes, and made serious threats to burn government buildings.

Shays' "army" soon disintegrated into a handful of fugitives, with Shays himself fleeing to Vermont when the governor of Massachusetts declared the state "in a period of rebellion" and ordered the militia into active status.

NAT TURNER'S REVOLT: This significant rebellion on the part of some of Virginia's 400,000 slaves has been covered by numerous books—

FIGURE 2.2. *Nat Turner (1800–1831). American slave leader. From a nineteenth-century American wood engraving. Reproduced with permission from The Granger Collection.*

[6]Summarized with permission of T. J. Fleming from "Revolt in America," *This Week* (Sept. 1, 1968), © United Newspapers Magazine Corp., pp. 2–8.

one, *The Confessions of Nat Turner*, written by William Styron, received an excellent response.

Nat Turner launched an insurrection in Southampton County, Virginia in 1831. On the night of August 21, he and a few companions murdered several farmers and their families throughout the countryside. Twenty farms were attacked, and before the rampage was brought to an end by the county militia, at least forty Negroes died in the fighting and twelve were executed. The death toll of the whites totaled approximately fifty-seven.

Nat Turner was subsequently hanged, and although his insurrection was neither the first nor the last Negro revolt, its mindless violence was "so appalling, he [Turner] silenced all hope of emancipating the Negro by peaceful vote, as Thomas Jefferson and James Madison had for decades pleaded."

THE DRAFT RIOTS: In 1863, President Abraham Lincoln's administration had decided that the war was going badly, and the North was in need of a considerable increase in manpower. Therefore, the draft was initiated as a desperate measure. Unfortunately, Congress in its efforts to "push through the Bill," constructed a rather unfair—that is, unfair to the poor—draft law (a substitute could be hired for $300 to take the place of the drafted person), which precipitated the infamous draft riots in New York City on July 13, 1863.

Approximately 800,000 draft-eligibles resided in New York City, and about 10,000 people protested the drawing of names for the city's first draft on July 11, 1863. With the assistance, in the opinion of some

FIGURE 2.3.   *The New York City Draft Riots of July 13–16, 1863. Wood engraving from a contemporary German-language American newspaper. Reproduced with permission from The Granger Collection.*

historians, of Confederate soldiers who had infiltrated the city, the mob surged down Broadway to 29th Street, where the Federal Provost Marshal was scheduled to draw more names of those eligible for the draft. Police officers, attempting to control the situation, were severely beaten—some critically. The "demonstrators" forced the Provost Marshal and his staff to withdraw and devastated the building, eventually setting it on fire.

The riot continued for four days and on several occasions, troops were forced to use point-blank artillery fire to disperse howling charges. (federal authorities had eventually dispatched troops to the embattled city.) On the fourth day, battle-tired regiments from the Army of the Potomac poured into the city, and the draft riot was brought to a halt.

THE GREAT STRIKE: In 1877, America was in its fourth year of a terrible depression. At this particular period, the four largest railroads in the country announced that wages were going to be decreased by at least 10 percent. Because the nonunionized employees were being paid very poor wages (approximately $1.75 per day) and a single railroad, the Pennsylvania, reportedly showed net profits of $25,000,000 a year, the attempt to slash the workers' pay touched off a national crisis.

Employees on the Baltimore and Ohio, the Pennsylvania, the New York Central, and the Erie refused to work—in essence, they struck. The strikers seized the railroad yards in Baltimore and did not permit any trains to move. Freight and buildings were destroyed. And the rioters' numbers grew to an estimated 15,000. President Rutherford B. Hayes responded to the plea from the governor of the state and dispatched 500 federal troops to Baltimore. The disturbance subsided almost immediately upon the show of force.

In Pittsburgh, the strikers followed the same pattern, but there they were far better organized, and their leaders were men with wilder ideas. It was necessary, therefore, to rush 650 state militiamen from Philadelphia. Upon their arrival, they fought a battle with the strikers, killing approximately 25. The rioters forced the Philadelphia militia into the Pennsylvania roundhouse and bombarded them with bricks; in fact, in several instances, the dissenters utilized firearms. Freight cars were burned, and the Philadelphia militia was forced to "fight their way out from the roundhouse and retreat."

Like a contagious disease, the strike moved from city to city; Omaha, San Francisco, and St. Louis felt the sting of the reactionary mob. In New York and Buffalo, the Central yards were seized. Rioters stormed through the streets of Chicago, forcing workers to quit their jobs, shutting down factories, stores, and construction projects and intimidating officials into signing papers promising to raise wages.

Acting on advice from a Civil War general, President Hayes actually ordered a proclamation prepared declaring that the unruly rioters were

FIGURE 2.4. *The Great Railroad Strike of 1877. Wood engraving from a contemporary American newspaper. Reproduced with permission from The Granger Collection.*

"levying war" against the United States. However, before the proclamation was made, the great strike had begun to be brought into control by state militiamen, local policemen, and on several occasions, federal troops.

JACOB COXEY'S "INDUSTRIAL ARMY": In 1894, Jacob Coxey, a reformer, led a group of unemployed in a march on Washington. In order to sustain themselves, his followers stole food as they advanced. However, Coxey soon saw that a majority of the people of the United States were extremely hostile to his "industrial army." He gathered only 1,200 protestors in Washington instead of the 100,000 he had so confidently predicted prior to the march.

The riots, mob disturbances, and all-out rebellion described above certainly do not represent the entire scope of disturbances that have taken place in the United States. There have been other times when Americans were extremely concerned, fearing that the nation was on the fringe of anarchism. For example, when the Industrial Workers of the World issued a cry for removal of the system utilized to set wages and called for strikes to sabotage the war effort during World War I, Americans were very apprehensive. The federal government quickly took the union leaders into custody and filed charges of sedition. Such tactics eliminated them as a force in American labor. In 1932, 15,000 World War I veterans assembled in Washington in the "Bonus March" to demand from Congress immediate payment on certificates that had been issued for their war service, and which were not legally due until 1945. The majority returned home peacefully when Congress declined to pass the bill they wanted. The president reluctantly ordered the army to expel the 300 who refused to leave the Capitol grounds.

Nature, Scope, and Extent of
Contemporary Police-Citizen Confrontations

In the 1960s, we witnessed numerous savage urban disorders in American society. It is apparent that attacks upon both representatives of government agencies (i.e., police, firemen, National Guardsmen, court and correctional personnel) and property are ageless manifestations of social problems. The events that touch off violent mass disturbances are deeply rooted in the neighborhood, the community, the family, the times in which we live and, as we shall see, the *administration of the criminal justice system and process* (i.e., police, courts, and corrections).[7] Some of our contemporary problems have centered around the Vietnam War; the radical transformations in com-

---

[7]Much of the information in this section relating to population change was adopted with permission from D. L. Lohman, "Race Tension and Conflict," in Watson, *Police and the Changing Community*, pp. 42–47. See also *The National Commission Report on Urban Problems* (Washington, D.C.: U.S. Government Printing Office, 1968).

munity life of our time; and the transition of urban populations, which involves the wholesale settlement of minority-group members and causes problems of housing, of income, etc. These changes within metropolitan regions, along with the more liberal attitude of college students, have generated problems of crime control which ultimately have resulted in the use of law enforcement personnel.

The following observations were made after a brief examination of urban disorders and police-community relation problems during the past two centuries.[8]

1.   Major disorders or riots have occurred frequently in the cities of the United States.

2.   The causes of riots have been consistently identified as major social issues—for example, labor strikes; wartime conscription; social, racial, ethnic, religious, and nationalistic prejudice, and reactions to it.

3.   Major disorders generated by social movements or by the reaction to government and all nonspecific "others" nearly always take the form of police-mob conflicts.

4.   In disorders which involve two or more struggling factions, the police invariably become engaged as a third faction in an effort to restore tranquility. Their participation may assist or appear to assist the cause of one of the factions or, barring that, may invite the animosity of both factions, neither of which welcomes the attempt to end the contention.

5.   Although riots and poor police-community relationships have both been frequently described in histories of the United States, the two phenomena have rarely been joined in a cause-effect relationship. Before the present decade, there was no mention of strained police-community relationships as a contributing factor to community disorders. On the other hand, there were several depictions of police commanders who, to their later benefit or detriment, established great riot suppression reputations during major disorders.

6.   Following virtually every major disorder, according to contemporary published accounts, the police have been criticized for (a) forbearance in the presence of public disruption and insults to the rule of law and (b) use of excessive force in dispersing mobs and restoring order. Additionally, the police have consistently been accused of (a) slowness in the deployment of force against riotous crowds or (b) a too-quick, provocative use of force, which nourished the full-scale disorder.

7.   Riots usually result in the arrest of many persons—with varying quality of identification and substantiation of charges. Disposition of the cases, however, has nearly always been discharged without prosecu-

[8]V. G. Strecher, *The Environment of Law Enforcement: A Community Relations Guide* (Englewood Cliffs, N.J.: Prentice-Hall, Inc., 1971), pp. 50–51.

tion, even when the number of deaths and serious injuries and the destruction of property have been great. This fact is seldom deplored in contemporary accounts of riots, even in those by police historians. It is as if there is tacit acknowledgment that grave social issues are being worked out.

One of the most significant problems causing discontent and subsequent entrance of law enforcement personnel has been the emergence of the Black inner cities which have developed in the 1950s and early 1960s.

The Changing American Scene: Black Inner Cities

There are basic changes taking place in the community, and these affect the problems that confront law enforcement officials. Cities are becoming the residence of black minority groups, while the whites are moving to the suburbs.

Between 1960 and 1970, the twelve largest cities of the United States lost over two million white residents. In that same period, when white residents were moving beyond the formal municipal limits into the modern metropolitan region, the cities gained almost exactly the same number of nonwhite residents. *Two million blacks moved into the places evacuated by two million white residents.*[9] People came as foreign immigrants to move into the great cities. Residents of the older portions of these cities had social and economic success, and the young people moved on to the widening circle of residential resettlement, the middle-class suburbs. It is well known that many of the problems of law and order are concentrated in particular neighborhoods and involve the trials and tribulations of those groups in transition. But the neighborhoods have now burgeoned into veritable cities in transition. Vast sections of cities have been occupied by the new immigrant people. In places like Baltimore, Detroit, Cleveland, Chicago, Washington, D. C., and St. Louis, as much as a third of the city is made up of these new immigrant groups. So the transition is a transition of cities rather than a transition of neighborhoods.[10]

The consequences of this trend is a new way of life for many people. Diverse groups with conflicting customs and interests suddenly find themselves side by side. And there have been changes in the relative wealth and power of various groups. From these many changes have come special problems, such as housing, which throw groups into competition with one another and thereby become police problems.[11]

[9]Lohman, "Race Tension and Conflict," p. 46.
[10]Ibid., p. 47.
[11]Ibid.

The National Commission on Urban Problems recently released a study which reports that if present trends continue, "America by 1985 would be well on the road toward a society characterized by race classification along racial and economic lines as well as geographic separation."[12]

A projection of population figures by a team of demographers shows that by 1985 central cities will have gained ten million more nonwhites—a 94 percent increase. This would be an acceleration of the trend begun in 1960 of increasingly Black inner cities ringed by burgeoning white suburbs.

Unhappily, the projection vividly portrays the geographic fulfillment of the fears expressed by the President's Commission on Civil Disorders— that American society is becoming apartheid society—that is, divided into two societies, black and white, separate and unequal.

A study by Patricia Leavuy Hodge and Philip Hauser of the University of Chicago points out that although nonwhites are expected to increase numerically in the suburbs to 6.8 million in 1985 (from 2.8 million in 1960), "they will be all but lost in the sea of whites with the non-white suburban population increasing from only five to six percent of the total." Hodge and Hauser also pointed out that, because of their high fertility rates, nonwhites will increase at a greater rate throughout the nation than whites, their proportion of the total population rising from 11 percent in 1960 to 14 percent in 1985.

However, in the central cities, the increase in nonwhites is expected to be greater by 1985. According to projections, the white population there will have dropped to 69 percent (82 percent in 1960), and the nonwhite population will have increased to 31 percent (18 percent nonwhite in 1960), with many major cities having nonwhite majorities. As an example of this situation (black inner cities), the Newark, New Jersey Housing Authority estimates that since 1950 some 200,000 whites have moved out of Newark, while 85,000 blacks have moved in. More than half the population of Oakland, California will be black by 1983 if present trends continue, the President's Commission on Civil Disorders stated in its recent report. Washington, D.C. and Newark, New Jersey are already at that point, the Commission noted. The Commission listed other cities where blacks would be in a majority in 1984 if the present trend continues: New Orleans, Louisiana and Richmond, Virginia in 1971; Baltimore, Maryland and Jacksonville, Florida in 1972; Gary, Indiana in 1973; Cleveland, Ohio in 1975; St. Louis, Missouri in 1978; Detroit, Michigan in 1979; Philadelphia, Pennsylvania in 1981; and Chicago, Illinois in 1984. In addition, in 1985, Dallas, Texas; Buffalo, New York; Cincinnati, Ohio; Harrisburg, Pennsylvania; Louisville, Kentucky; Indianapolis, Indiana; Kansas City, Missouri; Hartford, Connecticut; and New Haven, Connecticut will probably have black majorities.

12*The National Commission Report on Urban Problems*, p. 8.

The majority of black immigrants are often deficient in education and job skills. Some of them must be supported by public welfare, and many do not know how to live in cities. Obviously, dialogue and communications are difficult; therefore, these specific features of the discontent and deprivation are separately and together an expression of radical changes in population distribution. The central features of the times which are commonplace in our society make up the context in which we must identify all problems. And if we so identify them, it may be possible that we will see them quite differently. In any event, if there are those in America who expect groups in our society to act differently than they currently do, they should realize that this will happen only if the necessary conditions come about.

The question then arises, What is the role of the police in our contemporary society? With the transition of the urban community generating conditions that promote and sustain social problems, the role of law enforcement agencies will expand rapidly. In Chapter One we reviewed the role of a contemporary policeman handling his tasks during a routine day. We will now attempt to examine the role of law enforcement in our rapidly changing society.

Many demands for change in important areas of our national life are being made. These in turn generate controversies and produce a great deal of resistance to the proposed changes. Most of us in the police field recognize that there is a need for change because of the constantly rising crime rates and the increasing number and intensity of instances of disorder and violence. Likewise we are faced with a demand for many different kinds of services than we were formerly expected to perform. Moreover, people are looking to the police for effective programs to prevent crime and violence, a matter in which we have not been notably successful.

That the police have problems with change cannot be denied. Some people agitate for change and others balk at change. The net result is trouble. The police find themselves often in the unenviable position of having to oppose certain people who wish to see changes made because of the police commitment to enforcement of the law. This was expressed very well by William L. Cahalan, Wayne County Prosecuting Attorney, in an address to the Michigan Chiefs of Police Association in June, 1969, when he said:

> In Los Angeles, when a prominent peace advocate was murdered, his followers asked, "Where are the police?"
>
> A few months later in Chicago, when many of his followers were advocating their cause, they asked, "Why so many police?"
>
> In short, the police represent and enforce the existing order. In an open society committed to change, the existing order is always open to challenge. Hence, the American pastime of challenging the authority of

the policeman—at one time asking for his protection, at another time scorning him as an oppressor. It is bad enough to incur the disfavor of the lawless, but the policeman frequently finds himself incurring the disfavor of all who disagree with the existing policy of government, a policy he did not form.

No one is suggesting that the police set the policy of government or that the police abandon their role of enforcing and maintaining the existing order. It is finally being recognized, late though it is, that the policeman's role is not only complex and taxing, but that the policeman, more than anyone else in government, represents the balance between anarchy and totalitarianism, between the desire of people to be both free and secure.

The point of our discussion is that we often run into trouble with change because of the way people perceive it. In other words, it is not the change itself but what people think it means to them which makes the difference. . . .

. . . Our society today is undergoing major changes in a number of important ways, many of them painful to a lot of people. The old order, referred to as "the establishment," is being bitterly criticized and seriously challenged by many. The charge is that the establishment has failed and those who would change it advocate courses of action ranging from a continuing orderly evolution within the system to outright revolution by violence. Some critics do little more than deplore and cry for change but, aside from handwringing, propose no solutions; others advocate elaborate new systems involving the violent wresting of power from the "ins"—from the establishment.

That the so-called establishment has failed in some respects we must honestly acknowledge. There is no question that we have failed to control crime. We certainly have not been successful in correcting or rehabilitating offenders—witness the disgraceful rates of recidivism. Clearly the distribution of power, which means in a very real way the distribution of wealth and of opportunity, is uneven. How many times have you heard someone say it is not what you know but who you know that counts? How many times have you heard that you can't fight city hall? How many good men have lost out to the boss's son? How many people have been discriminated against because of religion, race, color, political affiliation and similar factors?

We are now being warned that we are in grave danger of annihilating the human race by polluting our air and water. We have been poisoning our soil with DDT and other chemicals. The automobile and airplane, both so essential to our lives, are mixed blessings. Atomic energy—a technological advance of unimagined potential—is at the same time a curse. The Pill, an effective means of attack on one of our most dangerous threats, the population explosion, is at best a calculated risk.

The war in Viet Nam is regarded by some as the height of moral commitment—commitment to liberty, freedom, and human self-determination. To others it is an immoral, unconscionable, inexcusable interference in the affairs of a sovereign nation in which we are pursuing what is, in the final analysis, a selfish national interest.

The problems arising out of the ways people perceive change often produce fallout which means work for the police. It is highly unlikely that any change of significance would be unanimously approved. There will always be some people opposed to it. Generally people split up on crucial issues so that at one extreme there are more or less militant advocates of the change and, at the other, vocal and adamant opponents. In the middle is what has come to be known as the great silent majority.

It seems clear that the more one is likely to be affected by the change, the more strongly he will react to it. If he feels threatened, he will be opposed. If he believes the change will benefit him, he will be all for it. As an example, consider the case of a Halfway House for prisoners soon to be given full release. A man may feel that this is a promising way to ease convicts back into society as productive citizens and he may approve of the Halfway House as a constructive step in the correction process. He approves, that is, until he learns that the house is to be located in his immediate neighborhood. Then, all of a sudden he is up in arms against it. I guess it depends upon whose ox is being gored.

We must realize that change produces stress. Occasionally, the stress reaches crisis proportions. A very real matter of concern is society's capacity for coping with crisis piled on top of crisis. Our law enforcement agencies are usually geared to handle normal conditions. A big crisis such as a huge natural disaster is beyond their resources to handle without help. Now what we must worry about is what we as a people are going to do when social unrest generated by racial clashes is compounded by the addition of the stress of war. Add to that natural disaster, pollution, racial strife, food shortages, economic recession and other problems and you soon come to question the ability of our system to withstand the cumulative effects of these multiplying crises piling on top of one another.

The job of policing a society in which there are many complex cross currents of social change is a very difficult one. There are disorganizations and deviance, norms that are cherished by some and rejected by others, visions of the promised land and visions of powerful gatekeepers barring the way. There is nothing new about the fact that age is shocked by the antics of youth. Yet, we are shocked. There is nothing new about the fact that people are shocked by the rebellion of those who feel disadvantaged and depressed. Yet, we are shocked. Social dislocations and upheavals have always been with us. Many of our social institutions feel the impact of these conditions and especially the police are often put in the position of taking the brunt of the resulting conflicts.

It seems clear to me that if we, as a society, fail to give every man his due, if we fail to make substantial and visible progress toward equality of opportunity, we shall see increasing dissatisfactions and conflicts. You are undoubtedly familiar with the frustration-aggression theory and, if that theory is correct, our failures to resolve frustrations will result in greater aggression, more protests, demonstrations and even riots. The police are in the unfortunate position of being the visible and immediately accessible symbols of what are regarded as the agents of frustration and much of the aggression will be directed against them.

Some of the problems center around the concept of xenophobia—suspicion, mistrust, and dislike of the unlike. This is one of the factors at the roots of the clash between youth and age. Older people see the young as refusing to live by "tried and true" moral standards—standards of sexual morality, for example, although how different they are I am not sure. Changing styles in haircuts, dress, and speech, while only superficial trappings, are somehow thought to be indicative of sinister decay of cultural and moral standards. Many people seem to find something much more alarming about kids being one of the "hippies" than they did about kids a couple of generations ago being one of the "flappers." There is something much more sinister in the expression, "Cool it, baby!" than there was in "So's your old man!" And, of course, there are those who equate slum with scum.

The primary mission of police forces is the promotion and maintenance of order in the community. The laws and the police procedures related to them are prescriptions used by police agencies for the purpose of maintaining order. Many of the things police must do result in prohibiting people from doing what they want to do or in requiring them to do what they do not want to do. That is not the way to win a popularity contest! Now, if we add to the natural irritation people feel when subject to police control a strong conviction that the control is being exercised unjustly because of race, social class, or personal prejudice, we have a situation ripe for explosion.

There are a great many things police are called upon to do which are not specifically law enforcement activities, but which have to do with maintaining order in the community. Some of these are related to crime prevention, but many fall upon the shoulders of police simply because, like the mountain to be climbed, they are there. If there is an accident, people look to the policeman. He is the public authority, the take-charge guy. He is supposed to step in. If the neighbor's children are trampling the petunias, call the police! Many nowadays wouldn't think of speaking to the parents about it as they did when I was a boy.

Let us conclude with a few "if or unless" points.

If our society continues toward increasing complexity, present standards of admission to police ranks will be even more inadequate than they are today. It will take better prepared men to handle the great variety of police duties. This will require higher recruiting standards and more and better police training—and for this we are going to have to pay more.

Unless we find ways of reducing the disparity between the poor and otherwise disadvantaged and the great middle class, we shall experience continuing and most likely increasing social disorganization—crime, violence, and disorder. This will put heavier burdens on the police and, as police officials see themselves being more and more hard-pressed to contain crime and disorder resulting from society's failures, they will involve themselves more and more in clearly and forcefully pointing out those failures and pressing for community solutions.

If the police are to make real progress in the crime prevention aspects of their work, they will have to devise new and effective methods of marshalling the power of public opinion and the support of large numbers of people. It is especially important that these efforts reach and enlist people in high crime areas. This cannot be achieved by community relations specialists alone; every officer must play a part. The average officer must come to realize the importance of his role in establishing and maintaining good working relationships with the people for whom he works. It is my belief that a proper understanding of the relationship between the maintenance of order in the community as the principal objective and the enforcement of the law as a tool to be used in achieving it is an important first step.[13]

Racial Violence:
A Contemporary Dilemma

Needless to say, because of the problems mentioned in the previous section, violence was to be expected. A general view of antisocial behavior relating to mob violence holds that such actions are not in and of themselves the *problem* but instead are the *product* of various social conditions in our society. (Mob behavior will be covered extensively in a later chapter.) Indeed, it is a fact that some individuals in all societies and in all classes of society respond to economic, social, and psychological pressures by violently acting out their objections.

Although violence is to be expected when social change is rapid, the disorders of the 1960s were unusual, irregular, complex, and unpredictable social processes. Like most human events, they did not unfold in an orderly sequence. Furthermore, the violence in the metropolitan urban areas was often perpetrated by the black members of the community who resided in that particular area and who had the assistance of blacks who lived outside the community. The initial confrontation with law enforcement

[13]N. A. Watson, "The Perception of Change in Contemporary Society," in R. W. Kobetz and C. W. Hamm, *Campus Unrest: Dialogue or Destruction* (Washington, D.C.: International Association of Chiefs of Police, 1970), pp. 9–15. By permission of the publisher.

FIGURES 2.5, 2.6.   Although the police always try to eliminate bloodshed in the streets, it is difficult and, during riots, injuries and death unfortunately do occur. Photos courtesy of the San Francisco Police Department, San Francisco, California.

agencies and other agencies (i.e., firemen and the National Guard) began in 1965 in Watts—an outlying area in Los Angeles, California. The damage in terms of property was in the millions; in terms of human tragedy, it was impossible to calculate. Soon after the Watts riot, numerous other riots followed—in Detroit, Newark, Chicago, San Francisco and Oakland, California and many other black urban communities throughout the United States. As an example, during the first nine months of 1967, 164 disorders were reported; eight (5 percent) were major in terms of violence and damage; 33 (20 percent) were serious but not major; 123 (75 percent) were minor and undoubtedly would not have received national attention as riots had not the nation been sensitized by the more serious outbreaks. In seventy-five disorders studied by a Senate subcommittee, eighty-three deaths were reported. Eighty-two percent of the deaths and more than half of the injuries occurred in Newark and Detroit. Ten percent and 38 percent of the injured were public employees, primarily law officers and firemen. The overwhelming majority of the persons killed or injured in all the disorders were black civilians.[14]

Initial damage estimates were greatly exaggerated. In Detroit, newspaper reports first estimated damage at from $20 million to $500 million; the highest recent estimate is $45 million. In Newark, early estimates ranged from $15 million to $25 million. Monthly damage was estimated at $10.2 million, over 80 percent in inventory losses.[15]

The basic causes for the 1960s turmoil specifically involving blacks in all American communities was discussed in Chapter One. However, in again addressing ourselves to the question of why this happened, it is important to focus on the relationship of the black in the subordinate social status to American society as a whole. In the South, social position is still so rigidly defined as to constitute a caste system, and even in the North and West, in spite of a certain amount of equality with respect to civil rights, the black is still generally subjected to social ostracism and economic discrimination. This had been explicitly pointed out by noted authors in the field of criminology and law enforcement. For example,

> Every community has dominant and subordinate groups. Whites first dominated Negroes in the United States through slavery. When slavery was abolished as a social institution, the value system of racism became embedded in folk beliefs of the Southern states as an informal control system, supplementing the formal controls expressed in laws of segregation and disenfranchisement. Among Southern whites, the race attitudes became part of morality and religion. In the North, the value system of racism is also present, but it is deluded by humanitarian ideals and adherence to values of equal rights under the Constitution.

14Ibid.
15Ibid.

But in both regions, the informal system exists as a latent barrier to racial equality. The current disturbances in the North demonstrate clearly the stress of this informal control system and in spite of the lack of legalized segregation and disenfranchisement. These disturbances occur because the civil rights movement, as directed in the North, has succeeded in enforcing the informal control system to the overt level of expression.[16]

This exposure of the "hidden informal control system to the overt level of expression," along with the transition of populations in our urban areas, made an explosive mixture which sparked the riots discussed here and elsewhere in this volume.

There is no doubt that both the black and white citizenry are guilty of lack of sound judgment. There has been overreaction on both sides. It appears that the nation's black leaders, with the exception of the late Dr. Martin Luther King, have not been forceful enough in condemning violent revolt as a definite threat to civil liberties.

King advocated a doctrine of non-violent direct action by marches, demonstrations, sit-ins, and similar methods, which he feels "dramatize" the injustices and prick the consciences of the nation's citizenry. He feels that the entire society must be confronted with the problem and that nothing will change the social order without exposure of tensions and prejudices.[17]

But such wishes by black leaders have been barely audible above the call to arms by black militants. In Newark, the National Conference on Black Power degenerated into a cry for black racism, as its leaders threatened a separate black nation. In Detroit, the worst riot in the nation's modern history exploded in the face of a progressive city leadership that had wrested from Washington more than $200 million in federal aid. And nowhere was the base side of the upheaval more sharply etched than along Detroit's Grand River Avenue, where black and white looters roamed and thieved in integrated bands.

As a result of the mass disturbances, local law enforcement has found itself placed in an extremely sensitive position. The decisions relating to protecting the public and property on one hand and individuals on the other cause a great deal of concern regarding the degree of police power

[16]E. H. Johnson, "A Sociological Interpretation of Police Reaction and Responsibility to Civil Disobedience," *Journal of Criminal Law, Criminology and Police Science,* 58, No. 3 (Sept. 1967), p. 407.

[17]J. L. LeGrande, "Non-Violent Civil Disobedience and Police Enforcement Policy," *Journal of Criminal Law, Criminology and Police Science,* 58, No. 3, (Jan. 1972), p. 396.

to be utilized. It is important to point out that the degree of police power required to provide a society freedom from chaotic racial disorders would be such that all individual liberty would be destroyed. Similarly, rejecting the concept that such disorders can be reduced and better controlled would result in anarchy, or the complete absence of government and law. Law enforcement must continue to strive to balance these two alternatives. The use of police power in civil disturbances must be carefully weighed if it is not to be a barrier against long-term changes of the community's social structure and the sociological forces pressing the community to change.

Few men had more insight into America than John Quincy Adams, son of a president, himself a president, close enough to Thomas Jefferson to be called his adopted son. Adams visualized clearly the delicate balance between good and evil on which the United States as a nation rests. In referring to the country's democratic system, he once stated, "The American Government is an experiment upon the heart."

There were some statesmen involved in framing the Constitution of the United States who believed that human nature could not be trusted with freedom. They were certain that if the right to protest, to resist injustice, and to criticize the government itself were accorded to the citizen, the inevitable result would be revolt, violence, and anarchy.

During the last decade, there has been a great deal of anxiety on the part of a significant number of Americans that the pessimists may have been correct after all. Riots have left their marks on our cities and have disrupted our educational systems; tragic assassinations of John Kennedy, Dr. Martin Luther King, Jr., and Robert Kennedy have, without doubt, taken their toll on the confidence of many citizens in the ability of America to survive and continue as a free society. *However, the problems confronted by the American people throughout their history serve as a reminder that contemporary violence is not a new problem.*

THE ONLY WORLD WE HAVE: REMEMBERING THE LESSONS OF HISTORY[18]

Our religious, ethical, and political beliefs tend toward the proposition that man is a perfectible being, spiritually if not physically. However, the person who deals daily with human failings—whether a policeman, psychiatrist, or marriage counselor—jeopardizes his own emotional and mental health if he clings too tightly to this vision of trouble-free man and, by extension,

---

[18]This section adopted from V. G. Strecher, *The Environment of Law Enforcement,* pp. 97–99. Courtesy of the publisher.

trouble-free society. Neither exists, and for the realistic enforcer of the law, neither should be expected or even hoped for.

What you, as a policeman, *can* expect and hope for during your career must be a product of your informed, skeptical, honest perspective of your working place—urbanized society. And your perspective of the present-day community depends upon your having an equally thorough understanding of the past and present. Only by extending your knowledge beyond personal experience and learning from the past can you hope to escape a narrow interpretation of current conditions. Those in every generation who deplore the decay of morality, the demise of respect for policemen, the loss of respect for authority in general, the lack of consensus in human affairs, and the sudden loss of security in our cities have simply not paid attention to the lessons of the past.

Certainly change occurs; both cyclic change, in which history appears to repeat itself with minor variations, and permanent, cumulative change, which presents the world with new and unique conditions. But change nearly always brings effects that are beneficial and detrimental to the quality of human life. They are rarely as bad as the viewers-with-alarm would have it or as rosy as the technology glamorizers claim.

The public service or law enforcement perspective which emerges from these understandings of present and past vary from man to man, but it should squarely confront the following observations.

1. Human groups, whether large or small, are subject to internal and external insecurities, which are largely the products of human behavior. Throughout history, group insecurities and the behavior which produced them have brought about responses of group leadership or institutions intended to manage the tensions and behavior.

2. In comparatively recent times, managing behavior and group insecurities has become increasingly the business of institutions, particularly governmental and educational institutions. It has been less influenced by moral consensus—that is, human regulation has largely moved from the sacred toward the secular domain.

3. Change in human living patterns occurs as a result of the interactions of values, cultural institutions, social structures, technology, and the environment. Most change probably results from the combined effects of these factors upon the behavior of millions of persons, both as individuals and in their many groupings. Some of the resulting change is desirable to most persons; some is deplorable and frightening to virtually everyone. But, given the dimensions and momentum of its underlying forces, change has not yet become subject to human management and control, despite wishful beliefs to the contrary.

4. Styles of human life appear to change considerably from one generation to the next. Much of this change is regarded by short-run observers as either progress or social decay. Evidence is increasing, however, that much of the change in lifestyles actually consists of change in the visibility of human

behavior and change in attitudes toward that behavior, rather than in change in the kind or amount of behavior. This is particularly apparent when, as in the case of human sexual activity, powerful values interact with a form of behavior.

5. Paramount and substantial change, rather than cyclic and seeming change, may be found in certain recent social responses to technological innovations, especially in transport and communication. As a result of some innovations, change has apparently speeded up. This has made critically important the longstanding time lag in the response of institutions to new demands made upon them. These institutions—the government, schools, churches, and labor unions—have not yet adapted to the change of pace. Law enforcement, always involved with the working out of conduct standards and social response to deviations from them, is very much affected by the newly critical importance of lag in its response to new conditions.

6. The design of democracy in the United States imposes special demands upon police officers in this country. In the pull between security and individual freedom, we tend slightly toward the side of *inefficient* social control—purposely. Those in law enforcement who find this difficult to accept should review their commitment to constitutional government. Those who cannot accept this factor of inefficiency to the extent that personal freedom may require it should not endure the frustrations of a law enforcement career.

When policemen gain the historic and contemporary perspectives, they lose both the security and insecurity which result from ignorance. The security is a form of false confidence, which literally sprays the man's environment with negative side effects as he blunders about in his sensitive and important work. The insecurity represents a tendency to "gut react" and stampede with others who are insecure when politically and socially sensitive catchwords are attached to ordinary forms of social change or to harmless unconventional behavior. Recognizing true social hazards and subversion—which indeed exist—is not work for men who suffer from tunnel vision. Neither is it work for those who reason from insufficient or unverified information or who know what is best for everybody else. In America such men are not meant to be part of the law enforcement system.

SOCIAL UNREST: IMPLICATIONS FOR IMPACT ON LAW ENFORCEMENT

"Police work" is a phrase that conjures up in some minds a dramatic contest between a policeman and a criminal in which the party with the stronger arm or the craftier wit prevails. When a particularly desperate or dangerous criminal must be hunted down and brought to justice, there are heroic moments in police work, but the situations that most policemen deal with most of the time are of quite another order. Much of American crime, delinquency, and disorder is associated with a complexity of social conditions: poverty, racial antagonism, family breakdown, or restlessness of young people. During the last twenty years, these conditions have been aggravated by such profound social changes as the technological and civil rights revolutions, and the rapid decay of inner cities into densely packed, turbulent slums and ghettos.

It is in the cities that the conditions of life are the worst, that social tensions are the most acute, that riots occur, that crime rates are the highest, that the fear of crime and the demand for effective action against it are the strongest. This is not to say, however, that the crime rates have shown an increase only in the big cities of the United States. Actually, crime has shown a drastic increase everywhere in the United States. Serious and violent crimes (particularly murder, assaults and forcible rape) soared across the nation in 1974, according to a nationwide summary of police statistics gathered by the Federal Bureau of Investigation.

One of the most fully documented facts about crime is that the common, serious crimes that worry people the most—murder, forcible rape, robbery, aggravated assault, and burglary—happen most often in the slums of large cities. Studies in city after city, in all regions of the country, have traced the variations in the rates for these crimes. The results, with monotonous regularity, showed that the offenses, the victims, and the offenders were found most frequently in the poorest, the most deteriorated, and the most socially disorganized areas of cities.

Studies of the crime rate in cities and of the conditions most commonly associated with high crime rates have been conducted for well over a century in Europe, and for many years in the United States. The findings have been remarkably consistent. Burglary, robbery, and serious assault occur in areas characterized by low income, physical deterioration, dependency, racial and ethnic concentrations, broken homes, working mothers, low levels of education and vocational skills, high employment, high proportion of single males, overcrowded and substandard housing, high rates of tuberculosis and infant mortality, low rates of home ownership or single-family dwellings, and high population density. Studies that have mapped the relationship of these factors and crime have found them following the same pattern from one area of the city to another.

Crime rates in American cities tend to be highest in the center of the city and tend to decrease in relationship to distance from the center. This pattern has been found to hold fairly well for both offenses and offenders, although it is sometimes broken by unusual features of geography, enclaves of socially well-integrated ethnic groups, irregularities in the distribution of opportunities to commit crime, and unusual concentrations of commercial and industrial establishments in outlying areas. The major irregularity found in the clustering of offenses and offenders beyond city boundaries is caused by the growth of satellite areas that are developing such characteristics of the central city as high population mobility, commercial and industrial concentrations, low economic status, broken families, and other social problems.

The city slum has always exacted its toll from its inhabitants, except where those inhabitants are bound together by an intensive social and cultural solidarity that provides a collective defense against the pressures of slum living. Several slum settlements inhabited by people of Oriental ancestry have shown a unique capacity to do this. However, the common experience of the great numbers of immigrants of different racial and ethnic backgrounds who have poured into the poorest areas of our large cities has been quite different.

An historic series of studies by Clifford R. Shaw and Henry D. McKay,[19] of the Institute of Juvenile Research in Chicago, document the disorganizing impact of slum life on different groups of immigrants as they moved through the slums and struggled to gain an economic and social foothold in the city. Throughout the period of immigration, areas with high delinquency and crime rates kept this high rate, even though members of new nationality groups moved in to displace the older residents. Each nationality group showed high rates of delinquency among its members who were living near the center of the city and lower rates for those living in the better, outlying residential areas. Also, for each nationality group, those living in the poor areas had more of all the other social problems commonly associated with life in the slums.

This same pattern of high crime rates in the slum neighborhoods and low crime rates in the better districts is true among the blacks and members of other minority groups who have made up the most recent waves of migration to the big cities. (Minority groups and crime will be discussed in another chapter.) As other groups before them, they have had to crowd into areas where they can afford to live while they search for ways to live better. The disorganizing personal and social experiences of life in the slums are producing the same problems for the new minority-group residents, including high rates of crime and delinquency. As they acquire a stake in urban society and move into better areas in the city, their crime rates and the incidence of other social problems drop to lower levels.

SUMMARY

Racial tensions, civil disobedience, and mob violence are *not* new phenomena in the United States. Such problems have been a part of society from the beginning of civilization. The rapid growth of the population, particularly in urban areas, with attendant social problems in housing, education, employment, and social welfare services has accentuated social unrest to a degree that has caused law enforcement officers to become the symbols of social ills. They have been placed in a difficult position of attempting to

---

[19]*Juvenile Delinquency in Urban Areas* (Chicago: University of Chicago Press, 1942).

enforce societys' laws as well as concerning themselves with a variety of social conditions.

This chapter presents brief summaries of a few major historical disturbances, as well as describing contemporary disorders in the United States, in an effort to point out that they are often quite similar. Antisocial behavior as it relates to mass disturbances and violence is not in itself the *problem* but, instead, a *product* of various social conditions. In fact, individuals in all societies and in all classes respond to economic, social, and psychological pressures by acting-out behavior. The social change that emerged during the displacement of huge populations to suburban areas and the migration of the minorities to the metropolitan areas have had a great effect on law enforcement agencies. While population growth has changed central city concentration little, the "flight to the suburbs" has drained it of those groups which traditionally were forces for social control and stability.

Chapter Two discusses complaints of minority groups regarding police behavior. Most often, these complaints concern the *attitudes* displayed by law enforcement officers rather than their *tactics* per se. There are conflicting viewpoints held by both parties involved—minority groups and police officers. Thus there remains a serious communication gap which urgently needs to be closed.

The perception of change in contemporary society focuses on the many demands for change in important areas of national life as well as the controversies these changes produce and the resistance to such proposed changes. The job of policing a society in which there are many complex cross-currents of social change is a very difficult one. There is disorganization and deviance, as well as norms that are cherished by some and rejected by others.

The topic of social unrest and its implications on police work is discussed. In this particular section the authors discuss the amount and type of crime that has been generated, or aggravated, by profound social changes such as the technological and civil rights revolutions and the rapid decay of the inner cities into densely packed, turbulent slums and ghettos. Deviant behavior is usually generated by unhealthy social conditions, and such conditions are named and briefly discussed within the chapter.

DISCUSSION TOPICS

1. Discuss the major riots throughout United States history, utilizing Appendix A in this text as well as material in this chapter.

2. Discuss social change and its implications on law enforcement.

3. Discuss the lack of communication between police and members of the minority groups, utilizing the conflicting viewpoints held by both parties involved. List some of these conflicting viewpoints.

4. In this chapter, N. A. Watson elaborates on "The Perception of Changes in Contemporary Society." What does he mean?

5. Discuss the impact of social unrest on law enforcement.

6. Why is it so important that policemen gain historic and contemporary perspectives of societal disorder?

ANNOTATED REFERENCES

BAYLEY, D. H., AND H. MENDELSON, "The Policeman's World," in Charles E. Reasons and J. L. Kuykendall, eds., *Race, Crime and Justice.* Pacific Palisades, Cal.: Goodyear Publishing Co., Inc., 1972. This is an excellent chapter discussing the occupation of law enforcement and the necessity to understand the world as it is for better police-community relations.

BROWN, C., *Manchild in a Promised Land.* New York: The Macmillan Co., 1965. An excellent work discussing the black's psychological problems in American society.

BYRD, R. C., "Police Brutality or Public Brutality," *The Police Chief,* 33, No. 2 (Feb. 1966), pp. 8–10. The author discusses the lack of public support for the police officer in the United States, taking a hard line with those he feels are attacking the laws of our nation and making such laws impotent. The author's lack of sympathy toward these individuals might be of some interest to the reader who may *over-identify* with such groups.

KEILEY, J. A., AND T. W. O'ROURKE, "An Appraisal of the Attitudes of Police Officers toward the Concept of Police-Community Relations," *Journal of Police Science and Administration,* 1, No. 2 (June 1973), pp. 224–31. An assessment of police personnel attitudes toward the concept of police-community relations prior to their participation in a police-community relations program under the auspices of the University of Illinois Police Training Institute.

KOBETZ, R. W., AND C. W. HAMM, *Campus Unrest: Dialogue or Destruction?* Washington, D.C.: International Association of Chiefs of Police, 1970. This work provides an extensive study of student disorders and the political and social impact of such protests on police and college administrations.

MURRAY, D., *America's Crisis in Authority.* Chicago: Claretian Publications, 1971. A pamphlet touching on some of the many problems confronting today's criminal justice system. This book attempts to view the problem of law enforcement in a society faced with a rise in the demand for civil liberties as well as an increase in the crime rate.

Report of the National Commission on the Causes and Prevention of Violence, *Rights In Conflict*. Washington, D.C.: U.S. Government Printing Office, 1969. The investigation of the civil disorders and the police actions surrounding the Democratic National Convention of 1968.

SKOLNICK, J., ed., *The Politics of Protest*. Task Force Report, National Commission on the Causes and Prevention of Violence. New York: Simon & Schuster, 1969. A publication with a collection of contributions dealing with the facets of protest and politics.

STRECHER, V. G., *The Environment of Law Enforcement: A Community Relations Guide*. Englewood Cliffs, N.J.: Prentice-Hall Inc., Essentials of Law Enforcement Series, 1971. An excellent discussion of the environment within which police officers operate. Focuses on the policeman who works in a variety of settings—territorial, social, and organizational. A highly recommended paperback, in nontechnical language—a must for a police library.

WATSON, N. A., "The Fringes of Police-Community Relations Extremism," *The Police Chief*, 33, No. 8 (Aug. 1966). The late Dr. Watson examines the "extremists" in our society, who plant the seeds of disorder. With actual cases which have a great deal of impact.

WHITEHOUSE, J. E., "Historical Perspectives of the Police-Community Service Function," *Journal of Police Science and Administration*, 1, No. 1 (March 1973), pp. 87–92. This article ties in nicely with the historical and contemporary aspects of police-community relations discussed in this chapter.

SOCIAL PROBLEMS AND CONSTITUTIONAL GOVERNMENT:
Impact on Law Enforcement

3

Historically, there has always been some form of restriction placed upon the police by the government—regardless of who the police may be and who the government may be. In various societies throughout history, the complexity of enforcing law within governmental restrictions has varied greatly. This complexity, however, began to increase steadily in Western civilization with the Magna Carta. American law enforcement has encountered a steady rise of such complexity, beginning with the Bill of Rights and the Fourth Amendment and followed by a steady progression of similar influences molding the relationship between government and law enforcement.

Later chapters will cover a wide variety of police activities, many of which bear directly upon various social problems. For example, police activities such as *family crisis intervention* will be discussed in a context that suggests a broadening rather than a restricting of law enforcement responsibility in terms of social problems. Of course, this merely emphasizes the *prevention* of crime rather than the *control* of crime, but it is nevertheless an expansion of the scope of law enforcement in a constitutional form of government.

But a police activity such as family crisis intervention is only one of many police functions that are expanding. The complexity of enforcing law is expanding and, of course, the scope of enforcement is expanding. In effect, complexity can restrict law enforcement by complicating matters, but in most instances, complexity expands law enforcement—at least within the relationship between police and American government.

The relationship between police and government itself also varies widely. Nevertheless, one factor remains consistent in all government-police relationship structures in all societies and throughout history. All governments conceive of police as responsible for maintaining a sufficiently stable environment to permit government to exist. An orderly environment, then, is of crucial significance.

GOVERNMENT AND ORDERLY ENVIRONMENT

Many years ago a student of nature expressed a belief that a small child isolated from human society would likely grow into an adult *homo ferus*— a hairy man who walks on all fours and lacks an intelligible language. Linnaeus, the Swedish naturalist was the scholar who held this belief, and there has since been occasional corroboration.[1] But insofar as government is concerned, the individual human being must be thought of as a talking member of society who walks upright like his fellow man. More importantly, the individual must be thought of as depending on government to provide a safe or at least an orderly environment.

Entire volumes have elaborated the many ways in which the individual depends on society for a safe or orderly environment. One of the more obvious ways has to do with regulating human behavior. When primitive man had advanced sufficiently to acquire the rudiments of a language, the necessity of regulating behavior was not long in developing, at least not long by historical standards. This is not to say that with language came the civilized philosophy *Cogito, ergo sum* ("I think therefore I am"). Indeed, primitive man tended to assign as much entity to stones or animals as he assigned to himself. But primitive man, nevertheless, soon contrived methods of regulating the behavior of human beings—particularly, when it became apparent that doing so was necessary for survival.

The biblical Cain's assault on his brother, Abel, posed (at least from Abel's viewpoint) the continuing need for society to regulate behavior. The absence of such regulation proved grossly unfortunate to Abel. For in the absence of deliberate and concrete efforts at such regulation, man has historically demonstrated an inclination to foster his own survival and well-being at the expense of his fellow man.

An individual's relationship to his society is one of dependence. In exchange for permitting his own behavior to be regulated, the individual depends on his society to provide *personal safety* for him. In this context, society is, or should be, an enforcer. And because human beings present such great variety in their willingness to be regulated, this enforcement function becomes necessary for society's very existence.

[1]K. Davis, *Human Society* (New York: The Macmillan Co., 1949), p. 204.

Still another consideration in evolving an orderly environment has to do with the freedom extended to the individual by his society. All societies provide for the personal safety of individuals who permit their own behavior to be regulated (although some regulations at times appear virtually impossible to either observe or enforce). But in societies that permit great personal freedom, as is the case with modern constitutional governments, the individual can acquire property or property rights. Such societies obviously differ from those in which the State attempts to retain the rights of all property. The question of property rights relates to government enforcement of rules, and the retaining of an orderly environment when there are as many potential property violations as there are property owners becomes far more complicated than when the State is the owner of all property. The rules regulating human behavior, along with the standards of enforcing these rules, obviously increase in complexity accordingly.

Early societal rules that ultimately become criminal law might then be thought of philosophically as being society's first effort to promote an orderly environment. If the individual is to remain willing to permit his behavior to be regulated, he must believe that enforcement will be impartial, predictable, and consistent; being provided with an orderly environment will not serve as an inducement to him.

In seeking to promote an orderly environment, government restricts human behavior to protect the freedom of all, or it restricts behavior for the sake of controlling the individual. In either case, impartiality is necessary to convince the individual that there exists a definite relationship between conformity and personal safety (as well as property security in free societies). But in either case, the main function of government is to maintain an orderly society.

With the goal of an orderly society, government, particularly constitutional government, must take into consideration the relationship between the society's power and the power of man's *will*. Much of what is called the wisdom of the ages probably deals with this very relationship in one way or in another. So also does this very relationship define most of what are called social problems. For in the final analysis, the individual power of the person is equally potent whether in support of or in dissent from the society's system of providing personal safety and property security.

FOR EXISTING GOVERNMENT OR AGAINST

War is frequently discussed as one of many major influences on social conditions defined as problems—particularly when it is defined as a problem involving societal power and the power of an individual's *will*.

Regardless of whether the individual is *for* existing (established)

FIGURES 3.1, 3.2. The impact of the late Vietnamese conflict resulted in demonstrations by organized and unorganized groups. Some of these demonstrations have not been peaceful. Thus they created problems for police. Photo courtesy of the San Francisco Police Department, San Francisco, California.

government or against it, problems such as these would appear likely to influence *against* government. This would seem likely if for no other reason than the jeopardy in which the government's existing system of providing an orderly environment is placed by changes inherent in solving such problems. For in attempting to solve problems such as these, existing government, or the *Establishment*, as it is known to many, often finds itself choosing between two rather restrictive alternatives: *suppress change* or *make change*. And to whatever degree the position of suppression of change is taken, to *at least* that degree there is certainty of opposition—surely from those seeking solutions through changes in the governmental system of providing an orderly environment.

Law enforcement obviously retains a crucial interest in governmental reaction to social problems. Suppression of change has conspicuous implications in this context but so have governmental decisions to make changes. Determining precisely *what* changes are being sought and *by whom* frequently becomes a concern of law enforcement, *whether law enforcement desires to become involved or not.*

Emphasis should be placed upon the complete lack of option for law enforcement to ultimately become "involved"—even though *initial* involvement of police often lags behind existing needs. "Community services offered by the public and private sector usually lag far behind the population demand. Public recreation, police services, health services, cultural opportunities, and business services cannot catch up with population growth until there is a leveling off of the growth rate."[2] Involvement, then, has to do with *timing*—the "timing" of police involvement in community affairs.

The student unrest of the 1960s is an example of police finding themselves deeply involved in social change without any choice. Student revolt, although only one of many signs of unrest, might serve as an example of how law enforcement becomes caught up in social problems and governmental efforts to retain orderly environment.

Constitutional Government and Student Unrest

Of course, the notion of student nonconformity is by no means new. Even before panty raids and goldfish swallowing, most college campuses had accumulated a history of incidents in which segments of the student body had drawn attention to themselves via nonconformity. But insofar as the Establishment was concerned, there was little reason to believe that questions were being raised regarding the very system of providing an orderly environment.

---

[2]Patricia Hunsicker, "Community Services Project, Orange County, California," *Better Ways to Help Youth: Three Youth Services Systems* (Washington, D.C.: U.S. Department of Health, Education and Welfare, 1973), p. 29.

FIGURES 3.3, 3.4. *From November 1968 through May 1969, the San Francisco Police Department was confronted with daily student unrest at San Francisco State College. Professional police action was one of the major factors in settling the unrest. Photo courtesy of the San Francisco Police Department, San Francisco, California.*

A somewhat different pattern of dissent began to emerge on college campuses at approximately the time of enrollment by students whose parents had been directly involved in World War II. By the early 1960s this new pattern had drawn mass attention through student demonstrations

FIGURE 3.5. *America has changed in many ways. When there are changes in the very tangible world then changes in the social world should be no surprise. But change may not always be of a positive nature. Photo courtesy of the San Francisco Police Department, San Francisco, California.*

supporting demands ranging from free speech to preventing campus recruitment by the military forces or defense industry. The deluge of publicity given to draft-card burning dramatized the increasing focus on the Establishment as the source of considerable student unrest.

In the spring of 1968, a survey by the National Student Association noted 221 demonstrations on 101 campuses across the nation—in 59 cases, involving the virtual takeover of an administration building. At the October 1968 convention held at the University of Colorado by the Students for a Democratic Society (SDS), a call was made for a national student strike to disrupt the pending presidential election. The eruptions at the political conventions are profound comments on the magnitude of the unrest. So also are the violent outbreaks on many campuses since—Columbia University and San Francisco State College serving as particularly salient examples in 1968.

Student revolt is merely *one* sign of unrest, and only *one* social problem. Many other problems, perhaps of greater immediate concern to law enforcement, are dealt with throughout this volume. But student revolt, as it functions under a constitutional government that guarantees the right

FIGURE 3.6 (a).   *Courtesy of the Berkeley Police Department, Berkeley, Cal.*

FIGURE 3.6 (b). *Courtesy of the Berkeley Police Department, Berkeley, Cal.*

of dissent, may provide many clues to the process of interpreting social tension—a process of vital importance to the police in a changing community.

Interpreting the Degree of Extremism

If there was a time when panty raids were thought to be the behavior of extremists, the nature of current student nonconformity certainly modifies this view. However, it is possible to analyze the most extreme philosophy—racial philosophy—by examining the relative militancy in the beliefs of Black Muslims, Black Panthers, and the Third World in relation to the position of the National Association for the Advancement of Colored People (NAACP) and that espoused by the late Martin Luther King. Of course, depending on the orientation of the observer, the views of any or all of the foregoing could be called extreme. Their *degree* of demand for change might therefore prove a more effective way of assessing the potential impact on law enforcement. For with the tremendous social changes occuring, today's "extremist" or "activist" may (by comparison) be tomorrow's "con-

FIGURE 3.7.   *Black Panther demonstration on May 1, 1969 to "Free Huey Newton." Courtesy San Francisco Police Department, San Francisco, Cal.*

servative." This knowledge becomes important because interpreting social tension requires acknowledging a distinction between consequential and inconsequential patterns of change.

In part, the significance of such knowledge is demonstrated by the *absence* of such knowledge—particularly in the virtual "uprising" of students during the 1960s. This absence probably relates to a continuing belief of many police that such knowledge is merely part of many factors over which police have no control, and possibly no interest:

> Most policemen feel that the police-community relations problem is caused by factors over which they have no control—lack of jobs, poverty, frustration, and others. If more people in our slum areas had jobs and adequate housing, tensions would be reduced. Alleged brutality, accusations of improper search and seizure, clamor for civilian review boards, and public apathy are a culmination of citizens' misunderstanding and mistrust of police in general. It is this misunderstanding and mistrust which we must seek to abolish through community relations programs. When groups get to know one another, suspicion and mistrust usually fade away.
>
> Not many years ago everybody knew the policeman on the beat, and he was accepted as a member of the neighborhood. People in his area knew him by name, and he could count on them to help him, just as they could count on him.
>
> With the advent of the automobile and the two-way radio, concepts

of police administration and patrol planning began to change. It became obvious that the mobile criminal would have to be apprehended by a mobile police officer using a two way communications system that keeps him in close, but impersonal, contact with the public.[3]

There were, of course, many other reasons for police to feel less than appropriately involved in campus life. In addition to increasing mobility that reduces direct public contact, law enforcement entered the 1960s with a concept of college campus problems as composed of such things as "poor grades" and "tough courses." From such a frame of reference, it was easy to *ignore* student unrest—at least for a little while.

Student unrest in itself may or may not be of consequence to law enforcement. Whether or not a student feels satisfied with his grades is of little concern to police. But when large groups of students violently demonstrate to deny local draft boards access to grade records, it is clearly a police problem. Again, this is a matter of degree.

As a model of how law enforcement might interpret social problems well enough to anticipate direct involvement, student grades might be thought of in a context similar to complaints about public assistance and ghettos. The point becomes of course, what is (or is not) being done to relieve this stress before the problem erupts into violent demand for law enforcement intervention.

Returning to the example of student unrest, a number of matters are of concern, among which is the virtual certainty that bureaucracies, colleges included, treat individuals as abstractions or statistics rather than as persons. This being the case, a student's concern about grades may often be merely a symptom of the problem rather than the problem itself. But the student concerned enough about grades or other scholastic problems usually raises another meaningful issue—the issue of relevance.[4] It might also be noted that, with equal uniformity, the inhabitants of ghettos expressed dissatisfaction with a number of public assistance programs prior to violent outbursts. Relevance may then be viewed by the student as crucially significant in much the same way that power to influence his own destiny is seen by the ghetto inhabitant. The student's desire for *relevance* and the ghetto inhabitant's desire for sufficient political and economic power to modify an unfair system both relate to their needs in a changing society.

A college student's grades per se would seem to remain outside the scope of police concern. But when students collectively decide that they are receiving grades for subjects that fail to meet the needs of either the students or society, police intervention may ultimately be required, particu-

[3]Col. Curtis Brostron, "Police-Community Relations," *FBI Law Enforcement Bulletin,* 37, No. 3 (March 1968), p. 3.

[4]Western Interstate Commission for Higher Education, *WICHE,* XV, No. 1 (Nov. 1968), pp. 3–7.

larly if these very same grades influence standing with a selective service system for a war effort opposed by large numbers of the students. *The increase in police concern is based on the recognition that dissent and protest are not likely to be viewed a success unless and until they bring about a system that is deemed to be relevant.* The frustration resulting from a lack of success makes predictable greater demands for significant changes, and with the increased demands comes the increased jeopardy of violence. For law enforcement, the question becomes one of overall governmental response to mounting demands—frequently a difficult question in constitutional forms of government. Police interest in the developmental stages of social unrest, whether on the campus or in the ghetto, can no longer be denied.

But there are those who consider social unrest in terms of a positive outcome—at least the *potential* for a positive outcome:

> It is one of the ironies of social existence that the greatest progress often occurs at times of greatest social unrest. Indeed, it is the threat of violence that is frequently the most powerful force to promote change in the institutions of society. History attests to the fact that the most dramatic technological advances have occurred during periods when our nation was imperiled by war. There is little question that when "under the gun" we are able to marshal our resources, we can reappraise our priorities, and we can alter our institutions to enhance our survival as a social order.
>
> Today threats of violence are legion—not so much from without as from within our society. Are we prepared to undertake critical appraisal of our institutions and alter them to insure survival? If the past is prologue, we will; there are signs that the necessary changes are taking place.[5]

The ever-increasing demand for police recognition of social unrest need not be "negative."

Against this background of the relationship between law enforcement and social unrest, attention is now directed to the influence on constitutional government of other social changes—changes in patterns of Supreme Court power and civil rights.

CONSTITUTIONAL GOVERNMENT AND THE INFLUENCE OF SOCIAL CHANGE

In a rather profound manner, Warren Freedman commented on social change as follows:

[5]Morton Bard, "The Role of Law Enforcement in the Helping System," *Community Mental Health Journal*, 7, No. 2 (June 1971), p. 151.

In the chaotic growth of modern society the individual is being coerced, conformed, and threatened in new and unique ways by social changes. At the same time, "society is on trial," for we must determine whether or not the dynamics of society are equal to the task of coping with the slow-to-change laws and legal processes which measure the social values of the individual's right amid disturbing social, political, and economic conditions.[6]

Freedman's comments cast the judicial process inherent in constitutional government in a significant role insofar as social change is concerned. For it is the judicial process, particularly Supreme Court decisions, that more often than not influences government response to mounting social demands.

Of equal or even of greater importance in the response of constitutional government is the legislative process. Indeed, the judicial process, including Supreme Court decisions, necessarily flows almost entirely from the legislative process. However, notwithstanding the power of the legislative process, it remains abundantly clear that the judicial process through Supreme Court decisions has had far more direct effects and dramatic impact on law enforcement than any other single aspect of governmental response to social change.

Supreme Court Decisions

It has been said that American courts function as social controls of values and attitudes toward law, while at the same time reconciling grievances—grievances between either the State and the individual or between individuals.[7] And while the press has carried prominent articles about the need for strong judicial measures on behalf of the State in every decade for the past fifty years,[8] only recently has general concern focused directly on court reconciliation of grievances between the State and individuals.

A traditional role of law enforcement in constitutional forms of government is *apprehending* law violators, leaving *punishment* to the judicial process. Philosophically, at least, such a role permits crime prevention to be a mutual, although secondary, responsibility of both police and courts. But in recent times, police and courts are increasingly faced with "crimes" stemming from growing demands for social reform rather than merely from the violation of criminal statutes. One apparent reaction by the courts, particularly the Supreme Court, has been a number of decisions tending to have great impact on police procedure in general, and on the relationship of police to social change in particular. In effect, the Supreme Court has

[6]W. Freeman, *Society on Trial: Current Court Decisions and Social Change* (Springfield Ill.: Charles C. Thomas, 1965), Preface.

[7]W. Amos and C. Wellford, *Delinquency Prevention* (Englewood Cliffs, N.J.: Prentice-Hall, Inc., 1967), p. 208.

[8]R. W. Winslow, *Crime in a Free Society* (Belmont, Cal.: Dickenson, 1968).

handed down rulings that judge not only the lower courts' functions but the police function as well.

Much of the basis of the increasing Supreme Court assessment of police practice is the Fourth Amendment, and to some degree the Ninth Amendment. The implications of the Fourth Amendment to the police function have received more than adequate concern in the literature.[9] Nonetheless, a brief review of the highlights of the more significant court decisions may serve to clarify these implications.

In 1914 the United States Supreme Court ruled in *Weeks v. United States* that a federal court could not accept evidence that was obtained in violation of search and seizure protection, which is guaranteed by the Fourth Amendment. In 1963 the Supreme Court ruled on the appeal case of *Gideon v. Wainwright*. The effect of this ruling was that a new trial could be demanded by anyone convicted of crime who had not had legal counsel. Moving closer to the function of the police, in 1964 a decision was handed down in the case of *Escobedo v. Illinois*. This decision, based on a five to four majority, held it the constitutional right of an indigent to be provided with legal counsel at the time of the police interrogation. In June 1966, again by a five to four majority, the Court ruled on the case of *Miranda v. Arizona*. The *Miranda* decision had the effect of providing legal counsel during police questioning for persons *suspected* of crimes. Because this and the previous rulings were made on the basis of "constitutional rights," law enforcement found itself compelled to regard many traditional investigative methods as unconstitutional. So if constitutional rights have been violated by certain previously practiced police methods, the question becomes one of alternate approaches. And determination of such approaches is at best difficult when the overall function of the courts is undergoing change, resulting from Supreme Court interpretations of the United States Constitution.

Fortunately, the pattern of Supreme Court decisions in recent years has been to reduce the *direct* impact upon law enforcement—at least when compared to the Supreme Court decisions of the 1950s and 1960s. Indeed, if a pattern is discernible at all, it appears to show faint signs of recognizing the implications of the following:

> America decries her rising crime rate, people board themselves into their homes at night, they walk the darkened streets with dread. More and newer laws are enacted. While all along the police officer knows

---

[9]E. L. Barrett, "Personal Rights, Property Rights, and the Fourth Amendment," in *1960 Supreme Court Review* (Chicago: University of Chicago Press, 1961), p. 65. See also C. R. Sowle, ed., *Police Power and Individual Freedom* (Springfield, Ill.: Charles C. Thomas, Publisher, 1962); and W. H. Parker, "Birds Without Wings," in *The Police Yearbook*, 1965 (Washington, D.C.: International Association of Chiefs of Police, 1965).

the solution: rehabilitate in an all-out effort those criminals who are salvable; those who have proven themselves unrehabilitable should be permanently incarcerated for the protection of society.

Failure to cope realistically with crime and the criminal has caused wide-spread suspicion of government among the police. The policeman distrusts his government and its facilities for justice, while at the same time he fears the elements of turmoil and crime operating almost without restriction. This places the policeman in the unenviable position of truly being the middle man. Intellectuals, reformists, and government-sponsored groups attack the police from one side; criminals, revolutionaries, and anarchists attack from the other side, and the police find themselves even more alienated, defending a precarious middle ground they are not sure anyone values.[10]

Beyond doubts of law enforcement personnel regarding the value of the middle ground being defended, the Supreme Court looms large in the area of defining the "interests" of the community as opposed to the "interests" of the *individual*—critically significant contrasts for police in attempting to integrate these conflicting interests.

Police cope with the conflicting "interests" of groups representing themselves as the community, but in any given situation the Supreme Court exerts its influence on police practice through the individual. A clear definition of such interest is called for.

Regardless of the importance of defining interests, such a task cannot be easy in an era of articulate yet divergent explanation of interests. The difficulty is increased still more by Supreme Court decisions that influence not only the definition of what *due process* is but also the definition of the *interests* served through due process. Nevertheless, defining *interests* remains crucial to law enforcement.

Civil Rights and Power

Supreme Court decisions since World War II have influenced a number of interesting definitions—particularly in terms of educational opportunity and civil rights. In the majority of Supreme Court treatments of these areas, there is an implied definition of the individual's interest in political power. For indeed, insofar as constitutional government is concerned, there is little value in guaranteeing equal distribution of educational opportunity and civil rights if there is not a corresponding equality in the power to influence both. Put another way, the individual cannot gain equality either in educational opportunity or in civil rights unless and until he also commands political power—as much as is guaranteed to all—to modify both.

[10]Charles W. Sasser, "Cops Are Conventional People, But. . . ," *Law and Order*, 19, No. 8 (Aug. 1971), p. 50.

In discussing this, a Lutheran minister, Reverend Joseph R. Barndt, writes:

The central problem of the ghetto is powerlessness, and its result is a physical and emotional paralysis. The deepest need of the ghetto resident, as an individual and as a part of the whole community, is the power of self-determination.

The first tragic mistake we make in analyzing the needs of the ghetto is to confuse the symptoms with the disease, to fail to separate cause and result. The symptoms are poor education, over-crowded housing, unemployment, and underemployment, welfare, etc. But these are the results and not the causes of the ghetto resident's deep distress. If the four R's—rats, roaches, rape, and lack of recreation—were eradicated tomorrow by the magic wave of a wand, along with the rest of the symptoms of ghetto living, the disease would not be cured, the ghetto would not disappear. The ghetto will disappear only when the disease itself is dealt with efficiently, when power is returned to the people from whom it has long been withheld.

The second mistake we make is to pretend there is no sickness, but only a lack of will. A medical doctor who fails to diagnose illness in a patient, and who in addition, accuses the patient of pretending to be sick, should be sued for malpractice at the very least. A society that fails to diagnose the existence of a serious illness of the black slum ghetto, but instead accuses the patient of pretending or being lazy, is committing the same inexcusable action. The only possible explanation for our failure to diagnose the sickness is that if we did so we would have to recognize ourselves as the cause of the illness.

We have all too often and far too long been inaccurate in describing the condition of a person born and raised in the low income, minority ghetto. He has been portrayed as an ambitionless, lazy man, lacking the initiative necessary to raise himself to the same level of success as his middle and upper income brothers. The premises on which such a portrayal is based—that he has equal opportunity, that no preventive forces restrict him, and that the fault lies within people inside the ghetto walls—are false. In order to portray the resident of the low income minority ghetto accurately, we must understand this falsity. The ghetto resident is prevented from improving his own situation simply because he has been rendered powerless by, and is controlled by, outside forces. Although these forces are frustratingly invisible to the ghetto resident, some of their representatives are visible daily, performing their various tasks inside the ghetto walls. They include the slumlord, the case worker, the inspector, the politician, *the policeman*, the War on Poverty worker, and many, many more. In any other community, these people would at least represent cooperative forces that join the individual to assist him in the self-determined directions of his life. In the ghetto, however, these forces completely determine the individual's life, leaving him powerless for self-determination.

Furthermore, these outside forces effectively determine not only the life of the individual but also that of the collective community.[11]

Beyond recognizing the constitutional-government implications of these observations, a trend is clearly emerging within many law enforcement organizations that may well sustain this recognition:

> Most large metropolitan police departments seem to be moving toward a goal of creating integrated law enforcement agencies, while simultaneously removing, or at least decreasing, discriminatory behavior and practices among policemen as co-workers and within police departments as administrative units. Furthermore, there seems to be some question among citizens and law enforcement officials as well as among social scientists, as to whether the black policeman is accepted, respected, and cooperated with in his work within black communities.[12]

Still another trend that may be on the verge of perceptible development is the recognition that police interest in such things as poverty is on the basis of social unrest and *not* on the basis of *crime* as such:

> Poverty does not cause crime; poverty and crime are correlated with many other variables, such as employment, income, family stability, housing, illegitimacy, education, and welfare dependence. The crucial factor appears to be income, since income has a more significant relationship to crime that do the other variables. However, we cannot deal with income without also dealing with employment, job training, education and welfare.
>
> The poverty and crime thesis is based on studies of the characteristics of individual offenders caught in the web of justice, and, from the characteristics of individual offenders, we construct rehabilitation programs. It is another example of a crime prevention program set up to work through the rehabilitation of the individual offender, an assumption which runs throughout positivistic criminology. So long as we insist on designing crime control programs around the characteristics of individual offenders, rather than around the environment in which crimes are committed, we are going to emphasize changing the individual offender and not changing the environment.[13]

Social problems of any kind are remedied or relieved through power—political and economic power. The absence of such power almost assuredly leads to resentment among those on whom social problems have their

[11]J. Barndt, *Why Black Power* (New York: Friendship Press, 1968), p. 31.

[12]James D. Bannon, and G. Marie Wilt, "Black Policemen: A Study of Self-Images," *Journal of Police Science and Administration*, 1, No. 1 (March 1973), p. 21.

[13]C. Ray Jeffrey, *Crime Prevention through Environmental Design* (Beverly Hills: Sage Publications, 1971), p. 141.

greatest direct impact. This resentment, whether expressed or implied, is of critical interest to law enforcement in an era in which Supreme Court decisions and civil rights legislation often tend merely to dramatize the frustration that results from trying to achieve the power needed to influence one's own destiny. This frustration has emerged as the greatest single social problem having direct impact on law enforcement in a changing community.

Compounding the law enforcement problems in this regard is the obscurity of definitions of either crime *or* delinquency. Simple *violation of law* is no longer seen as a clear definition of either crime or delinquency in constitutional governments because virtually *everyone* violates *some* law. Crime and delinquency are of course violation of the law. *But is every violation of law crime or delinquency?* Indeed, is every violation of *criminal* law crime or delinquency?

If the answer to the first question is "yes," then it is probable that virtually *every* American is a "criminal." Even if the more technically restrictive second question is answered "yes," the suggestion is made that the overwhelming majority of Americans are "criminal" or "delinquent." It has been suggested by some that this *is* the case—that most Americans *are* "technically" criminal or delinquent. Specifically, the relatively frequent assertion that virtually all American adults have violated some law is now being applied to juveniles as well—an assertion that most juveniles have committed acts defined as "delinquent." Indeed, some claim findings to the effect that "delinquents" consider other "delinquents" *less* delinquent than juveniles in general:

> Even the most delinquent teenagers characterized their own friends as being *less* delinquent than *teenagers* in general. No matter how frequent or serious their offenses, they did not see themselves and their friends as the town's toughest, meanest, and most rebellious teenagers. This finding challenges the "delinquency subculture" theory. The classic "hood" is always somebody else, not them, not known to them. The stereotype of teenager as hoodlum has become so wildly accepted in American society that nearly all young people from ages 13 to 16 subscribe to it as unquestioningly as do a high percentage of adults . . .
> . . . The mythical American Delinquent casts a shadow over what might loosely be termed the delinquency-prevention industry. He dominates the juvenile courts and obscures the reality important to researchers, law-enforcement officials, social workers, the courts, the media, and the public. As a result, current treatment and prevention programs are, in a word, misdirected. Starting with false assumptions about who commits delinquent acts, they aim the wrong programs at the wrong groups . . .[14]

[14]Bill Haney, and Martin Gold, "The Juvenile Delinquent Nobody Knows," *Psychology Today*, 7, No. 4 (Sept. 1973), p. 55.

These kinds of considerations of course bear on the *prevention* of crime and delinquency in another context that will be developed later in this chapter—the context involving the idea of a sequence, with juvenile delinquency occurring before adult crime. But in the immediate context of considering the proportion of American population involved in law violation, many consider the growing evidence that most Americans violate American law as evidence that the *society,* rather than the people, is "criminal." A more subtle version of the "sick society" reasoning is the idea that society, rather than law violators, is currently on trial.

Whether or not it is sick or on trial, it is clear that preventing and controlling crime and delinquency is *not* the same as preventing and controlling law violation—at least *every* law violation. Moreover, preventing and controlling crime and delinquency is not the same as declaring virtually every American either "criminal" or "delinquent." Of course this poses what appears to be a contradiction and possibly a significant paradox.

Adult Status and the Influence of Face-to-Face Relationships

There are many reasons for this seeming contradiction in *distinguishing* between crime or delinquency and law violation—some reasons simple, some reasons complex. *All* reasons for such a contradictory distinction, however, have in common a relationship (either direct or indirect) to the current American definition of "adult"—adults who are potentially "criminal" or "potential delinquents" *become* after maturation:

> When we ask what qualities an adult in society must have, it is useful in answering to think of societies ... points along a continuum of complexity. First is a communal, face-to-face society in which a man knows personally all the members of his relevant social environment ... second is a society that includes relations at a distance, or what some sociologists call secondary relations. In such societies, a man's daily activities include interactions, both economic and social, with people he does not know personally. A nonindustrial society of craftsmen, merchants, and farmers, spread over a geographic area with travel between different towns, exemplifies the larger type of society. America of the eighteenth and early nineteenth centuries and preindustrialized Europe are concrete cases that illustrate such a society.[15]

The definition of an adult in twentieth-century America includes considerations of both face-to-face relationships and secondary relationships. Urbanization, along with many other social changes, tends to *reduce* face-to-face relations for adults and brings about a great deal more emphasis on the secondary relationships. In other words, becoming adult may mean becom-

---

[15]James S. Coleman, *Adolescents and The Schools* (New York: Basic Books, 1965), p. 88.

ing "less personal." There is no clear definition of the *nature* of either relationship, face-to-face or secondary, once adult status has been reached. "Friendship" neighbors or other personal relationships are often the only face-to-face, whereas organizations tend to be the secondary relationships. Confusing this matter is the relationship between the willingness to participate in active prevention of crime as a part of secondary relationships but for "personal" or face-to-face reasons.

For example, many American adults maintain face-to-face relations with those who find no difficulty rationalizing the violation of vehicle speed laws or traffic laws in general. Driving faster than the posted speed limit is O.K. when the "traffic is right"; stopping at a stop sign is "silly when no cars are in sight." The fact that law has been violated seems to function in such cases as "merely incidental"—if it functions at all.

Organizations in which secondary relationships may occur may well support the "letter of the law," and even actively support community efforts to prevent crime. The individual effort required, however, may not be forthcoming when a contradiction between primary and secondary relationships occurs. For it is the ability to express positive concern about crime *without* involving face-to-face personal relations that permits the secondary relationships within organizations to focus against crime and delinquency.

Imagine for a moment that community organizations, in which secondary relationships occur, agree on the need to prevent crime and delinquency. Further imagine that the crime and delinquency that these organizations seek to prevent is "fudging on tax" and "joyriding." Finally imagine that a significant segment of the personal face-to-face relationships of members of these organizations consist of persons who "fudge" on their tax returns and who participate in joyriding in someone else's car. From this frame of reference, consider whether or not the following stands any chance of real success:

> The spectrum of anticrime efforts appropriate for citizens is so wide that almost everyone has many opportunities to promote and pursue crime prevention activities—and on a number of the involvement levels described earlier. Seizing a fair share of such opportunities need not inconvenience anyone; on the contrary, because of the variety, they are more likely to complement, and constitute an outlet for, one's natural interests.
>
> A major category of crime prevention activities pertains to those efforts aimed at what many consider to be the infrastructure of crime: insufficient education, inadequate job skills, unavailable recreation opportunities, and the like. Citizen action in this area constitutes crime prevention in the positive sense of the term. That is, the objective is to fill vacuums in the lives of individuals who might otherwise be drawn dangerously close to the line that separates the legal from the illegal.

These kinds of crime prevention activities are brought to bear outside of the criminal justice system and are designed to reduce significantly the need to utilize the sanctions of that system.

Another major category of citizen action encompasses those crime prevention measures that are closely related to the three components of the criminal justice system—police, courts, corrections. In general, these activities seek either to complement the operation of one of the components, as a citizen crime commission might, or to strengthen the component, as probation volunteers might. Efforts in this area constitute crime prevention to the extent that the criminal justice system is thereby improved and thus becomes a more effective crime deterrence.[16]

The crime and delinquency that is to be "fought" here is definitely not "fudging on tax," or minor traffic violations. Nevertheless, to whatever degree there is a difference between the secondary relations of organizations attempting to prevent crime and the personal face-to-face relations, to the same degree does the actual potential of prevention efforts diminish.

Of course there is a great deal more involved in the distinction between law violation and crime than merely recognizing that a great deal of law violation is not thought of as crime—that things friends do are not *really* criminal or delinquent. Beyond acknowledging that many law violations are not considered part of the crime problem, consideration of the stereotyped criminal is important. The entertainment medium has given a fairly consistent image of the adult "criminal." Delinquent juveniles are similarly stereotyped:

Each of us carries in mind pictures of a variety of social statuses; among these is one of the juvenile delinquent. Our basic conceptions of the juvenile delinquent, and those of other contemporary figures, are imbedded in these pictures. Consequently, research frequently does not progress deeply enough to offend and thus qualify our conceptions. Research typically is guided by basic conceptions rather than being designed to question them.

Our picture of the delinquent consists of the basic assumptions we make about him. Currently and for almost one hundred years our assumptions about the delinquent have been those of the positive school of criminology. My main purpose in this book is to question and modify the positivist portrait. Since assumptions are usually implicit, they tend to remain beyond the reach of such intellectual correctives as argument, criticism, and scrutiny. Thus, to render assumptions explicit is not only to propose a thesis; more fundamentally it is to widen and deepen the area requiring exploration. Assumptions implicit in

[16]As appears in *Working Papers for the National Conference on Criminal Justice*, January 23–26, 1973, Washington, D.C., pp. CC13–14.

conceptions are rarely inconsequential. Left unattended, they return to haunt us by shaping or bending theories that purport to explain major social phenomena. Assumptions may prompt us to notice or to ignore discrepancies or patterns that may be observed in the empirical world. Conceptions structure our inquiry.[17]

Recognizing the powerful influence of stereotyping is useful in approaching the influence patterns that mitigate against defining all law violation as criminal or delinquent. In other words, when it is believed that what "delinquents" (or "criminals") *are* is visible, many believe that such a stereotype also provides a definition of what delinquents and criminals are *not*. With incredible ease, then, "knowing" what delinquents and criminals "do" affords knowledge of what criminals and delinquents do *not* "do"— and personal face-to-face relations, not being delinquent or criminal, *never* involve "real crime."

In the complexity of twentieth-century urbanized America, this realization need not lead to cynical conclusions. It is probably impossible to avoid violating some federal, state, county, local, or military law in a lifetime. Even within the academic study of criminal justice, certain forms of law violation tend to be seen as less criminal—check-forgers compared to armed robbers, embezzlers compared to rapists, petty thieves compared to burglars, car thieves compared to extortionists, etc. Even the statistical proportions of those violating the law seem to influence the degree of criminality perceived.

> One of the facts of fundamental importance in criminology is that as far as arrests and convictions are concerned, women are far less commonly involved in crime than men. In most Western countries, about six boys are convicted for every girl among juveniles, and ten men for every adult woman; in other parts of the world the proportions of male offenders is even larger. This remarkable discrepancy between the sexes has to be borne in mind when considering the biological, psychiatric, and psychological causes of crime. Where any particular factor (e.g., mental illness) is fairly equally distributed between the sexes, one must account for its different effect upon criminality in the sexes.[18]

Crime and delinquency, then, are more matters of degree than matters of laws violated. The *degree* to which law violation is tolerated within the face-to-face context, along with the *sequence* in which toleration of law violation occurs, becomes critically important. Tolerance thresholds actually

---

[17]David Matza, *Delinquency and Drift* (New York: Wiley & Sons, 1964), p. 1.

[18]T. C. N. Gibbens and Robert H. Ahrenfeldt, eds., *Cultural Factors In Delinquency* (Philadelphia: J. B. Lippincott Co., 1966), p. 36.

determine the point at which prevention can succeed. In other words, this degree is the point at which the organizational secondary relationships stand some chance to succeed in organized prevention efforts. This of course acknowledges that formalized secondary relationships within community organizations constitute the only *real* potential to prevent (or control) crime and delinquency.

This then is the context in which the enforcement of law operates in relation to a constitutional government that is attempting to cope with widespread frustration.

SUMMARY

This chapter examined the impact of social problems on law enforcement and the influence of constitutional government on the solution of such problems.

There are various limitations and restrictions on law enforcement in the context of "free" constitutional government. These include property rights; free speech, with the right of dissent; and the right to seek alternate methods of affording an orderly environment—orderly environment seen as a primary responsibility in all forms of government.

Unrest is a consequence of disparity between the interests or needs of individuals and governmental methods of dealing with such interests or needs. In this regard, student concern with "relevance" was presented in this chapter as a model for examining various social problems. Such terms as *extremists* and *activists* were discarded in favor of assessing the degree or level of the demand for social change.

Both the legislative and especially the judicial process in constitutional government have an immediate impact on law enforcement in a changing community. The United States Supreme Court decisions have had an immediate effect on law enforcement and an indirect impact on decisions that tend to call attention to the gross limitations of political and economic power available to some individuals—often individuals seeking such power merely to achieve solutions to social problems. Power is equated with educational opportunity and civil rights, and is a prime requisite in remedying chronically unresolved social problems in constitutional government.

DISCUSSION TOPICS

1. Elaborate the law enforcement implications of the introductory remarks on government influence over police.

2. Discuss what was presented initially in the chapter as the "common factor" of all governments expecting all police to retain sufficient stability to *permit* government to exist.

3. What are the obligations of a free constitutional government to the individual who permits his behavior to be controlled?

4. Name five social consequences of World War II. Discuss the relationship of each to law enforcement.

5. What is the most significant difference between current student unrest and student nonconformity of the past?

6. Discuss the role of police in solutions to social problems in general; in demonstrations, in particular.

7. What bearing have Supreme Court decisions on social problems in general? On police, in particular?

8. How is the acquisition of power by minorities an advantage for the majority? For law enforcement?

ANNOTATED REFERENCES

AMOS, W., AND C. WELLFORD, *Delinquency Prevention*. Englewood Cliffs, N.J.: Prentice-Hall, Inc., 1967. Chapters 9, 10, and 11 deal effectively with the relationship of economics, police, and the judicial process in the community.

BANNON, JAMES D., AND G. MARIE WILT, "Black Policemen: A Study of Self-Images," *Journal of Police Science and Administration*, 1, No. 1 (March 1973). Excellent article on the current state of developing intra-organization approaches to the same problems confronting police from "outside."

BARD, MORTON, "The Role of Law Enforcement in The Helping System," *Community Mental Health Journal*, 7, No. 2 (June 1971). Places law enforcement in the general context of facilitating reduction in problems of social unrest.

BARNDT, J., *Why Black Power*. New York: Friendship Press, 1968. An excellent treatise which identifies and isolates the *positive* value of political and economic power for minorities.

COFFEY, ALAN R., *Criminal Justice Administration: A Management Systems Approach*, Englewood Cliffs, N.J.: Prentice-Hall Inc., 1974. Chapters 9 and 10 elaborate organizational techniques for coping with governmental influences on law enforcement; see also Chapter 15.

COFFEY, ALAN R., AND VERNON RENNER, eds., *Criminal Justice Readings*. Englewood Cliffs, N.J.: Prentice-Hall, Inc., 1974. A wide selection of articles about criminal justice in the context of constitutional government.

FREEMAN, W., *Society on Trial*. Springfield, Ill.: Charles C. Thomas, Publisher, 1965. An exceptionally detailed review of modifications in modern judicial process.

FLOCKS, R., ed., *Conformity, Resistance, and Self-Determination: The Individual and Authority.* Boston: Little, Brown, 1973. A fine collection of contributions affording a classical analysis model for virtually all modern social problems.

MAY, E., "The Disjointed Trio: Poverty, Politics, and Power," *National Conference on Social Welfare: Social Welfare Forum,* 1963, pp. 47–61. An excellent discussion of the relationship of power to poverty through the medium of politics.

THE PROBLEM
OF POLICE IMAGE
IN A CHANGING COMMUNITY

4

Police across the nation are confronting the most difficult task in the history of law enforcement. We live in an era of growth, expansion, and change that is unprecedented. Law enforcement is more directly affected by the changes than perhaps any other agency of government.

Numerous methods used by the police in the past have been declared unconstitutional. Decisions handed down by the higher courts of the land and the United States Supreme Court, as well as new laws, make the work of police in protecting the general public much more difficult.

In the nation's large cities and in many small cities and towns as well, the need for strengthening police-community relationships is critical today. Blacks, Puerto Ricans, Mexican-Americans, Indians, and other minority groups are taking action to acquire rights and services which have historically been denied them. As the most *visible* representatives of the society from which these groups are demanding fair treatment and equal opportunity, law enforcement agencies are faced with unprecedented situations which require that they *develop policies and practices governing their actions when dealing with minority groups and other citizens.*

Even if fair treatment of minority groups were the sole consideration, police departments would have an obligation to attempt to achieve and maintain a positive police image and good police-community relations. In fact, however, much more is at stake. For police-community relations have a direct bearing on the character of life in the cities and on the community's ability to maintain stability and solve its problems. At the same time, the police department's capacity to deal with crime depends to a large extent upon its relationship with the citizenry. Indeed, no improvement in law enforcement is likely in this country unless police-community relations are substantially improved.

The last decade has seen an increasingly enlightened public. Many of the mass disorders during the 1960s damaged the police image and made the public increasingly critical of police service. As a result of such criticism, some of which has been without validity, thousands of loyal, capable, and professional officers throughout the nation are extremely perplexed and apprehensive of the future. The complexity of contemporary law enforcement in conjunction with the rapidly growing problems of traffic control has demanded frequent citizen contact, not only with the criminal element but also with the law-abiding citizen. Thus, because of the closer, more personal contact, there is a greater need to present a positive police image.

Police-community relations cannot be viewed as an isolated problem —one which confronts only those agents who have a vested interest in administration of the criminal justice system and process. When we discuss the problem of police-community relations, police image, and human relations in general, we really have many things in mind. Because practitioners in the field of community justice are primarily concerned with working with people—every one of them an individual in his own right—it is vital for police personnel, as well as those associated with the judicial and correctional process, to understand that there is a common denominator—a sharing of one very important feature. *This common feature is the awareness that every human being has his own aspirations, hopes, and standards of behavior.*

It is not the intention of this chapter to address itself to police-community relations *programs;* this is a major topic of Chapter 12. Instead, emphasis will be on the effect of negative police image and the problems confronting law enforcement agencies in developing and maintaining a positive police image. As indicated in Chapter one, a good police image tends to affect favorably the individual's willingness to observe the law voluntarily. Therefore, police retain a vital interest in good image.

THE COMMUNITY AND THE POLICE:
CONTROVERSY OVER POLICE ROLE

A great deal of controversy exists today over the role police should play in our contemporary society. The responsibility of the police officer is *basically* to regulate the conduct and minister to the needs of people from all classes of life. All of these individuals are equally entitled to the services of law enforcement agencies. There are other duties which have fallen within the

FIGURE 4.1   *Officers of Los Angeles County assist victims of a disaster. Courtesy Los Angeles County Sheriff's Department, Los Angeles, Cal.*

purview of law enforcement, but basically, all fall within the scope of protection of personal life and property and regulation of the conduct of *all* individuals within our community while administering to their needs.

The primary police-citizen contacts are, contrary to popular belief, primarily with those members of our society who request assistance and protection. These individuals turn to the police officer for assistance with problems which are extremely difficult and important—at least important to them. Although these problems may be viewed as minor or insignificant to some, "it is imperative that matters of such vital personal importance be approached with understanding, compassion, and magnanimity."[1]

In analyzing the number and character of contacts the policeman has with members of the public during his tour of duty, we see that he spends very little time chasing criminals or locking people up. Dr. Michael Banton commented on the community service function of the police:[2]

[1]D. L. Kooken, *Ethics in Police Service* (Springfield, Ill.: Charles C. Thomas, Publisher, 1957), p. 21.

[2]"Social Integration and Police Authority," in N. A. Watson, ed., *Police and The Changing Community: Selected Readings* (Washington, D.C.: International Association of Chiefs of Police, 1965), p. 29.

A POLICEMAN . . . is a kind of professional citizen, administering the moral standards defined and accepted by his community. . . . He earns public cooperation and esteem by the manner in which he exercises good judgment in performing his duties, and the foundation of his good judgment is an awareness of the public's point of view. . . . He is a Defender of the Peace more than an Enforcer of the Law, possessing authority as well as power. His authority gives him the willing obedience of the public, thus including a moral element which compels obedience that is not necessarily rightful. . . . He will suppress his personal feelings in disintegration troubles to identify with his Department if it is committed to professional policing and has a morality of its own. . . . His role should be based upon the moral authority of his office rather than its legal powers, particularly in districts of racial and cultural differences.

How a police officer handles the inherited "police power" is often a factor in the public's view of law enforcement in the community. Law must be enforced if civilized man is to survive. Society cannot depend completely upon simple persuasion to induce law observance, and therefore it must require enforcement of law. This enforcement, then, is necessarily a part of the police role. But the manner in which it is viewed by the public often determines whether the police image is good or bad. Neither the policeman nor the public finds it easy to differentiate between the law and its enforcement. This is pointed out by the late D. L. Kooken: "The public generally are inclined to look upon policemen not so much as representatives of government and agents of law enforcement, but more in the light of policemen being the law in themselves."[3] The late Bruce Smith also pointed out that "relatively few citizens recall ever having seen a judge; fewer still a prosecutor, coroner, sheriff, probation officer or prison warden. The patrolman is thoroughly familiar to all. His uniform picks him out from the crowd so distinctly that he becomes a living symbol of the law—not always of its majesty, but certainly of its power. Whether police like it or not, they are forever marked men."[4]

Police are engaged in traditional occupations, which are being loaded down with new requirements because of the changes and social unrest in our society.

Nothing is tougher than being a policeman in a free society. For one thing, the U.S. Constitution guarantees as much individual liberty as public safety will allow. To uphold that elusive ideal the policeman is supposed to mediate family disputes that would tax a Supreme Court

[3] *Ethics in Police Service*, p. 31.

[4] "Municipal Police Administration," *Annals of the American Academy of Police and Social Science*, 40, No. 5 (1972), p. 22.

Justice, soothe angry Negroes despite his scant knowledge of psychology, enforce hundreds of petty laws without discrimination, and use only necessary force to bring violators before the courts. The job demands extraordinary skill, restraint, and character—qualities not usually understood by either cop-hating leftists who sound as if they want to exterminate all policemen, or by dissent-hating conservatives who seem to want policemen to run the U.S. in a paroxysm of punitive "law and order."

The U.S. policeman is forbidden to act as judge and jury—for that way lies the police state. Yet, he also has enormous discretion to keep the peace by enforcing some laws and by overlooking others. How does he exercise that discretion? Largely on the basis of common sense and common mores, plus his own private attitudes. Unfortunately, he faces an era of drastically changing mores that challenges his most cherished creeds and preconceptions.[5]

The essay continues by noting that the American public is confused in their expectations of the role of law enforcement officers in the United States: "We ask our officers to be a combination of Bat Masterson, Sherlock Holmes, Sigmund Freud, King Solomon, Hercules, and Diogenes.... Indeed, the U.S. often seems lucky to have any cops at all. Plato envisioned the policeman's lofty forebear as the 'guardian' of law and order and placed very near the top of his ideal society, endowing him with special wisdom, strength and patience. The U.S. has put its guardians near the bottom. In most places, the pay for experienced policemen is less than $9000 a year, forcing many cops to moonlight and some to take bribes. Fear and loneliness are routine hazards."[6]

The *Time* article concludes its analysis of the basic police problem by commenting that the average cop feels he is unappreciated or even actively disliked by the public he serves. Very often, he is right—and thus he is all the more apt to confine his entire social as well as professional life to his fellow cops, a group that all too often see the world as "we" and "they."

The Police: "We and They"

But the problem involves more than lack of understanding regarding police activities in our free society. There is increasing evidence that Americans of all races, creeds, and income groups share their reservations about the police. Some of these are for obvious reasons. Most people tend to come in direct contact with police only under rather unhappy circumstances —when they have parked the car "just a little bit illegally," when caught driving faster than the posted speed limit, or when they have been involved

---

[5]"Time Essay: The Police Need Help," *Time* (Oct. 1968), p. 26.
[6]Ibid.

in some "innocent" horseplay that misfired. Coupled with this is belief in the old adage: "When you happen to need a policeman, he's never there." Either way the police image comes out scarred.

According to a noted author, H. H. Toch, it is the broader connotations of police actions rather than their direct impact that may promote most of the antagonism on the part of society.[7] Although these connotations probably can be ameliorated through stronger emphasis on police courtesy and public relations, they can hardly be completely eradicated. Ultimately the social and psychological control role of law enforcement is one of essentially one-way communication against a backdrop of latent power.[8]

If it is limited to this type of contact, the policeman's role as a controlling agent within the community will be damaged. Furthermore, according to Toch, such one-way contact ultimately will prove psychologically harmful to the police as well as to the public. The policeman too often exaggerates the prevalence of apathy and projects hostility even where there is none. He interprets public antagonism as an indication of his inevitable separation from the "mainstream" of the community.[9]

POLICE: SYMBOL OF SOCIAL PROBLEMS

There is no doubt that the policeman is the symbol of authority and middle-class values. With his standard equipment of the uniform, the gun, the insignia of rank, and the baton, the policeman on occasion tends to think of himself as part of a paramilitary unit, which is certainly not too far from the truth. However, unlike the military, the police have a requirement to keep good relations between themselves and the community. Law enforcement is more dependent upon public support than any single branch of government or any other profession. The average police officer is likely to come from a middle-class community in which he lives a well-regulated life according to middle-class standards of ethics and morality. But he works at law enforcement in an area populated by people who are largely alien to him. He finds the language, customs, and emotions of minority groups strange, hostile, and aggravating. Professionalism has not resolved this problem. Identification with fellow officers is reinforced, "forging a social bond . . . at the same time it generates a great deal of mutual suspicion."[10]

[7] "Psychological Consequences of the Police Role," *Police*, 10, No. 1 (Sept.-Oct. 1965), p. 22.

[8] Ibid.

[9] Ibid.

[10] D. J. Dodd, "Police Mentality and Behavior," *Issues in Criminology*, 3, No. 1 (Summer 1967), pp. 56–57.

Statistics indicate that there is a definite increase in assaults against policemen. Thus, confronted with hostility and fearing physical injury, the policeman is constantly "on guard". This contributes to his isolation and his view of the community, in which he sees

everything taking place around him as a configuration of events designed to attack him. His natural reaction is to strike first. The idea of the symbolic assailant illustrates one of the two principal variables which make up the working personality of the police officer—reaction to danger. The other is his reaction to authority.... His natural suspicion, plus his natural conception of his work as a way of life, reinforce the tendencies previously noted, and draw him further away from the public he intends to serve and protect.

... This is especially so in lower class areas where the cop is seen as standing for the interests and prejudices of dominant [white] society in the role of the oppressor, and where each party sees the other as a misfit.[11]

It may be paradoxical that the same people who are the most victimized by crime are the most hostile to the police, but it is not remarkable because the policeman is the symbol of middle-class society and values.

In a fundamental sense, it is wrong to define the problem solely as hostility to police. In many ways, the policeman symbolizes much deeper problems. Responsibility for apathy or disrespect for law enforcement agencies would be more appropriately attributed to

a social system that permits inequities and irregularities in law, stimulates poverty and inhibits initiative and motivation of the poor, and regulates low social and economic status to the police while concomitantly giving them more extraneous non-police duties than can actively be performed.[12]

The ongoing daily affairs of the people of the community are the result of an interplay of social, economic, psychological, and biological forces which influence the behavior of all citizens, whether clerics or criminals, educators or demonstrators, merchants or police. Police problems are not unrelated to welfare problems. Dropouts are obviously not solely the problem of school administrators. Unemployment, bad housing, discrimination, improper family structures, illegitimacy, and disease produce results that directly aggravate those problems more generally regarded as police matters—crime, violence, and the like. Moreover, to the extent that persons

[11]Ibid.

[12]R. L. Derbyshire, "The Social Control Role of the Police in Changing Urban Communities," *Excerpta Criminologica*, 6, No. 3 (1966), pp. 315–16.

living under these conditions see themselves as victims of social oppression, the police can expect much of the rebellion to be focused against them.

Everyone certainly agrees that the police cannot be expected to solve all the ills of the community. Many do not realize, however, how directly involved the police are in conflict with the problems these ills generate. It is easy enough to see how the police are involved when there is a demonstration, riot, or minor or major disorder, but the less spectacular day-by-day accumulation of social costs and police involvement, though not so dramatic, is nonetheless enormous. When such disorders break out, nearly everyone assumes that the role of the police is to stop them; that is clear. What is not generally understood, however, is that in their daily performance, the police, along with other governmental structures, inevitably tend to view things in terms of community mores. People in general go about their daily lives with a sort of unverbalized understanding that "this is the custom; this is the way things are." And for most people in most facets of their daily existence, it is comfortable to be able to rely on things "being the way they are." The police realize this—perhaps more so than most because they are so close to the conflict potential that accompanies pressures for change. The fact that the police do not take the initiative to change things is not just a case of not wanting to "rock the boat." The police alone are not in a position to change community mores even if they wanted to and knew how.

To a considerable extent, then, the police are the victims of community problems which are not of their making. For generations, minority groups and the poor have not received a fair opportunity to share the benefits of American life. The policeman in the ghetto is the most visible symbol of a society from which many ghetto residents are increasingly alienated.

> At the same time, police responsibilities in the ghetto are greater than elsewhere in the community since the other institutions of social control have so little authority: The schools because so many are segregated, old and inferior; religion—which has become irrelevant to those who have lost faith as they lost hope; superior aspirations, which for many young Blacks are totally lacking; the family, because its bands are so often snapped. It is the policeman who must deal with the consequences of this institutional vacuum and is then resented for the presence and measures this effort demands.[13]

The policeman, as a symbol not only of law but of the entire system of law enforcement and criminal justice, becomes the tangible target for grievances against shortcomings throughout the system. When a suspect is held for a long period in jail because he has no money to pay a fine, when

[13]National Advisory Commission on Civil Disorders, p. 157.

the jail or prison is physically dilapidated or its personnel brutal or incompetent, or when the probation or parole officer has little time to give a prisoner and he is given inadequate counsel from the public defender system that is very often understaffed and overworked, the police are blamed. Following is a description of a familiar courtroom process that exemplifies this.

[The] lawyer goes through row after row of spectators and defendants in the court room, calling out his client's name. The chances are that he has seen the client only once in his life before—months ago, when the client's case was in the arraignment stage. Today is the trial date and he keeps calling out his man's name, looking over the rows of faces. "Williams? Harry Williams?" he calls, and finally a man stands up, shrugs his shoulders to get the tension out of them and says, "Yeah."

"Just wanted to see you were here," says the lawyer, and tells the client to sit down again and reassures him that he will return shortly. He glances at the wad of papers in his hand, arrest warrants, arraignment records, writs, and all the paper foundations of justice. Then he heads out of the courtroom, where a melee of policemen are moving about, chatting and joking, talking to lawyers, waiting for cases to be called.

The lawyer finds the name of the officer who made the arrest and, because he is familiar with these small type criminal cases, he soon spots him in the crowd. "You got Williams today?" he asks. The officer nods.

The two then set about a bargaining session. Let's say Williams, the defendant, has been arrested perhaps a year before, the way court calendars go today—for carrying a pistol. It was found in a shake-down as he was coming home one night under a "stop-and-frisk" ordinance. He was hurrying because he was late coming from his job, and a hurrying Black man is a suspicious person to many police officers. He offered no resistance and the officers made a search for weapons. The gun was found and he was charged with a felony, one which might carry a prison term of several years.

"Can we do business?" the lawyer asks in the crowded court room. And the policeman has to think. In most states, stop-and-frisk laws also provide that the officer have "reason to believe" that a felony has been committed or was about to be. In this case, the officer might be letting himself in for trouble. "Did the suspect show the gun?" the judge might ask. "How was he acting suspiciously?" The officer wants to avoid this, and agrees that a better charge might be a misdemeanor, such as failure to register a firearm or some such, depending on the state law.

Soon he suggests a lesser charge, the lawyer nods and the two go—more often than not—to stand in line to wait to talk to whichever prosecutor will be handling the case. When they see the prosecutor, he looks at whatever reports he has and generally agrees to allowing a guilty plea on the lesser charge.

The lawyer goes back to Williams, assures him that if he is willing to "cop out" he will receive probably a maximum of 90 days in the county jail, whereas if he pleads innocent to the other more serious charge, he could, if convicted, go to prison for several years. Williams, confused, and afraid of prison, accepts the lesser of two evils.

The practice, roughly akin to buying a rug in an Oriental bazaar, is called "plea bargaining," and it goes on day after day, year after year.[14]

A more critical look at the manner in which the courts and adult corrections (California) operate in the field of human relations is given in an article in the *Los Angeles Times* on July 12, 1970.[15] This article examines the problems of the administration of criminal justice system and process (police, courts, and corrections). The author points out that blacks usually receive longer prison sentences than whites for most criminal offenses. A study of persons convicted of burglary and auto theft in Los Angeles County, most of them first offenders and unskilled laborers, revealed that on the average whites were treated much less severely than blacks. Forty-five percent of the white and 27 percent of the blacks were given sentences for these crimes of four months' imprisonment or less, or probation. Forty-two percent of the whites and 47 percent of the blacks received four to nine months; and 13 percent of the whites and 27 percent of the blacks got 10 to 20 months. Some of the most glaring disparities occur in sentences imposed for capital crimes. According to the Bureau of Prisons, 3,857 persons were executed in the United States between 1930 and 1966; 53.5 percent of these were black, 45.4 percent were white, and 1.1 percent were members of other minority groups. Not only is it less likely that a white person will be sentenced to death, but the workings of executive and administrative discretion are such that, once condemned to die, a white person is more likely to have his sentence commuted to life imprisonment by a governmental executive, board of pardons, or similar agency. Marvin E. Wolfgang, the noted criminologist, reports that among those condemned to die, between 10 and 20 percent more blacks than whites were actually executed.

Once again, at the risk of repetition, remember that when such situations exist, it is the *police officer* who arrested the citizen and started the process who will probably be given a large share of the blame.

The policeman assigned to the ghetto is a symbol of increasingly bitter social debate over law enforcement. The Commission on Civil Dis-

---

[14]David Murray, *America's Crisis in Authority* (Chicago: Claretian Publications, 1971) by permission of the publisher.

[15]The article was written for the *Los Angeles Times* by Haywood Burns, then national director of the Conference of Black Lawyers.

orders noted that one group, disturbed and perplexed by sharp rises in crime and urban violence, demands that what police need to maintain law and order is better and more sophisticated equipment. They perceive the police role as seeing that the law is strictly enforced. Those who transgress are to be dealt with, with dispatch and without pampering. Those who hold this view exert a great deal of pressure on police for tougher law enforcement. Another group, blaming police as agents of repression, tends toward defiance and believes that order is maintained at the expense of justice.

Because the police are a symbol of society's social ills and the shortcomings of the administration of criminal justice system, it is incumbent upon police to take every possible step to allay grievances that flow from a sense of injustice and increased tension and turmoil.

Several years ago, a report was prepared for the President's Commission on Law Enforcement and Administration of Justice that dealt with police-community relations. One of the areas the study focused on was public attitudes toward the police. It revealed a number of prejudices common in communities throughout the United States. A summary of these biases against police will be useful now to help us understand the problems of the police in achieving or obtaining the confidence of the public. The following are excerpts of this study.

THE PUBLIC VIEW[16]

Characteristically, there is a divergence of opinion in the "public view" of police-community relations. In San Diego the divergence is based upon race rather than upon geography, economics, or social class position. Opinions about the status of police-community relations tend to arrange themselves around "positive" and "negative" poles; the majority of the white community tending generally to feel that the situation is "good," with some possible minor exceptions; the minority Negro and Mexican-American communities —regardless of social class position—feel that police-community relations are poor. Because of the clear division of opinions and concepts along these ethnic lines, the following discussion arranged according to majority- and minority-group views.

White Middle Class

When asked to evaluate the state of police-community relations in San Diego, middle-class Caucasians typically responded that the relations

---

[16]This section adopted from J. D. Lohman, and G. E. Misner, *The Police and the Community: The Dynamics of their Relationship in a Changing Community,* report prepared for the *President's Commission on Law Enforcement and Administration of Justice,* Vol. 1 (Washington, D.C.: U.S. Government Printing Office, 1966), pp. 50–55.

were either "outstanding," "extremely good," "favorable," or "exceptional." A number of persons contacted emphasized that from their own personal experiences or observations, police-community relations were better in San Diego than in other cities where they had previously lived, cities such as Chicago, Los Angeles, Buffalo, or Baltimore. One individual commented spontaneously that "in comparison with other cities, the San Diego Police Department has tried to do a missionary job here and has done pretty well."

Many persons believe the protection of property to be a prime police function and their positive assessment of the police and community relations is based, in part, on the effectiveness of the department in this direction. A resident of a high-income area, who describes police-community relations as "quite good," recalled favorably an incident in which the police, while working on a burglary case in the area, checked with him to say that his garage door was open and inquired whether any items were missing.

In support of their positive view of police-community relations, many persons mentioned the "honesty" of the police and their "efficiency" in combating crime. Several people stated their belief that the police department is dedicated to a high standard of performance and that policemen enforce the law equally for all members of the community, without regard to race or national origin.

Some persons stated that everyone accepts the *status quo* in San Diego; therefore, the community does not want any changes in the police department. The degree of support which white middle-class residents give the San Diego police is evident in their attitudes toward the border check station[17] and, in certain instances, their attitudes toward "stop and chat" procedures used with juveniles. One lawyer, opposed to the border check, explained,

> I discussed this a couple of years ago with a group that I thought would be willing to support a lawsuit to test the constitutionality of just this practice. And, to my surprise and shock, the civil liberties group concerned about these matters . . . happened to be composed of a lot of parents with a lot of teenaged kids, and they all took the position that they were glad to see it being done. They felt, however, that it probably was a constitutional deprivation.

Several lawyers, though agreeing this procedure is unconstitutional, nevertheless felt that a *reasonable* basis for it could be found and, if necessary, the federal government should then assume responsibility. Several lawyers recognize that juveniles are apt to be stopped more often than adults for the same actions, yet they justify this on the grounds that youngsters repre-

---

[17]The border check station is manned by San Diego Police Department personnel and is an attempt by the department to screen young people who attempt to cross the border and enter Tijuana and to prevent those under 21 years of age who do not have parental consent from entering Mexico.

sent *the group* that is "going to cause the problems." One lawyer felt that the "parents are pretty happy for in the majority of cases, the police are looking out for the kids a bit when the kids are out away from home." Another lawyer stated that "field interrogation to me, where they ask a person to produce identification in a brief restraint of complete freedom of action, is certainly not *that* repugnant to constitutional guarantees."

The white middle-class citizens interviewed generally had limited first-hand knowledge of the San Diego Police Department's enforcement activities, except in the area of traffic contacts. While most of their opinions concerning police-community relations were favorable, traffic control is singled out by many people for unfavorable comment. The consensus is that too many traffic citations are issued and that the motive for this is revenue rather than public safety. One prominent citizen stated that the San Diego Police Department is "corruption-free, tough, well-disciplined and obsessive regarding traffic control." Another person felt that citations were written in situations where a warning could serve as well or better.

The experience of our research staff suggests that much of the middle-class Caucasian community has little personal contact with the police. (The only exception to this is, of course, in the area of traffic regulation and enforcement.) A striking feature of the data collected in this research is the fact that the general law-abiding citizen has limited knowledge and interest in the overall operations of the police department of this city. The only exception to this generalization is the one fact that middle-class Caucasians who actively participate in social justice organizations have substantial knowledge of police administration and operations. Furthermore, these persons were not reticent about expressing an opinion on the matter of police-community relations. For the most part, however, the prevalent attitude among middle-class Caucasians may be summarized as follows: "As long as criminals are caught, and as long as good citizens are protected and otherwise left alone, community relations are good!"

Despite the generally favorable impression which the middle-class Caucasian community had on the subject, there were some "problem areas" which were cited in interviews with the research staff. These problem areas are important, not so much because they give an accurate appraisal of the situation, but rather because they give an insight into the view which middle-class Caucasians have of "their world." Many persons associated "community relations" with minority groups, implying that this was the *only* possible problem area. Many persons were quick to say that San Diego had no racial problem. At the same time, most of these persons recognized that minority group persons do have some "special economic and social problems."

The attitude was expressed by some persons that *despite* what Blacks may think, police-community relations in San Diego are good. A segment of the white community believes that although the police are willing to hear complaints, the minorities frequently tend to look for things about which to complain. These same persons think that the police still have much to do to *educate* the minorities about the police role, the difficulty being that Negroes are prone to be biased against the police and they are unable to state publicly that the department is doing a good job. Many of those interviewed recognized that the police do constantly look at people in the poverty bracket with suspicion, but they believe this is justified because a high proportion of the poor *are* involved in crime. Some believe that although individual police officers may abuse their power and authority, this is not too frequently the case. One individual added that relations are good if you are "white and clean."

A number of persons regarded the formation of the Community Liaison Unit as a positive step forward. The orientation of one segment is that it is necessary for the police department to *explain* and *make the public aware* of the police service function and that a community relations program involved getting the police department's image known and improved. One description termed the Unit as one representing a "press agent" for the police department and offered the suggestion that actions, rather than words, are of importance. Although white residents, generally, felt they had access to the police department, several expressed the view that there exists only a one-way flow of communication, rather than an exchange between the public and the community. Some in fact think that the Community Liaison Unit is naive if it believes it is really reaching and winning the support of people at the grassroots level, especially since the program is primarily one of "public relations rather than community relations."

The Minority Groups

Regardless of class position, Blacks and Mexican-Americans are almost uniformly critical of the present state of police-community relations. Despite this unanimity of criticism, middle-class minority persons were quick to recognize the importance of the role which properly oriented police agencies could perform for society. It may be said, therefore, that these persons are *not* anti-police, despite the intensity of their disapproval of present police policies and procedures. It should also be emphasized that many middle-class minority persons felt that the police department was making some positive efforts in the direction of *meaningfully* improving the status of police-community relations. At the same time, these persons were quick to point out that only a beginning had been made. In any case, they are reserving final judgment about the sincerity of police efforts in this regard.

Although many *middle-class* Blacks agree that the San Diego Police Department is "honest and clean," and is attempting to improve relations with the public, their criticisms of police policies and actions are stronger and more widespread than those expressed by the white community. Many view the community relations program as a product of the police concern over poor relations and of pressures which have been exerted by civil rights groups. Several who know something about the functioning of the Community Liaison Unit, however, believed that its present orientation is unsatisfactory and unrealistic. Their reasoning is that to be effective any such program needs sufficient authority over patrolmen.

Although middle-class Blacks indicate an awareness of the police side of the problem, they emphasize consistently that the Black community in general neither trusts nor respects the police. The department is viewed only as a punitive agency. Several residents believed that lower-class members of their race are becoming more hostile. Others pointed out that the major part of the problem is with youths, aged 16 to 25 years.

The middle-class Blacks believed that the police view Logan Heights, a minority-group poverty area, as an undesirable place to serve and that the police are inclined to prejudge residents there. Instances of police practices—including field interrogations, overpatrolling, physical brutality, verbal abuse, racial harassment, and unequal enforcement of laws—are cited in criticism of the police department's relations with minorities.

The *lower-class* Blacks interviewed presented a position of strong dislike and distrust of the police. No one indicated that he had any means of communicating with the police. In the opinion of the lower-class Black, a dialogue or structure for dialogue with the police is nonexistent. They are not aware of the police department's community relations program. A typical attitude toward the police is reflected in the following quotation by a member of a social action group:

> 'Cause there is this feeling about cops. Let's face it. Kids nowadays . . . a cop is someone who is unfriendly and it's only the one that stands on the crosswalk guiding them to school that they really take a liking to.

A common belief among those interviewed is that the police are inhuman and are insensitive to the Blacks' need to be respected and treated with dignity. This produces frustration and a rebellious spirit. One youth stated that he had been arrested several times and then released without being charged, and finally, because of this, he was repeatedly late to work and lost his job. He felt that the police did not care or consider what would happen to him.

Other statements indicated a belief that a complete lack of communication exists between the police and the lower-class Black: "I wouldn't be no . . . . police . . . . . Why? 'Cause I'm black. I wouldn't be no police." The following quotation is taken from a street interview with a youth:

QUESTION: What are your attitudes about the police?

ANSWER: I don't like them, man. They're chicken shit, but you can't tape that.

QUESTION: Sure, I can tape that. I don't want to know your name or anything. I just want your opinion.

ANSWER: I feel they are very belligerent people. They don't have no understanding of your problems. I mean, if you have a problem, they don't listen and try to understand you or nothing, man. Only thing, the police, you do what I say, that's the policeman.

QUESTION: Have you ever been stopped by the police?

ANSWER: I been fighting the police.

QUESTION: How do you plan to fight them?

ANSWER: With these, [pointing to hands] that's the only thing I got. And I'll keep on until they put me in jail. They put me in jail two or three times for fighting, and they'll put me in jail again if they mess with me again, the same way.

FIGURE 4.2. *July 29, 1973, Dallas, Texas. Downtown Saturday afternoon after a memorial march for the slain Santos Rodriguez erupted into chaos. These two police motorcycles were set afire and destroyed. Several downtown store windows were also broken. Courtesy of Wide World Photos.*

The *Mexican-American* community in San Diego is not highly organized and communication with the police department is practically nonexistent. Community leaders express the belief that Mexican-Americans do not have good relations with the police. Despite these generally negative reactions to the department, there is also a realization that part of the problem stems from language barriers, the impact a different culture has upon their highly authoritarian family structure, and the "neutral" function of the American policeman as compared with the judgmental one of the Mexican policeman.

Mexican-American leaders have expressed the belief that the police in San Diego "exist for the protection of the Caucasian [Anglo] community" and that they have only "restraining and punitive" functions. It has also been stated that police "impose themselves upon the community." Generally, it was felt that residents are "scared" of the police; they believe police do not understand Mexican-Americans, nor do they attempt to do so.

Several police practices were singled out for unfavorable comment. It was felt that police were discriminatory, condescending, and paternalistic. This is evidenced by indiscriminate stopping and frisking of both minority adults and juveniles; the use of degrading terms, such as "pancho, "muchacho," and "amigo," and excessive patrolling within the Mexican-American community.

Although some middle-class minority persons were in favor of the principle behind recent efforts of the police department to improve communications, many were frankly skeptical of the results which could be expected. There was general approval of the recent hiring of a Black sociologist to teach human relations to recruits in the police academy; many stated, however, that improvement in the present state of police-community relations would take more than the hiring of *one* Black to teach an *occasional* course at the academy. Since training in human relations is limited to newly recruited officers, many minority-group persons were skeptical of the department's sincerity in this field when it apparently determined that older officers are to be "immune" from such training.

A study in Philadelphia[18] by the same team on the same subject (i.e., public view of law enforcement) reached identical conclusions. Both studies, in other words, pointed out that the public's view of law enforcement differs depending upon economic and ethnic considerations and the position the members occupy in their particular community.

Frequency of Police Contacts with Citizenry:
Part of the Problem

Needless to say, because it is the primary duty of the police to enforce laws that restrict behavior, the very nature of their work will lead to both private and public resentment:

[18]Lohman and Misner, *The Police and the Community.*

Really favorable conditions will never be provided so long as misuse of police authority continues to bulk large in the public mind. Notwithstanding the rapid expansion of the policy of moderation in exercise of law enforcement powers, the tide of general opinion still runs strongly against the police. The reasons for this condition are easily identified. Universal use of the automobile invites an increasing volume of restrictions upon the motoring public, and the old easy division of the community into law-breakers and law-observers is thereby destroyed. Today, all are law-breakers, and a large and important minority are deliberate offenders.[19]

Therefore, the frequency of police contacts with the whole population (usually through the mass media) has thrown enforcement of the law into sharp collision with general standards, to which neither police nor public has reacted well. The public has—because of occasional "lawless" enforcement by the police (police abuse of constitutional rights)—become cynical about its own police officers and its legal system. This, in turn, has resulted in an almost universal phenomenon wherein police officers have isolated themselves from the community they serve and have banded together in condemning anyone who levels criticism at them. Because of the policeman's possible aloofness and egotistical and arbitrary demeanor, each "collision" results, on one hand, in the swelling of his authority complex and, on the other hand, in a *new* birth of antagonism in some large (or "minority"-group) segments of the community.

COMPLAINTS OF HARASSMENT AND BRUTALITY
AS THEY AFFECT THE POLICE IMAGE

There is a strong belief among many members of nonwhite minority groups that they get rougher treatment at the hands of the police than whites do.[20] A 1970 report by the U.S. Civil Rights Commission declared that although "most police officers never resort to brutal practices," the victims of police abuse, when it does occur, are almost always those "whose economic and social status afford little or no protective armour—the poor and racial minorities." In other words, if police brutality or harassment does occur, such incidents are directed to the poor (regardless of race), who usually include a large proportion of members of the minority groups—including Blacks, Mexicans, Puerto Ricans, Indians and other minorities.

The subject of physical police brutality is one that continues to be surrounded by controversy. Police spokesmen have protested angrily against such charges. Quinn Tamm, executive director of the International Associa-

[19]B. Smith, *Police Systems in the United States* (New York: Harper & Row, 1969), p. 10.

[20]This belief is dispelled somewhat in a study by Albert J. Reiss, "Police Brutality," *Trans-action* (Jul.-Aug. 1968).

tion of Chiefs of Police, declared that he "knew of no period in recent history when the police have been the subject of so many unjustified charges of brutality, harassment, and ineptness." Tamm contended, "Never have we been singled out so mercilessly and so wrongfully as the whipping boys by demonstrators for so-called sociological evolution and by out-and-out hoodlums who have abandoned the banner of civil rights to engage in senseless insurrection."

Yet many believe that all the denials and explanations will not dispel the deep-seated suspicion that police sometimes practice a double standard in dealing with certain members of the community. In fact, the more intimate the person's knowledge of the ghetto, the stronger his feeling that brutality is a fact; the converse is equally true. The consensus among authorities in the field of race relations is that, while there may be *some* cases of brutality with racial overtones, brutality, if it does occur, does not generally have racial overtones. It does, however, have impact on socio-economic groups. However, press reports of police dispersals and arrests of civil rights demonstrators—particularly but by no means exclusively in the South—are said to have reinforced in many people a view of the policeman as a defender of the in-group and the oppressor of protesting minorities. Many civil rights leaders remain unconvinced, to put it mildly, that policemen always act "in the strict line of duty in terms of racial cases." As a result, hostility toward the police has become an increasing problem in neighborhoods having large minority populations.

Police administrators continue to respond heatedly that brutality is not condoned in law enforcement agencies and disciplinary actions are immediately taken. These administrators quickly point out that sometimes police procedures that are disliked by minorities are branded as examples of police brutality. Often they may be evidence of police harassment rather than physical brutality.

A lawyer expresses his belief that the police crack down on card games and drug addicts more in North Philadelphia [where most Blacks reside] than elsewhere. He views this as "harassment." Another lawyer points to the fact that the police enter homes without search warrants. The problem of the searches is not limited to the apartments of adults in the North Philadelphia ghetto. He said, to his knowledge, teenagers are searched and patted down when coming out of a dance. Their cars may be stopped and they may be questioned at some length. This is "general harassment." One instance of brutality as reported by a woman who is active in community affairs is the breaking down of doors and the searching of homes without warrant in the Hawthorne [another ghetto area in Philadelphia] community.

Verbal abuse or verbal brutality is not widely mentioned, but some persons do state that policemen resort to name-calling. One youth worker comments, "Verbal abuse goes on much less than one would suspect." Several persons cautioned that the Black community has until recently been inclined to take its lumps and keep quiet. It is the opinion of a settlement house worker that there are few instances of outright brutality. Rather, he feels that the more serious problem is one of mental abuse and a kind of demeaning of people in the area. He describes it as a mental brutality rather than a physical brutality.[21]

Because a community's attitude toward the police is influenced by the actions of individual officers on the streets, courteous and tolerant behavior by policemen in their contacts with citizens is a must. According to a report by the President's Commission on Law Enforcement and Administration of Justice, there have been instances of unambiguous *harassment* and *physical abuse*. The late Nelson A. Watson gave the following report at a police administrators' conference regarding police action:[22]

So far as police *action* is concerned, there are things that come to my attention on that, too. I hear of the incidents from police and from civil rights workers. I read about them in the press, in magazines, and books. I cannot vouch for the accuracy of these reports because we all know how easily things can get distorted and misinterpreted. But accurate or not, it is vitally important that we all remember that people form opinions and take action on the basis of what they hear and what they believe without checking its accuracy. Things like the following illustrate what people are saying, what they believe, and what is back of the way they behave:

Case No. 1. "The cops pulled us over and came up to the car with guns in their hands. This one cop [incidentally, the officer was a Negro] told me to show him my license and registration. When I asked him why, he told me to do as I was told and not get smart. Then they made us all get out of the car while the other guy looked inside. When they couldn't find anything wrong, they told us we could go. I asked them what it was all about, and the one cop said they had a lot of stolen cars around there lately so they had to check up."

Case No. 2. A newspaper reported that a man had complained about the actions of an officer which he felt were uncalled for. It was reported the officer had arrested a man and had handcuffed him. For some reason, the man fell to the ground and the complainant said the

---

[21]Lohman and Misner, *The Police and The Community*, Vol. 2, p. 67. See also *The Challenge of Crime in a Free Society*, report prepared for the President's Commission on Law Enforcement and Administration of Justice (Washington, D.C. U.S. Government Printing Office, 1967), p. 102.

[22]N. A. Watson, "The Fringes of Police-Community Relations," paper read at Police Administrators' Conference, June 29, 1966, at Indiana University. (Mimeographed)

officer then put his foot on the man's neck. The complainant said the arrested man was not fighting the officer and, after all, he was handcuffed. He cited this as an example of police brutality.

Case No. 3. An officer patrolling a beach where kids had caused trouble approached a teen-aged boy who was sitting by himself on a bench drinking from a bottle. Drinking liquor by minors was forbidden by law. The officer asked the boy what he was drinking and the boy replied that it was Coke. The officer took the bottle and smelled the contents. Finding that it contained no liquor so that he had no basis for arrest, the officer poured the remainder of the drink onto the sand and ordered the boy to move along.

Case No. 4. A man reported a fight in progress and said some shots had been fired. He later complained that it took the police nearly an hour to respond and charged that the same report from a white neighborhood would have brought them on the double.

Case No. 5. A Black who witnessed a robbery was asked by two officers to come with them to see whether he could identify a suspect who was working in a gas station. The place was miles away across town. When they got there, the suspect had left. The officers put the witness out of the car saying they were too busy to take him back home.

Case No. 6. A Black was observed walking in a white neighborhood one evening about 10:00 o'clock. Two officers stopped and asked him to explain his presence there. He told them it was none of their business, that he had a right to walk on any street any time he felt like it. He refused to answer questions so they took him to headquarters for further interrogation. It turned out he was a minister who was very active in the civil rights movement. He had no criminal record and had done nothing to sustain any charge in this instance. He complained that the officers' action was indicative of the attitude of police toward all Negroes.

Case No. 7. With respect to the Puerto Rican disturbances in Chicago recently, the Christian Science Monitor reported as follows: "There was little doubt that the presence of police—and their handling of Puerto Ricans over a period of several years—was the center of the controversy in this conflict. We heard no other argument or issue in the seven hours we worked the streets. . . . Despite careful guidelines, police tactics were not uniformly discreet. One instance took place before we began breaking up the congestion at Division and California. Most of the young men had gone, and we had been thanked by the sergeant on the corner. Suddenly a police captain with a dozen blue-helmeted men stormed across the street. I was standing inside a restaurant at the time because the street was virtually clear. The captain and three men pushed into the restaurant where more than 50 people, in family groups, were quietly eating their evening meal. In a loud voice, he demanded to see the owner. Moving to the kitchen, he demanded that she clear the place and close up. Then he stalked out, shaking his fist and shouting: "I'll give you 15 minutes to get everybody out of here, you understand. Fifteen minutes." Then he slammed the door with such force the storefront windows rattled. In less than a minute, he had changed quietness into anger.... A spokesman for the police department said it was only one of several complaints about the same captain. At 10:50 P.M., only a handful of people were left on the street. A lieutenant and a group of policemen raced to the upper floor of a three-story building on Division Street and hauled out two men who someone said had been seen with crude anti-police signs in a window. Then the police closed a restaurant below where there were a number of young Puerto Ricans. Those in the restaurant scattered as ordered. But two youths, walking slowly a block away were spotted by a sergeant who cursed them, saying to the lieutenant: "Those guys were in the restaurant. Let's go get them." At this point, the only incident of undue physical roughness I observed during the entire night took place. Two police searched one of the youths, and then gave him a hand shove that sent him sprawling toward the police wagon. The lieutenant and sergeant stood on the curb discussing what they could charge the two youths with since they had only been walking down the street...."

Watson concluded this portion of his address to the conference by stating:

... I cannot vouch for the accuracy of these reports. I suspect there is a considerable bias in them. I also realize that when they are shaved down in the retelling, there may be significant facts omitted. *But the point is that these are the kinds of things people hear and it is on the basis of such stories they form their opinions about police.* [Italics added.] Then, when approached by an officer they expect rough, inconsiderate, impolite treatment.

I know and so do you that it sometimes takes pretty strong talk and forceful action to get the police job done. However, I am sure we can agree that an officer who uses profanity is definitely out of line. So is one who is so prejudiced that he cannot treat the objects of his prejudice as ordinary human beings. An officer who generates resentment, who makes people rise up in anger by the things he says or does or the way he acts toward them is a source of trouble. An officer who would stand by and watch someone being beaten is violating his oath. One of the things that we must attend to in our effort to improve relations with the people in our communities, therefore, is the way our officers are doing their job on the street day in and day out. This is not to say that *all* the fault lies in police behavior, but, to the extent that *any* of the fault lies there, we must accept the blame and correct it.

The President's Commission observed that physical abuse is only one source of aggravation in the ghetto. In nearly every city surveyed the Commission heard complaints of harassment of interracial couples, dispersal of social street gatherings, and stopping blacks on foot or in cars without an objective basis. Such things, together with contemptuous and degrading verbal abuse, have great impact in the ghetto—impact in the area of attitudes toward law enforcement personnel. Such conduct, relates the Commission, strips the black of the one thing he may have left—his dignity, "the question of being a man."

Harassment or discourtesy, according to the President's Commission, may not be the result of malicious or discriminatory intent of police officers. Many officers simply fail to understand the effects of their actions because of their limited knowledge of the black community. Calling a Black man by his first name may cause resentment because many whites still refuse to extend to adult Blacks the courtesy of the title "Mister." A patrolman may take the arm of a person he is leading to the police car. Blacks are more likely to resent this than whites because the action implies that they are on the verge of flight and may degrade them in the eyes of friends or onlookers.[23]

Commission observers have also found that *most* officers handle their rigorous work with considerable coolness and with no pronounced racial pattern in their behavior. However, in the words of O. W. Wilson,

> the officer must remember that there is no law against making a policeman angry and he cannot charge a man with offending him. Until the citizen acts overtly in violation of the law, he should take no action against him, least of all lower himself to the level of the citizen by berating and demeaning him in a loud and angry voice. The officer who withstands angry verbal assaults builds his own character and raises the standards of the department.[24]

These views are accepted by all responsible police officials. Although all departments have written regulations setting standards of behavior, in many departments these are too generalized. Where standards are violated, there should be a thorough investigation of complaints and prompt, visible disciplinary action where justified.

THREATS AND CHALLENGES IN POLICE WORK[25]

In many everyday situations on the street, a policeman finds himself threatened or challenged. How many times has an officer encountered a

---

[23]*Challenge of Crime*, the *President's Commission on Law Enforcement and Administration of Justice*, p. 102.

[24]*Police Administration* (New York: McGraw-Hill, 1963), p. 73.

[25]This section adopted from N. A. Watson, *Issues in Human Relations: Threats and Challenges* (Washington, D.C.: International Association of Chiefs of Police, 1969), pp. 9–22. (Courtesy of the publisher)

FIGURE 4.3 (a). In responding to calls for assistance, particularly in riot situations, the arresting officer(s) must exercise utmost care and professionalism. The manner in which he (arresting officer) effects an arrest, interviews witnesses and, in general, assumes control may very well determine the extent and amount of further damage or injury. Courtesy Berkeley Police Department, Berkeley, Cal.

FIGURE 4.3 (b). *Courtesy San Francisco Police Department, San Francisco, Cal.*

traffic offender who, as a "friend" of the chief or the mayor, threatens to have him transferred or fired? How many times has an officer found himself facing a man with a gun? Not infrequently a suspect makes threatening moves and remarks when being arrested. In riots, police are under the serious threat of being injured or killed. Police generally regard the attitudes and behavior of the Black Panthers and certain other organizations of black youths as threatening. Some of the behavior of campus protesters is challenging to the police and some of it is threatening. The deliberate provocation and insults of the New Left on the campuses are seen by some as challenges.

For the purposes of improving our understanding of human relations, it may be useful to describe various levels or kinds of threats:

Verbal Emotional Release. Some people become upset under pressure and they blow off steam by becoming verbally abusive and threatening.

They have little possibility of actually doing what they are threatening to do and no real intention of trying it. It is often apparent that the chatter is just so much "hot air." The officer calmly proceeds to write the ticket or to hold the prisoner for the paddy wagon without getting involved in a verbal free-for-all. He knows the best procedure is simply to let the person talk, in the meantime maintaining his composure and his control of the situation.

Real Threats. Some people are not "badmouthing" just to relieve the tensions; they mean it and eventually they will try to follow through. This is not always easy to ascertain, however. If a suspect pulls a gun, however, action should be immediate and decisive. This is not the time to wait to find out whether or not he really means it.

Threats Intended as Offensive Weapons. Some threats are made in a calculated manner, the intention being to provoke the officer into a response. In a sense, these threats are challenges. There really is no intention to follow through if the officer does not "take the bait." The challenge is issued to goad the officer into some injudicious or unprofessional conduct which can then be used as a basis for charges of abuse or brutality. Strict adherence to professional standards is the best defense against this type.

Latent Symbolic Threats. The three types of threats just described occur on a face-to-face basis during interpersonal contacts. This fourth type, which is really as important as the others, does not necessarily involve face-to-face matters. It is based upon certain kinds of beliefs. A person may come to believe, either as a result of personal experience or because of things he has been told, that certain objects, situations, or people are potentially dangerous. We call such threats *latent* because, like attitudes, they are always there just below the conscious level ready to spring into action when the symbol with which they are associated is perceived. We call them *symbolic* because the thing that activates them is possibly only a representative of a general class of things—in other words, a symbol.

To clarify, let us take an example. Suppose a hoodlum has been arrested on several occasions for robbery, assault, and carrying a concealed weapon. He has been convicted of robbery and has served time. Under the stop and frisk law he has been questioned a number of times, resulting in arrest and conviction for carrying a concealed weapon. To him, anyone wearing a uniform and a badge is a latent symbolic threat. His perception of the police as a threat is activated when he is planning a "hit" and every time he sees an officer or a patrol car. Both the uniform and the patrol car are symbols in which the essence of the threat is concentrated.

This is a human relations mechanism to which we must be alert in our own work. As human beings, police officers are as much subject to this psychological process as anyone else. If we are not knowledgeable about such things, we may well be misled by latent symbolic threats. For example, one could make the mistake of regarding all college students who wear beards, sandals, and "odd" clothing as being anti-police. The same is true of young Negro males, all of whom may come to be regarded as potentially dangerous and criminal.

Situational Threats. These are the obvious or the most subtle threats we face. They operate unilaterally on an intrapersonal basis. They are implicit in many of the situations and circumstances commonly encountered in our daily lives. They often operate without our realizing it. The subtlety in these threats results from the fact that, though they influence our behavior much like any threat, we do not think of them as threats. Moreover, they are deeply personal and do not affect everyone the same way. What any individual does about them depends heavily upon his social conditioning, his sense of values, his aspirations, and many other personal characteristics. These situational threats are steeped in tradition and culture and very important in governing our conduct.

Some examples of situational threats may be helpful here. For instance, it is generally accepted that a police officer is supposed to be thoroughly masculine. Without even realizing it, he may be careful to act in speech and deed the way he thinks a man should act. He dares not run the risk (expose himself to the threat) of being thought weak. This leads some officers to act *unnecessarily* tough.

Another example: Say you are a policeman hoping for promotion to sergeant. Your lieutenant, who is an opinionated person who insists that things be done by the book, will be the person who prepares your performance rating. A situation arises in which you must take action. In your opinion, it seems clear in this case that the best procedure both for the department and for the person involved is to make an exception to regulations. However, if you do this, you might incur the wrath of the lieutenant, causing him to give you a lower rating. The threat to your ambition to be promoted is very real. ·

Threats to police officers are more implied than overt. The policeman is regarded by most people as a powerful person and an open threat is deemed to be rather risky. Most people would, therefore, threaten by implication. This puts the officer in the position of *assuming* the making of a threat. Because officers are assaulted or perhaps verbally abused rather often, it is often easy to assume that a person is threatening when he really is not. When a person shows an attitude of hostility, he may or may not be dangerous. The same may be said for attitudes of fear, anger, or unusual excitement. In other words, these attitudes do not always produce dangerous behavior. It must be admitted, however, that they do often enough to warrant caution and preparedness.

Much the same might be said about challenges. A new, young officer assigned to patrol on foot in a slum area may meet an implied challenge from members of a gang. These youths are going to test the officer. One way or another, he has to meet the challenge or he will not be able to continue patrolling there. This does not necessarily mean that he must resort to physical combat, though that may be what the gang members have in mind. Finding a way to handle the challenge without physical violence is preferable.

The process of communication is seriously curtailed because of people's reaction to latent symbolic threats and situational threats. An important factor in both types is that these threats often involve the perception of other people as "different" and therefore unfriendly—maybe even dangerous. Many people have a tendency to suspect and dislike people who are unlike themselves. People who are "different" may be perceived as the embodiment of latent symbolic and situational threats. This would produce a negative position on the pleasant-unpleasant dimension.

One of the several elements of the culture of youth has been called the "conspiracy of secrecy." Youths sense the embodiment of latent symbolic and situational threats in their elders (and vice versa, by the way). This makes them wary and interferes with effective communication.

Police often complain that Negroes are uncooperative in criminal cases in that they withhold information that might lead to a solution. This is the conspiracy of secrecy in another setting. The circumstances are familiar to policemen everywhere. A detective looking for a suspect questions people in the neighborhood, all of whom claim they never heard of the man even though the officer knows the suspect has lived there for years. The detective is convinced they are not telling the truth and are, in fact, protecting the suspect. It must be admitted that this can be a result of antipathies between the police and some people. Clearly, to the extent that this feeling exists, the resulting "conspiracy of secrecy" works to the disadvantage of society.

The same mechanism is at the bottom of demands for police review boards. Charges have been made that police themselves engage in a protective "conspiracy of silence." The idea is that no policeman is going to tell the whole truth about a case in which a fellow officer is accused of harassment, abuse, or brutality toward a complainant. The natural follow-up to this belief is that any investigation conducted *by* police *of* police will turn out to be a whitewash. The so-called conspiracy of silence and the conspiracy of secrecy run head on into each other. As a result, some people believe it is futile to complain about police abuse and feel they must take matters into their own hands outside the law.

The reduction of the threat potential in these latent symbolic and situational types would undoubtedly relieve the tensions associated with them. A more productive level of communication would result and the entire atmosphere would be improved.

The Professional Approach

What happens in many cases in which an officer is challenged is that the challenger is trying to get the officer to step out of his professional role. It is as though he were saying, "Look, Buster! You wouldn't be such a big shot if you didn't have that gun and badge." As the wielder of public power and authority, the officer is the dispenser of public discipline. In this capacity, he is required by law to exercise his authority according to rules. The rules do not allow him to vent his personal spleen on anyone. They do not provide for the administration of punishment by the police. Vindictiveness or harassment by an officer is as much against the rules as are criminal actions.

A policeman is not an ordinary person. He is a professional, and as such, his conduct must conform to the rules. It is offensive to be called a "pig," but no retaliation can be permitted in violation to the rules because to do so threatens destruction of the system the policeman is sworn to defend. Moreover, to abandon the professional prescriptions for conduct is to walk into a trap, and this is the objective of the challenger.

The widely held concept of the police role provides an overemphasis on the police-violator relationship. Seldom is a policeman thought of as a helper, even though a large part of his time is spent in rendering various kinds of service. The common concept of the role of a fireman, on the contrary, emphasizes the helper notion. Unfortunately, it is unrealistic to expect that anytime soon we are going to be able to persuade people that the policeman is a helping person, despite the fact that each time a violator is brought to justice the public good is promoted.

Adopting the professional role as a model for conduct and conforming to it in the face of provocation, frustration, and temptation is not only correct and commendable, it is also a source of great strength for an officer. It tilts the balance of power in his favor. Officers who are consistently professional in conduct and bearing are in an advantageous position. They are clearly demonstrating their superiority, and as a result, people give them the respect and admiration their professional behavior has earned. When an officer weakens and abandons his professional posture, the conduct that results may assume several forms, all of which are seen by the public as deserving of condemnation. Depending upon the circumstances, nonprofessional conduct may consist of anything from vulgar language and petty abuse to unwarranted physical punishment and harassment up to outright criminality. Those who seriously challenge the policeman want him to shed his professional armament. They want to reduce him to their level. The best way to handle such people is to adhere steadfastly to the professional code.

Needless to say, an officer should not make threats he cannot or does not intend to carry through. To do so weakens his position and leaves a residue of animosity that will plague him and other officers in the future.

Group Reactions and Police-Community Relations

One of the most important aspects of human relations involving threats and challenges, especially the former, concerns the expectations held by the parties to the encounter. There are many references in police literature to the effect that Black slum or ghetto residents, Puerto Ricans, Mexican-Americans, and other minority persons *expect* to be treated rudely or abusively by police. For their part, many police officers expect to meet with hostility and resistance or even violence from these same people. These very expectations come to be regarded as threats and inevitably they produce behavioral reactions. The behavioral reactions are then taken by the other group as evidence of existence of the threat and we have a "self-fulfilling prophesy." It is a vicious circle and if the tensions and hostility are to be reduced, we must find a way to break it.

Probably all experienced officers have encountered people who think the world is against them. Such people are not necessarily psychotic. Some of them may have gotten off to a bad start from the time they were born. People like this expect others to be cruel or at least indifferent. Because they expect to be hurt, they often reject others in advance in order to keep from being rejected by them. As a matter of fact, sometimes these people even reject themselves. For them, police may be especially significant. Police have been chosen as the representatives of all those hostile others who have been cruel or indifferent and who wish to keep them down. Therefore, in the police they see concentrated the threats of the hostile world.

People who believe themselves unfairly disadvantaged may react by becoming aggressively militant. Some minority groups, for example, convinced that their troubles stem from white racism, agitate aggressively for change and may even riot. They may physically attack whites or if none are available, they may attack their property—"Burn baby, burn." Of course, because the police, most of whom are white, are always there, they are natural targets for the militants. The militance may take other forms such as writings, speeches, marches, or picketing. Not all militancy is undesirable. A strike by a labor union is a form of militance. It is entirely legitimate for people to be militant in order to advance themselves as long as they remain within the law. Aggression can be a legitimate way to meet threats and challenges.

There is an opposite kind of reaction. Instead of attacking the source of threat or frustration, people may elect to move away from it. They may withdraw into a world of their own, give up, or perhaps deny that there is a problem and try to ignore it. The withdrawal can take a variety of forms. People who withdraw can take solace in all kinds of substitute adjustments. Among the havens often used are hobbies, religion, and even antisocial or abnormal activities such as crime, drug addiction, and neurotic or psychotic personality disorders.

It is interesting and disturbing to note that some people claim to see similar kinds of behavior on the part of some policemen. It has been said that the police are themselves a minority group and as such are subject to certain disadvantages and discriminations. Some police have been charged with what amounts to aggressive militance in their behavior toward certain groups such as campus demonstrators, hippies, and black people. Some claim that the police, in giving expression to their militance, have been violent, that they have used unnecessary force, that they have been bigoted and intolerant, and that they have overstepped the bounds of their authority. Frequently this alleged behavior is attributed to the recruitment of the policeman chiefly from the lower classes, where physical aggression is more

FIGURE 4.4.   San Diego police community relations officer discusses with school children the role and importance of obeying the law. Courtesy San Diego Police Department, San Diego, Cal.

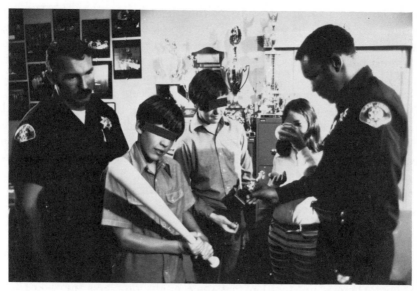

FIGURE 4.5.   *San Jose Police Athletic League (P.A.L.) and other such P.A.L. activities have been quite instrumental in deliquency prevention. Courtesy P. Crawford, San Jose Police Department, San Jose, Cal.*

often a reaction to frustration. Low pay, little education and inadequate training, and low social status are also said to contribute to the problem.

It should be obvious that among a group of 400,000 people—an estimate of the number of police officers in the nation—there will be all kinds of personalities. It is to be expected that some policemen will meet their problems aggressively, just as people in other occupations do. It is also expected that some will withdraw just as other people do. The important point is that the policeman's best approach to his problems is reliance on the professional code. Although it may be all right for the average citizen to follow his personal inclinations, it is not so for a policeman.

The police in many places have taken constructive steps toward dealing with threats and challenges of those who dislike and/or fear them. This is one of the objectives of police-community relations programs. Training programs in human relations for police have been offered. Efforts have been made to reach out to the people through Boys' Clubs, block parent plans, crime check or crime stop programs, juvenile recreation programs, storefront operations to bring police service closer to the locality, and similar activities.

Often in police meetings and training schools, the officers say, in effect, "We're willing, but what about them? Who's telling them? There has to be some give on both sides; it can't be a one-way street." They are so right! There must be a change of attitude on both sides. In fact, a large part of the problem lies in the widespread and unquestioned acceptance of the existence of "sides." The vast majority of the people and the police should be allied in the fight on crime and the pursuit of justice and order.

The hard and practical fact that we must accept is that it is the police who have to tell "them." In some cases, the police themselves go directly to the people In others, the "telling" is done by community organizations with which the police work. Obviously, not everyone can be reached and despite our best efforts, there will always be a lot of residual hatred and hostility. But a well-conceived, realistic approach to the human relations problems in police-citizen contacts must be an indispensable part of the daily activities of every police officer before real progress can be made.

Overcoming mistrust and hostility—as far as the police function in the community is concerned—is a *police* problem. Overcoming mistrust and hostility—as far as the broad social problems of our time are concerned— is a problem for all people, toward which public and private effort must be directed. There is no question that some of the problems the police face result from the failures of society at large. And in this sense, it must be understood that there are no community problems which are not to some extent police problems because of the "fallout" resulting in crime and disorder. The police mission per se, however, must be carried on both at the police level and by each individual officer in his daily performance of duty.

Large numbers of people who now see the policeman as a threat must be convinced through good human relations practices by officers that they and the police are seeking the same goals and that, therefore, law enforcement people are not a threat. The only ones for whom police should be threatening are criminals and those who seriously abridge the rights of others. The relationship between the policeman and the ordinary citizen of any race, creed, or political persuasion should be characterized by mutual respect and good will. This becomes very important when making contacts with the public. The policeman must always strive to make the other person feel that he's doing his best to see justice done.

Minimizing the Effects of the Threatening Police Image

Every officer should be aware that he is symbolically threatening to many people. He is regarded as a disciplinarian, a wielder of power, someone to be feared. His very presence constitutes a threat to many people even when they are not doing anything wrong. It is a common experience for people to slow down when they see a patrol car, even though they are not exceeding the speed limit. Undoubtedly, a lot of people immediately make a behavioral inventory (Am I doing anything wrong?) and become wary when they see a policeman approaching. This apprehension is part of the aura of threat with which the police are surrounded.

The fact that many people see the officer as a threat has some undesirable consequences. The tendency to avoid him is one. Another is refusal or unwillingness to cooperate. Still another is the belief that the police are enemies; this often produces overt aggressive behavior. It has been suggested that if we disarm the police they would not seem to be so threatening. We are not willing to go along with that suggestion. It would certainly be wonderful as an ideal, but in the harsh realities of today's urban jungles, it would be foolhardy.

The fact that a policeman is regarded as a threatening person by law violators is legitimate; he should be a threat to such people. But law-abiding citizens and police should be pulling together in a common cause: the prevention of crime and the promotion of justice and order.

What can police officers do about problems growing out of human relations in which threats or challenges are significant issues? There are some human relations techniques which policemen can cultivate with good effect. Learning how to be an effective person is essentially a matter of developing skill in relating to others. Following are some guidelines to help improve human relations skills:

1. Don't be trapped into unprofessional conduct by a threat or a challenge

2. Make sure everything you do is calculated to enhance your reputation as a good officer—one who is firm, but fair and just.

3. When you are faced with a threat and you can't tell how serious it is, try to "buy time" in which to size up the situation by engaging the person in conversation. Make a comment or ask a question to divert his attention if possible.

4. Don't show hostility even if the other fellow does. Often a calm and reasonable manner will cause his hostility to evaporate or at least to simmer down.

5. Reduce your "threat" potential. Avoid a grim or expressionless countenance. Be an approachable human being. Too many officers habitually appear gruff and forbidding.

6. Cultivate a pleasant, friendly manner when making nonadversary contacts. Be ready with a smile, a pleasant word, a humorous comment when appropriate.

7. Let your general demeanor and especially your facial expression and tone of voice indicate that you respect the other person as a human being.

8. Let the other fellow know by your reception of him that you don't expect trouble from him and that you don't consider him a nuisance. (Maybe you do, but don't let it show.)

9. Show an interest in the other fellow's problem. Maybe you can't do anything about it, but often it is a great help just to be a good listener.

10. Go out of your way to improve police-community relations. Even though your department may have a unit that specializes in community relations,

never forget that you are the real key. The essence of good working relations between the people and the police is to be found in the way you handle yourself.

11. Always leave the people you deal with feeling that they have been treated fairly. When you render a service or react to a request, show some interest and give some explanation. This will promote good feelings which if carried on consistently by the entire force will have a cumulative effect resulting in vastly improved human relations.

12. Try in every way you can to encourage people to work with the police for their own protection. Let the average citizen know that, far from being a threat, you are interested in being a help. Drive home the point that the citizen is threatened by crime and disorder, not by the police.

In conclusion, it seems wise to caution readers to be realistic about the threats and challenges posed by others. Remember that some threats are real. Don't let your guard down while trying to be reasonable and decent. At the same time, do not assume that everyone is out to get you. Do conduct yourself according to the best professional standards and traditions. Keep calm and try to get threateners and challengers to see reason. But don't hesitate to use legitimate force to protect yourself from physical harm.

SUMMARY

Chapter Four discusses the problems of the police relationship to the community, including the lack of respect for law enforcement. During the last few years, particularly during the period after the Watts Riot in Los Angeles, there have been more and more attacks, both physical and verbal, on the police by minority groups composed of people from all social strata. These people, protesting situations they perceive as unjust, have demonstrated in varying degrees of violence. Police reaction to such behavior has been to try to prevent personal and property damage, but this has been difficult in the face of increasing hostility to authority.

This chapter discusses the nature of police work which leads to both private and public resentment. It is pointed out that a certain amount of resentment is natural and must be expected. Policemen, then, must be realistic—they must realize that the people they serve will not universally like or respect them. Every officer must be aware that he is symbolically threatening to many people. Thus he must utilize practices that will minimize the effects of such a threatening image. For this, the policeman must realize that it is his own attitude that is most important in bringing about good will and respect. Also, the proper training and educational procedures are instrumental in helping individual officers maintain a professional demeanor. However, policemen should realize that some threats are authentic and must be dealt with realistically. Professional standards and traditions relating to arrest, search and seizure, handling of demonstrators, threatening mobs, etc., must be implemented at all times.

The late Nelson Watson's report at a police administrator's conference indicates the "uphill fight" confronting law enforcement officers' attempts to improve their image.

The President's Commission on Law Enforcement and Administration of Justice, when investigating complaints of harassment and brutality, observed that there are many kinds of abuse that cause aggravation of citizens against police. It was stressed throughout the chapter that respect for and understanding of other human beings was a primary need of all law enforcement officers to counter the hostility of the community.

In order to promote and maintain a good police image, it is of great importance that law enforcement personnel thoroughly understand minority groups—their reason for being, their methods of dealing with their world, their desires, and their tactics. The police must be tolerant under all conditions—even in the face of intense provocation. In this respect, they must: (1) use techniques that will maintain order by means of legitimate goals; (2) uphold the law by steadfastly using the law; and (3) be able to isolate and arrest those guilty of illegal acts without indiscriminate attacks on the innocent.

DISCUSSION TOPICS

1. Discuss the role of the police officer in our modern democratic society.
2. Discuss the social and psychological control of law enforcement as presented by H. H. Toch.
3. List the guidelines, as presented by N. A. Watson, in ameliorating the threatening image of the police to many people.
4. What is suggested by the statement, "the policeman *symbolizes* much deeper social problems"?

ANNOTATED REFERENCES

Aaron, T. J., "Education and Professionalism in American Law Enforcement," *Police* (Nov–Dec. 1965), pp. 27–31. This article discusses the fact that professionalism in police work is a *must* if the problems relating to police-community relations are to be resolved.

Boer, B. L., and B. C. McIver, "Human Relations Training: Laboratories and Team Policing," *Journal of Police Science and Administration*, 1, No. 2 (June 1973), 162–67. The authors comment on the "sound and fury" type of human relations training available, contending that such training does not fill police needs for adequate human relations training.

DEVLIN, P. A., "The Police in a Changing Society," *Journal of Criminal Law, Criminology and Police Science*, 57, No. 2 (June 1966). An excellent discussion of the impact of social change on traditional law enforcement roles.

DODD, D. J., "Police Mentality and Behavior," *Issues in Criminology*, 3, No. 1 (Summer 1967), pp. 47–67. This affords a particularly good commentary on police culture and police officers' view of the community they serve.

ELDEFONSO, E., A COFFEY, AND R. C. GRACE, *Principles of Law Enforcement*. New York: Wiley & Sons, 1974. Chapter 16 of this volume is an updated version of the problems confronting law enforcement agencies throughout the United States and suggests programs, guidelines, and opinions that can assist the police officer in alleviating or combating poor police-community relations.

ESBECK, E. S., AND G. HALVERSON, "Stress and Tension—Team Building for the Professional Police Officer," *Journal of Police Science and Administration*, 1, No. 2 (June 1973), pp. 153–61. The authors discuss the changing social role of today's police officer and criticize the lack of *specialized* training available to help create a more positive image of the police.

FLEEK, T. A., AND T. S. NEWNAN, "The Role of the Police in Modern Society," *Police* (Mar.–Apr. 1969), pp. 21–27. This article explores the image of police in the urban community, police power, and definition of role. Captures the problem of law enforcement in a changing community.

HANLIN, O., "Community Organizations as a Solution to Police-Community Problems," *The Police Chief*, 32, No. 3 (March 1965), pp. 16–22. This article outlines relations between the police and community organizations. The author presents logical corrective solutions which take cognizance of changes in community life and the structure of the urban areas.

WALKER, W., *Rights in Conflict*. New York: Bantam Books, 1970. An investigation of the civil disorders and the police reaction surrounding the Democratic National Convention of 1968.

WATSON, N. A., "Threats and Challenges," *Issues in Human Relations*. Washington, D.C.: International Association of Chiefs of Police, 1969. This short pamphlet gives an excellent account of the dimensions of human relations, the nature of threats and challenges.

THE POLICE: EQUAL JUSTICE, COMMUNITY TENSION, AND MINORITY-GROUP ATTITUDES

PART 2

CONSTITUTION of the UNITED STATES

PREAMBLE

ARTICLE I.
ARTICLE II.
ARTICLE III.
ARTICLE IV.
ARTICLE V.
ARTICLE VI.
ARTICLE VII.

AMENDMENTS

Published by GEORGE BURR McLANNAN, Taft Building, Hollywood, California. For Best Results this Parchment Should be Mounted on White Backing.

RACE AND PREJUDICE

5

Man is a complex animal—so baffling, in fact, that since the first syllable of reported time, the "man on the street" has responded to the riddle "What is man?" in terms of glib and totally erroneous generalizations. Not only is such erring all too human, it is further compounded by a set of genuine but contradictory facts; human behavior is characterized by (1) an *essential sameness* and (2) *multifold differences*.

Many fallacies have been attached to the term *race*, and the most popular one has been the assumption that *race* is what distinguishes segments of mankind.

RACE: MYTH AND REALITY

Race, as the term is popularly defined, evolves from (1) *mutations* (markedly different specimens that appear in a species for no apparent reason and then pass on their unusual characteristics to their offspring through hereditary forces); (2) *isolation* (whether geographical, self-imposed, or whatever, it results in interbreeding that tends to perpetuate and magnify original eliteness); and (3) *inbreeding* (the usual outcome of a combination of mutation and isolation factors).

The most frequently used criteria for racial identification are skin color; hair color; hair form; eye color; ratio, multiplied by 100, of head width to length (cephalic index); ratio of nose width to nose height times 100 (nasal index); distribution of body hair and beard; stature; and prognathism (lower facial projection). These particular criteria are used because it is assumed that they are: (1) relatively stable, that is, more or less un-modified by the environment and essentially inherent in the genes; and (2) easily measured.

But in studying the distribution of these characteristics in the human species, it has been discovered that there is a *wide variation* in each of them; thus, human types range through every conceivable combination of such factors. Are there not, however, large numbers of peoples who have a *combination* of these characteristics in common? Earlier research did suggest that the world population could be divided into three distinct "clusters" of people—each distinguishable by the fact that the individuals in it shared a combination of physical characteristics not shared by individuals in other clusters. The following types were suggested by such early theorists: (1) *Negroid*—long-headed, wide-nosed, dark-skinned, dark-haired, dark-eyed, more or less hairless, tending toward tall stature, having tightly coiled hair, highly prognathous; (2) *Mongoloid*—medium stature, straight-haired, yellow-skinned, "Slant-eyed (the mongolian fold is merely a drooping of the eye-lids), medium-headed, medium-nosed, medium-eyed, mildly prognathous, and relatively free from body hair and beard; (3) *Caucasoid*—light-haired,

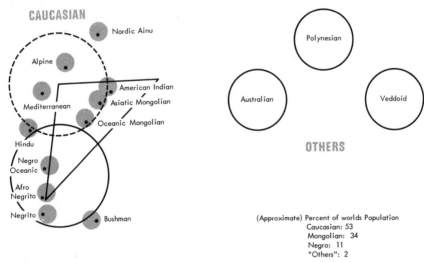

FIGURE 5.1 *That "races" differ from one another only slightly and through a continuing series of graduation (i.e., differences of degree or intensity—not of kind) is apparent. From the strictly genetic standpoint there can be no such thing as a pure race or human type because every single individual is literally a mixture of genes. The graphs above indicate the general groupings—and subracial groupings—of mankind. There are some groups ("Others") which defy accurate classification owing to overlapping of physical character-istics.*

light-eyed, light-skinned, medium or tall stature, round to medium head shape, relatively hairy, long-nosed, wavy- or curly-haired, nonprognathous. Those groups of individuals that did not fit into any of these clusters were either ignored or squeezed into one of the three racial pigeonholes, regardless of their lack of conformity.

We now know that no individual fits exactly into the definition of a particular race because the definition itself is a *statistical average* of traits of the whole group. Thus, if we say a man is Negroid, we imply that, to some degree, he has all of the Negroid characteristics listed above. In actuality, we find among the so-called Negroids the tallest and the shortest people on earth; people with light tan skins and bluish-black skins; those with long, thin noses and flat, broad noses; and people having heads which are elongated and heads which are "round." The same scattered array of racial traits marks the Mongoloid and Caucasoid. In the last analysis, more people do *not* fit these type-descriptions than do fit them! In reality, most people are neither distinctly Mongoloid nor Negroid nor Caucasoid but show some mixture of all the listed characteristics. Whatever the origin of man— multiple or single—biologists and anthropologists concur on one point: *there is no "pure" race.* A pure race could exist only if its people had lived throughout its history in complete and total isolation—with *no* cross-breeding whatsoever with other groups.

We find, then, that there are no pure races in any serious sense of the word and no large numbers of people who are reasonably identifiable as distinct types (who share numerous characteristics in common). We are left, therefore, only with the fact of the existence of many small groups that may share in common certain genetic features by which they are identifiable and distinguishable. The biological fact of race and the myth of "race" should and must, then, be distinguished. *For all practical social purposes "race" is not so much a biological phenomenon as a social myth.* We cannot, therefore, scientifically account for differences in group behavior in terms of differences in group biology. The events overwhelmingly point to the conclusion that "race" and "race differences" are not valuable concepts for the analysis of similarities and differences in human group behavior.

Whatever classification[1] of races an anthropologist might concur with, he never includes *mental characteristics* as part of the classifications. It is generally recognized in today's social science circles that *intelligence tests* do not in themselves enable us to differentiate safely between what is due to innate capacity and what is the result of environmental influences, training, and education (the usual estimate: 65 to 70 percent inheritance).

---

[1]For more detailed and illustrative data on the weakness of racial classifications, see R. W. Mack, *Race, Class, and Power* (New York: American Book Co., 1963), pp. 33–94; and H. S. Becker, ed., *Social Problems: A Modern Approach* (New York: Wiley & Sons, 1967), pp. 339–56.

In fact, wherever it has been possible to make allowances for differences in environmental opportunities, the tests have shown essential similarity in mental characteristics among all human groups. One of the more famous studies in this area provided conclusive data on the point: Blacks newly arrived in New York City from the Deep South obtained far lower intelligence quotients than did American-born whites when they first arrived in the city. But several years later—acclimated to the city's competitive, literacy -stressing, fast-geared environment—the same Blacks' IQs were statistically identical with those of the whites! As another example of the huge role of cultural conditioning in structuring intelligence, consider the numerous well-documented cases of identical twins (who have identical intelligence) reared apart. IQ differences of 20 and 30 points have separated twins reared in favorable versus unfavorable environments. *In short, given similar cultural opportunities to realize their potentialities, the average achievement of the members of each and every ethnic group is virtually identical.*

Not only are there no innate cultural, social, or intellectual differences among the races, but there is no evidence whatsoever that race mixture produces biologically "bad" results. As was stated earlier, each race is in fact an intricate amalgam of cross-breeding with other racial strains. No race (or nation), then, is biologically any more or less pure than any other; races are "inferior" only in the sense that they are defined as inferior by the ethnocentric values of people such as "white supremacists."

A Tragic Error

The idea of race, as one authority has noted, represents one of the greatest—if not the greatest—error of our time, and the most tragic. Everyone seems to know, and is only too eager to tell, what race is. Well-intentioned or otherwise (the latter is most often the case), the mythical "man on the street" is abysmally ignorant and almost totally ill-informed on the matter. For the student, in particular, the facts must be put straight.

"Though the concept of race is genuine enough," famed anthropologist Clyde Kluckhohn once observed, *"there is perhaps no field of science in which the misunderstandings among educated people are so frequent and so serious."* One of the basic misunderstandings to which Kluckhohn refers is the confusion between *racial* and *ethnic* groupings of mankind.

Ethnic Group

Where race refers, of course, to hereditary ties, the term *ethnic* connotes social and cultural ties. Thus, when people confuse racial and ethnic traits, they are confusing what is *given* by nature and what is *acquired* through learning. What, then, is an ethnic group? The Jews, the American

Indians and the Nordics are *not* racial entities—but ethnic units—in the sense that they largely *share a common cultural heritage* and set of values. But even the label *ethnic* is conducive to gross oversimplification. Take for example, the category Jew. The German, Russian, Spanish, English, and Polish Jew (which together comprise some 95 percent of American Jewry) differ radically from one another not only in cultural terms but in the realms of religious belief and dogma, too. Further, there is a profound split within the Jewish religion—among Orthodox, Conservative, and Reformed. Also, in America fewer offspring of Jewish parents are Jews in the *religious* sense than are the children of Protestants Protestant or of Catholics Catholic. Similarly, the generic term *Indian* encompasses a people whose original tribes differed from one another linguistically and culturally as much as modern Americans differ from ancient Chinese.

RACIAL PREJUDICE

We have all known people whom we can justly label prejudiced. Many of the readers of this book, in fact, are in all probability quite intolerant toward one or more of the ethnic or racial groupings—toward Jews, Blacks, or some other group of "foreigners." Prejudice toward outsiders (out-groups) is so frequent an aspect of American society—of all known societies—that it is literally a universal phenomenon. Despite the contention of many racialists, however, prejudice is *not* inherent in man as man; it is *not* a biogenic trait. To effectively probe the how and why of prejudice, then, it is crucial that we recognize that like stature or IQ, prejudice is not a thing that a person either has or does not have, but is a matter of degree and intensity. We cannot, for example, legitimately assert that a man who is 6 feet tall is "tall" and a man who is 5 feet, 11 inches is "short," or that a person with a recorded IQ of 140 is "near-genius," while one whose IQ is 139 is merely "bright." Nevertheless, there are tall people, geniuses, and highly prejudiced persons. And the authors' concern throughout the remainder of this chapter will largely be with the highly prejudiced.

Definition of Prejudice

Prejudice is, specifically, thinking ill of a person or a group without sufficient justification; a feeling (favorable or unfavorable—though we shall be concerned with the latter aspect here) that is prior to, or not based on, actual experience. It is of course not easy to say how much "fact" is required to justify a judgment. A prejudiced person will almost certainly claim that he has sufficient cause for his views. He will tell of bitter experiences he has had with refugees, Koreans, Catholics, Jews, or Blacks, Mexicans, Puerto Ricans, or Indians. But in most cases, it is evident that his facts are both scanty and strained. He typically resorts to a selective sorting of his own memories and mixes them up with hearsay and then he over-generalizes. No one can possibly know *all* refugees, Koreans, Catholics, etc. Hence, any negative judgment of these groups as a whole is, strictly speaking, an instance of thinking ill without warrant, or justification. We can further elaborate our basic definition of prejudice to include an avertive (avoiding) or hostile attitude toward a person who belongs to a group, simply because he belongs to that group and is, therefore, presumed to have the objectionable qualities ascribed to the group. Another essential attribution of prejudice is that of giving and applying a stereotyped name or *label of difference* to members of a given group.[2]

Targets of Prejudice

Historically, the targets of prejudice have been determined by the particular configuration of conflicting values and opposing groups; they have been determined largely by the particular cultural and social situation of the time and place. *And the most evident targets of prejudice have been those particular group relationships which are marked by competition or other forms of opposition.* Often a group may be singled out for a period of time and then replaced by another group.

At the outset of our history, the first targets of strong prejudice were the British, who opposed our efforts toward independence. But there was also a certain amount of sectional division among the states. As the struggle for the extension of slavery became more and more a factor in national politics, a split between the industrial North and agrarian, slave-geared South became evident. After the Civil War, the whole situation changed in the South, with the appearance of the color-caste system, which still continues. Later, as the black moved into the North in response to sordid conditions at home and the lure of freedom and economic betterment, he came into direct competition with the northern urban white. And a certain amount of anti-black prejudice began to emerge in such places as Chicago, Detroit, Los Angeles, and New York City. Then, with the flood-tide of immigrants fleeing poor political and economic conditions in Europe, new objects of prejudice took their place in the sun.

The black and immigrant groups constituted a handy set of specific targets of intolerance, discrimination, and prejudice on the part of native-born or longer-established American citizens. Though economic competition was a crucial factor in the earlier outbreaks of prejudice (for immigrants willing to work for lower wages often eased American workers out of jobs

---

[2]A *stereotype* is a conception of a particular group held by the general public in the absence of specific knowledge of the characteristics of the individual members of that group. Stereotypes function, in a sense, as a substitute for knowledge.

in this era of rapid industrialization and explosive capitalism), one of the symbols of hostility pertained to an ideological conflict between the Protestantism of the Americans and the Catholic faith of the immigrants. This was especially true after 1890, when southern Europeans began to outnumber immigrants from Germany, Britain, and Scandinavia. The Protestant-Catholic friction—with native enmity less often directed toward Catholicism per se but toward the very "different southern European brand of culture—erupted in the growth of "native American" or nativist movements. Foremost of these movements was the Ku Klux Klan.

Two Basic Types of Prejudice

Granted that prejudice is so widespread that it is "normal," who are the persons likely to manifest the *most* prejudice? Although prejudice is essentially a matter of degree, there are two basic types of prejudice: culture-conditioned and character-conditioned.[3]

Culture-Conditioned Prejudice. We shall consider the former first, for it is by far the most typical. As its name might imply, culture-conditioned prejudice is primarily learned or acquired in the *normal* process of social interaction. Thus it is the rare southerner who views the black without antipathy. For he has been taught—deliberately and by subtle examples—that the black is both different and inferior; he has known no other explanation from childhood on. It cannot be overemphasized that *typically* the formation of prejudiced attitudes is not a product of "distorted" personality development. Prejudiced attitudes are, in fact, formed through the same process as other attitudes; they are derived from group norms. Within a group where patterns of prejudice prevail, it is the individual who *conforms* to the group (i.e., the most "normal" or "well-adjusted" person) who is likely to be the most prejudiced; conversely, lack of prejudice in such a group implies nonconformity. And studies of the growth of ethnic prejudice in children indicate that such prejudice arrives largely through contacts with prevailing social norms rather than through individual contacts with members of the out-group in question. Once a small child accepts the prejudicial norms of his parents, and, through osmosis, of his schoolmates, the negative outgrowth stereotypes he has learned become internalized; that is, they slide into his subconscious and become a functioning part of his personality configuration. In his adult years when he "feels" an aversion for the out-group he learned to dislike in childhood, he will defend his attitude with all manner of "reasonable" rationalizations.

[3]For a lucid analysis of *culture-* and *character-conditioned prejudice*, see T. W. Adorno et al., *The Authoritarian Personality* (New York: Harper & Row, 1950); G. Allport, *The Nature of Prejudice* (Reading, Mass.: Addison-Wesley, 1955); and H. M. Hodges, Jr., *Social Stratification* (Cambridge, Mass.: Schenkman Publishing Co., 1964).

There are, however, differences in susceptibility to the culture-conditioned brand of prejudice even among individuals reared in the same general culture. Thus, the more highly prejudiced person, in contrast with those less prejudiced, is more likely to (1) be older; (2) have had less formal education; (3) be either a farmer or in an unskilled or semi-skilled occupation; (4) live on a farm or in a very small town; (5) take less interest in civic affairs, be less informed on public issues, and vote less often, and (6) earn a lesser income. Many of these sociological factors, it is apparent, are intercorrelated; that is, they almost automatically "go with one another" (e.g., education, age, income, occupation, etc.). Closer analysis has revealed that of all these sociological variables *formal education* is the most crucial. Other social cultural determinants appear to be downward mobility and social-economic insecurity.

The particular target of prejudice will depend upon a number of factors; but it is currently most likely to be the Black in the North and South; the Puerto Rican, Mexican, and Jew in large urban areas; and in the more rural sectors of the Middle West, the big-city eastern intellectuals or "aristocrats." The particular *scapegoat* or object of prejudice will often, however, be a group sanctioned as "inferior" by people in general or a person or group too weak to strike back when attacked.[4]

Culture-conditioned prejudice *can* be "unlearned"; although the process is not as effortless as many well-intentioned and naive people believe. Because such attitudes are not formed in a piecemeal way and they are usually deeply ingrained within the personality structure, attempts to legislate prejudice out of existence, on some occasions, have had the opposite effect. Almost as unsuccessful have been efforts to "educate" people, to shame them (by appeals to their religious ethics or Americanism), or to bring them into "contact" with minority groups. Lecturing, like legislation, requires expert and subtle direction, if it is to avoid alienating its subjects. Social contact and situations such as living in an interracial housing project have often, when poorly handled, increased friction and hostility. Because the particular highly prejudiced individual is conformistic and cautiously attuned to his group's values, he is unlikely to alter his basic beliefs unless the group's beliefs change too.[5] To lessen prejudice with any degree of effectiveness, then, we must either change the basic values or attitudes of entire groups, or we must somehow transfer the prejudiced person's alle-

---

[4]Scapegoating has always been with us; people have traditionally found it uncomfortable to blame themselves when "things are going wrong." Projecting blame onto another source (displaced aggression) has long been a popular way to ease such unpleasant tensions.

[5]The authors do not intimate that such legislation (Civil Rights Act, 1964) is inappropriate; active government intervention in areas of unjustified ethnic prejudice is an absolute "must." However, such efforts will only cause frustration or "false hopes" if there are "unenforceable" laws or if such laws are not intelligently executed.

FIGURE 5.2. *Equal treatment by the courts and the police—as well as society in general —is a necessary ingredient in our American way of life. Courtesy Wide World Photos.*

giance to another group (or "reference group"). Educating the young child is, of course, a far simpler undertaking than changing ossified adult attitudes. However, such educational programs must reach the child during his lower-elementary school years, must be skillfully handled (preferably with the help of visual aids), and must strongly compete against extracurricular influences, such as the family and lower-culture values, which are frequently enormously potent.

Character-Conditioned Prejudice. This type of prejudice is quite firmly imbedded in the personality makeup, and attempts to rid people of it must be, quite needless to note, far more formidable than the just-cited techniques of eradicating culture-conditioned prejudice. As will become clearer later in this chapter, the person victimized by character-conditioned prejudice almost *has* to hate, and if one of his scapegoats or objects of venom is somehow eliminated from focus, he will inevitably seek out some other victim.

A psychologically prejudiced person (one having character-conditioned prejudice) is more dangerous than the sociologically prejudiced or culture-conditioned prejudiced person in a twofold sense. He is (1) present in all areas of the population—among the educated, the wealthy, and influential as well as the poor and ill-educated, and he is (2) more likely to be actively prejudiced and in a position whereby he can translate his hatred into effective political or social action. Postwar studies of the more avid Nazis and of potent native American Fascists have uncovered all the earmarks of the *character-conditioned* brand of prejudice.

Like culture-conditioned prejudice, the character-conditioned variety has its roots in childhood. But unlike the former, specific sets of prejudice, such as anti-Black or anti-Semitic, are seldom acquired in the early years. Rather, a basic outlook on life is learned during this formative period—an outlook that will warp the entire life of its victim. How does the childhood of such psychologically prejudiced persons differ from the normal person's? It differs at many—and as the subconscious will affirm—crucial points. It is worth recalling, at this juncture, how vitally important the formative years are in shaping one's entire personality.

It is abundantly clear, in summation, that the more deeply prejudiced person—one who looks down on *many* minority groups rather than one or two specific out-groups—is marked by a distinct personality makeup. He is, in short, a "sick person." His sickness is not of his own doing but rather is the outcome of a strict and undemocratic upbringing. As a result, his entire life will be marred by deeply imbedded frustrations, vague hatreds, and insecurity. He is already a target for demagogues of the far Right and far Left. He will be unhappy with both the Republicans and the Democrats, and can only be satisfied with a totalitarian order.

Forms of Prejudice

What is racism? The word has represented daily reality to millions of racial minorities for centuries (particularly the black people), yet it is a difficult term to define. *Racism* may be defined as the prediction of decisions based on considerations of race. Furthermore, such decisions or policies are intended to subjugate a minority racial group for the purpose of maintaining or exerting control of that group.

Minority problems are problems of intergroup relations, in which each minority is the subject of prejudice and discrimination by the majority. The majority itself is made up of many minorities and, indeed, is sometimes but the dominant minority of a group of minorities holding key positions. As previously indicated, prejudice is an attitude arrived at without sufficient exploration of the facts. It is prejudging, in the sense of making a judgment before or independently of the relevant facts in the matter. *Discrimination,* although related to prejudice, is *not* the same thing. Discrimination implies the unequal treatment of different people according to the group to which they belong.

The Functions of Prejudice

Among the functions that prejudice against minority groups may perform are the following:

1. It provides a source of egotistic satisfaction, through invidiously comparing others with oneself.
2. It affords a convenient grouping for people one is ignorant of. Lumping such people together under a popular stereotyped description saves time and thought and affords a convenient grouping.
3. It provides a convenient group or person to blame when things go wrong in one's personal life or in the community (scapegoating).
4. It provides an outlet for projecting one's tensions and frustrations onto other people.
5. It symbolizes one's affiliation with a more dominant group.
6. It owes justification for various types of discrimination which are thought to be of advantage to the dominant group.[6]

The Functions of Discrimination

Among the functions performed by discrimination against minority groups are the following:

[6]For a thorough analysis of minority-group problems, see J. S. Roucek and R. L. Warren, *Sociology, An Introduction* (Totowa, N.J.: Littlefield, Adams & Co., 1956), pp. 146–48.

1. It tends to reinforce prejudice concerning the group's alleged inferiority.
2. It assures members of the majority group various types of economic advantages.
3. It limits the effectiveness of possible competition from members of the minority group in business, education, political office, and so forth.
4. It affords an avenue to economic exploitation of the minority group.[7]

Elimination of Prejudice

Because much prejudice is based on stereotyped thinking, education in the matter of group differences—where they are found—should provide the necessary intellectual basis for a change of attitude. It is for this reason that various organizations like the National Conference of Christians and Jews, the National Association for the Advancement of Colored People, the Urban League, and the Anti-Defamation League carry on extensive educational programs. However, as was mentioned in an earlier section, prejudice is almost by definition an irrational attitude. Knowledge is not enough. A change of attitudes—attitudes conditioned by norms found acceptable by the group—must be the ultimate goal. Several "techniques" have been found to be successful in achieving this goal: (1) changing group norms (values, folkways, mores) through discussion, lectures, and the use of communication media (TV, newspapers, books, radio, etc.); and (2) encouraging association with members of the minority group. Quite often, the removal or suspension of discrimination subsequently provides an opportunity for experiencing mutual social participation and leads to a reconsideration of the prejudiced conception held by majority-group members. Because prejudice is largely irrational and emotional in nature, emotional appeals to the alleged values of democracy are sometimes effective, though they frequently have little permanent effect. Educational campaigns seem to be effective over a longer period of time.[8]

Reduction of Discrimination

Most sociologists and social psychologists are of the opinion that the attempt to eliminate prejudice under conditions of widespread discrimination is almost destined to fail, "for it separates verbal symbols and behavior, and the verbal symbols of tolerance and understanding are largely ineffective if daily life reinforces habits of discrimination. Hence, many people see the resolution of the problem in a constant agitation to defeat discrimination wherever possible, and to make it illegal where this is within the power of the law."[9]

[7]Ibid.
[8]Ibid.
[9]Ibid.

Therefore, antidiscriminatory laws have proven to be effective, although not without conflict. There are *some* indications of an improvement in the conditions surrounding minority groups—particularly the black minority. The U.S. Supreme Court has made several important decisions pertaining to desegregation—i.e., in education, housing, use of public facilities, and voting. Furthermore, because the black is becoming much more sophisticated politically and his vote is growing larger with every election, politicians are taking cognizance of the black's might. Also, many new types of employment were opened up for large numbers of Blacks during World War II, the Korean Conflict and the Vietnam War: These jobs have "opened the door," and labor unions have displayed a willingness to admit black workers to their membership. Nevertheless, the range of discrimination is still great and constitutes a challenge to any country claiming to be a democracy.

Prejudice: Related Effects

There are some segments of our population—notably blacks and other nonwhite minorities—that have been systematically excluded for generations from effective participation in the society. They have been locked into a self-perpetuating pattern of poverty, substandard living conditions, inadequate education, lack of skills, and unequal protection of the law, all mutually reinforcing one another. Their efforts to break out of this vicious cycle have been frustrated by subtle and not-so-subtle biases that have denied them access to educational opportunities, to jobs, to unions, to loans —in short, to all potential points of entry into the system.

Members of these groups have now gone beyond the earlier civil rights movement in insisting that their right to full participation in the society implies not merely the removal of legal barriers, but active affirmative efforts to open up opportunities to them and to assure that they will be in a position to take advantage of these opportunities. Moreover, they are insisting on the right to their own identity—the right to be included in the system on their terms, without having to adopt the values, lifestyles, and other cultural trappings of the white middle-class majority.

Two black assistant professors of psychiatry at the University of California Medical Center, William H. Grier and Price M. Cobbs, conclude in their book that riots express personal pain and rage provoked by the severe psychological and emotional pressures of living in a racist society.[10] Many other authorities in the field of race relations are of the same opinion. The psychological pressures and fear derive from a history of

[10]*Black Rage* (New York: Basic Books, 1968). See also E. E. Thorp, *The Mind of the Negro* (Ortlieb Press, 1961), and F. K. Berrien, *Comments and Cases in Human Relations* (New York: Harper & Row, 1951).

FIGURE 5.3. *"Activists" representing the Black minorities have been extremely vocal in demanding equality in education, employment, political and social opportunities. Courtesy San Francisco Police Department, San Francisco, Cal.*

oppression and capricious cruelty. This is clearly pointed out by Louis E. Lomax:

> The American Negro spent the first half of the twentieth century adjusting to and recovering from the all-pervasive reality of legalized segregation. Fear of white people being advanced was the basic motivation of Negroes during those years, and I suppose there is some validity in the analysis. But I doubt that fear was the only force shaping Negro activities and behavior; self-realization in an essentially hostile world, I suggest, is a no more accurate description of what the Negro was about. Fear, to be sure, was one of the techniques of that self-realization. After all, when the entire legal structure is against you and your very life is in daily peril, fear is an understandable emotion. Denied modern weapons with which to defend yourself, and hauled before openly hostile courts when you fight back with sticks and stones, you will do well to pretend fear even when you are not afraid.[11]

Not surprisingly, according to Grier and Cobbs, paranoid psychosis (or persecution complex—quite exaggerated) is the most typical type of

[11]*The Negro Revolt* (New York: Harper & Row, 1963), p. 42.

serious mental illness among blacks. The authors assert that the problem has its genesis during the formative years at the most crucial stage of development—sexual identity. A black mother, because she is afraid of the "penalties" of white society, will strive to maintain stringent control of her son. She must "intuitively cut off and blunt his masculine assertiveness and aggression lest they put the boy's life in jeopardy." Furthermore, this pattern of attempting to eliminate assertiveness and creativeness does not stop when the child reaches the adolescent stage but continues under the guise of the parents' discouraging of education. Black families, Grier and Cobbs write, tend to discourage their sons from seeking degrees by using hostility, scorn, and hatred as well as praise. Black families feel that having a degree may force their children into direct and dangerous competition with whites.

Unable to withstand the pressure of daily living in the ghetto, many black families are simply unable to function. This disintegration can be seen in the high percentage of fatherless homes. Sociologist Daniel P. Moynihan, in a well-publicized report, argues that lack of job opportunities prevents the black father from asserting authority in his household, so that, *psychologically emasculated* and humiliated, he leaves his family. The emasculating force is not economic but social; the father feels impotent and helpless because, living in prosperous American society, he is unable to provide for his family and protect it from harm.

For many blacks, self-respect has become almost impossible. Traditionally, a large number are preoccupied with hair straighteners, skin bleaches, and the like, which illustrates a most tragic aspect of American racial prejudice—blacks have come to believe in their own inferiority. Recently, however, there have been some encouraging signs. For instance, blacks have begun to advocate the "beauty of dark skin and kinky hair." And there has developed a new culture pride (e.g., natural Afro hair styles and African style of dress) which has had a positive effect on their mental health.

Discrimination Against Minority Groups

Discrimination takes several forms as it applies to minority groups. *Economic discrimination* involves unequal treatment in the economic sphere of individuals who are members of certain minorities. *Educational discrimination* results in school segregation and inferior facilities for educating those individuals who reside in poorer school districts owing to *economic* deprivation. This is particularly true in the case of the blacks and Spanish-speaking Mexican-Americans and Puerto Ricans. *Political discrimination* is exercised against minority groups *despite* constitutional amendments (because of "apathy in enforcement procedures") designed to assure citizens the right to vote. Political discrimination is particularly important because it is largely through federal legislation that minorities can expect to gain protection against the many other types of discrimination.

Another aspect of political discrimination is the manipulation of political boundaries and the devising of restrictive electoral systems. In areas where there is a large "bloc" of minority-group residents, it is not unusual for the political "machinery" of the dominant group to have gerrymandered such neighborhoods so that their true voting strength is not reflected in political representation.

Social discrimination is perhaps the most difficult form to eliminate through legislation. This may be attributed to the strong belief of many people that it is their basic democratic right to associate with whom they please and to bar whom they please from membership in associations to which they belong. So, for example, many fraternities will not admit members of certain minority groups. Also, restrictive covenants in housing operate to exclude minority groups from certain residential areas. The recent United States Supreme Court decision regarding open housing has not eliminated this problem, nor has the Rumford Act in California. Social discrimination is important because it hinders a closer association between the members of different groups and thus reinforces stereotyped prejudicial thinking which arises through ignorance.

Although racial prejudice and discrimination have been a problem to other racial groups, blacks have been so victimized by discrimination that they have been referred to as second-class citizens and the "underdog's underdog." Blacks comprise roughly 12 percent of the U.S. population. The *difference* in life expectancy of Blacks and whites is perhaps the best indication of the condition of Blacks as a minority group. The average nonwhite male, according to the United States Department of Health, Education and Welfare, has a life expectancy at birth nine and one-half years less than that of the average white male. The corresponding figure for the average nonwhite female is nearly eleven years less than for the white female.

POLICE AND PREJUDICE

All parties agree that the elimination of police misconduct requires selecting police for duty in ghettos with care. This is partly because police responsibility in these areas is particularly demanding and sensitive as regards ghetto residents' attitudes, and often it is rather dangerous as well. The highest-calibre personnel is required to overcome feelings of inadequate protection and unfair discriminatory treatment by the police. Of late there has been some effort to recruit minority-group members into the police department. The feeling is that with minority-group members as part of the police department patrolling the ghettos and barrios, the people within these residential areas will feel the police as more a part of the community rather than as an outside occupational force of the white establishment.

Policemen Representing Minority Groups

Generally speaking, if government is to be for all the people, it must be *by* all the people. However, that portion of the government that is known as law enforcement has tended to be underrepresented by minority groups. Yet there has been a great deal of tension between minority-group members and the police. Probably one of the better ways of resolving some of this tension would be to encourage minority-group members to be full participants in the governing process. This means that they need to become involved in law enforcement activities. "Not of least importance is the fact that the very stresses and tensions between the protective services and minorities which hinder recruitment are not likely to be resolved until these services are more representative of the minority community.[12]

Generally speaking, recruitment of minority-group members to the police department can only come about if these members do not view the police as enemies of the people. This means that acts of police brutality and police harassment must be punished swiftly by top municipal and police officials. It also means, as discussed in Chapter Four, that there must be training in human relations for police officers.

Mounting a one-time minority recruitment campaign by the police department tends to be ineffective. There should be an ongoing recruitment. This, however, is not an easy matter. The problems facing the black policeman are quite extensive[13] and may cut down his effectiveness a great deal. On the other hand, Bannon and Wilt indicate that policemen who are also members of a minority make a substantial contribution.

> This should not be such a surprising finding, but much of the current literature on the subject contradicts this statement. In light of that literature, we felt that if further studies by ourselves and others add more data to support these findings concerning the positive characteristics of black policemen, this should help to overcome many of the hesitations which sociologists and policemen alike have concerning black policemen.[14]

[12]R. J. Margolis, A Report of the United States Commission on Civil Rights, *Who Will Wear The Badge?* (Washington, D.C.: U.S. Government Printing Office, 1971), p. 3.

[13]See N. Alex, *Black in Blue: A Story of the Negro Policeman* (New York: Appleton-Century-Crofts, 1969).

[14]J. D. Bannon, and G. M. Wilt, "Black Policemen: A Study of Self-Images," *Journal of Police Science and Administration,* 1 (March 1973), p. 29.

Minorities in Police Work: Some Problems and Answers

It is important at this juncture to point out that the problems of economic, educational, political, and social discrimination have been continually under attack by local, state, and federal governments, not to mention private organizations and groups. The federal, state, and local governments "affirmative action" (i.e., hiring of minorities) hiring policy has had a definite impact on resolving some of the *economic* problems confronting these racial minorities. Along these lines, the Department of Justice's Law Enforcement Assistance Administration (LEAA) equal opportunity guidelines (see Appendix B) have generated a great deal of concern on the part of police administrators, and the recruitment of minorities has been accorded top priority. *Furthermore, rulings by federal courts relating to the "ratio hiring" of minority personnel, although appearing to civil service commissions and police unions and associations to be discrimination in reverse, have been handed down throughout the states.* In San Francisco, for example, entrance-level examinations and the examinations used for promotions to sergeant have been declared discriminatory. According to federal judge Robert F. Peckham, they prevented minorities from being able to compete on an equal level with the dominant group in the community. However, "federal court supervision of city employment policies, ..." Peckham said, "cannot substitute for enlightened leadership by city and police officials. Court intervention, at best, stimulates concerned parties to develop and implement policies which not only comply with the law but would also be an advantage to general community interests." "Affirmative action" is certainly not the *only* answer to the hiring of minorities. Its use as a "political ploy" will defeat its purpose. A strong statement regarding such misuse was made in a speech by Robert Weigle which applies to all segments of the criminal justice system:

> There will be a special place in hell for those who knowingly misuse Affirmative Action. Like the hucksters who use Christianity in order to fleece congregations, their sin is made worse because it betrays the trust of honest men and women and does so while hiding behind a worthy cause.
>
> Corrections, because of its ongoing interest in social justice, is particularly vulnerable to the charlatan. To religious zealots, a man's holiness is frequently weighed by how often he shouts "Jesus!" or "Hallelujah!" In corrections there is a tendency to judge a man's social awareness by how often he shouts "Prejudice!" Both groups had better keep an eye on their wallets.
>
> In Ventura County, Affirmative Action was used as an excuse to destroy standards related to the hiring of probation officers. Are "stand-

ards" ever used solely for keeping out minorities? Damn right they are, but is it always so? Is it so in Los Angeles County? Standards as applied in Los Angeles County may not have the same intent and purpose as they do in Jackson, Mississippi.

In some counties, quotas are being set up as the sole criteria for employment or advancement. Merit and ability are being dumped. Personnel departments have become employment offices. Legitimate hiring standards have become troublesome road blocks.

What kind of professional development is being served? Where are we headed? You cannot say, on the one hand, that a job is important and difficult to do and then turn around and say that anyone can do it. You cannot talk about improving the quality of the work and, in the next breath, state that *merit* and *ability* are merely secondary virtues. You cannot speak of measuring the quality of the work, but deny that it is possible to measure the quality of the worker. No one, white, black, or brown, can maintain his moral or intellectual balance taking part in that kind of a high wire act. Sooner or later everyone falls off. And there's no safety net to catch them.[15]

Police departments throughout the United States appear to be aggressively pursuing the goal of integration and are seriously concerned about discriminatory practices and behavior within their own organizations. Focusing on the most *predominant* minority group, the blacks, numerous research studies have provided some insight into this problem. Bannon and Wilt investigated the role of the black policeman within two social contexts: "(1) as a member of a specially and institutionally defined bureaucratic functional setting, the police department; and (2) as a person functioning within a dually defined and enacted role of public servant and figure of authority within black communities or residential areas."[16] Regarding the first context:

> police-community relations can best be improved in black neighborhoods by the department setting up strict rules of courtesy and insisting that they be adhered to. These rules should stress the importance of treating each individual citizen regardless of race or social status with the dignity of a human being. Until such time that a person acts otherwise, decent treatment is his right. Abuse of this right is the basic cause of poor police-community relations. The black community is not well-organized and it is therefore up to the police department, which is well-organized, to move toward gaining the respect and trust of the black community. This is at best a very difficult job but it is not impossible. The great majority of the black community fully realize

[15]R. Weigle for California Probation, Parole and Corrections Association (Jan. 1974), p. 4.

[16]"Black Policemen: A Study of Self-Images," pp. 21–25.

that the major beneficiary of community-police dissension is the criminal element of the black community which is protected by the community and ignored by the police.[17]

Regarding the second issue, concerning a person functioning in a dual role, the opinion of the study's respondents was that:

> integration is an unrealistic, undesirable red herring invented by whites as a stumbling block to equality. The key to police-community relations is professional, well-trained adequate police.
>
> I think that police-community relations can definitely be improved by placing more black officers in *all* areas of both the black and white community. This way both communities will begin to trust and have confidence in the police department as a whole, be it black or white officers they have contact with.
>
> [An increase in black policemen is needed] only if these officers are of a high caliber—mediocre personnel who do inadequate work will only worsen a bad situation.[18]

The statements made by the respondents reveal, acording to Bannon and Wilt, a deep concern, particularly on the part of black officers, regarding the issue of hiring more black officers.

> These men state that they favor the hiring of more black officers, but express a concern that standards not be reduced to facilitate this goal. It appears that the underlying reason for this concern is that present black officers have the attitude that if they could pass the more rigid standards, so should new recruits.
>
> It seems that what is functioning here is an awareness that, as minority officers, their performance has been thoroughly scrutinized by their white counterparts much more critically than for other recruits. Along with this is perhaps the unconscious awareness that the whites tend to identify all blacks as equivalent to each other.
>
> The black officers seemed to be concerned that should standards be lowered and inferior officers hired, then demonstrate deficiencies, their common color will tend to cause all blacks to be equated with the inferior performer. In other words, just because they are black, others will assume that all blacks hired were in fact below standard, regardless of the individual's capacity. On an empirical basis, we suspect that this fear is not altogether groundless.
>
> As blacks have been more and more accepted, their assignments have become much more challenging. Thus, they have been placed in positions which have allowed them to demonstrate their equal or superior abilities vis-à vis their white counterparts. They naturally do not want

[17]Ibid., p. 25.
[18]Ibid., p. 26.

to regress because of a new wave of stereotyping. Old-line black officers have seen the painful and lengthy process of escape from "black jobs" within the law enforcement establishment. They recognize that this progress was only possible through the performance of truly superior black policemen who had to be better than anyone else to escape the stereotype.

It has been a long and tortuous road since it was common to hear "he's a good colored officer" with the implication that this was not only rare, but that it was limiting or relative. He was "good" only in relation to other "colored" officers—he was not being equated with officers who were white. In other words, it was polite variation on an old theme: "That's surprising for a black." Now these officers are more commonly referred to as "good cops," without the limiting adjectives.[19]

Some members of the ghetto, most significantly the "middle-class residents," are of the opinion that the black officer is a "victim of the system"; "lower-class" residents are not so kind! Prevailing sentiment is that the Mexican-Americans and Puerto-Rican officers will be given the same contempt.

It is an important, and most often an overlooked factor, that "black citizens who distrust black policemen essentially do not want any policemen. Others [respondents] felt that those who are going to cooperate will do so with any police officer. The general consensus was that about 95 percent of all blacks have a high regard for black policemen. They believe that distrust exists because many blacks do not view law enforcement as being to their advantage."[20]

A key to the effectiveness of community relations may very well lie in the attitude of black members, as well as other minorities, of police agencies, and whether or not there is active recruiting of young people for the police service. Ongoing recruitment should make police–minority-group relations more effective and meaningful.

Anthropologists, in their studies of varying social groups the world over, have identified and emphasized the importance of recognizing cultural factors in dealing with problems of our own American society. Such groups as Puerto Ricans, Italians, and Blacks often maintain their own cultural systems and social groups as completely as do natives living in New Guinea. Such cultural systems are composed of and supported by characteristic behavior and attitudes shared by all members. These attitudes and behavior patterns, and *not* those of the surrounding dominant culture, define what is considered right and "moral" by the group members. It is not possible to understand the actions of an individual from a point of view outside his cultural system or subculture, any more than one can judge an iceberg from its visible fraction above the water. One must know,

[19]Ibid., p. 26.
[20]Ibid., p. 23.

then, the values a subculture imposes upon its members, especially as those values differ from one's own values. A person's actions must be examined in a context of his own group.

SUMMARY

Race is popularly defined as being traceable to (1) *mutations,* (2) *isolation,* and (3) *inbreeding.* There are no *pure* races in any serious sense of the word and no large numbers of people who are reasonably identifiable as distinct types (who share numerous characteristics in common).

The biological fact and the myth of "race" must, then, be distinguished. *For all practical social purposes "race" is not so much a biological phenomenon as a social myth.* We cannot, therefore, scientifically account for *differences* in group behavior in terms of differences in group biology. The events overwhelmingly point to the conclusion that "race" and "race differences" are not valuable concepts for the analysis of similarities and differences in human group behavior. Whatever classification of races the anthropologist might concur with, he never includes *mental* characteristics as part of those classifications. Furthermore, intelligence tests too do not enable us to differentiate safely between what is due to innate capacity and what is the result of environmental influences, training, and education.

The term *ethnic* connotes social and cultural ties. Thus, when people confuse racial and ethnic traits, they are confusing what is *given* by nature and what is *acquired* through learning.

Prejudice is defined as thinking ill of others without sufficient justification—a feeling (favorable or unfavorable) toward a person or group which is not based on actual experience.

Essentially, there are two basic types of prejudice: *culture-conditioned* (sociologically prejudiced) and *character-conditioned* (psychologically prejudiced. This chapter discusses fully the manifestations of such prejudices and analyzes the personality makeup of those who fall into each group.

Chapter Five also discusses the extremely sensitive area of police recruitment of minorities. Minorities in police work are concerned about professionalism; therefore, regard the hiring of *unqualified* minority-group members as a negative practice.

In the area of politics, education, and economics, there has been improvement in that discriminatory processes have lessened somewhat.

DISCUSSION TOPICS

1. Briefly discuss mutations, isolation, and inbreeding.
2. Is there a pure race? Discuss.

3. Discuss the difference between ethnic groups and race.
4. Define prejudice.
5. Discuss culture-conditioned and character-conditioned prejudice.

ANNOTATED REFERENCES

ADORNO, T. W., et al., *The Authoritarian Personality*. New York: Harper & Row, 1950. This book still is a classic in the field of the study of authoritarianism.

ALLPORT, G., *The Nature of Prejudice*. Reading, Mass.: Addison-Wesley, 1955. This textbook provides an excellent discussion in the area of bias and bigotry.

ANDERSON, W., *The Age of Protest*. Pacific Palisades, Cal.: Goodyear Publishing Co., 1969. This volume deals with essays, articles, and studies relating to significant protest movements and actions in areas of civil rights, education, peace, and religion. Also discussed are the roots of violence in American society.

GRIER, W. H., AND P. M. COBBS, *Black Rage*. New York: Basic Books, 1968. This book discusses the role of rage in black violence. The social emasculation of the black male is also examined, along with an intuitive explanation of the severe psychological injury suffered by the black male and female.

MARGOLIS, R. J., *Who Will Wear The Badge?* A Report of the United States Commission on Civil Rights. Washington, D.C.: U.S. Government Printing Office, 1971. This is an excellent study of minority recruitment efforts in protective services.

Mexican-Americans And The Administration of Justice in the Southwest. Summary of a Report of the United States Commission on Civil Rights, Washington, D.C.: U.S. Government Printing Office, 1970. This pamphlet investigates the biased treatment that Mexican-Americans receive from law enforcement agencies in the Southwest.

REESE, C. D., "Police Academy and its Effects on Racial Prejudice," *Journal of Police Science and Administration*, 1, No. 3 (September 1973), pp. 257–68. This article is well worth reading for potential law enforcement officers.

SWETT, D. H., "Cultural Bias in American Legal Systems," *Law and Society Review 3*, August 1969. The sections "Recruitment into the Police Culture," and "The Police Value System" are excellent, covering many areas discussed in this chapter.

EQUAL JUSTICE
AND
MINORITY GROUPS

6

In the "Pledge of Allegiance", every American school child learns the phrase, "liberty and justice for all." These words, if truly accepted as expressing a national goal, carry broad implications not only in regard to equal treatment by the courts and the police but also in regard to the general functions of society.

The courts and the police are the institutions of society generally examined with reference to injustice. However, it would be more logical to start an investigation of injustice by examining minority-group treatment within the general society. In 1967, over 70 percent of minority-group members lived within ghettos.[1] A ghetto is defined as "an area within the city characterized by poverty and acute social disorganization and inhabited by members of a racial or ethnic group under conditions of involuntary segregation."[2]

When discussing Spanish-speaking minorities, the word *barrio* is often used instead of *ghetto*. Barrio is Spanish for precinct, district, or quarter. However, when discussing the poor, *barrio* is often used instead of *barrio bajo*, which translates to *slum*.[3]

Keeping these definitions in mind, one soon realizes that the slum-

[1]*Report of the National Advisory Commission on Civil Disorders* (Washington, D.C.: U.S. Government Printing Office, 1968), p. 31.

[2]Ibid., p. 6.

[3]S. Ramondero, ed., *The New World Spanish-English and English-Spanish Dictionary* (New York: Signet Book, New American Library, 1969), p. 82.

ghetto dweller, because of the limited nature of his environment, does not enjoy liberty or freedom to pursue any goals. In this chapter, to help in our understanding of injustice as it exists for minorities in the United States, we will examine the black ghetto, and later the barrio. Blacks are the largest single minority group in the United States; the Spanish-surnamed minority is the second largest.

THE BLACK GHETTO

Almost every large city in the United States has a black ghetto. Such ghettos have a constantly growing concentration of blacks within the central city. A breakdown of blacks in the United States shows that approximately 69 percent live in metropolitan areas. Furthermore, approximately 56 percent live in the central city.

Studies show that during the past three decades, there has been a great shift of blacks from the rural southern areas to the large cities of the North and West. (However, during the 1970s there has been a counter-migration from the large cities of the North and West to the large cities of the South.) In 1910, the number of blacks in the metropolitan areas of the United States was approximately 28 percent of the total black population.[4]

It is obvious that more and more of the black population has become urbanized during the past sixty years; however, so has most of the population of the United States. The difference is that most blacks moved into and concentrated in the inner core of cities, while whites moved to the urban suburbs.

Furthermore, approximately 1 percent of the total population of the nation consists of poor blacks who come from disadvantaged neighborhoods. This 1 percent represents from 16 to 20 percent of the total black population in the central cities. Therefore, within the central city, there is a high concentration of very poor persons of a particular ethnic background —in this case black people.

It is speculated that the population shifts which have led to the formation of large black ghettos have been caused by three factors: (1) the migration of southern blacks to the cities in pursuit of employment (this has accelerated during the past thirty years), (2) the concentration of blacks in segregated big-city neighborhoods, and (3) the rapid growth of the black population because of better medical care coupled with a high fertility rate.[5]

By 1966, approximately two-thirds of all black people who lived outside the South were residents of the twelve largest cities of the United

[4]Report of the *National Advisory Commission on Civil Disorders,* pp. 115–20.
[5]Ibid.

States. Most of them were residents of the central city. These cities are New York, Chicago, Los Angeles, Philadelphia, Detroit, Baltimore, Houston, Cleveland, Washington, D.C., Milwaukee, St. Louis, and San Francisco. For the most part, blacks move into ghetto-type segregation. Like other migrants and immigrants, they first move into the older sections of cities. But unlike migrants from Europe, the black man's color barred him from leaving these poor neighborhoods even when he became financially able to do so. The predominantly white society which has absorbed the immigrant has, by and large, refused to absorb the black man. Until quite recently this segregation was effected by local housing ordinances and real estate codes coupled with violence and intimidation. Often when a black man moved into a white neighborhood, whites moved from the area, causing vacancies which were, in turn, filled by black citizens, and the whole character of the neighborhood was changed. Unscrupulous real estate agents often used this so-called "block-busting" technique to increase sales and, consequently, real estate commissions.[6]

Racial segregation has existed in American cities for decades. However, recently it seems to have increased to a higher degree in every large city in the United States. A study by Karl and Alma Taeuber shows this quite graphically.[7] These authors devised an index to measure the degree of residential segregation. This index indicated the percentage of black Americans who would have to move to other blocks from where they lived to bring about a perfectly proportioned unsegregated distribution of the population. The average segregation index for 207 of the largest cities of the United States in the year 1960 was 86.2. This means that an average of over 86 percent of all blacks would have had to relocate to create an unsegregated population distribution. This index indicates quite strikingly that by and large blacks live in segregated areas of the city. The houses in these segregated areas are not necessarily of the best quality and therefore we should examine the housing facilities available to the person who lives in the central city.

Ghetto Housing

Housing has been described in a federal government report as follows:

If the slums of the United States were defined strictly on the basis of dilapidated housing, inadequate sanitary facilities, and overcrowding, more than five million families could be classified as slum inhabitants.[8] To the inner-city child, home is often characterized by a set of rooms

---

[6]Ibid.

[7]*Negroes in Cities* (Chicago: Aldine, 1965).

[8]See the *Report of the Task Force on Individual Violence, Crimes of Violence* (Washington, D.C.: U.S. Government Printing Office, 1970), Chapter 14.

shared by a shifting group of relatives and acquaintances, furniture shabby and sparse, many children in one bed, plumbing in disrepair, plaster falling, roaches and sometimes rats, hallways dark or dimly lighted, stairways littered, air dank and foul.

In such circumstances, home has little holding power for a child, adolescent or young adult. Physically unpleasant and unattractive, it is not a place to bring friends; it is not even much the reassuring gathering place of one's own family. Indeed, the absence of parental supervision early in the slum child's life is not unusual, a fact partly due to the conditions of the home.[9]

It should be noted that the actual number of urban whites in substandard housing, generally known as slums, is two and one-half times the number of urban blacks in such housing. However, the important thing is that the proportion of the black population in inferior dwellings has run from a low of 18.1 percent in Los Angeles to a high of 58.9 percent in Pittsburgh. Approximately 25 percent of the black population in central cities lives in substandard housing, compared with 8 percent of all Caucasian. Furthermore, in six of the fourteen largest cities, 40 percent of black housing was below standard less than fifteen years ago. Generally speaking, black housing is far more likely to be substandard and quite aged when compared with white housing. Furthermore, it is far more likely to be overcrowded. Approximately 25 percent of black housing in American cities is overcrowded, while approximately 8 percent of housing for whites is overcrowded. This means that proportionately, approximately three times more blacks live in substandard housing than whites. When this figure is looked at in another light, it indicates that approximately one-fourth of the black population live in overcrowded housing.[10]

Seemingly, this overcrowding is directly related to the fact that blacks tend to get far less for their housing dollar than do whites. Often they cannot get housing similar to that of whites without paying much more for it. This particular situation seems to prevail in most slum areas. This fact, plus the predominantly low income earned by black ghetto dwellers, results in a large percentage of the family income being spent for housing. As a matter of fact, in many cities blacks use from 35 to 40 percent of their income for housing. Needless to say, this severely cuts into the ghetto resident's funds for other items.[11]

Landlords often victimize ghetto residents by ignoring building codes; probably because they know that their tenants are restricted, by economic

[9]The National Commission on the Causes and Prevention of Violence, *To Establish Justice, To Insure Domestic Tranquility* (Washington, D.C.: U.S. Government Printing Office, 1969), pp. 30–31.

[10]Report of the National Advisory Commission on Civil Disorders, p. 257.

[11]Ibid.

FIGURE 6.1. *Typical Houses of the slums.*

or ethnic background, to live in the ghetto. Broadly speaking, these circumstances along with others that will be expanded later, are those that minority groups refer to when they state they are being treated unjustly by society.

There is some feeling that ghetto dwellers might have a better chance of leaving the ghetto if they were able to earn better incomes. On the other hand, there is evidence that when they do obtain a better income, blacks feel uncomfortable moving away from their old neighborhoods; consequently, they may stay in the black neighborhood even though they have the monetary resources to move.[12] It is important to note that ghetto residents have problems obtaining jobs. Therefore we should examine job possibilities as they relate to ghetto residents.

Jobs and Ghetto Residents

Unemployment and underemployment are among the most serious and persistent problems of disadvantaged minorities. These problems contribute a great deal to civil disorders in the ghetto. Despite many efforts, and even during times of economic prosperity, blacks tend to have problems getting useful jobs at reasonable wages. Possibly because of the growing demand for skilled persons in an economy that is becoming more and more automated, attaining full employment has become increasingly difficult for the ghetto resident.

Even more important than unemployment is the related problem of the undesirable nature of many jobs open to blacks. Black ghetto dwellers are often concentrated in the lowest-paying and the lowest-skilled jobs in the economy. These jobs usually involve substandard wages, great instability, and uncertainty of steady employment. As a result, the income of black families has tended to remain below that of white families.

12J. White, and J. Boyce, "America's Rising Black Middle Class," *Time* (June 17, 1974), p. 28.

Because of these factors, residents of black ghetto neighborhoods have been subject for decades to social, economic, and psychological disadvantages. The result is a vicious cycle of failure; the employment problems of one generation breed similar problems in the following generation.

Getting a good job is harder than it used to be for those without preparation, for an increasing proportion of all positions require an even higher level of education and training. To be a Negro, an 18-year-old, a high school dropout, a resident of the slums of a large city, is to have many times more chances of being unemployed than a white 18-year-old high school graduate living a few blocks away. Seventy-one percent of all Negro workers are concentrated in the lowest paying and lowest skilled occupations. They are the last to be hired. Union practices, particularly in the building trades, have always been unduly restrictive toward new apprentices (except those related to union members), and this exclusionary policy has a major impact on young blacks. The unemployment rate, generally down in the last few years, remains twice as high for non-white than for whites and for black teenagers in the central cities in 1968 the unemployment rate was 30 percent, up a third over 1960.

Success in job hunting is dependent on information about available positions. Family and friends in middle-class communities are good sources for obtaining information about employment. In the ghetto however, information about job openings is limited by restricted contact with the job market. The slum resident is largely confined to his own neighborhood, where there are few new plants and business offices, and unfortunately state employment services have been generally ineffective even when used.

Most undereducated youngsters do not choose a job. Rather, they drift into one. Since such jobs rarely meet applicants' aspirations, frustration typically results. Some find their way back to school or into a job training program. Some drift fortuitously among low-paying jobs. Others try crime, and, if successful, make it their regular livelihood; others lack aptitude and become failures in illegal as well as the legal world—habitues of our jails and prisons. And there are those who give up, retreat from conventional society, and search for a better world in the private fantasies induced by drink and drugs.[13]

So far we have seen that the ghetto is a portion of the central city that is characterized by poor housing. People who live there tend to have less education and consequently fewer job opportunities and, in general, they are poorer than the average American.

The one bright hope most Americans in earlier periods had for their

[13]The National Commission on the Causes and Prevention of Violence, *To Establish Justice, To Insure Domestic Tranquility* (1969).

future generations lay in the schools. But schools in the black ghettos leave a great deal to be desired. An examination of educational facilities in the ghetto appears to be appropriate at this time.

Education in the Ghetto

A good education has traditionally been the means by which people have escaped from poverty and discrimination and, consequently, from the ghetto. Therefore, education within the ghetto is a particularly acute problem. By and large, schools in black ghettos have failed to liberate the people from their plight. This failure has caused the resentment of the black community against the schools. This resentment is not wholly unfounded.

An indication of what happens in a ghetto school is summarized in the following excerpt:

> The low-income ghetto child lives in a home in which books and other artifacts of intellectual interests are rare. His parents are usually themselves too poorly schooled to give him the help and encouragement he needs. They have not had the time—even had they the knowledge—to teach him basic skills that are routinely acquired by most middle-class youngsters: telling time, counting, learning the alphabet and colors, using crayons and paper and paint. He is unaccustomed to verbalizing concepts or ideas. Written communication is probably rare in his experience.
>
> The educational system in the slum is generally poorly equipped. Most schools in the slums have out-dated and dilapidated buildings, few texts or library books, the least qualified teachers and substitute teachers, the most overcrowded classrooms, and the least developed counseling and guidance services. These deficiences are so acute that the school cannot hold a slum child's interest. To him it is boring, dull, and apparently useless, to be endured for a while and then abandoned.
>
> The school experience often represents the last opportunity to counteract the forces in a child's life that are influencing him toward crime and violence. The public school program has always been viewed as a minor force for the transmission of legitimate values and goals, and some studies have identified a good school experience as a key factor in the development of "good boys out of bad environment."[14]

Unfortunately, as time passes, the record of public education for ghetto children seems to be becoming worse. In the critical verbal skills of reading and writing black students in the ghetto schools fall further and further behind with each year of school completed. The U.S. Department of Health, Education and Welfare published a report[15] which indicated that

[14]Ibid., pp. 32–33.
[15]*Equality of Educational Opportunity* (Washington, D.C.: U.S. Government Printing Office, 1966).

on the average, minority-group children from the ghetto are somewhat below white children in respect to educational levels upon entering first grade. However, by the sixth grade, standard achievement tests indicate that black students from the ghetto are 1.6 grades behind, and by twelfth grade they are 3.3 grades behind the white students who have started school with them.

As a result of this, many minority students drop out of school. Black students are three times as likely to do this as white students. Unfortunately, a very high proportion of the dropouts are not equipped to enter the normal job market, and when they do, they tend to get low-skilled, low-paying jobs.

The vast majority of inner-city schools are involved in de facto segregation. Racial segregation in urban public schools is principally the result of residential segregation, combined with widespread employment of neighborhood school policy. This, of course, transfers segregation from housing to education. Many of the students in the segregated schools are poor. Many come from families whose adults were products of inadequate rural school systems of the South, which had very low levels of educational attainment. Children from these families most often have limited vocabularies and are not well-equipped to learn rapidly. When these disadvantaged children are racially isolated in ghetto schools, they are deprived of a significant ingredient of quality education—exposure to other children who have strong educational backgrounds. Most educators and sociologists believe that strong socioeconomic backgrounds of pupils in a school exert a powerful impact upon the achievement of other students in that school. By the nature of the ghetto school, this is denied to most minority-group pupils. Teachers in inner-city schools say they have many emotionally disturbed, retarded, and maladjusted students and few facilities to deal with these students. Another criticism of ghetto schools is that curricula and materials used there are ordinarily geared to middle-class white suburban students, and textbooks make little or no reference to Negro achievements and contributions to American life. Because the schoolwork has little or no relevance to the ghetto youngster's life experience, the youth tends to conclude that education is not relevant to his life.

Many black residents of the inner city are angry about the inadequacies of their schools. Unfortunately, communication between the community and the school administrators tends to be quite poor. Probably this is because the teachers and administrators tend to live outside the ghetto and do not fully understand its problems. On the other hand, most ghetto parents lack much formal education and generally believe they have little voice in changing school matters. However, they do feel the schools are not providing an adequate education for their children, and they regard this as unjust.[16]

[16]Ibid., p. 20.

Housing, school, and employment are part of the problems in the ghetto. However, there are other problems for the ghetto resident.

Problems of the Typical Ghetto Family

For years criminologists have known that crime rates are always higher in poor neighborhoods, whatever their ethnic composition. The black ghetto is no exception. The black resident's sense of personal security is certainly undermined by the frequency of crime in the big-city ghetto. The ghetto may have as much as 35 times as much serious crime per 100,000 residents as does a high-income white district.

Crimes in ghettos are committed by a small minority of the residents. Most of the victims are law-abiding people. It is difficult for middle-class whites to understand how insecure these law-abiding ghetto dwellers feel. In poor black areas a person is 75 percent more likely to be the victim of a major crime than residents of high-income areas.[17]

Because of this high crime rate, many blacks have bitter feelings toward the police. They feel they do not receive adequate protection from law enforcement agencies, and this tends to be one of the black person's principal grievances against the police. It is important that law enforcement personnel be aware of this.

Poor families are usually found to have poor diets, poor housing, poor clothing, and poor medical care. Generally speaking, about 30 percent of such families suffer from chronic health problems that have adverse effects upon employment possibilities. Although black ghetto residents have many more health problems, they spend less than half as much per person on medical services as white families with comparable incomes. There are several reasons for this: (1) black families are usually larger than white families, (2) necessities often cost black people more than white people (e.g., housing costs for blacks versus housing costs for whites), (3) fewer medical facilities and personnel are available to poor blacks, generally because doctors prefer to practice in high-income areas, and (4) general environmental conditions in the black ghetto are not conducive to good health. Among these are poor sanitation and overcrowding, the lack of decent facilities for storing food, and serious rodent problems.

The ghetto neighborhood itself is one of the problems of the ghetto family.

> In many center city alleys are broken bottles and snoring "winos"— homeless, broken men, drunk constantly on cheap wine. Yards, if any, are littered and dirty. Fighting and drunkenness are everyday occurrences. Drug addiction and prostitution are rampant. Living is crowded, often anonymous. Predominantly white store ownership and

[17]The National Advisory Commission on Civil Disorder, p. 83.

white police patrols in predominantly black neighborhoods are frequently resented, reviled, and attacked, verbally and physically. Municipal services such as garbage collection, street repairs and utility maintenance and the like are inadequate and, at times, all but nonexistent.

Many ghetto slum children spend much of their time—when they are not watching television—on the streets of this violent, poverty-stricken world. Frequently, their image of success is not the solid citizen, the responsible, hard-working husband and father. Rather, the "successful" man is the cynical hustler who promotes his own interests by exploiting others—through dope, selling numbers, robbery, and other crimes. Exploitation and hustling become a way of life.[18]

Seemingly, the family structure is affected by living within the ghetto. Because the men of the family often cannot obtain jobs in legitimate enterprises that enable them to support their wives and children, their status and self-respect are affected. Frequently wives are forced to work so the family can be provided for economically. Often the women earn more money than the men, and this too may affect the status and self-respect of the husband. With the husband feeling inadequate, the possibility of divorce or separation increases. This, in turn, leads to more and more ghetto families being headed by females rather than males. A related factor is that welfare payments are often tied to the absence of the father in the home. This means for the mother and children to survive economically, the father often deliberately absents himself from the home. The result of these two factors is that almost three times as many black families are fatherless than white families. This situation in turn has a great impact upon the attitudes of children in these homes. A report of the federal government indicates the following about these families:

> Inner-city families are often large. Many are fatherless, permanently or intermittently; others involve a conflict-ridden marital relationship; in either instance the parents may communicate to their offspring little sense of permanence and few precepts essential to an orderly, peaceful life.

> Loosely organized, often with a female focus, many inner-city families bestow upon their children what has been termed "premature autonomy." Their children do not experience adults as being genuinely interested or caring persons. These children may, rather, experience adults as more interested in their own satisfactions than those of their children. Consequently, resentment of authority figures, such as policemen and teachers is not surprising. With a lack of consistent, genuine concern for children who are a burden to them, the parents may vacillate from being unduly permissive to becoming overly stern. Child-rearing problems are exacerbated where the father is sometimes

[18]*To Establish Justice, To Insure Domestic Tranquility,* p. 32.

or frequently absent, intoxicated, or replaced by another man; whose coping with everyday life, with too little money for the size of the family leaves little time or energy for discipline.[19]

It is easy to see why the ghetto resident, particularly the young person, may believe he has no stake in the "system" and therefore little to gain by patterning himself by society's rules. In fact, there seems to be little to lose by not conforming to society's rules. It is easy to believe that the odds against succeeding in a legitimate enterprise are greater than the odds against succeeding in criminal activities. With this sort of conditioning, violence—either individual or group—in the ghetto is understandable.

THE SPANISH-SPEAKING MINORITY

The Spanish-speaking minority is the second largest minority in the United States. In many respects, the lot of these people has been similar to that of the black citizens of the United States. By and large, the Spanish minority lives in a separate residential district which has come to be known as the barrio. In the southwestern part of the United States this is often a residential district separated from the rest of the population center by a highway or railroad track. Housing within the barrio, as within the ghetto, is dilapidated, aged, and substandard.

When discussing this minority group, it is necessary to remember that it is composed of several groups of people with somewhat different backgrounds. In the five southwestern states of Arizona, California, Colorado, New Mexico, and Texas, the Spanish-speaking people are Mexican-Americans. This means that they were either born in Mexico rather than in another Latin American country or that their ancestors originally came from Mexico. The Spanish population of New York, New Jersey, and other eastern states, on the other hand, is largely of Puerto Rican descent. The persons with Spanish surnames who live in Florida generally trace their ancestry to Cuba.[20]

The minority group of the barrio has almost all the problems that are associated with blacks in the ghetto. To compound the difficulty, there is a language problem. Most of this group learns Spanish as a first language. In a limited study in 1968, it was found that only 24 percent of the children and 15 percent of the parents used English all the time. Furthermore, 37 percent of the parents of these children and 15 percent of the children themselves spoke Spanish in their everyday life.[21]

19Ibid., p. 31.

20United States Commission on Civil Rights, *Mexican-American Education Study* (Washington, D.C.: U.S. Government Printing Office, 1971), p. 15.

21J. G. Anderson, and W. H. Johnson, *Social and Cultural Characteristics of Mexican-American Families in South El Paso, Texas,* paper prepared for presentation

The child who learns Spanish as a first language often has a problem when he or she enters the American public school where English is the language used. For a time in the 1920s and 1930s, Spanish-surnamed people were considered to be less intelligent because of their problems with school-work. Since that time, however, there has developed an awareness of the many variables that affect school achievement, such as socioeconomic factors, cultural elements, past educational experiences, and health and nutritional status as well as language inadequacies.

The problem of overcoming the handicap of learning English as a second language, coupled with segregation of the Spanish-speaking students in school, has had its negative effect. Until the late 1940s there was segregation of the Mexican-Americans on a *de jure* (legal) basis in the southwest.[22] Presently there still is de facto segregation of such students within the school system. This segregation is related to residential patterns.

Unfortunately, a member of the Spanish minority tends to have a problem receiving a good education in English. The result is that this person has problems selling his or her services on the job market. This in turn continues the cycle of poverty.

But the solution to the language problem is not rectified by a simple course in English. Many children with Spanish surnames, who are second- and third-generation American citizens, speak Spanish as poorly as they do English. Many of them speak a combination of English and Spanish slang that is quite difficult for language instructors to deal with.

The problems of both the ghetto and barrio are sometimes felt to be a reflection of the general social structure of the society and its lack of concern for equal justice among the minority groups. The institutional structure of the courts and their history have had a telling effect upon the present social structure of the ghetto and barrio. Lest it seem, however, that the courts have been wholly responsible for the present situation, one must remember that to a large extent they have been responsible for some of the changes for the better that are happening to minority groups in the community.

EQUAL JUSTICE IN THE COURTS

The great majority of persons accused of crime in this country are poor. The system of criminal justice under which they are judged is rooted in the idea that arrests can be made only for good cause and that those arrested are presumed innocent until proven guilty. By and large, the accused are

---

at the Joint Meeting of the American Association for the Advancement of Science with the National Council of Teachers of Mathematics, December 27, 1968, Dallas, Texas, p. 7.

[22]Commission on Civil Rights, *Mexican-American Education Study,* pp. 13–14.

entitled to pretrial freedom to aid in their own defense. A plea of guilty should be voluntary, and all the allegations of antisocial behavior are to be submitted to the adversary system that is referred to as the "bar of justice." The courts are quite important, even though relatively few cases reach trial. It should be noted that those that do so establish the legal rules for all cases and affect the public image of justice as a whole.

To examine this system as it relates to minority-group members, some consideration should be given to the history of the court's treatment of minority groups.

Historical Highlights of Courts and Minority-Group Members

The most appropriate place to start examining minority-group treat-ment before the courts is the *Dred Scott* decision,[23] which was handed down by the Supreme Court in 1857. This case concerned a Negro slave who had lived with his master for five years in Illinois and Wisconsin Territory. At the time these were free states, while the southern states were slave states. The court decided that because Scott was a slave, he was therefore not a citizen. Consequently, he could not even sue in court.

This decision quite plainly indicated that a little over 115 years ago, people of a minority group had no rights whatsoever in court. However, in 1868, the Fourteenth Amendment to the Constitution was passed and stated in part:

> All persons born or naturalized in the United States, and subject to the jurisdiction thereof, are citizens of the United States and the State wherein they reside. No State shall make or endorse any law which shall abridge the privileges or immunities of citizenship of the United States; nor shall any State deprive any person of life, liberty, or property, without due process of law; nor deny to any person within its jurisdiction the equal protection of the laws.

The Amendment clearly established that members of a minority group were to be treated equally under the law. However, for many years fol-lowing this, the courts interpreted the law in light of a doctrine which was known as "separate but equal rights." The case of *Plessy v. Ferguson*,[24] decided by the United States Supreme Court in 1896, upheld this doctrine as it related to the civil rights of American Negroes. In many areas, espe-cially regarding schools, the doctrine of separate but equal was prevalent. In most cases, however, facilities may have been separate, but they were far from equal. Obviously, for the minority groups, they were inferior.

A study by Guy Johnson, which covers the years 1930 to 1940, indicates

[23]*Dred Scott v. Stanford*, 19 How. 393 (1857).
[24]*Plessy v. Ferguson*, 163 U.S. 537 (1896).

that in most southern courts Negroes who committed offenses against other Negroes were dealt with no more severely than white persons who committed crimes against other white persons. Differentiation was made when a Negro perpetrated a crime against a member of the Caucasian race; at this point he was dealt with quite severely.[25] The Johnson study did not take into account the probability that more accused persons of the Negro race were convicted than were members of the Caucasian race. A great deal of the reason for this has to do with the fact that Negroes, in general, were poorer than Caucasians, and unfortunately, a great discriminating factor in criminal justice is whether or not the accused has sufficient financial means. Persons who have money are much more likely to be treated leniently by the courts than persons who do not.

Recently, the Supreme Court has made some rulings which should change this. One of the first landmark decisions regarding equality of justice was *Shelly v. Kraemer*.[26] This struck down restrictive covenants in housing. Theoretically at least, it made it possible for members of a minority to legally buy a residence wherever they wished to. From a practical standpoint though, it was necessary to resolve each issue with new litigation. However, part of the reasoning of this case led to another landmark case.

In 1954 the *Brown v. Board of Education* ruling declared that the separate but equal doctrine that had been used to segregate the public schools was unconstitutional.[27] This case was specifically concerned with the board of education of Topeka, Kansas. Similar cases in Virginia, Deleware, and South Carolina were decided at the same time. This ruling by the Supreme Court began the process of correcting injustice to minority-group members.

It should be noted that segregated schools for Mexican-American youngsters were found to be a violation of due process and equal protection of the law guaranteed under the Fifth and Fourteenth Amendment earlier—in 1947 in California[28] and in 1948 in Texas.[29] Essentially, then, separate but equal schools have been ruled inappropriate for all minority groups.

The Supreme Court has actively led this country toward a fuller understanding of the high ideals set forth in the Constitution. Through various decisions it has begun to equalize a poor person's chances before the bar of justice with that of someone who has more money. This is most impor-

---

[25]G. B. Johnson, "The Negro and Crime," in M. Wolfgang, L. Savitz, and N. Johnson, eds., *The Sociology of Crime and Delinquency* (New York: Wiley & Sons, 1962), pp. 145–53.

[26]*Shelly v. Kraemer*, 68 Sup. Ct. 836 (1948).

[27]*Brown v. Board of Education*, 347 U.S. 483 (1954).

[28]*Mendez et al. v. Westminister School District of Orange County et al.*, 64 Supp. 544, affirmed 161 F, 2d 774 (9th Cir. 1947).

[29]*Delgado v. Bastrop Independent School District*, Civ. No. 388 (D.C. WD Tex. (1948).

tant to minority-group members because they tend to be poorer than members of the white majority. Among the cases that probably did most for minorities in this indirect manner was *Gideon v. Wainwright*,[30] decided in 1963. Essentially, Gideon was charged with breaking and entering a poolroom. At his trial in Florida he was refused counsel. When the U.S. Supreme Court reviewed the case, it decided that legal assistance is the right of anyone charged with a crime and is fundamental to a fair trial. (It should be noted that when Gideon, with competent counsel, was later retried, he was found not guilty).

A second case of interest is *Miranda v. Arizona*.[31] This case, decided by the Supreme Court in 1966, concerned a confession admitted as evidence in a rape charge. It developed that Miranda had not been informed of his constitutional rights to remain silent and to have legal counsel. The Supreme Court reversed his conviction on the grounds that a person arrested for a crime should be given a fourfold warning before he is questioned: he has a right to remain silent; anything he says may be used against him; he has a right to have an attorney present during the questioning; and if he is indigent, he has a right to have an attorney furnished to him without charge. (Miranda was retried and again found guilty of the crime of rape.)

A third case that was important in bringing about equal justice for minority groups was *in re Gault*, which was decided in 1967.[32] Gault, a minor, was found to be a "delinquent youngster" and was committed to a state facility in Arizona. However, at the time of his arrest he was not given the full warning that the court felt reasonable for an adult; furthermore, he had not been provided an attorney, and was given no opportunity to face his accusers. All these rights, had, before this time, been spelled out for adults. In the Gault case, the Supreme Court ruled that they should also be applied to minors being tried in a juvenile court. The Gault case is important because from 40 to 50 percent of the persons arrested for crimes in the United States are juveniles. In addition, as with adults, a disproportionate number came from minority groups. These minority groups in turn tend to be poor residents of the ghetto or barrio.

The next most important court decision that affects minorities, principally Spanish-surnamed minorities, was a 1974 decision known as *Lau v. Nichols*.[33] This case concerned a Chinese youth who spoke only a Chinese dialect. Because of this it was impossible to educate him in the San Francisco public school system. The Supreme Court ruled that he must be provided an education in his primary language, rather than in English. The

---

[30]*Gideon v. Wainwright*, 372 U.S. 335 (1963).

[31]*Miranda V. Arizona*, 384 U.S. 436 (1966).

[32]*In re Gault*, 387 U.S. 1 (1967).

[33]*Lau v. Nichols*, 42 U.S. Law Week 4165 (1974).

importance of this ruling to the Spanish-speaking minority can only be estimated at this time. However, it would seem that it could be a great benefit for the children who come from families in which Spanish is the primary language.

Another process of the court system which has posed some inequities is the bail system.

Bail and Other Methods of Release

Traditionally, criminal cases begin with an arrest. This is followed by detention until a magistrate can decide on the amount of bail the accused may post before trial for his release. In its present form the bail system discriminates against and consequently punishes the poor. The affluent can afford to buy their freedom, while the poor go to jail. Because of this, the defendant without monetary funds may lose his job and his present earning capacity. All this transpires before the trial and before there has been a determination of guilt or innocence. This, in effect, may result in a person being punished severely for being poor rather than for being guilty.[34] Many changes have been taking place recently regarding the bail system. Some of these show promise for more equal justice for the poverty-stricken and, consequently, for minority groups in general.

More and more, law enforcement agencies are coming to the conclusion that in certain circumstances there are alternatives to arrest. There is no question that arrest and detention is needed if the crime is serious or if there is danger of the defendant fleeing from court jurisdiction. Police may feel that the defendant needs to be fingerprinted and photographed as well as searched and questioned. However, generally speaking, an arrest followed by detention is not usual in traffic matters, and there is reason to believe that arrest for certain other offenses does not need to be followed by detention. Offenses involving petty crimes and local code violations may well be handled in another way.

Alternatives to routine arrest and detention have been developed by several states and federal courts. These alternatives generally take two forms. In the first situation, a judicial officer issues a summons upon complaint of the prosecutor. In the second situation, a police officer issues a citation or a notice to appear much like a traffic ticket. There have been a number of areas in which citations are used for misdemeanant offenses. In these circumstances, unless an arrest is necessary to protect the community, the court process, or the defendant, a misdemeanor suspect is released at the scene of the offense upon identifying himself. The arresting officer decides upon the summons process after he checks with head-

[34]R. Goldfarb, *Ransom: A Critique on the American Bail System* (New York: Wiley & Sons, 1965).

quarters through the computer-based police intelligence network system.

A number of states and the federal government have developed a second method of processing persons arrested for criminal acts without subjugating them to posting of bail. In this method, people are released on their own recognizance.[35]

Indications are that moves of this kind by the justice system have tended somewhat to improve chances of the poor defendant for equal treatment before the court. Furthermore, release of persons accused of crime before trial has apparently not posed a serious threat to the community or the justice system per se.

As far as can be determined, in many matters of criminal justice, the courts have made an increased effort to treat minority-group members much more fairly. It is possible, however, that the emphasis on criminal court problems has somehow screened out the need for reform in civil problems that are peculiar to the poor.

The Poor and Civil Litigation

According to Thomas E. Willinge, the major barrier to justice for poor people is the inability to receive expert legal counsel.[36] Although adequate counsel is a necessity for successful litigation, our efforts to provide good counsel for the poor have not worked out very well. For example, a poor person who believes that his landlord may be right or that the alleged debt he owes is just, usually does not bother to show up in court. The person who does come to court feels that he has a good case, nevertheless, because he has been treated unjustly. But for the most part, lawyers represent the businessmen, and they usually win judgments against the bewildered, intimidated poor. Too often, the poor leave the courtroom as losers, without any feeling that justice has been done. Consequently, equity in civil matters is often not the case for poor people.

A second factor, of course, is the financial barrier. Under our system of justice, the Constitution guarantees free access to civil courts for all citizens. However, many poor people are frightened by the court system, which they view as being rigged against them because they are frequently unsuccessful litigants. Therefore, they are faced with loss of time and money as well as court costs if they lose a case.

There have been some efforts at changing such inequities. These efforts have come from the persons who have been involved in organizing con-

---

[35]The *President's Commission on Law Enforcement and Administration of Justice, Task Force Report: The Courts* (Washington, D.C.: U.S. Government Printing Office, 1967), pp. 40–41.

[36]"Financial Barriers and the Access of Indigents to the Courts," *The Georgetown Law Journal*, 57, No. 2 (Nov. 1968), pp. 253–306.

sumer protection agencies. Although consumer protection generally has been a concern of the middle class in the United States, it certainly has great importance for the poor. Its implications are such that continued review of its progress, as well as some knowledge of the laws, and knowledge of where an individual might go for redress of his grievances, would probably be quite useful to every patrolman. If patrolmen were able to direct persons with grievances of this sort to the appropriate agencies, this in itself could be a community relations gesture well appreciated.

After this brief examination of the society and of the courts, we should turn our attention to law enforcement agencies and their handling of minority groups in relation to equal justice.

POLICE, MINORITY GROUPS, AND EQUAL JUSTICE

In most instances the decision to initiate criminal prosecution is a matter of police judgment. Supposedly, this judgment is based upon the legal definition of crime. However, in many instances in which a violation of the law has occurred and the police know of this violation, they do not act. Some of the factors that cause this discrepancy are: (1) the volume of criminal law violations and the limited resources of the police, (2) the enactment of laws which define criminal conduct in a generalized manner, and (3) various pressures reflecting the attitudes of a particular community.

An example of this dilemma is social gambling. In most jurisdictions gambling is illegal. However, there is good reason to believe that complete enforcement of anti-gambling laws is neither expected nor intended. For example, in September 1974, a number of people were arrested for playing "penny-ante" poker in a senior citizens' home in San Francisco. The court dismissed the charges against these citizens although within the definition of the law they were probably guilty. Law enforcement agencies are left with the responsibility of deciding whether or not to enforce anti-gambling statutes in the communities they serve. Because of this, bingo may be tolerated at church functions, and book-making in the community may be prosecuted. Also, the police may be confronted with the problem of deciding whether gambling in a private home constitutes a violation of the anti-gambling statutes. For the average white middle-class American, a small game of poker within the confines of one's own home is possible because the indoor living space is adequate. On the other hand, in the crowded ghetto, where indoor living space is at a premium, games of chance are often moved to a dead-end street or alley. When police are informed that such a game is taking place in a ghetto, they generally respond and arrest the players. They justify their intervention by saying that such arrests serve to prevent crime because past experience shows that card games in the ghetto frequently end in fights; those played in suburban areas generally do not.[37] Consequently, although the police intention might be quite noble, the practice gives the appearance of improper class and racial discrimination.

Another example of the discrepancy in prosecution is the handling of assaultive-type offenses. These offenses come to the attention of law enforcement agencies quite frequently because they occur in public, because police wish to intervene before more harm is done, or because the victim is found to be in need of medical aid by a patrol unit. Although the perpetrator of the assault is known to the victim in a large percentage of the cases, frequently there is no arrest, or if an arrest is made, it is followed by release of the alleged assailant without prosecution. Seemingly, this is especially true in ghetto areas owing, according to law enforcement personnel, primarily to an unwillingness on the part of the victim to cooperate in the prosecution. Even if the victim should cooperate during the investigation stage, this willingness to cooperate often disappears at the time of trial. It might be possible for police to achieve some success in assault cases by subpoenaing the victim to testify. However, the subpoena process is seldom used. Instead, the path of least resistance—the decision not to prosecute—is followed when the victim appears unwilling to testify. Police justify this action by pointing out the high volume of cases and other compelling demands made upon the agency. This decision is further rationalized on the grounds that the injured party was the only person harmed and he does not wish to pursue the matter. Cases of this sort can be written off statistically as cleared cases, which then constitute an index of police efficiency.

These kinds of police practices, particularly in the ghetto, give rise to the question of the degree to which police tolerance of assaultive conduct results in the formation of negative attitudes on the part of ghetto residents toward law and order in general.[38] How can a ghetto resident consider law enforcement fair when attacks by a ghetto resident upon a person residing outside the ghetto generally results in a vigorous prosecution?

Many minority-group members believe that police brutality and harassment occur repeatedly in black neighborhoods. This is one of the main reasons for minority-group resentment against the police. To a large extent, however, research reported by the federal government seems to show these beliefs are unjustified.

> One survey done by the Crime Commission suggests that when police-citizen contacts are systematically observed, the vast majority are

[37]The President's Commission on Law Enforcement and Administration of Justice, *Task Force Report: The Police* (Washington, D.C.: U.S. Government Printing Office, 1967), pp. 21–22.

[38]Ibid., p. 22.

handled without antagonism or incident. Of 5,339 police-community contacts observed in slum precincts in three large cities, in the opinion of the observer, only 20—about three-tenths of one percent—involved excessive or unnecessary force. And almost all of those subjected to such force were poor, more than half were white.[39]

In another study conducted by the Center of Research on Social Organization, the data seemed to support the same kind of conclusion.[40] In this study, observation of police arrests was conducted in Boston, Chicago, and Washington, D.C., seven days a week for seven weeks. Professional observers accompanied policemen on their calls and to the stations where bookings and lock-ups were made. There were 643 white suspects and 751 black suspects in the sample. Twenty-seven of the whites and 17 of the blacks experienced undue use of force when they were arrested. This yields an abuse rate of 41.9 per thousand white suspects and 22.6 per thousand black suspects.

Thus, physical abuse does not seem to be practised against minority-group members in a greater degree than it is practiced against majority-group members. However, physical abuse is certainly not the only source of irritation to the ghetto resident. Any police practice that degrades a citizen's status, restricts his freedom, or annoys or harasses him is felt to be an unjust use of powers by police enforcement personnel. A policeman talking down to a person or calling him names is particularly objectionable; this type of treatment strips people of their dignity. Police, too, are often inclined to command minority-group members to "get going" or "get home." Because homes in ghetto areas tend to be overcrowded, young ghetto residents are the most likely target of this type of authority. This is true especially during the hot summer months when ghetto youth spend most of their time in public places or walking the streets because they have no other place to go.

In an article by Sam Blum, an incident of police harassment was described. The incident, which occurred in Washington, D.C., involved a man who had been arrested three times in two weeks' time—once for littering when he dropped a paper cup and twice for drinking in public. The latter occurred when the man was found drinking a beer while sitting behind a laundromat.[41] Incidents of this type are generally regarded as police harassment by ghetto residents.

Everyone agrees that each police officer needs to be able to act in a judicious manner in innumerable situations. However, there seems to

[39]National Advisory Commission on Civil Disorder, p. 159.

[40]A. J. Reiss, Jr., "Police Brutality—Answers to Key Questions," *Trans-Action*, 5 (Jul.–Aug. 1968), pp. 10–19.

[41]"The Police," in S. Endleman, ed., *Violence in the Streets* (Chicago: Quadrangle Books, 1968), pp. 417–33.

be further evidence that for a better understanding and a better ability for the police as an organization to deal with the public, that police organization needs to be able to understand all the public it serves. There are those who feel that ethnic minorities cannot be understood by anyone other than a member of that ethnic minority. Whether or not this is true—which by the way the authors don't necessarily believe—is unimportant. The important fact is for the public that is served to believe that it is understood. Consequently, every effort needs to be made to get fair representation of ethnic minorities into law enforcement.

SUMMARY

The inadequacies of justice for minorities were examined from three aspects: (1) minority treatment within the ghetto or barrio, (2) minority-group treatment by the courts, and (3) minority-group treatment by the police.

The black ghetto was examined in some depth because blacks represent the largest minority in the United States and because it was felt that certain generalizations could be made about all types of minority groups who live in slum areas from this examination. The main thrust of this chapter's concern with Spanish-speaking minorities revolved around education.

The ghetto and barrios are characterized by poverty and social disorganization. Mainly because of poverty and segregation, much of the housing in these areas tends to be substandard, overcrowded, aged, and deteriorated. Underemployment and unemployment are critical problems of the ghetto and barrio dweller and may well be the key to his poverty. For example, twice as many black people as white people are unemployed, black people are three times more likely to be underemployed. These circumstances help to strengthen the poverty cycle. For the Spanish minority, the problem of English being a second language affects the ability to succeed in school; this in turn affects job potential—another continuation of the poverty cycle.

Poverty and family disorganization, as well as tension and insecurity, are part of the ghetto and barrio community. Crime rates are far higher than in other areas of the city. Narcotics addiction, juvenile delinquency, veneral disease, poor health services, and dependency on welfare are all prevalent in these areas. The law enforcement student is reminded that the high crime rate causes the residents of these areas to feel bitter toward the police because they believe they do not receive adequate protection from law enforcement.

Neighborhood schools in these areas tend to be the worst in the school system. The result of this is that far more minority-group students leave school before graduating than majority-group students. The regrettable part of this is that a good education has traditionally been the means by which people have escaped from poverty and moved toward more equal treatment within the society.

In this chapter, we reviewed the historic court decisions and statutes that have been instrumental in changing minority-group treatment. Certain other Supreme Court decisions concerning the legal rights of indigent persons were also discussed. Because minority-group members are often without monetary funds, these decisions should have a far-reaching effect on their treatment in the courts. A short critique was made of the bail system, as well as of the handling of civil cases by the courts, to show how persons without funds are often adversely affected by the judicial process.

Police practices and their effect on equal justice regarding minorities were examined. Particular attention was devoted to the police tendency to enforce certain types of violations differently in the ghetto and barrio than elsewhere. An example of this is enforcement of anti-gambling laws in poor sections as opposed to the lack of rigid enforcement in the suburbs.

According to research done by the federal government, acts of police brutality seemingly are not related to minority-group prejudice. Causes of police brutality seem to be more closely related to poverty than to ethnic background. Police harassment, often called police brutality by minorities, is a good example of the problem in communication between police and minority groups. Incidents of police harassment seem to be highest among the youth of ethnic minorities. It is felt that when each individual law enforcement officer understands some of the minority-group complaints regarding unequal justice, he will be better-equipped to understand members of minority groups and to communicate better. Such meaningful communication will lead to the solution of many of the problems in the area of police-community relations.

DISCUSSION TOPICS

1. What is a ghetto? What is a barrio?

2. What does a ghetto or a barrio have to do with equal treatment for minorities?

3. Why should the conditions in a ghetto or barrio be of concern to law enforcement personnel?

4. What does learning English as a second language have to do with the poverty cycle?

5. Explain why it is felt that the courts have changed their attitudes toward minorities over the past 115 years?

6. In what area have the courts been slow in acting in the best interests of minorities?

7. How can consumer protection agencies help alleviate tension in the ghetto and barrio?

8. Explain the difference between police brutality and police harassment.

ANNOTATED REFERENCES

CLEAR, VAL, AND S. CLEAR, "Horizons in the Criminal Justice System", *Crime and Delinquency,* 20, No. 1 (Jan. 1974), pp. 25–32. A concise treatment of changes in the Criminal Justice System.

Department of Health, Education and Welfare, *Equality of Educational Opportunity.* Washington, D.C.: U.S. Government Printing Office, 1966. This report is an extensive study of the education received in ghetto schools as it compares with that of suburban schools. This study is often referred to as the Coleman Report.

ENDLEMAN, S., ed., *Violence in The Streets.* Chicago: Quadrangle Books, 1968. This is a collection of essays regarding violence and police response to criminal behavior. The writers represented in this work seem to form a broad spectrum of political persuasion.

HARRIS, R., *Justice: The Crisis of Law, Order and Freedom in America.* New York: Avon, 1970. An exceptional and perceptive work of political and social analysis.

The *National Commission on the Causes and Prevention of Violence, To Establish Justice, To Insure Domestic Tranquility.* Washington, D.C.: U.S. Government Printing Office, 1969. This is the final report of several Task Force Reports that were concerned with the problem of violence, both group and individual, in the United States.

The *President's Commission on Law Enforcement and Administration of Justice, Task Force Report: The Courts,* Washington, D.C.: U.S. Government Printing Office, 1967. This is part of the supporting material for the Commission's report *The Challenge of Crime in a Free Society.* It provides a very good description of the criminal courts and how they function.

The *President's Commission on Law Enforcement and Administration of Justice, Task Force Report: The Police.* Washington, D.C.: U.S. Government Printing Office, 1967. This is also part of the supporting material for *The Challenge of Crime in a Free Society.* All law enforcement students should probably take time to familiarize themselves with the materials in this book.

Report of the National Advisory Commission on Civil Disorders. Washington, D.C.: U.S. Government Printing Office, 1968. This is a comprehensive study of several of the riots that occurred during the 1960s. It also is an extensive investigation of conditions within the ghetto. This report is often referred to as the Kerner Report.

United States Commission on Civil Rights, Mexican-American Education Study. Washington, D.C.: U.S. Government Printing Office, 1971. This report concerns itself with problems of education of Spanish-speaking children, particularly Mexican-American students in the Southwest.

THE ENFORCEMENT OF LAW DURING SOCIAL CHANGE AND COMMUNITY TENSION

7

Relating the concept of community tension to the concept of social change does not appear to be a difficult task—initially. Once beyond the simple generalizations about change, however, the relationship becomes more complex.

But complex or not, understanding the relationship between change and tension is crucial to understanding *successful* approaches to law enforcement in a changing community—a changing community with high levels of tension.

Perhaps the greatest clarity of the concept of change can be gained by first noting that change is *not optional*. The Grand Canyon is becoming deeper at the rate of one inch a year, whether people approve of such change or not. Scotland moves toward Ireland about eight feet annually, and Europe and the United States are moving about one foot apart each year. London sinks a fraction of an inch annually, while the North Pole moves southward one-half foot.

When you note such changes in the tangible physical world, then changes in the social world should be no surprise. Any difference in human behavior over a period of time is *change*, and differences in human behavior are constantly observable. But change may not always be of a positive nature.

Police family crisis intervention, which we will discuss in greater detail in Chapters eleven and twelve, serves as a good example of the relationship between social change and law enforcement. Police involvement in domestic problems at the present level would have been patently unthinkable before the civil disobedience and riots of the 1960s. Even in jurisdictions in which there existed sophisticated recognition of the proportion and seriousness of police involvement in family affairs, great social change has been necessary to evolve the concept of family crisis intervention. And this is only one of many major modifications of the police function that has followed the social changes of the 1960s. Perhaps the most appropriate way to begin consideration of social change, then, is to discuss the very beginnings of the American culture.

SOCIAL CHANGE

For the most part, early American culture developed in the rural areas. Farmers in the North depended mainly on the labor of their children, and the agrarian economy of the South depended on the labor of slaves. The main source of energy was human beings. Of course inventions in the field of agriculture and the use of tools helped to make human energy more effective, and early rural America enjoyed many labor-saving devices. Nevertheless, the primary source of energy was human effort.

The transition from agriculture to industry, known as the Industrial Revolution, tended to displace both the northern workers and the newly freed southern slaves, forcing them to the cities. These same cities were busily replacing human labor with machinery, however, and at an even faster pace than farms were being mechanized.

One immediate result of the Industrial Revolution was increased leisure for many. In the case of those who worked, the mechanization of labor reduced the amount of time needed to achieve desired production levels. For those unable to gain employment in urban factories, leisure also increased dramatically, if not desirably—at least during periods when employment was being sought. In either event, the dawn-till-dusk workday of the farm began to fade from the American scene. With it also faded the security of the dreary but certain continuation of living out a predictable life on a farm or plantation. Several major wars and a never-ending elimination of jobs by machinery have done little to give the modern urban worker security similar to that of yesterday's farmer—in spite of, and perhaps because of, ever-increasing leisure.

Clearly, America has changed in many other ways, but it is the changes producing the greatest abundance of leisure time that were the sources of many community tensions.

Leisure

Most people would agree that leisure has a great number of positive factors. Discovery of tools and the use of animals along with numerous other sources of energy placed prehistoric man on a path utimately leading to enough free time for the creation of the *arts and sciences*—neither of which was conceivable until sufficient leisure was available.

In this context, leisure tends to gain a favorable connotation, probably because it can be equated either with recreation or productivity. But not all leisure is recreational or productive, and herein lies a source of community tension. Among the unemployed and underemployed of the ghetto, leisure may mean idleness—providing more time in which to get into trouble.

It is worth noting that leisure time in the first half of the 1970s witnessed significant changes for those individuals who were *not* in ghettos and *not* either unemployed or underemployed—the American middle class. Entertainment, in both movies and nightclubs, for example, became increasingly permissive. Middle-class men and women became able to spend some of their leisure time in pursuits that a decade earlier would have generated massive police response in most jurisdictions. The point is, that leisure time *does* relate to law enforcement in recreational areas *outside* the ghetto, even though our general focus of concern is the "nonrecreational" leisure within ghettos or other high-crime areas.

When American "buying habits" are examined, it might seem that the increasing leisure of affluence has been dominated by recreation. Beginning in the World War II decade of 1940 through 1950, expenditures for sports equipment and toys increased threefold, musical instruments and sound equipment fivefold. Money spent for opera and legitimate theater doubled, with opera companies increasing in number from two to thirteen. In the same decade, twice as much money was spent on books, the amount spent on foreign travel increased nearly nine times, and the number of classical music concerts held outside New York City more than doubled. The twenty years that followed showed the same trend.[1]

Such data imply widespread affluence in our country. But not everyone has enjoyed affluence to the same degree; some have not enjoyed it at all. One view of adversity that is dealt with in the literature is that it is more or less a natural consequence of "progress."[2] Of course, to accept such a view without challenge is to question the possibility or at least the advisability of programs geared to alleviate the adverse consequences of social

[1]F. Turck, "The American Explosion," *Scientific Monthly* (Sept. 1952), pp. 187–91.

[2]H. Meissner, ed., *Poverty in Affluent Society* (New York: Harper & Row, 1966), p. 19.

change. But if community tension is to be reduced, the negative results of social change that produce increased leisure *must* be conceived of as correctable. Correction, however, depends on a number of variables relating to the political and economic power. The key variable, in an increasingly automated society, is educational opportunity.

Education

The demand for education grows with social changes that result from increases in technical knowledge. With each discovery of new sources of energy and machinery to replace human labor, there is a corresponding demand for increased sophistication in methods of productivity. *Automation, cybernetics,* and *electronic data processing,* on the one hand, close many avenues of employment by displacing employees. On the other hand, they create many new and promising opportunities, but only for the well-trained and educated. The significance of education then necessarily increases.

Unemployment in America is traditionally a stigma. The moralistic Puritan ideas that developed many of the American work mores drew heavily on the belief that labor is not only imposed by nature as a punishment for sin but is also an ascetic discipline willed by God.[3] This Puritan heritage has led segments of the population to hold some quite rigid tenets. Individuals raised to believe in the necessity for and the value of work are likely to feel that persons who are not employed are simply lazy. Such an oversimplification, of course, ignores the vast complexity involved in examining the *true* nature of competition for meaningful employment. It also reduces the usual confusion in sophisticated analyses of the necessity of *access* to education in order to compete for jobs. But law enforcement personnel who are *increasingly confronted with the violent consequences of such oversimplifications must seek a far more sophisticated view of the causes of unemployment and the role of education in alleviating joblessness.*

Before examining equality of *access* to education, some thought might be given the concept of social change as it relates to education in general. The occupational field of law enforcement itself serves as a model of the lag between the growth of social institutions and the rate of change in modern America. In cities having growing populations, for example, there are fewer police per 10,000 inhabitants than in cities with decreasing populations.[4] In like fashion, certain school programs for the disadvantaged child have lagged far behind the growth in the numbers of these children in the educa-

[3]H. Stein and R. Cloward, *Social Perspectives on Behavior* (New York: The Free Press, 1967), p. 273.

[4]W. Ogburn, "Cultural Lag as Theory," *Sociology and Social Research* (Jan.–Feb. 1957), pp. 167–74. Also, *Social Characteristics of Cities* (International City Managers Association, 1937).

FIGURE 7.1.   Courtesy Elizabeth Police Department, Elizabeth, New Jersey.

tion system.[5] This lag has continued in spite of the compulsory school attendance that distinguishes the United States from much of the world.[6]

Social change, bringing increases in leisure, brings attention to education in two ways. As already noted, an increased demand for technical skill accompanies the discovery of new sources of energy and labor-saving machinery. Here there is, of course, an obvious role for education and training. But social change draws attention to the *length of time* necessary for a student to complete his education.

Both family and the public have traditionally been prepared to support a child's education through at least grade school and often through high school. But what about college? And how much college?

Before the "knowledge explosion" following the technical advances of World War II, college was not a requisite in most people's education. But automation, combined with government sponsorship through the GI Bill and other subsidized college programs, has rapidly focused attention on college training as a crucial part of the educational process. To many, this social change has unveiled vast new horizons of opportunity. To others, it has even further widened the gap between affluence and poverty. For unlike the masses of middle-class families prepared and motivated to support children through the increasing expenses of education, poverty-stricken families necessarily consider the child of high school age a potential source

[5]R. Kerckhoff, "The Problem of the City School," *Journal of Marriage and the Family,* 26, No. 4 (Nov. 1964), pp. 435–39.

[6]E. Friedenberg, "An Ideology of School Withdrawal," *Community,* 35, No. 6 (June 1963), pp. 492–500.

of income, for some relief from the drain on limited family income. The relatively small number of college students from poor backgrounds should not then be surprising, even in the rare instances in which *adequate* high school programs were available.

There are many sources of community tension, but none are so great as the social changes that increase the disparity of opportunity to control one's destiny. Education is increasingly the prime ingredient in the potential of ultimate control.

Of course there are as many "solutions" to community tension as there are sources—education merely serving as a prime influence and sometimes as a common denominator of sources. The community development concept is often cited as a solution somewhat removed from the direct influence of education—but it is cited without acknowledgment of the attendant problems.

> Those who use the term "community development" (their number is legion) are enthusiastic for vague reasons. They are strongly in favor of "community" (whatever that may be). And they are equally in favor of "development" (as long as this moves toward their preferred objectives).
>
> But the enthusiasts encounter difficulties when they become specific. They do not agree upon what "the community" is that they hope to develop. Their confusion reflects the fact that ordinary citizens have lost or are losing the sense of community, the experience of community. Whether the people live in older apartments or in new housing developments, in inner-city slums or in unincorporated urban fringes, in affluent or in not-so-affluent suburbs, in smaller cities and towns or in sparsely settled areas in trailers or in lodgings for transients, they find neighborly relationships difficult to maintain and less than satisfying.[7]

Bearing in mind that *all* "solutions" to community tension encounter similar problems, we will now turn our attention away from the powerful influence of the educational element in solving community tension problems to the problems of community tension itself.

THE POTENTIAL IMPACT OF COMMUNITY TENSION

There are numerous causes of community unrest. Many of these lie beyond the scope of law enforcement or of criminal justice. There is, nonetheless, a significant relationship between law enforcement and certain aspects

---

[7]William W. Biddle, with Loureide J. Biddle, *The Community Development Process—The Rediscovery of Local Initiative* (New York: Holt, Rinehart and Winston, 1965), p. 1.

FIGURE 7.2.   *Courtesy Los Angeles Police Department, Los Angeles, Cal.*

of unrest. As noted, symptoms of unrest frequently foreshadow direct intervention by law enforcement agencies. Moreover, law enforcement may even become involved in various casual aspects of community tension. The relationship of law enforcement to such community unrest has been placed in excellent context in Frank Remington's comments on arrest practice:

> ... from the point of view of either the individual or the community as a whole, the issue is not so much whether police are efficient, or whether the corrective system is effective, but whether the system of criminal justice in its entirety is sensible, fair, and consistent with the concepts of a democratic society. ... [8]

In this context, at least part of the community tension can be thought of, first, as a disparity between various citizens in terms of their potential to control their own destiny. Second, unrest may be thought of as a reaction to the method of enforcing conformity to a system that creates or permits this inequality. In other words, a system that is not "sensible, fair, or consistent with the concepts of a democratic society" may become as much a source of community tension as the social changes that created the original disparity.

[8]F. Remington, Foreword, in W. LaFave's *Arrest* (Boston: Little, Brown, 1965).

As noted elsewhere throughout this volume, the person's position within the overall society influences the belief in the system's fairness or lack of it.

The plight of millions of impoverished Americans has captured the attention of the press, welfare agencies, local, state, and federal bureaus and the general public more than any other possible domestic aspect of our contemporary society, with the possible exception of civil rights. There is also a rapidly growing body of professional literature on poverty, coming from workers in many disciplines. Many of the researches on which these reports are based are relevant not only to applied, practical problems such as allocations of funds or administration of educational programs, but also to more theoretical considerations concerning human development, learning and the relationship between culture and personality.[9]

Beyond concern for the influences flowing between culture and personality, there is the law enforcement concern for what position the individual *believes* himself to be in as a result of these influences. More to the point, *are there possibly methods through which law enforcement can influence all positions to strive for a sensible and fair system?*

Unrest Without Violence

Of course determining what is sensible, fair, and consistent with democratic concepts may not be completely possible for law enforcement in an era of grossly divergent and constantly changing demands. But to whatever degree law enforcement is able to achieve a system having these attributes, to at least that degree is community tension likely to be reduced.

The significance of such a reduction is probably most perceptible in distinguishing between a demonstration and a riot. Throughout this book this distinction is discussed in terms of the *behavior* of the group involved. And more often than not, the behavior itself relates directly to law enforcement. It would seem reasonable to generalize that rioters rarely conceive of law enforcement as sensible, fair, and consistent, whereas possibly many demonstrators do not riot simply because they believe the police have nothing to do with social changes that cause tension. But in many instances police have borne the brunt of violence erupting out of demonstrations protesting social problems having no connection with law enforcement. It remains a valid area of conjecture that at least the *degree* of violence relates to the attitude of the rioter toward law enforcement.

Regrettably, having enforcement systems that satisfy the criteria of

---

[9]Salvador Minuchin, Braulio Montalvo, Bernard Guerney, Jr., Bernice L. Rosman, and Florence Schumer, *Families of The Slums—An Exploration of Their Structure and Treatment* (New York: Basic Books, 1967), p. 21.

making sense and being fair does not *insure* favorable attitudes toward enforcement.

The Impact of Publicity

Beyond the criteria of making sense and being fair, attitudes toward enforcement are often shaped by publicity—often by *sensational* publicity.

"Sensationalism," as it is often called, is the kind of press coverage of police matters that emphasizes the "incident" more than the "causes"— emphasizes the "dramatic" more than the "rational." Not surprisingly, such publicity often obscures rather than clarifies how an enforcement system "makes sense" or is "fair."

While police could scarcely control the often unfavorable impact of sensational publicity, a great deal could be done to foster other forms of publicity that encourage a more positive attitude toward police. Actively calling press conferences to present progressive programs is one possibility.

But simply presenting a "progressive program" may not, in itself, attract publicity, favorable or otherwise. However, where matters with public "appeal" are *featured*, the chances of attracting favorable publicity improve. Consider, for example, the hiring of minorities or women in police service, as features of some "progressive" program.

There is no doubt that police, in general, could improve the general approach to press relations and, in turn, improve the impact of publicity. Consider the following:

> It is a fact of newspapering that most seasoned police reporters know more about the inner workings of law enforcement agencies than the peace officers know about the principles of journalism. Accordingly, for many reporters of good will, educating the cops is an ongoing ambition. We want police to recognize the public's right to know about their operations. We want them to realize that it is news media's constitutional obligation to fulfill that right.
>
> In any educating process, it takes two to tango. The police must be willing. If they are, and the learning begins, the eyes of both "sides"— press and police, attempting in their own ways to serve a shared community—are likely to be opened wider. . . .[10]

Sensationalizing problems and the causes of problems tends to aggravate community tension not so much through the distortion of facts as through the distortion of *perspective*. In the many contacts of law enforcement with all segments of the public, some abuses of police power are real, some are fancied. Both are frequently reported. But when the abuses of power are *real*, this is newsworthy because it is *not* expected.

[10]Carter Barber, "A Magna Carta for Media-Police Relations," *The Police Chief*, 37, No. 9 (Sept. 1970), p. 28.

FIGURE 7.3. *Student unrest on campuses throughout the United States has had a tremendous effect on police tactics, manpower, and financial resources. Photo courtesy of the San Francisco Police Department, San Francisco, California.*

Reporting of a sensational type about police brutality may serve two functions; law enforcement should be aware of both in its struggle for an equitable system. *First,* sensational news is of high commercial value. *Second,* it has great attention-gaining value to any group seeking relief for actual or imagined social ills. This realization on the part of law enforcement personnel will help to anticipate the *causes* of sensationalism that may lead to community tension. As a result, there will be better communication between police and the community.

Improving Police-Community Communication

Perhaps the era of the riot has passed. There appears a quieting of the more violent forms of campus demonstrations of the variety that marked the 1960s. But police responsibility to understand and deal realistically with social change will remain. This responsibility, of course, includes the anticipation and prevention of overwhelming social tensions flowing from social change. In meeting this responsibility, and in order to prevent the polarity that tends to exist between the police and the community, law enforcement must be aware of the implications of the following quotations:

> ... Professionalism has brought a necessary raising of standards into municipal policing, and has served as a vehicle for the introduction of

much-needed technological and managerial reforms. Its inherent autonomy, however, has interfered with its ability to change to meet new citizen expectations. It is clear that the public endorses a more aggressive program of minority recruitment than most police departments now pursue. Citizen involvement at a routine level of policy making is also supported. Little evidence emerged from the latter survey to support the claim of professional policemen that police operations should be determined and evaluated on a largely internal basis.

These shifts in concern are significant because they involve an occupation that has become increasingly insular, in response not only to its professional ideology but also to rising public pressures for effectiveness and greater representation. This insularity threatens to increase existing antagonism between the police and segments of the public, unless police leaders recognize the degree to which citizens would support their efforts for a more flexible approach to police policy making.[11]

The American police service is founded upon the principle that the police are a part of and not apart from the people. This principle dictates that the police make a determined effort to seek information from the public, to weigh conflicting demands and ideas, and to arrive at considered judgments. It also requires that the police inform the people how to protect themselves against crime as well as how to cooperate with police to reduce crime.

Effective two-way communication between the police and the public helps the public understand police decisions and helps the police measure their success or failure in enforcing the law and in fulfilling community expectations. Information from the public reflects the degree of trust and confidence that the people have in their police and government. The public's attitude toward the police—including hostility and its causes—should be considered by police administrators in allocating resources and developing programs.

Some segments of society have little confidence in their government and no confidence in their police. This lack of confidence could become a chasm of total misunderstanding without communication. Obviously the police task is much more difficult if police are feared rather than trusted by the people.

Police agencies have responded in a variety of ways to local situations in establishing programs to facilitate bilateral communication with their communities. The following programs have had varying degrees of success; they are offered as illustrations of possible approaches, not as standards to be adopted by all police agencies.

One common method of soliciting community suggestions and determining community attitudes toward police agencies is through neighborhood meetings between members of the public and beat officers. The Berkeley, California, Police Department's Neighborhood Work-

---

[11]Gene E. Carte, "Public Attitudes toward the Police," *Journal of Police Science and Administration*, 1, No. 2 (June 1973), p. 200.

shops and the "Coffey Klatches" that have been instituted by many agencies are examples of programs using the home of a neighborhood volunteer as a setting for informal discussions between officers and members of the community.

In several cities, Citizen Advisory Councils advise police agencies on formulation of policies and development of community crime prevention programs. Such councils, if truly representative, can serve as an effective means of determining the needs and expectations of the community as well as a forum for explaining and encouraging acceptance of policies developed in response to those needs.

Although community-police advisory councils have been established by city ordinance in cities such as Berkeley and Seattle, most do not have a formal basis of authority. The success of community advisory councils, both formal and informal, depends largely upon how representative of the community the council members are, and upon the willingness of police agencies to consider and act on their recommendations. Therefore, police agencies should attempt to insure the independence of the council and be receptive to its recommendations.

Several large police agencies have established "storefront centers" to provide greater public access to a wide variety of referral services. These centers serve as a way to communicate with the public, as well as aiding them.[12]

Although not the primary source of community tension, public apathy and indifference to crime provide an excellent barometer for measuring the success or failure of police efforts to communicate with the community. In terms of such apathy and indifference, consider the following:

1. *Citizen apathy and indifference contribute to the spread of crime.* If we are to reduce crime, what is needed is a willingness on the part of every citizen to give of himself: his time, his energy and his imagination. Judging by the size of the crime problem, our record is not impressive. Preferring to ignore the frustration and rage that produces crime and developing a ponderous bureaucracy to deal with symptoms has substituted for striking at the core of the problem itself.

Enlisting the American conscience on behalf of community crime prevention is at once an ironic and necessary procedure. It is ironic because of the hue and cry about the current volume of crime. There appears to be a widespread assumption that it is the business of the criminal justice system to respond to this demand and to marshal all available resources to choke off crime at its roots. This viewpoint neglects the certainty that unless a worried citizenry can translate its indignation into active participation in the search for and implementa-

---

[12]As appears in *Working Papers for the National Conference on Criminal Justice,* Washington, D.C., Jan. 23–26, 1973, p. P-137.

tion of an effective solution, the criminal justice system must inevitably fall even further behind in its crime control and rehabilitation efforts. Awakening the conscience of America is a *necessity* because if the multiplicity of factors that produce crime and delinquency are not recognized and remedied, more crime will occur, more of it will go undetected, and the inadequacies of the system will thus become even stronger incentive to further illegal activity.

How does one enlist the public conscience as the initial step in a concerted *community* effort at crime prevention? How is social sensitivity and awareness to be substituted for indifference? Where does a campaign begin to replace widespread apathy with enlightened and responsible citizen action? The answers to these and a litany of similar questions become apparent if we can successfully define community crime prevention as an urgent national priority.

There must be an energetic national campaign whose aim is to sensitize communities to the dimensions of the problem and the level of effort necessary to provide a solution. The commission report contains suggestions for action at the local level and offers guidelines for individual citizens, communities and organizations who may wish to cooperate in voluntary and governmental activity directed against crime and its causes. The commission believes that effective crime prevention is possible only through broad-based community awareness and involvement. Many communities have already recognized this reality and acted on it and the report cites numerous examples of crime and delinquency prevention programs and projects. Hopefully, these success stories will serve as a catalyst and incentive to new efforts in all our states, cities and communities.

2. *Private and public agencies and institutions outside the criminal justice system contribute to rises and declines in the incidence of criminal behavior.*

A major focus of the report is on more efficient and responsive delivery of general services—education, manpower development, recreation, medical and other social services. Better delivery of these services should increase the confidence of citizens in public and private institutions and thus foster cooperation with these institutions—including those of the criminal justice system.

There is an abundance of evidence to indicate that delinquency and crime occur with greater frequency where there is also poverty, illiteracy, unemployment, inadequate medical, recreational and mental health resources. To the extent that effective and responsive delivery of public and private services promotes individual economic and social well-being the Commission believes this will contribute to a reduction in crime.

Perhaps a quotation from a section in the citizen action chapter called "Attacking Crime's Infrastructure" will focus on this principle. Having called for citizen attention on such social priorities as employment, education and recreation, the discussion continues:

This is not to say that if everyone were better educated or more fully employed that crime would be eliminated or even sharply reduced. What is meant is that unemployment, substandard education, and so on, form a complex, and admittedly little understood, amalgam of social conditions that cements, or at least predisposes, many individuals to criminal activity.

Thus a job, for example, is just one wedge by which to break this amalgam. Increased recreational opportunities represent another. Though one wedge may not have much effect on an individual's life style, two or three might.

3. Community crime prevention efforts include demonstrable benefits for existing institutions and agencies organized toward the achievement of other primary goals.

The Task Force on Community Crime Prevention recognized the need to enlist the cooperation and assistance of institutions, agencies and groups already existing in communities. School systems, manpower resources, rehabilitative and social welfare agencies, mental health clinics, labor unions, private businesses and industry, churches, clubs and social organizations all serve people in a variety of ways by responding to different needs.

An employer who sponsors a drug education or treatment program for his employees thereby advances his own economic interests and contributes to a decline in the incidence and dangers of drug abuse in his community. School-sponsored job counseling and referral services can effectively reduce the number of dropouts and many young people will therefore avoid the idleness and boredom that may contribute to juvenile delinquency. Churches and community clubs willing to make their facilities and personnel available on a broader basis can attract new members to their programs while at the same time providing expanded recreational and social opportunities to many heretofore excluded.

There must be a clear recognition on the part of community organizations, agencies and facilities that the degree of imagination, efficiency and enthusiasm they bring to their own work impacts directly on crime prevention. Accordingly, individual chapters of this report address themselves to citizen involvement, public school education, employment, recreation, the church, drug abuse prevention programs, and a heightened responsiveness of governmental services. Institutions are not asked to redefine themselves and their functions to accommodate the purpose of this Task Force. Rather, suggestions are provided for ways to harmonize efforts toward community crime prevention.[13]

As already noted, community tensions, in a large measure, reflect social changes over which the police have no control. But the area of contact between police and public is singularly susceptible to community relations

---

[13]Ibid., p. CC–1–3.

programming. (Refer to Appendix C). And just as change is inevitable, the obvious methods of meeting the problems of change through awareness must be *feasible*. To remain of value, the manner in which all justice is dispensed, particularly in a changing community, must remain functional, problems of change or not.[14] The ultimate initiative always falls on the shoulders of law enforcement personnel when avoiding gross civil disruption is the goal.

Accepting responsibility for such initiative of course means many things to law enforcement. But above all else, it means developing a *systematic* and *effective* organizational approach to the problem. The final chapter of this volume will present the concept of programming such activities, but brief consideration of police programs of this nature may prove useful in clarifying police concern with social change, community tension and public communication.

Every police agency should recognize the importance of bilateral communication with the public and should constantly seek to improve its ability to determine the needs and expectations of the public, to act upon those needs and expectations, and to inform the public of the resulting policies developed to improve delivery of police services.

1. Every police agency should immediately adopt policies and procedures which provide for effective communication with the public through agency employees. Those policies and procedures should:

   a. Ensure that every employee having duties which involve public contact has sufficient information with which to respond to questions regarding agency policies; and

   b. Ensure that information which he receives is transmitted through the chain of command and acted upon at the appropriate level.

2. Every police agency which has racial and ethnic minority groups of significant size within its jurisdiction should recognize their police needs and should where appropriate develop means to ensure effective communication with such groups.

3. Every police agency which has a substantial non-English speaking minority within its jurisdiction should provide readily available bilingual employees to answer requests for police services. In addition, existing agency programs should be adapted to ensure adequate communication between such non-English speaking minority groups and the police agency.

4. Every police agency having more than 400 personnel should establish a specialized unit responsible for maintaining communication with

---

[14]A. Coffey, "Correctional Probation: What Use to Society?" *Journal of the California Probation and Parole Association*, 5, No. 1 (1968), p. 28.

the community. In smaller agencies, this responsibility should be the chief executive's, using whatever agency resources are necessary and appropriate to accomplish the task.

a. The unit should open and keep open lines of communication between the agency and recognized community leaders and should elicit information from the citizen on the street who may feel that he has little voice in government or in the provision of its services.

b. The unit should be no more than one step removed from the chief executive in the chain of command.

c. The unit should identify impediments to communication with the community, research and devise methods to overcome those impediments, and develop programs which facilitate communication between the agency and the community.

d. The unit should conduct ongoing evaluations of all programs intended to improve communication and should recommend discontinuance of programs when their objectives have been achieved or when another program might more beneficially achieve the identified functional objective.[15]

As will be noted in Chapters Eleven and Twelve, police efforts to open greater channels of communication afford many advantages in terms of the *overall* law enforcement program—advantages related to police image and the prevention of development of law enforcement problems. Police can, with effort, determine in virtually all areas of criminal justice the degree to which the public supports or fails to support the system of justice.

SUMMARY

This chapter discussed the concept of *social change* as it relates to unrest and tension in the community. *Change* is seen as an ongoing process, subject not to prevention but only to control. As an elaboration of the social problems discussed earlier, major social changes in society were discussed in relationship to law enforcement.

The Industrial Revolution that changed America from a rural agrarian economy to a culture of urbanized automation was a prime mover toward greater leisure—leisure that is an advantage to the employable and a disadvantage to those without employable skills. The ensuing demand for employable skills are part of the changing cultural focus on access to higher education. Education is not available equally and, therefore, can be an additional source of community tension.

The unemployment accompanying the Industrial Revolution must be

[15]*Working Papers for the National Conference on Criminal Justice*, p. P-136.

considered in the context of Puritan ethics. Law enforcement personnel must acquire a more sophisticated understanding of the true factors in poverty if greater community unrest is to be avoided.

Community tension per se flows from many social changes, the majority of which are beyond the control of law enforcement. Nevertheless, a system of enforcing law that is sensible, fair, and consistent with democratic concepts is an important method of reducing community tension.

The response of law enforcement to social change and community tension must be functional. The detrimental impact of sensationalizing alleged abuses of police power is unusually susceptible to correction through programs geared to reduce community tension (or at least to increase public confidence in the system of enforcing law).

DISCUSSION TOPICS

1. Contrast social change and community tension in the context presented in the introduction to this chapter.

2. Elaborate the rationale for considering the relationship between social change and community tension as being more complex than it appears.

3. Discuss the concept of change. Of *social* change.

4. Discuss the sources of increased leisure in America. The variety of uses to which leisure is put. The nature of leisure.

5. Relate social change to community tension.

6. Relate community tension to law enforcement.

7. Relate community tension and the access to education.

8. Discuss education and automation as they relate to poverty.

9. What is the usual impact on community tension of sensationalizing alleged abuses of power by the police?

ANNOTATED REFERENCES

COFFEY, ALAN R., *Criminal Justice Administration: A Management Systems Approach.* Englewood Cliffs, N.J.: Prentice-Hall, Inc., 1974. Full, in-depth and comprehensive elaboration of the management technology required to develop programs of the nature suggested at the conclusion of this chapter.

COFFEY, ALAN R., AND VERNON RENNER, eds., *Criminal Justice: Readings.* Englewood Cliffs, N.J.: Prentice-Hall, Inc., 1974. A widely varied selection of relevant articles bearing directly and indirectly upon police and other criminal justice functions during an era of social change.

LaFave, W., *Arrest*. Boston: Little, Brown, 1965. An extremely comprehensive coverage of the power boundaries of law enforcement in the community.

Meissner, H., ed., *Poverty in Affluent Society*. New York: Harper & Row, 1966. A collection of contributions dealing with the many influences of poverty on the community.

Minuchin, S., B. Montalvo, B. Guerney, B. Rosman, and F. Schumer, *Families of the Slums*. New York: Basic Books, 1967. Excellent coverage of the subject—particularly of corrective measures for the problems such families encounter.

Noel, D., "A Theory of the Origin of Ethnic Stratification," *Social Problems*, 16, No. 2 (Fall 1968), pp. 157–72. A plausible explanation of the social separation of ethnic grouping.

Smith, A. B., and H. Pollack, *Crime and Justice in a Mass Society*. Lexington, Mass.: Xerox College Publishing, 1972. The nature of social control in American society is discussed in layman terms. Many other areas, pertinent to Chapter 7 of this text, are analyzed.

Stein, H., and R. Cloward, *Social Perspectives on Behavior*. New York: The Free Press, 1967. A varied, comprehensive sociological coverage of the nature of human conduct.

SIGNIFICANCE OF ATTITUDES IN POLICE WORK

8

Hostile attitudes of citizens toward the police are probably as disruptive of order as is police malpractice. But citizens probably will not get the complete protection their taxes are paying for until they change their viewpoint toward law enforcement officers. In many ways this presents a paradox in that, generally speaking, the people who display the most animosity toward the police need their protection the most. Many minority-group members harbor a resentment against authority and have doubts about American ideals. In consideration of the history of race relations as well as ghetto conditions in the United States, these by-products should be expected.

A report by the federal government expresses this problem most succinctly:

It is ... almost ... a truism that ghetto residents will not obtain the police protection they badly want and need until policemen feel that their presence is welcome and that their problems are understood. However, in the effort to achieve this state of affairs, the duty of taking the initiative clearly devolves on the police, both because they are organized and disciplined and because they are public servants sworn to protect every part of the community.[1]

[1]The *President's Commission on Law Enforcement and Administration of Justice*, *The Challenge of Crime in a Free Society* (Washington, D.C.: U.S. Government Printing Office, 1967), p. 100.

The major problem with the police taking the initiative is that they first must have some understanding of people's motives and attitudes, how they were formed, and how they can be changed. The rest of this chapter will provide a basis for this understanding.

APPROACHES TO STUDYING HUMAN BEHAVIOR

The behavior of mankind can be studied from two points of view. The first focuses on the group processes of mankind. Broadly speaking, this is the *sociological* approach. The second is the *study of the individual.* This chapter will concern itself with the latter approach.

Obviously, these methods cannot be completely independent of one another. Because man is a social being as well as an individual, they are interdependent. To better study the behavior of the individual, we will use a framework that views social behavior as being influenced by various factors.

According to S. Stanfeld Sargent, there are five major factors that influence social behavior: the nature of the social situation, the norms of the social group, the individual's personality, his transitory condition, and his perception.[2]

The Nature of the Social Situation. An onlooker might cheer for a fighter in the boxing ring but not at a street fight. The two fights are generally considered different social situations.

The Norms of the Social Group. A delinquent gang member and a middle class teenager react to the police in different ways.

Personality. A person who has an authoritarian personality will act more rigidly in social situations. Personality is the result of both heredity and environment.

Transitory condition. An angry individual will probably react to a peace officer in a much different manner than one who is not angry. Transitory conditions include various physical and emotional states, such as illness, drunkenness, etc.

Perception. If a person perceives the police as a Gestapo-like organization, he will react to them in a much different manner than if he perceived them as friends.

---

[2]*Social Psychology: An Integrative Interpretation* (New York: Ronald Press, 1950), pp. 242–71.

ATTITUDES

When social scientists wish to describe how an individual perceives situations and objects and how his behavior is affected by these perceptions, they do so in terms of *attitudes*. David Krech and Richard S. Crutchfield define attitude *as a long-lasting perceptual, motivational, emotional, and adaptive organizational process concerned with a person or object.*[3] Attitudes may be either negative or positive. Basically, this means that an individual might be favorably or unfavorably predisposed toward a person or object.

It can be seen that by this definition prejudice can be regarded as a kind of attitude. Prejudice categorizes persons or objects in a good or bad light—usually in a bad light—without regard to the facts.

Attitudes are regarded as having various dimensions and attributes. There are five dimensions which appear to be most descriptive of attitudes. These dimensions have been suggested in works by Krech and Crutchfield[4] and Klineberg.[5] In this text we have modified and adapted them to fit the subject. They are briefly described and illustrated below:

1. *Direction*: What is the direction of the attitude? Is it for or against the person or object?
2. *Degree*: How positive or negative is the attitude?
3. *Content*: Although various individuals may dislike the police in the same degree, this does not necessarily mean that their attitudes are the same. Investigation of the content of their attitudes may show that they perceive

FIGURE 8.1. *An opinion pollster gathering information.*

[3] *Elements of Psychology* (New York: Alfred A. Knopf, 1960), p. 692.
[4] Ibid., pp. 672–73.
[5] O. Klineberg, *Social Psychology* (New York: Holt, Rinehart & Winston, 1954), pp. 489–90.

the police in markedly different ways. The attitude of one may stem from unpleasant personal contacts, while another may feel antipathy to police because as a child he was taught to dislike them.

4. *Consistency:* Attitudes differ in how they are integrated and related to other attitudes that a person may hold. One person, for example, may show enmity toward police because he sees them as enforcers for the power structure. Another may have a dislike for the police that does not fit into his general framework of beliefs and attitudes. Consistency relates to the dimension of strength.

5. *Strength:* Some attitudes continue for a long time despite data that contradict them. These are known as strong attitudes. Weaker attitudes are those that are easily changed.

It can be seen that attitudes may serve many functions. Generally speaking, a man's ability to react consistently in situations is made possible by his attitudes. These combine his many feelings and experiences, creating a meaningful totality. How this comes about has been speculated upon by many social scientists. Two theories that we will examine are the *psychoanalytical theory* and the *learning theory*. These theories will be looked at more closely because they have been used considerably more frequently than other theories to explain the development of attitudes by minority-group members and/or ghetto residents.

Minority-Group Attitudes and the Psychoanalytical Theory

Psychoanalytical theory is concerned with the development of the individual from early childhood, as well as with motivational conflicts that might occur at any time. Basically, development is a kind of unfolding of the sexual impulses, certain transformations being the result. This theory emphasizes changes within a person, with a stronger emphasis on biological maturation than on social and environmental influences. Greatly simplifying the matter, we can say that culture and experience affect sexual impulses, and these, in turn, affect behavior and attitudes. (On the other hand, the *learning theories* suggest that culture and experience directly affect behavior and attitudes.)

One psychoanalytical theory of how attitudes are acquired by minority-group members is set forth by William H. Grier and Price M. Cobbs, using the Black as an example.[6] According to these authors, everyone in the United States grows up with the idea of white supremacy. Some Americans, furthermore, find that it is a basic part of their nationhood to despise black people. No one who lives in this country can avoid this hatred. Black people are no exception, and in essence, they are taught to hate themselves.

[6]*Black Rage* (New York: Basic Books, 1968).

Grier and Cobbs believe that these attitudes have been rooted in American life since the days of slavery. Black people have been oppressed and treated as inferiors so many times and in so many ways that they themselves are often convinced that they are inferior. Their thinking has been so perverted that they even feel there is a connection between high status and fair skin. For instance, the black woman's personality is undermined from girlhood. She is the antithesis of the "American" concept of beauty, for her blackness is the opposite of the creamy white skin that seems so desirable in the American culture.

Conversely, the black man occupies a very special sexual role in American society. He tends to be thought of as possessing great masculine vigor. However, at the same time, he is rendered socially, politically, and economically impotent. Very often, he even lacks the power to fulfill the fundamental role of providing a good living and protection for his family. Consequently, the Negro males' attitudes toward American society and toward law enforcement, the guardian of that society, are often greatly affected by their own self-concepts. It is obvious that the self-concept of blacks needs to be enhanced, particularly in the school, economical, and political areas. The slogan, "Black is beautiful" and all that this entails is an attempt to improve this self-concept.

Minority-Group Attitudes and the Learning Theory

Learning theory, in its broadest sense, suggests that a person is born into a social environment, and his personality is shaped as a result of his interaction with other human beings in this social environment.

The distinguishing characteristic of a culture is that it contains a body of behavioral patterns such as skills, habits, and activities. Also, certain types of thought patterns may be as much a part of the culture as are behavioral patterns. Thus, it can be seen that attitudes and opinions may well be determined by culture and, in turn, may reflect that culture and/or subculture.

The subculture of the ghetto tends to be made up of persons from the low class, by virtue of their inability to succeed economically. As explained in Chapter Six, this inability does not appear to be the ghetto resident's fault in most cases. According to Walter B. Miller, lower-class culture has a set of attitudes that are passed on to each succeeding generation. "A large body of systematic interrelated attitudes, practices, behaviors, and value characteristics of lower-class culture are designed to support and maintain the basis of the lower-class structure."[7]

The lower-class attitude toward the police tends to be hostile. A study

---

[7]See "Lower-Class Culture as a Generating Milieu of Gang Delinquency," *Journal of Social Issues*, 14, No. 3 (1958), pp. 5–19.

by Hollingshead and Redlick describes this hostility thus: "A deep-seated distrust of authority figures pervades ... [lower socioeconomic class] persons from childhood to old age. Suspicion is directed toward police, clergymen, teachers. ..."[8]

In addition to frequently being a member of the lower class and being thoroughly indoctrinated with the values of his class, the black person has had experiences which have further alienated him from law enforcement. By and large, one of the more important contacts the black man makes with white society has been through the white policeman. Therefore, the policeman has personified white authority. In the past, he not only enforced laws and regulations but also the whole set of social customs associated with the concept of "white supremacy." Historically, law enforcement was on the side of the slave-master. In more recent times, the so-called Jim Crow laws (primarily found in the South) of separate facilities were stringently enforced by the police. Minor transgressions of caste etiquette were punished by the policeman on an extrajudicial basis.[9]

A REVIEW OF SOME STUDIES OF ATTITUDES TOWARD THE POLICE

Opinions are closely related to attitudes. The term *attitude* implies a preparation to act, while *opinion* refers to what we believe is true. Because what we believe to be true affects our readiness to act in a certain way, it can be seen that opinions and attitudes are intertwined. Because of this,

FIGURE 8.2. *Typical of the South before the mid 1950s. (See the Report of the National Advisory Commission on Civil Disorder, 1968, pp. 92, 112.) Separate facilities were the rule.*

[8]A. B. Hollingshead, and F. C. Redlick, *Social Class and Mental Illness: A Community Study* (New York: Wiley & Sons, 1968), p. 130.

[9]A. Rose, *The Negro in America* (Boston: Beacon Press, 1948), pp. 170–88.

we shall be concerned with both attitudes and opinions while reviewing studies of attitudes toward the police.

Another thought to be considered when reviewing studies of attitudes is that, at this time, it is not possible to apply the scientific approach to human behavior with the same degree of certainty that it is applied to the physical sciences. We know, for example, that just amassing data does not necessarily lead to understanding human behavior. It is not, however, necessary to make exacting evaluations of all the factors that operate in regard to human behavior. Rather, from a practical standpoint, we will identify only the major trends of behavior so we can understand human behavior and attitudes more fully.

Task Force Report: The Police[10]

A great deal of research has been conducted into the public's attitude and opinions regarding the police. The best gathering and reporting of research information, despite its age, is still the 1967 *Task Force Report: The Police*. It drew upon a number of sources for its information, such as a 1966 Harris Poll, a 1965 Gallup Poll, and a survey conducted by the National Opinion Research Center.

The results of these three surveys showed substantially the same thing. The Harris Poll indicated that the public rated local law enforcement as good or excellent 65 percent of the time, state law enforcement as good or excellent 70 percent of the time, and federal law enforcement good or excellent 76 percent of the time. The Gallup Poll found that 70 percent of the public had a good deal of respect for the police, 22 percent had some respect, and only 4 percent had hardly any respect for the police. The National Opinion Research Center, which is affiliated with the University of Chicago, conducted similar studies in 1947 and in 1963. In 1947, 41 percent of those polled indicated that they thought the police had an excellent or a good standing in the community. In 1963, 54 percent were of this opinion. No other occupational group achieved such a striking improvement in its image as did the police during that sixteen-year period.

The *Task Force Report* cites a number of other studies which suggest that there is no widespread police-community relations problem. However, the report goes on to point out that these surveys only show *part* of the community's reaction. When a comparison is made between the Caucasian and the Negro community, an interesting difference of opinion and/or attitude becomes apparent.

The National Opinion Research Center surveys show that nonwhites,

[10]The *President's Commission on Law Enforcement and Administration of Justice, Task Force Report: The Police* (Washington, D.C.: U.S. Government Printing Office, 1967), pp. 145–49.

particularly Negroes, are much more negative than Caucasians in evaluating police efficiency. Nonwhites indicated only half as often as Caucasians that police gave protection to citizens at a very good rate. Furthermore, nonwhites tended to give a not-so-good rating twice as often as whites. According to the report, these differences are not merely a result of greater poverty among nonwhites; rather, the differences exist at all income levels, and among both men and women.

The *Task Force Report* further indicates that a bare majority (51 percent) of nonwhites, as recorded in the Louis Harris Poll, believed that local law enforcement was doing a good or excellent job. This is 16 percent lower than the rating among Caucasians. Another survey by John F. Kraft cited in the Task Force Report[11] indicated that 47 percent of Negroes believed the police did an excellent job, while 41 percent thought they were doing a not-so-good or a poor job.

Generally, the information seems to show that approximately two-thirds to three-fourths of the Caucasian community believe that police deserve more respect and are doing a good job, while approximately half the Negro community feels that police deserve more respect and are doing a good job. Percentage differences between what the racial groups think about police performance range from 16 to 25 percent. Obviously, the Negro population has a much less favorable attitude toward police than does the Caucasian population. However, the surveys may not accurately reflect the extent of minority-group dissatisfaction with law enforcement. When in-depth interviews are held with minority-group members, frequently neutral or even favorable statements at the beginning of the interview give way to strong statements of hostility before it is over. A study by Paul A. Fine reported upon in the Task Force Report points up the fact that there is intense hostility toward police in the Negro community.[12] This hostility is clearly pointed out when the factor of age is included. In most research studies, only adult attitudes are measured. When young minors of an ethnic minority were interviewed it became apparent that the anti-police attitude is much greater. In one study, it was found that approximately 30 percent of the black people over the age of 45 had anti-police attitudes, while approximately 60 percent of the black males between 15 and 29 thought there was a great deal of police brutality. Furthermore, over half of the black males under the age of 35 stated that they had been subjected to insulting remarks by police and to searches without good cause. Also, many felt that unnecessary force was used at the time of a police officer's arrest.

[11]Ibid., p. 146.
[12]Ibid., p. 147.

Report on Civil Disorders[13]

In an attempt to measure the attitudes of people in the cities in which riots have taken place, a survey team interviewed 1,200 persons immediately after the disorders occurred. This study identified the different types of grievances appearing to be of greatest significance to the Negro community in each city. Judgments with regard to the severity of a particular grievance were assigned a rank. These ranks were based on the frequency with which a particular grievance was mentioned, the relative intensity with which it was discussed, references to incidents that were examples of this grievance, and an estimate of the severity of the grievance obtained from the persons interviewed. The grievances were ranked from one to four—a weight of four points was assigned to the most severe, three points for severe, two points for the less severe, and one point for the mildest grievance. The points were added together for each grievance for all of the cities to create an intercity ranking. Although grievances varied in importance from city to city, the deepest grievances were ranked in three levels of intensity, as shown in Table 8.1.

As can be seen, police practices were a significant grievance in the intercity average. They also were a significant grievance in virtually all of the cities—often being one of the most serious complaints. Included in this

TABLE 8.1.

First Level of Intensity

1. Police practices
2. Unemployment and underemployment
3. Inadequate housing

Second Level of Intensity

4. Inadequate education
5. Poor recreation facilities and programs
6. Ineffectiveness of the political structure and grievance mechanisms

Third Level of Intensity

7. Disrespectful white attitudes
8. Discriminatory administration of justice
9. Inadequacy of federal programs
10. Inadequacy of municipal services
11. Discriminatory consumer and civil practices
12. Inadequate welfare programs

Source: Report of the National Advisory Commission on Civil Disorders.

[13]*Report of the National Advisory Commission on Civil Disorders* (Washington, D.C.: U.S. Government Printing Office, 1968), pp. 80–83, 344–45.

category were complaints about physical or verbal abuse of black citizens by police officers, lack of adequate channels for complaint against law enforcement personnel, discriminatory police employment and/or promotional practices with regard to black officers, a general lack of respect for black people by police officers, and the failure of police departments to provide adequate protection to black people.

A more complete picture of how these grievance categories were ranked in intensity can be seen from Figure 8.3, which was prepared for the National Advisory Commission on Civil Disorders.

This study was made in twenty cities. Nineteen of the cities were found to have significant grievances against police practices. In fact, grievances concerning police practices were ranked first in eight cities, second in four, third in none, and fourth in two cities. It should be noted that such grievances were present in five other cities; however, they were not ranked in the first four orders of intensity.

This research seems to indicate that negative attitudes toward police practices are related to riotous behavior.

Seemingly, the views of police officers toward most citizens suggests that they are seen as uncooperative at best, or even hostile. They feel that citizens generally do not cooperate with law enforcement and that law enforcement does not have the respect of most citizens. Furthermore, the police tend to feel that people obey the law only because they fear being caught.[14]

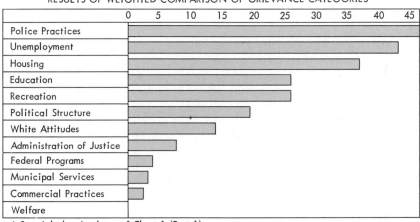

RESULTS OF WEIGHTED COMPARISON OF GRIEVANCE CATEGORIES*

* See right hand column of Chart 1 (Part 1).

FIGURE 8.3. *(Source: Report of the National Advisory Commission on Civil Disorders, Washington, D.C.: U.S. Government Printing Office, 1968, p. 83.)*

[14]James Q. Wilson, "Police Morale, Reform, and Citizen Respect: The Chicago Case," in D. J. Bordua, ed., *The Police* (New York: Wiley & Sons, 1967), p. 17.

This feeling by police seems to be prevalent despite the fact that surveys show it not to be completely true. Wilson suggests that this may be explained in the following manner:

> The average patrolman in a big city is most frequently in contact, not with the "average" citizen, but with a relatively small number of persons who are heavy users of police services (willingly or unwillingly), and his view of citizen attitudes is strongly influenced by this experience. By the nature of his job, the police officer is disproportionately involved with the poor, the black, and the young—partly because young males, especially poor ones, are more likely to be involved in criminal activities and breaches of the peace partly because even the law-abiding poor (who are, after all, the majority of the poor) must rely upon the police for a variety of services that middle-class families do not require (if they do, they obtain them from non-police sources). The police, for example, are routinely expected, in poor areas, to deal with family quarrels; in more affluent neighborhoods, such disputes are either less threatening to the participants or are kept by them out of the public view.[15]

To better understand the impact on the police officer of constant encounters that they may have with other than "average" citizens, the experience of George L. Kirkham should be examined. Mr. Kirkham holds a doctorate in criminology and is an Assistant Professor at Florida State University. Kirkham, academician, had strong feelings and correctional experiences in the humane treatment of the offender. After working on the Jacksonville–Duval County Police Force for six months he had the following to say about his attitudes:

> The same kinds of daily stresses which affected my fellow officers soon began to take their toll on me. I became sick and tired of being reviled and attacked by criminals who could most usually find a sympathetic audience in judges and jurors eager to understand their side of things and provide them with "another chance." I grew tired of living under the axe of news media and community pressure groups, eager to seize upon the slightest mistake made by myself or a fellow police officer.[16]

Dr. Kirkham goes on regarding his change in attitude:

> I would like to take the average clinical psychologist or psychiatrist and invite him to function for just a day in the world of the policeman;

[15] James Q. Wilson, "The Police in The Ghetto," in R. F. Steadman, ed., *The Police and the Community* (Baltimore: Johns Hopkins University Press, 1972), p. 61.

[16] "A Professor's 'Street Lessons,'" *FBI Law Enforcement Bulletin*, March 1974, p. 20.

to confront people whose problems are both serious and in need of immediate solution. I would invite him to walk, as I have, into a smoke-filled pool room where five or six angry men are swinging cues at one another. I would like the prison counsellor and parole officer to see their client Jones—not calm and composed in an office setting—but as the street cop sees him—beating his small child with a heavy belt buckle, or kicking his pregnant wife. I wish that they, and every judge and juror in our country, could see the ravages of crime as the cop on the beat must; innocent people cut, shot, beaten, raped, robbed, and murdered. It would, I feel certain, give them a different perspective on crime and criminals, just as it has me.[17]

The study of attitudes is important because they affect behavior. Consequently, most behavioral scientists feel that if a police officer has a biased attitude against a particular ethnic minority he will behave in a biased manner toward that ethnic group.

Interestingly enough, in research done in three cities for the President's Commission on Law Enforcement and the Administration of Justice, there were some surprises.[18] Careful records were kept of what more than 600 police officers said and did over a period of time. In this study, over three-fourths of the white officers working in black neighborhoods expressed negative attitudes against blacks. Also, almost 30 percent of the black officers working in black neighborhoods expressed negative attitudes towards blacks. However, black officers assigned to mixed neighborhoods expressed less prejudice against blacks than those in black neighborhoods. If attitudes lead to behavior, then the possibility of fair treatment for ethnic minorities appears to be rather poor.

However, observation of actual police behavior and practices did not support this contention. Rather, only in about 6 percent of the police-citizen contacts, which were over 5,000, could a negative attitude toward a particular ethnic minority be detected. The only generalization that can be made from this data is that when a citizen is deviant in behavior or disrespectful to an officer, no matter what his ethnic background, then police officers are more likely to react in at least a discourteous manner.

There are some encouraging implications that can be made from this study. The main one is that even though a particular police officer shows signs of a prejudicial attitude, he can still be taught to behave in a scrupulously fair manner. Consequently, an ethical commitment to fairness on the part of police and police administration is a must. In the attempt to develop a positive image within the total community, law enforcement

[17]Ibid., p. 17.

[18]D. J. Black, and A. J. Reiss, Jr., "Patterns of Behavior in Police and Citizen Transactions," *Studies in Crime and Law Enforcement in Major Metropolitan Areas* (Washington, D.C.: U.S. Government Printing Office, 1967), Vol. 2, Sec. 1, pp. 135–36.

officers should reflect an attitude that overtly shows a desire to uphold the rights of all the people who are served.

Of late, much has been said about the changing attitudes of the people of the United States. But little has been said about the changing attitudes of law enforcement personnel. The changing attitudes in the United States have largely been attributed to what have become known as the civil rights movement and the youth revolution. However, there is evidence that there are changes of attitude in the rank and file of law enforcement as well. During the past decade a whole new generation of law enforcement officers has entered the field. These men and women tend to be better informed and better educated, as well as more impatient, than their predecessors. Because of this, law enforcement has been changing also.

> Although very few policemen would use the term, they have in essence become as much "radicalized" as any other American minority group. In support of this point, one needs only to look at police picket lines around city halls, work slowdowns, "blue flu," job actions, boycotts, press releases to the media, court injunctions procured by their legal counsel, association representatives in state capitals lobbying for and against legislation affecting police, and active campaigning for political candidates. Their actions have generated outraged cries from the establishment—the same establishment that complained about similar efforts of ethnic minorities at various points in our history.[19]

Evidence of this sort indicates that police attitudes seem to be changing, just as all society's attitudes seem to be changing. Besides this evolutionary change in attitudes, there have been efforts to purposely change attitudes. These efforts generally come under the broad heading of education.

CHANGING ATTITUDES

Changes in attitudes are brought about in various ways. Some involve the change in an individual situation. An example of this would be the young man who develops a new attitude toward police when his brother becomes a policeman.

Change in group membership, too, may cause a shift in attitude. An example of this is the minor who quits his gang to go to school. This may well change his attitude toward police. Other changes in attitude are brought about through the impact of education. Derbyshire's study, done in Los Angeles, points this out rather well. This study, conducted with

---

[19]J. P. Kimble, "Crime Solutions: Bigger Guns or Better Cops?" *Crime and Corrections*, 1 (Fall 1973), p. 31.

third-grade youngsters, shows that social class and ethnic background influence children's perception of the police.[20] The sample was composed of thirty black youngsters from an area of low social and economic stability, thirty Mexican-American youngsters from a neighborhood having average to below-average socioeconomic stability, and thirty Anglo-American youngsters from an area of high socioeconomic stability.

The research consisted of asking the children to draw pictures of policemen at work. The results were analyzed and assigned basically into two categories. These categories were scored in terms of (1) aggressive police behavior, such as fighting, chasing fugitives, and shooting; or police assistance having negative overtones, such as searching a building, unloading a paddy wagon, driving in a car with prisoners, or giving a traffic ticket; or (2) neutral behavior, such as directing traffic, riding in a car, or walking; as well as assisting with positive overtones, such as talking with children or giving directions.

Black and Mexican-American youngsters differed significantly from the upper middle-class Anglo youngsters. The minority-group children were much more likely to picture police as aggressive or with negative behavior connotations. On the other hand, Anglo upper middle-class children tended not to see the policeman's task as aggressive, negative, or hostile, but rather as neutral, nonaggressive and assisting.

There is every reason to believe that these children accurately reflected the attitudes of their parents and/or other significant persons in their environment.

After the children had been tested, the Los Angeles Police Department, in conjunction with the Los Angeles Public Schools, exposed them to their *Policeman Bill* program. In essence, this program is one in which a police officer presents a twenty-minute discussion to first-, second-, and third-grade children. In it he describes the function of the police. After this discussion, the youngsters are taken outside the school building and allowed to sit in a police patrol car, blow the siren, etc.

When the thirty black children were retested two days after being exposed to the *Policeman Bill* program, their pictures revealed a somewhat different content. They showed significantly less hostility toward the police after this short contact.

This research seems to confirm the learning theory assumption that attitudes are learned from one's culture and/or subculture. The most significant finding for the practicing policeman, however, is that with a little effort, attitudes learned from one's culture can be changed.

From studies of this type it becomes apparent that leaving the devel-

[20]R. L. Derbyshire, "Children's Perception of The Police: A Comparative Study of Attitude Change," *Journal of Criminal Law, Criminology and Police Science*, 39, No. 2 (June 1968), pp. 183–90.

opment of this nation's childrens' attitude toward law enforcement to chance may be rather foolhardy. A child's parent is a rather significant educator of that child. Therefore, efforts should be made to influence the parent, who in turn will influence the child to develop a positive attitude toward law enforcement.

A second important developer of attitudes in children is the teacher. A study conducted in the Los Angeles area suggests that female school teachers and housewives tend to rate the police rather low.[21] Approximately 63 percent of the housewives and 87 percent of the school teachers did not rate the police very highly. These ratings may indicate that police departments need to direct public relations programs toward housewives and teachers, because they greatly influence the attitudes of children who are the citizens of the future.

In fact, law enforcement needs to be concerned with education of the public in the broadest sense regarding the police and the police role. To accomplish this, representatives of the police need to meet with and talk to all manner of groups and organizations. An alert, forward-looking police administration will make arrangements to see that education of this sort will be carried out.

The object of educating the public regarding the police and the police role is to try to improve attitudes of people toward the police. However, there may also be some room to improve police officers' attitudes toward the people they serve. Policemen need to appreciate the fact that the majority of their time is not spent strictly in law enforcement, but rather in what could be broadly called a social role. In all beginning training courses for police, as well as in all retraining courses, this matter should be covered. Badalamente et al., state this quite well in the following manner:

> Broaden the coverage of subjects pertaining to the policeman's social role in training programs, to include law enforcement, orientation to the behavioral and social sciences, human behavior and civil rights, minority culture patterns, needs, values, family structure, religious philosophies, and individual and group attitudes, concepts of mental health, alcoholism and drug abuse, among others.[22]

Further training in law enforcement is continually being recommended. There seems to be little doubt that training at this point is generally inadequate. Generally speaking, in the police academies throughout the United States, courses that come under the heading of "human relations"

[21]G. D. Gourley, *Public Relations and the Police* (Springfield, Ill.: Charles C. Thomas, Publisher, 1953), p. 78.

[22]R. V. Badalamente, C. E. George, P. J. Halterlein, T. T. Jackson, S. A. Moore, and R. Rio, "Training Police for their Social Role," *Journal of Police Science and Administration*, 1 (Dec. 1973), p. 453.

have the least affect on new patrolmen. Courses regarding arrest, first aid, and the use of weapons are taught by lecture and demonstration. However, the management of personal relations in a tense situation is not an easy thing taught in an academic setting. At least one authority in the field of police science feels that training in this area is inadequate.

It is the universal testimony of the officers that I have interviewed that training room discussions of minority groups and police-community relations have little impact and that such impressions that they do produce quickly evaporate when the officer goes on the street and first encounters hostility or suspicious behavior.[23]

Beside the alleged inadequacies in most community relations classes in police academies, Heaphy suggests that the emphasis of these courses leaves something to be desired. He feels that policemen need to study themselves better. Most of the present study that policemen devote to themselves consists of a sterile, theoretical picture of what police behavior should be. Police need to learn about themselves as persons and as members of a police group. Obviously, studying oneself is a very difficult task. However, because police are in a very sensitive role in the community, this is an essential part of police training. The policeman must learn to be better in touch with himself, his own feelings, and his own actions and reactions, so that he can better control them.[24]

Besides the formal kind of education, there is the education one receives through interpersonal relationships. This kind of education each policeman can do something about and hopefully can affect attitude changes through its use.

Each member of law enforcement should realize that he or she can have some positive effect on the public's attitudes toward police. Furthermore, each member of law enforcement should realize that treating every person as humanely as possible under the circumstances—circumstances that are often quite trying to say the least—is the best method of cultivating a positive attitude. This way of acting toward all people is education of the best sort.

SUMMARY

In this chapter we have discussed the nature of attitudes and their relationship to police-citizen contacts. Attitudes were defined as longlasting, conceptual, motivational, emotional, and adaptive organizational processes

[23]Wilson, "The Police in the Ghetto," p. 74.

[24]J. F. Heaphy, "Community Relations Training—An Alternate View," *Journal of Criminal Law, Criminology and Police Science,* 62 (Dec. 1971), pp. 570–73.

concerned with a person or object. There are five influences on social behavior: social situations, the prevailing social norm, a person's personality, his transitional condition, and the way he perceives and interprets a situation. Most social scientists regard the latter factor as being equivalent to attitude.

Attitudes have certain dimensions. The five most important are: direction, degree, content, consistency, and strength.

Both psychoanalytical and learning theories have been used to explain the acquisition of negative attitudes toward the police by minority groups. Psychoanalytical theory stresses culture and experiences as they affect sexual impulses, which, in turn, influence behavior and attitudes. Learning theory suggests that culture and experience *directly* affect behavior and attitudes. If attitudes are learned, then some effort can be made to change them into what could be called socially acceptable attitudes.

In this chapter some important studies of minority-group attitudes toward the police were reviewed, as well as police attitudes toward those they served.

Based upon the logic of learning theory, it appears that much can be done to improve attitudes. Generally speaking, education in its broadest sense is the best hope for changing attitudes. But this includes education of the police as well as of the people they serve.

DISCUSSION TOPICS

1. Of what concern to the police student is the study of attitudes?
2. What is the difference between attitude and prejudice?
3. Describe very briefly how attitudes may be acquired.
4. What do studies suggest about minority-group attitudes toward the police?
5. What do studies suggest about police attitudes about minority groups?
6. Discuss the idea that behavior changes may precede attitude changes.
7. What bearing does education have on attitude changes?

ANNOTATED REFERENCES

DERBYSHIRE, R. L., "Children's Perception of The Police: A Comparative Study of Attitude Change," *Journal of Criminal Law, Criminology and Police Science,* 59 (June 1968), pp. 183–90. This is an interesting report of a study done on children. The study concludes that negative attitudes toward police can be changed with a little effort.

GRIER, W. H., AND P. M. COBBS, *Black Rage.* New York: Basic Books, 1968. This book sets forth the psychoanalytical theory of the acquisition of attitudes for black people.

HOLLINGSHEAD, A. B., AND F. C. REDLICK, *Social Class and Mental Illness: A Community Study.* New York: Wiley & Sons, 1958. Although this book is primarily concerned with mental illness, it gives a very good picture of attitudes and behavior of the different social classes in the United States.

KIRKHAM, G. L., "A Professor's 'Street Lessons,'" *FBI Law Enforcement Bulletin,* March 1974, pp. 14–22. This is an interesting article by a college professor who became a policeman for six months. His experiences suggest that examining and discussing police attitudes and actions in the classroom may be quite different than reality.

KRECH, D., AND R. S. CRUTCHFIELD, *Elements of Psychology.* New York: Alfred A. Knopf, 1960. This text has a good working definition of attitudes. It also does a credible job of discussing the dimensions and the total concept of attitude.

MILLER, W. E., "Lower-Class Culture as a Generating Milieu of Gang Delinquency," *Journal of Social Issues,* 14, No. 3 (1968), pp. 5–19. This article is a classic in the field of defining attitudes of the dropout.

GROUP BEHAVIOR:
Implications
For Police Control and
Community Relations
Programs

SIGNS
OF THE PROBLEM

9

It has become commonplace among behavioral scientists to state that there are many signs of change in the social structures throughout the world. The evidence they point to is the great social unrest found in many geographic areas of the globe.[1]

The three main branches of behavioral sciences, anthropology, sociology, and psychology, each check on changes in social structure in their own manner. The *anthropologist* is concerned with any significant alteration in cultural patterns. Changes in technology, architecture, food, clothing, or art form, as well as in values, costumes, and social relationships, are the concern of the cultural anthropologist. The *sociologist* studies cultural change primarily through study of the alteration of the nonmaterialistic culture. Such things as values, mores, institutions, and social behavior are the means by which he examines social change. The sociologist usually finds a pattern of social changes following technological advances.

People's attitudes following technological advances are a concern of the *psychologist*, primarily the social psychologist. He feels that these attitudes either retard social change or allow it to progress at a rapid pace.[2]

Speculation is that attitudes have begun to change more rapidly in the last twenty to thirty years than previously. This is probably due to the advanced technology of communications. Now more persons can and do

[1]W. A. Heaps, *Riots U.S.A., 1765–1965* (New York: Seaburg Press, 1966), p. 1.

[2]S. S. Sargent, *Social Psychology: An Integrative Interpretation* (New York: Ronald Press, 1956), pp. 409–19.

express their views than in the past. Nevertheless, recorded history indicates that a certain portion of men in any particular place at any particular time have been dissatisfied with their lot. To control the overt expression of this discontent has been one of the responsibilities of government. And because of philosophical commitments, various forms of government tend to control or allow it in a different manner.

Built within each philosophy of government are certain concepts which bear on how dissatisfaction can be voiced. For example, in the philosophy of democracy are the cornerstone concepts of freedom of speech and the freedom of assembly. These freedoms create a different set of circumstances for the keepers of the peace in a democracy than are present in a nation governed in a different manner. An examination of the practical implications of these freedoms as they affect law enforcement will be made here.

DEMONSTRATIONS

In a democracy, the prudent person sees riots as threatening, irrational, and senseless behavior. On the other hand, within a democracy the prudent person feels that he has a legitimate right to "protest" unfair situations through the use of his oral and written language and through the use of peaceful assembly.

The practical implications for law enforcement regarding a citizenry that can assemble and peacefully demonstrate are quite significant. This is especially true when the demonstrations run the gamut from affluent college students to the poorly educated, economically depressed minorities of the ghetto.

Unruly College Students

The fate of college students involved in politically motivated mass public disorder is a rather new phenomenon on the American scene. However, there have been disorders at American colleges and universities before the decade of the 1960s. During the early nineteenth century there were a number of incidents of disorder and even riots at American colleges. Generally these incidents could be traced to inadequate living conditions, poor food, and/or harsh rules. Even today, complaints about campus living conditions are responsible for more campus disorders than is generally realized. However, nineteenth-century disorders in American colleges unlike disorders in European colleges, were largely apolitical.[3]

But to believe there has been little political influence in American colleges and universities before the 1960s is somewhat erroneous. The

[3]Report of the *President's Commission on Campus Unrest* (Washington, D.C.: U.S. Government Printing Office, 1970), p. 20.

President's Commission on Campus Unrest indicated the following regarding these earlier political activities within the American college.

> During the 1920's, there were campus protests against ROTC, denunciation of the curriculum for its alleged support of the established system, and attacks on America's "imperialistic" foreign policy. During the depression, there was still greater student discontent. Polls taken during the 1930's showed that one-quarter of college students were sympathetic to socialism and that almost 40 percent said that they would refuse to take part in war. There were many student strikes against war, a few disruptions, and some expulsions.
>
> Thus, it is not so much the unrest of the last half-dozen years that is exceptional as it is the quiet of the 20 years which preceded them. From the early 1940's to the early 1960's, American colleges and universities were uncharacteristically calm, radical student movements were almost nonexistent, and disruptions were rare. The existence of this "silent generation" was in part a reflection of the cold war. But as the tension of the cold war lessened, students felt less obliged to defend western democracy and more free to take a critical look at their own society. Once again the American campus became a center of protest.[4]

When disorders take place on a college campus, the college's only option may be to call law enforcement officers to preserve and restore order. Under the best of circumstances, the presence of a large contingent of law enforcement officers on a campus tends to be troublesome and troubling. It is troubling because it indicates that this institution, where reason should prevail, has had a breakdown in this reason. It is troublesome because any campus occupied by police or troops is a spectacle that is regretted by the American public.

Furthermore, American colleges and universities are not enclaves from which police are barred, as is true in some South American universities. Police are duty-bound to enforce the laws on the campuses as well as elsewhere within their jurisdiction. Whenever there is serious property damage or personal injury on the college campus, police must enforce the criminal law.[5]

On June 13, 1970, after a number of incidents of violence on college campuses in the San Francisco Bay Area; New York City, New Haven, Kent State, and Jackson, Mississippi, the President established a commission to investigate campus unrest. The Commission found that the subject was a difficult one to deal with inasmuch as "campus unrest" means many

[4]Ibid., pp. 20–21.

[5]Report to the *National Commission on The Causes and Prevention of Violence, Shut It Down! A College in Crisis* (Washington, D.C.: U.S. Government Printing Office, 1969), p. 154.

things to many people. In fact the term has become so generalized that it is used to describe the intellectual ferment which should exist in the university as well as peaceful and other type protests. The use of the term was found to be so differentiated in its meaning that the distinction between activities which university and society should engage in or must tolerate and those they should seek to prevent was somewhat obscure. The Report goes on to state the following:

> As a result of the muddling of the term "unrest," the university and law enforcement agencies find themselves under pressure to stifle even peaceful and legitimate forms of unrest and to condone its violence and illegitimate forms. Pressures of this sort can lead only to confusion and injustice. Throughout [the Report it is] stressed that campus unrest is in fact a complex phenomenon that is manifested in many kinds of protest activities. Many protests, even today, are entirely peaceful and orderly manifestations of dissent, such as holding meetings, picketing, vigils, demonstrations, and marches—all of which are protected by the First Amendment.
>
> Other protests are disorderly, that is, disruptive, violent, or terroristic. Campus unrest has taken each of these forms. Protest is disruptive when it interferes with the normal activities of the university, or the right of others to carry on their affairs. Obstructive sit-ins, interference with classroom teaching, blockading recruiters and preventing others from speaking or hearing speakers are further examples of disruptive protest.
>
> Violent protest involves physical injury to people, ranging from bloody noses and cracked heads to actual death. It involves the willful destruction of property by vandalism, burning and bombing.[6]

At the present time there are more than seven million college students in the United States. Of these, only a handful practice terrorism. In fact, some of the violence for which students are blamed is perpetrated by non-students. Despite their small numbers, the students who have adopted violence as a tactic have caused much destruction and evoked considerable sympathy from other students as well as a number of other people in the American society. Recommendations on how best to handle campus unrest has been set forth as follows:

> • Most student protestors are neither violent nor extremist. But a small minority of politically extreme students and faculty members and a small group of dedicated agitators are bent on destruction of the university through violence in order to gain their own political ends. Perpetrators of violence must be identified, removed from the univer-

---

[6]*Campus Unrest,* pp. ix and x.

sity as swiftly as possible, and prosecuted vigorously by the appropriate agencies of law enforcement.

• Dissent and peaceful protest are a valued part of this nation's way of governing itself. Violence and disorder are the antithesis of democratic processes and cannot be tolerated either on the nation's campuses or anywhere else.

•The roots of student activism lie in unresolved conflicts in our national life, but the many defects of the universities have also fueled campus unrest. Universities have not adequately prepared themselves to respond to disruption. They have been without suitable plans, rules, or sanctions. Some administrators and faculty members have responded irresolutely. Frequently, announced sanctions have not been applied. Even more frequently, the lack of appropriate organization within the university has rendered its response ineffective. The university's own house must be placed in order.

• Too many students have acted irresponsibly and even dangerously in pursuing their stated goals and expressing their dissent. Too many law enforcement officers have responded with unwarranted harshness and force in seeking to control disorder.

• Actions—and inactions—of government at all levels have contributed to campus unrest. The words of some political leaders have helped to inflame it. Law enforcement officers have too often reacted unethically or over-reacted. At times, their response has degenerated into uncontrolled violence.

• The nation has been slow to resolve the issue of war and race which exacerbate divisions within American society and which have contributed to the escalation of student protest and disorder.

• All of us must act to prevent violence, to create understanding, and to reduce the bitterness and hostility that divide both the campus and the country. We must establish respect for the process of law and tolerance for the exercise of dissent on our campuses and in the nation.[7]

Through the medium of television cameras, student unrest and the response to it is often under scrutiny. Images made by these cameras are relayed to millions of living rooms across the country. How law enforcement tries to handle demonstrations of all sorts needs to be considered to more fully understand the problem.

Peaceful Protests of Minorities

How effectively law enforcement agencies handle organized protests from the minorities of the ghetto may well make the difference between a peaceful demonstration or violence. As has been noted, members of minorities often view police with a great deal of resentment and hostility. Any

[7]Ibid., pp. 7–8.

police act that might be construed as imprudent could well trigger pent-up feelings to erupt into violent behavior. In many marches inspired and directed by the late Dr. Martin Luther King[8] are examples of peaceful protests by minority groups. It should be noted, however, that these protest marches remained nonviolent certainly as much through Dr. King's influence as through good handling by the police. The important point is that imprudent treatment of peaceful protestors of minorities by law enforcement agencies might well cause a large segment of society to revolt against constituted authority or at least to lose confidence in it.

Related to the handling of peaceful protests, which are guaranteed by First Amendment rights, are protests that are nonviolent yet disobedient of the law. These protests are generally attempts at changing laws that are felt to be unfair. How these nonviolent protestors are handled by law enforcement agencies is critical.

It is risky for a society to tolerate the concept of civil disobedience.

FIGURE 9.1.   A peaceful demonstration is an acceptable method of conveying displeasure with a situation or circumstance. Police must accept the responsibility of communicating with the leaders of the "scheduled" demonstration prior to the actual demonstration. Such communication may avert violence. Photo courtesy of the San Francisco Police Department, San Francisco, California.

[8]See nonviolent philosophy set forth in M. L. King, Jr., *Why We Can't Wait* (New York: Signet Books, 1964), pp. 25–26.

Yet, despite the compelling logic of opposition to civil disobedience, history will continue to note circumstances when it is not immoral even though it may be illegal. A good deal of the progress of the black people in the United States in the past twenty years can be traced to civil disobedience.

A caution regarding the use of civil disobedience as an approach to bringing about social change is that participants must willingly accept any penalty the law provides for. On the other hand, law enforcement officers should handle these acts of nonviolent disobedience in a positive professional manner. They must make legitimate arrests and they must do so without causing any incidents that may lead to grievances.

Civil disobedience, when handled poorly by law enforcement, tends to support the most militant elements and consequently can lead to full-scale riotous situations. In fact, those who engage in group violence as part of a political tactic advance the following logic:

1. Militants argue that the creation of turmoil and disorder can stimulate otherwise quiescent groups to take more forceful action in their own ways. Liberals may come to support radicals and while opposing their tactics; extreme tactics may shock moderates into self-examination.

2. Militants point out that direct action is not intended to win particular reforms or to influence decision-makers, but rather to bring out a repressive response from the authorities—a response rarely seen by most white Americans. When confrontation brings violent response, uncommitted elements of the public see for themselves the true nature of the "system." Confrontation therefore is a means of political education.

3. Militants believe that if the movement really seriously threatens the power of the political authorities, efforts to repress the movement through police-state measures are inevitable. The development of resistant attitudes and action towards the police at the present time is a necessary preparation for more serious resistance in the future.

4. Militants state that educated, middle-class, nonviolent styles of protest are poorly understood by working-class youth, black youth, and other "dropouts." Contact with these other sectors of the youth population is essential and depends upon the adoption of a tough and aggressive stance to win respect from such youth.

5. Militants recognize that most middle-class [persons] are shocked by aggressive or violent behavior. In the militant view, this cultural fear of violence is psychologically damaging and may be politically inhibiting. To be a serious revolutionary, they say, one must reject middle-class values, particularly deference toward authority. Militant confrontation gives resistors the experience of physically opposing institutional power, and it may force [some people] to choose between "respectable" intellectual radicalism and serious commitment to revolution, violence, or otherwise.

6. Militants respond to those who point to the possibility of repression as a reaction to the confrontation tactics by accusing them of wishing to compromise demands and principles and dilute radicalism. Militants believe that repression will come in any case, and to diminish one's effectiveness in anticipation is to give up the game before it starts.[9]

Handling Youthful Exuberance

Handling youthful exuberance can pose problems for law enforcement agencies. The high-spirited enthusiasm found at teenage dances and high school and college athletic events, if misdirected and mismanaged by police, can become a serious problem that can on occasion turn into outright rebellion.

When large crowds of young people assemble in one place, their vivacious, uninhibited behavior can be easily transformed. Incidents of this nature have occurred at Ft. Lauderdale, Florida; Seaside, Oregon; and Hamilton Beach, New Hampshire, among other places.[10]

Large gatherings of youth attending rock music concerts have also degenerated into disorderly gatherings which have become quite violent in nature. Controlling exuberant youths can be difficult for several reasons. Young people are often in the process of developing an identity separate from parents and adult authority. Because of this striving for individual identity, youth are often rather hostile toward authority per se. Consequently, the slightest mishandling of them in the group situation may precipitate serious civil disorders.

By and large, these disorders tend to be what sociologist Gary Marx called issueless riots.[11] Although many riots center around a generalized belief, in the issueless riot no such belief is present; these riots have slight implications for social movement or social change. These outbursts often occur during a holiday celebration, or during a victory celebration. They begin as merry-making activities, but often through mismanagement by agencies of law enforcement, degenerate into violent disorders.

An investigation made in 1967 indicated that one of the most frustrating tasks in police work today is controlling riotous situations. This study of how law enforcement personnel handled a number of riots was done in consultation with local and state police as well as with National Guard officials. The conclusions of the study were that most large city police departments have developed plans and some expertise in handling riot

[9]J. Skolnick, *Task Force on Violent Aspects of Protest and Confrontation, The Politics of Protest* (Washington, D.C.: U.S. Government Printing Office, 1969), pp. 81–82.

[10]The *President's Commission on Law Enforcement and Administration of Justice, The Challenge of Crime in a Free Society* (Washington, D.C.: U.S. Government Printing Office, 1967), pp. 118–19.

[11]G. T. Marx, "Issueless Riots," *Annals of the American Academy of Political and Social Science*, 391 (Sept. 1970), pp. 21–33.

situations. However, small police departments have much to learn in the area of handling unruly crowds.[12] This information is of significance when it is remembered that small community police departments are the ones frequently called upon to deal with youthful exuberance.

When a situation gets out of hand and develops into a civil disturbance it becomes a threat to the social order in a number of ways. Certainly from a theoretical framework, it can be argued that a riot is a threat to the authority of government and consequently a threat to the government itself. From the practical standpoint, there are numerous examples of governments being toppled by riotous actions. The classic example took place from 1789 to 1792 in France. Gustav LeBon described this in his account of the French Revolution,[13] in which violent civil disobedience resulted in the downfall of the reign of Louis XVI. Most acts of rioting, however, do not bring down governments; but they may well cause injury to persons and property.

CIVIL DISORDER AND INJURY TO PERSONS AND PROPERTY

The best-documented study of civil disorders and their cost during the past decade was made by a federal commission regarding the civil disorders of 1967. The investigation disclosed that about 10 percent of the persons killed in civil disorders during that year were public servants—these were primarily firemen and law enforcement officers. This indicates that 90 percent of the fatalities were civilian, and a great majority of these were black people. Of the injured, approximately 38 percent were public servants and 62 percent were private citizens.[14]

It should be remembered that deaths and injuries are not the sole measure, in human terms, for the cost of civil disorders. For example, the Commission found that the dislocation of families and individuals clearly could not be qualified in terms of dollars and cents. Other human costs were fear, distrust, and alienation—these occur in every civil disorder. Finally, it should be noted that even a relatively low level of violence and damage in absolute terms can very seriously disrupt a small or medium-sized community. This is an important consideration, particularly in view of the Commission's conclusion that violence is not limited to large cities. (A large city was defined as one having a population of more than 250,000 people.) Besides personal injury, much property damage was incurred in the cities through acts of civil disorder.

[12]*The Challenge of Crime*, pp. 118–19.

[13]*The Crowd: A Study of the Popular Mind* (New York: Viking Press, 1960).

[14]*Report of the National Advisory Commission on Civil Disorders* (Washington, D.C.: U.S. Government Printing Office, 1968), pp. 65–66.

In the twelve cities investigated by the Commission, nine reported less than $100,000 in damage. The other three reported damage of approximately $45 million, $10 million, and $1 million.[15] Where extensive damage occurred, it was generally caused by fire. The other great losses during civil disorders were caused by looting and/or damage to stock inventories, buildings, or both. Suffering the greatest loss through looting, in descending order, were liquor stores, clothing stores, and furniture stores. Generally speaking, public institutions were not the targets of serious attack, although police and fire equipment were damaged in approximately two-thirds of the riots and/or civil disorders investigated by the Commission.

Not all the listed damage was intentional or caused by the rioters. Some of it seemed to be a by-product of police and fire department efforts to control the situation. But although this damage was largely accidental, it was still of great consequences to certain individual businesses in the area where the riot occurred.

None of the damage figures include an estimate in dollars of the extraordinary administrative expense of municipal, state, and federal government caused by the disorder.

The Commission advised that the cost of civil disorder which erupts into rioting is enormous in terms of the threat to peace, persons, and property, and that such disorders should be prevented. To do so, it is necessary to be able to reasonably predict when these will happen. This seems very difficult to do, but there are some suggestions that it is possible.

Identifying the Potentials for Violent Disorder

It is imperative that a police department prepare long before violence occurs or even before the tension signals that disorder is about to break out. A competent and far-sighted police executive will be assessing the possibility of outbreaks of violence or of the staging of nonviolent demonstrations long before they happen. He will be making plans for action to be taken and should be especially involved in creating and developing a sound community relations program.

The law enforcement administrator is very much interested in maintaining a vigil against the possibility of violence erupting in his jurisdiction. According to William P. Brown, there is invariably ample warning of potential interracial imbalance long before any large-scale incident occurs.[16] Brown indicates that government officials, local or state, who believe that events occurring elsewhere are strictly the work of outside agitators and are therefore impossible in their city may well be in for a rude awakening.

---

[15] Ibid., pp. 66–67.

[16] "The Police and Community Conflict," *Police and The Changing Community: Selected Readings,* in N. A. Watson, ed. (Washington, D.C.: International Association of Chiefs of Police, 1965), pp. 3–12.

The sign of approaching problems seems to follow a definite pattern. Tensions rise rapidly, and responsible leaders on both sides of the question realize that it may erupt into violent disorder. Law enforcement officers can sense it when they find more and more hatred directed toward them. Incidents affecting the group in which discontent is rising—perhaps members of an ethnic group from a ghetto—are expanded out of all proportion to reality.

Nonviolent demonstrations, on the other hand, tend to occur more *spontaneously*. This is because the nonviolent demonstration is felt to be—indeed has legally been found to be—a means of legitimate protest, and as such, a much more likely enterprise for involvement of average citizens. If a sincere, courteous, and honest effort is made to communicate with the leaders of such a demonstration before it takes place, the probability of it turning into a violent disorder will be greatly diminished.

As far as possible, law enforcement personnel should request the leaders of demonstrations to disclose their plans. In most instances, these plans will be given in full. The pertinent laws and official policies which may govern the demonstration should be explained. Obviously, no law should be invoked against protestors that would not be directed against any other citizen in the community.

Law enforcement personnel in the jurisdiction in which a demonstration takes place must assume responsibility for the protection of the participants. When arrests must be made, they should be made quickly. Care should be taken that no unnecessary force or commentary is made by the arresting agency. It goes without saying that the arrest should be legally justifiable.

Returning our attention to tension situations capable of exploding into full-scale violent disorders, it should again be emphasized that major disorders are the culmination of a build-up process which is quite observable; they are set off by a final precipitating incident. When the development process is underway, law enforcement supervisory personnel should make an earnest attempt to understand it. If they fail to make a reasonably correct interpretation, the outcome could be disastrous for the community.

According to the late Joseph D. Lohman, mobilizing constructive community elements to deal with tensions of this sort is first of all an informational task.[17] Gathering such information can be done in a number of ways. Law enforcement must have knowledge about the tension, its relative state, and where violence is most likely to erupt. By the vast network and coverage of law enforcement agencies, the mood and tempo of the community can be assessed. Each law enforcement officer should be required to report incidents that might be stress-producing—particularly those

[17]*The Police and Minority Group* (Chicago: Chicago Park District, 1947), pp. 104–105.

involving ghetto and/or barrio residents. Also, an effort should be made to obtain information from such persons as school teachers, social workers, ministers, and reporters as well as employees of the transportation industry. Persons in these fields often can offer important data regarding the pressure build-ups. Informally obtained information from members of the business community, particularly tavern owners and liquor store operators, can often be most useful because incidents reflecting tension often occur in these types of public places.

All information should be screened by supervisory personnel. By evaluating the location and kinds of incidents that have occurred, they should be able to arrive at a conclusion as to the amount of tension present in a given area. As pressure rises, this should be reported to the head of the law enforcement agency and to other government agencies that would be interested in such information and in a position to act upon it.

George Edwards indicates that an important method of observing tensions and indeed of resolving or preventing conflict between police and members of the public is through communications.[18] He feels that police administrators must open and maintain contact with all sections of the community they serve, particularly with ghetto and barrio citizens. Furthermore, law enforcement supervisory personnel such as police captains or inspectors should know the local principals of high schools and junior high schools, the directors of social agencies, and the priests, rabbis, and ministers.

In each police precinct, open house should be held at least quarterly. Law enforcement officers should use these occasions to explain their work to the public. Also, an opportunity should be provided for people to air their complaints to the precinct commander or to a high-ranking officer the department has sent for just such an occasion. Making it possible for individuals to present their hostile feelings toward the police in this kind of situation, although probably difficult for the officers involved, may be tremendously valuable in dealing with openly antagonistic groups.

Communication with the public is not only valuable in helping to prevent problems, it can also be quite useful in preparing for problems that may arise. Law enforcement officers should be encouraged to attend various functions in the district they ordinarily patrol. Meetings of the PTA, neighborhood associations, block clubs, and the like are the types of meetings they should be interested in. At these meetings the officers might well discuss the problems of law enforcement.

According to Edwards, in Baltimore, members of an integrated community-relations unit of the police department work on a day-to-day basis

---

[18]*The Police on the Urban Frontier: A Guide to Community Understanding,* Pamphlet Series, No. 9 (New York: Institute of Human Relations Press, 1968), pp. 69–71.

with civil rights organizations.[19] This unit also meets periodically with teenaged groups in an effort to ward off trouble before it starts. Contacts like these may help weaken the picture of the police department as an "enemy occupation force."

Indications of the tensions mounting in a particular group may be ascertained through intelligence information and the appraisal of written material that any particular group may produce.

Gathering and Evaluating Intelligence

Law enforcement officials must have accurate, up-to-date information regarding civil disorders. Such information helps in a determination of whether or not, how, and when to act.

The intentions of militants and students regarding public demonstrations are most often announced. The grievances are proclaimed rather than concealed. Generally speaking, it is unnecessary to devise elaborate plans to discover information that is quite open to discovery by law enforcement officials. Most information-gathering techniques do not threaten anyone's privacy. On occasion, such techniques do require the use of undercover police agents and these do create some dangers. However, in most cases they are not necessary and they should not be used. In fact, simply by making a daily harvest of leaflets that are distributed, much information can be gathered.

Often within the ghetto, organizations write material setting forth their position. This is also true of the college campuses and most militant organizations. Frequently the material produced often verges on the libelous and/or seditious. From a law enforcement standpoint, these writings should be examined carefully with the old cliché "the pen is mightier than the sword" clearly in mind. As a measure of heightening tension, written material, when evaluated properly, can be an important informational asset to law enforcement. Disorders generally do not just spontaneously occur; they go through a definite build-up process.

The few cases in which the decision must be made to use undercover agents revolve around the fact that there are persons who apparently are plotting to burn and bomb and sometimes to maim and kill. Law enforcement officials must first attempt to determine whether or not such a plot is in progress, and if it is, they must attempt to keep it from being carried out. If this is impossible, they must try to identify, locate, and apprehend the participants after the fact. The best and sometimes the only means the police have to effect these purposes, especially the preventive one, is by a careful intelligence operation. However, the following cautions should be remembered about such operations:

[19]Ibid., p. 72.

FIGURE 9.2. *Signs of the problem: Written derogatory material distributed by militant organizations may serve as a catalyst for heightened tension in a community. Material courtesy of the San Francisco Police Department's Intelligence Section, San Francisco, California.*

Dangers provide compelling reasons to keep intelligence operations at the lowest possible level consistent with peace and security, to entrust intelligence activities to officers whose sensitivities and integrity are above suspicion, and to allow such activities to be undertaken only under strict guidelines and with close supervision. In the long run, clandestine police work cannot be more scrupulous than the department and men who carry it out.[20]

Routine Minor Police Matters as Precipitating Incidents

Civil disorders do not erupt as a result of a single precipitating incident. Instead, they are generated out of an increasingly disturbed atmosphere. Typically, over a period of time, a series of tension-heightening incidents become linked in the minds of the persons who become involved in the civil disorder. "One central fact emerges from any study of police encounters with protestors, anti-war demonstrators, or black militants; there has been a steady escalation of conflict, hostility and violence."[21]

This report goes on to state that the way police handle incidents tends to have a great bearing on whether or not civil disorder then develops.

In some senses we do demand more of the police than we do of other groups—or more accurately, perhaps, we become especially concerned when the police fail to meet our demands. But this *must* be the case because it is to the police that we look to deal with so many of our problems and it is to the police that we entrust the legitimate use of force. Moreover, unnecessary police violence can only exacerbate the problems police action is used to solve. Protestors are inflamed, and a cycle of greater and greater violence is set into motion—both in the particular incident and in future incidents. More fundamentally, the misuse of police force violates basic notions of our society concerning the role of police. Police are not supposed to adjudicate and punish; they are supposed to apprehend and take into custody. To the extent to which a nation's police step outside such bonds, that such nation has given up the rule of law in a self-defeating quest for order.[22]

An investigation directed toward the disturbances that occurred in ghettos in 1967 found that at some point in a potentially explosive situation a further incidence—often a routine or trivial one—became the so-called "straw that broke the camel's back."[23] And the tension spills over into civil disorder with the violence that this entails.

In approximately 50 percent of the disturbances, prior incidents which

[20]*Campus Unrest*, p. 173.
[21]*The Politics of Protest* (Task Force Report), p. 183.
[22]Ibid., p. 188.
[23]Report of the *National Advisory Commission on Civil Disorders* (1968).

increased the tension, as well as the incident immediately preceding the outbreak of violence, were *actions taken by law enforcement agencies*. Two examples follow that will illustrate this point.

The *first* example was the arrest of a black cab driver on July 12, 1967 in Newark, N.J. According to police reports, he was tailgating a Newark police vehicle. The man appeared to be a hazard as a cab driver. Within a short period of time he had had a number of accidents, and his license had been revoked. When the police stopped him for tailgating, he was in violation of the revocation of his license. As a result he was arrested and transported to the Fourth Precinct Station at about 9:30 P.M.

When the police arrived at the precinct with the cab driver, the cabbie either refused or was not able to walk. Therefore he was dragged by the officers from the car to the door of the station. Within minutes, civil rights leaders responded to the call from a hysterical woman, saying that a cab driver had been beaten by the police.

Shortly thereafter, crowds began to form across the street from the precinct station. As the people gathered, description of the purported beating grew more and more exaggerated. Three leaders of the black community—Thomas Still of the United Community Corporation, Robert Curvin of CORE, and Oliver Lofton, administrator-director of the Newark Legal Service Project—tried to disperse the crowd. They attempted to channel their energies into a nonviolent protest but were unable to do so. Although these men tried gallantly to calm the situation, by the next evening it had erupted into a full-scale civil disorder.

A second disorder which began with a rather routine incident points out another principle regarding civil disorders.

On September 28, 1966, a white patrolman in San Francisco saw several black youths in an approaching automobile. When they jumped out of the car and began to run away, the officer became suspicious. He claims that he fired three shots into the air before hitting one of the youths with the fourth shot. The youth—16 years of age—died just a few feet from his home. Four hours after his death, the automobile he and his companions had been riding in was reported stolen. When other blacks living in this section of San Francisco, who were reportedly members of a juvenile gang, viewed the body, they began breaking windows, looting stores, and burning buildings.[24]

Youths, particularly those who belong to juvenile gangs, are often in the forefront of civil disorders. Therefore it seems logical for law enforcement agencies to keep a close tab on activities of juvenile gangs. Out of their activities many serious incidents occur with increased tension or which precipitate incidents of civil disorder.

Once a demonstration or some form of civil disobedience begins, the

---

[24]C. Werthman, and I. Pelavin, "Gang Members and the Police," in D. J. Bardura, ed., *The Police* (New York: Wiley & Sons, 1967), pp. 56–98.

police can deal with it in a number of different ways. Two extremes in methods of handling situations will be presented here. From the standpoint of the police and public relations, the first was a rather unfortunate situation.

1. Demonstrations during the Democratic Convention of 1968. During the week of the Democratic Convention in Chicago in 1968, the police were targets of much provocation. Rocks, bathroom tiles, sticks, and even human fecal matter were hurled at the officers by demonstrators. Some officers responded to the extreme provocations in an unrestrained and undiscriminating manner. Considering that it often inflicted violence upon persons who had broken no laws, disobeyed no orders, and made no threats, this response was particularly inappropriate. Peaceful demonstrators, onlookers, and residents passing through the area where the confrontation between police and demonstrators occurred, were among the victims.

A report entitled *Rights in Conflict* indicates that a significant number of Chicago police units faced with this situation, which called for a great deal of discipline and restraint, simply dissolved into violent gangs and attacked protestors, press, and bystanders indiscriminately. The report went on to say that the situation was one which could be called a "police riot."[25]

It should be remembered that this report exemplifies a conflict between rights in which law enforcement was more or less in the middle. Rights such as free assembly for citizens as opposed to the rights of other citizens to access of the street for travel, and the right of news media to cover the action as opposed to law enforcement agencies' responsibility to control the movement of people in circumstances of public danger, were involved. As can be seen, these rights were in conflict and the result on this occasion was excessive violence on the part of the police.

2. Nonviolent Handling of a Demonstration. By and large, the police objective in a democracy is to handle demonstrations in a nonviolent manner. Therefore anyone interested in this aspect of police-community relations should be interested in viewing how other democracies have handled these kinds of situations on certain occasions. An example of this is a demonstration against the Vietnam War which occurred in London when a large crowd of people demonstrated in front of the United States Embassy. A situation of this type could easily have resulted in a violent confrontation between police and demonstrators.

A platoon system was worked out whereby squads of police relieved one another at intervals to avoid frayed nerves and short tempers resulting from being too long on the lines. In general, police strategy for handling the crowd was by linking arms to form a human wall capable of spreading

---

[25]D. Walker, *Rights in Conflict—Walker Report to the National Commission on the Causes and Prevention of Violence* (New York: Bantam Books, 1970).

FIGURE 9.3.   *How an assembly is handled may well determine its behavior—eruption into violence or peaceful demonstration? Photo courtesy of the Elizabeth Police Department, Elizabeth, N.J.*

a menacing crowd into harmless fragments. As the spearhead of the demonstration group plunged through, its members were isolated and propelled away from the line. This tussle continued, and the report indicates that it was viewed as a contact sport rather than a bloody riot.

At the end of the day a large group of tired demonstrators were singing "Auld Lang Syne." The British Bobbies joined in the singing, which somehow seemed to be a quite fitting tribute to the job well done by the police on this occasion.

Obviously, the social and cultural differences to be found in the United Kingdom are such that this particular method of handling demonstrators may not be capable of being utilized in the United States. However, examinations of how other democracies handle these kinds of demonstrations may give some insight in the handling of protestors per se.

Since the 1968 Chicago convention problem, there have been a number of incidents wherein the police in the United States have handled protest problems quite well. One such incident occurred on January 20, 1969. This was the so-called "counter-inaugural" protest in Washington, D.C. Many of the persons who organized this event were the same who had organized the protest at the Democratic National Convention in 1968. Many of the people who attended the protest in Washington were the same people who attended the protest in Chicago. Roughly equal numbers of persons attended these two protests. Yet the results of these events were markedly different. The situation in Chicago became out of hand. There, the authorities were restrictive in granting demonstration permits, and some of the police, after being goaded by verbal and physical attacks by a small number of militants, responded with excessive force. Their conduct, although it may have won the support of the majority, did polarize a substantial and previously neutral segment of the population against authorities and in favor of the demonstrators.[26]

The authorities in Washington were rather liberal in their issuance of demonstration permits. Although there was also provocative violence by some of the demonstrators in Washington, the police used only that force that was necessary to maintain order. This tactic could be considered quite successful in that there was little criticism of police behavior. The National Commission on Causes and Prevention of Violence concluded that the amount of violence that occurred during these demonstrations and the resulting effects on public opinion were directly related to the kind of official response that the demonstrators received on each occasion. These differences were described in the following manner:

> As the Chicago and Washington events differed in preparation, they differed in outcome. After minor skirmishes, trouble in Chicago escalated when throngs of demonstrators, having been denied permits to remain overnight, refused to leave Lincoln Park, their main gathering place. Dozens of police attempted to clear the park on three successive nights. In response to serious and deliberate provocation, but without coherent planning, some policemen clubbed and tear-gassed guilty and innocent alike, chasing demonstrators through streets some distance from the park. Particularly on the side streets, some bystanders who had taken no part in the demonstration were attacked by police officers. Several media representatives were clubbed and had their cameras smashed. Predictably, tension and anger rose. Extremists who would otherwise be ignored began to attract audiences. They urged demonstrators to fight back. The police were exposed to more and more jeers and obscenities and had to withstand heavy barrages of rocks and other missiles. During one of the first nights, 15 policemen were injured; two nights later, 149 were injured.
>
> In Washington, the cycle of escalating violence never got started. Both verbal and physical provocations by demonstrators were frequently

[26]Final Report of the *National Commission on the Causes and Prevention of Violence, To Establish Justice, To Insure Domestic Tranquility* (Washington, D.C.: U.S. Government Printing Office, 1969), pp. 71–72.

intense, but they were met with restraint. Provocation by police was rare; when it occurred it was terminated by police and city officials who intervened quickly to restore discipline. In general, police withstood physical and verbal abuse with great calm. In the end, the behavior of Washington officials and the police won praise in newspaper editorials and from leaders of the demonstration.

There were some radical leaders, however, who were more grateful for the official response in Chicago, for it appeared to validate their characterization of government as being "reactionary" and "repressive" and to increase support for other protesting groups. The chaos of Chicago also gave solidarity to the ranks of those who regarded all demonstrations, however peaceful, as irresponsible "punks." The overall effect was to increase polarization and unrest, not diminish them.[27]

SUMMARY

Anthropologists, sociologists, and psychologists have noted signs of change in the social structure in the United States during the past two decades. These changes tend to highlight people's dissatisfactions. This is not to say that some people have not been dissatisfied with the social structure from the beginning of recorded history. It does indicate that now more and more people are becoming aware of society's inadequacies. This awareness probably has been heightened by the advances in the field of communication, particularly television.

In a democracy, individuals are able to express these different dissatisfactions in approved manners. Law enforcement officers must allow people to express dissatisfaction as long as it is done in a lawful manner. From a practical standpoint, this is a very difficult job with many implications. The person who demonstrates his dissatisfaction may be any citizen from any social station; when demonstrations are not handled well by the police, the result is a loss of confidence in constituted authority, or worse—civil disorder.

When a situation of this sort gets out of hand, it becomes a threat to the social order. It may become a threat to the government itself, a threat to person or to property. Identifying those situations that have potential for violent disorder is a must for the well-functioning police department. The signs of an approaching situation seem to follow a certain pattern. Predictably, tensions rise rapidly, and responsible leaders on both sides of a particular question can perceive this build-up. Generally speaking, at such a time law enforcement personnel become the object of more and more hatred.

To diminish the chances of having a demonstration erupt into violence,

[27]Ibid., pp. 73–74.

a sincere effort should be made by law enforcement personnel to communicate with the demonstration leadership. Further, law enforcement must protect the right of demonstrators as well as the rights of the majority. Pertinent laws and policies should be explained to the demonstrators so that they can be aware of what constitutes a legally permissible demonstration and what constitutes an illegal demonstration. When and if arrests of demonstrators are made, they should be made quickly, and with as little force as possible.

A check of the build-up of tension is important. Gathering information regarding its rise should be done by patrol officers as well as by supervisory personnel and outside persons and agencies. Written material is another measure of heightened tension. When such material is screened, it can give law enforcement agencies important clues regarding the build-up of tension.

Police must handle with care a demonstration that is a lawful expression of discontent or else the protest may degenerate into a civil disorder or riot. When tensions are high, poor police handling can be disastrous.

DISCUSSION TOPICS

1. Name several ways behavioral scientists measure social change.
2. In what way does social change tend to cause civil disorders?
3. Explain what a precipitating incident has to do with civil disorders.
4. Explain what tension has to do with civil disorders.
5. In what way can the police evaluate tension within the community?
6. Why is the study of how other countries handle civil disorders of importance to persons interested in civil disorders in the U.S.?
7. Discuss the gathering of intelligence as it relates to civil disorders.
8. What do the predatory activities of juvenile gangs have to do with civil disorders?

ANNOTATED REFERENCES

BORDUA, D. J., ed., *The Police: Six Sociological Essays*. New York: Wiley & Sons, 1967. This book has six essays by different sociologists who are concerned with the work of law enforcement in a society in which freedom of the individual is of great concern.

EDWARDS, G., *The Police on the Urban Frontier: A Guide to Community Understanding*. New York: Institute of Human Relations Press, 1968. This pamphlet outlines relationships between the police and the public in a number of situations. It suggests some ways to modernize and improve law enforcement, particularly as it operates within the ghettos of large cities.

Final Report of the *National Commission on the Causes and Prevention of Violence, To Establish Justice, To Insure Domestic Tranquility.* Washington, D.C.: U.S. Government Printing Office, 1969. This report is concerned with the total problem of violence surrounding civil disorder.

HEAPS, W. A., *Riots, U.S.A., 1765–1965.* New York: Seaburg Press, 1966. This book covers the history of some of the riots and civil disorders during the 200 years of this nation's history.

KING, M. L., JR., *Why We Can't Wait.* New York: Signet Books, 1964. The late black leader tells about frustrations caused by the lack of black people's participation in the American society. The book gives some insight into Dr. King's decisions regarding nonviolent demonstrations for equal rights.

Report of the President's Commission on Campus Unrest. Washington, D.C.: U.S. Government Printing Office, 1970. This report discusses a number of incidents of civil disobedience that occurred on college campuses during the late 1960s. The report points out some of the inadequacies to be found in the college situation as well as the inadequacies of law enforcement in its attempts to quell disturbances on the campus.

SKOLNICK, J., *The Politics of Protest. Task Force Report on Violent Aspects of Protest and Confrontation.* Washington, D.C.: U.S. Government Printing Office, 1969. This report discusses the political aspects of civil disorders. Furthermore, it discusses some of the objectives and goals of militants who become involved in leading civil disorders.

WALKER, D., *Rights in Conflict. Walker Report to the National Commission on the Causes and Prevention of Violence.* New York: Bantam Books, 1970. This is the report of the investigation of the civil disorders surrounding the Democratic National Convention in Chicago in 1968.

IMPLICATIONS OF GROUP BEHAVIOR FOR POLICE

10

There seems to be no end to the many books, articles, conferences, speeches, and commissions which have analyzed, diagnosed, counselled, prescribed, or proscribed concerning violence. Violence is clearly a major social problem. Crimes of violence, riots in urban ghettos, and political assassinations have been responsible for the appointment of ... [a number of] recent national commissions: The President's Commission on Law Enforcement and Administration of Justice (1965), The National Advisory Commission on Civil Disorders (1967), ... The National Commission on the Causes and Prevention of Violence (1968) ... [and The President's Commission on Campus Unrest (1970)]. These commissions have engaged the efforts of many distinguished citizens and outstanding scholars.[1]

Investigation by scholars into civil disorders has given rise to concern with the ways knowledge and theories of the behavioral sciences can be applied to training programs and community relations programs. Because methods of handling civil unrest are of great importance to many people throughout the nation, a brief look at some behavior patterns might suggest alternatives to physical force in controlling unrest.

[1]J. F. Short, Jr., and M. E. Wolfgang, "On Collective Violence: Introduction and Overview," *Annals of the American Academy of Political and Social Science,* 391 (Sept. 1970), p. 2.

GROUP BEHAVIOR

Traditionally, mob behavior has been interpreted in two widely different ways. One has emphasized the group itself. This interpretation suggests that groups are more or less independent of the individuals of which they are composed. The other emphasizes the behavior of the individuals who make up the crowd. Gustav LeBon, associated with the first theory, illustrated his point with a description of the behavior of the aggressive mobs of the French Revolution. LeBon felt that a crowd might have a "group mind" which supersedes the minds of the individual participants. He believed that the individuals in such crowds are "swept up" and thereupon lose individuality. The crowd was considered uncivilized and irrational. The participant, no matter how rational or civilized a person he might be, could be reduced to a bestial level in a crowd.[2]

The opposing concept stresses that members of a crowd act as individuals, while recognizing that individual behavior changes in certain respects in the presence of other people. In most instances, their presence tends to have a restricting effect on behavior. However, under certain conditions there is a permissiveness about a crowd situation that induces individuals to act in a less restrained way. An individual may normally never think of looting a store, but when others are doing so, he may join them. The thought that "everybody is doing it" and the feeling that as an individual he cannot be singled out and punished for his act may be responsible for this change in behavior.

Because police sometimes need to intervene in the activities of various groups, a systematic study of the social, psychological, and cultural factors related to the behavior of people en masse should help prepare a police officer to discharge his duty more intelligently and effectively.

Behavioral scientists generally refer to people en masse as a *collectivity*. They use this term to denote crowds, groups, classes, and the public. Practically all group activity can be thought of as collective behavior. Group activities are made of individuals acting together in some form; in the action there is some fitting together of the different lines of individual conduct.

Because the collectivity that police are most concerned with is the crowd, the structure and function of crowds will be examined. This will be followed somewhat later by an examination of the individuals who make up the crowd.

[2]*The Crowd: A Study of the Popular Mind* (New York: Viking Press, 1960).

Types of Crowds

For our purposes, four types of crowds will be discussed. Herbert Blumer has described these types quite well.[3] The first type can be identified as a *casual* crowd. A group of people observing a display in a store window is an example. Characteristically, the casual crowd has a momentary existence. More important, it is loosely organized and has very little unity. The members of this crowd come and go, giving temporary attention to the object that has captured their interest. They have little association with the other members of the crowd. These individuals are classed a crowd because the chief mechanisms of crowd formation are present in the casual crowd.

A second type of crowd can be designated the *conventionalized crowd.* An example is the spectators at a football game. The spectators' behavior is essentially like that of the members of the casual crowd, except that it is expressed in established ways. For instance, the crowd at the game probably stands for each kickoff. This established way of being involved in an activity is what sets off the conventionalized crowd from other types.

The *expressive crowd* is the third type. Its distinguishing characteristic is that excitement is expressed in physical movement, and the excitement, instead of being directed toward an objective, is a form of release. This type of crowd is commonly found in certain religious sects.

The last type of crowd that will be considered is the so-called *acting or aggressive crowd.* Its outstanding feature is that there is an objective toward which activity is directed. An aggressive crowd could easily be classified as a mob. It is this type of crowd that is of concern to law enforcement personnel.

Using Neil Smelser's *theory of collective behavior,*[4] the so-called acting crowd can be divided into two subtypes. The first could be called "the crowd acting because of panic." The reaction of the audience to a fire in a theater provides an example. The second subtype could be called "the crowd acting because of a hostile outburst." This crowd is also known as a riot mob. It should be noted that panic and hostile outbursts frequently occur in sequence. There are many examples in which panic behavior by a crowd is followed by hostility and attacks on persons and agencies held to be responsible for the panic in the first place.

Because the appearance of a hated individual or symbol can transfer

[3]"Collective Behavior," in A. M. Lee, ed., *Principles of Sociology* (New York: Barnes & Noble, 1951), pp. 165–222.

[4]N. J. Smelser, *Theory of Collective Behavior* (New York: The Free Press, 1963).

a reckless crowd into a mob, we will now give some consideration to how a crowd is formed.

The Formation of Crowds

Most social scientists are in general agreement regarding the phases in the formation of a crowd. An exciting event which catches the attention of people and arouses their interest seems to be the *first* occurrence. In the process of being occupied with the event and the excitement generated by it, a person is likely to lose some of his self-control. Characteristically, impulses and feelings are aroused which tend to press one on to some type of action. A number of people stimulated by some exciting event, therefore, are inclined to behave like a crowd.

The second phase in the formation of a crowd involves a milling process. Characteristically, individuals who are aroused by some stimulating event are inclined to talk to one another and/or to move about, if this is possible. This tends to cause the excitement to become greater. Each person's excitement is conveyed to other people. Furthermore, excitement is reflected back to each individual, thereby intensifying the whole condition. The milling process seems to generate a common mood among members of the crowd and also to increase the intensity of that mood. Individuals are inclined to take on a common identity and are therefore much more likely to act as a unit than in other circumstances.

We will discuss other aspects of crowd formation in the section specifically dealing with the *acting* or *expressive crowd*. First it will be useful to examine some of the primary dimensions of a crowd.

Characteristics of a Crowd

Certain general characteristics apply to all crowds. Others apply only to certain types of crowds. Let us examine the general characteristics in turn.

Size. It is obvious that, under certain circumstances, the very size of a crowd may cause problems for police. The thousands of people at an athletic contest necessitates careful planning and organization, particularly regarding orderly movement. Police will also probably be quite concerned with plans for protecting people in case of an emergency caused by a disaster. However, with the possible exception of traffic control, generally speaking, the size of a crowd gives little indication as to the nature and seriousness of problems law enforcement officers will face. Problems regarding a crowd are usually related to other characteristics of the crowd. However, because ineffective handling owing to a lack of adequate police personnel may prove troublesome, it can be seen that the size of a crowd is an important dimension.

But a knowledge of size alone is not very satisfactory from the police operational point of view. It is too indefinite and does not provide a sufficient basis for deciding how many police may be needed. This leads to the conclusion that other dimensions must be taken into account. One of these is duration.

Duration. By duration is meant how long a group has been in existence. For example, a gang of boys may have existed a number of months before it congregates as a crowd on a street corner. Merely to chase the boys off the corner may disperse the crowd, but in actuality this brings more solidarity to the gang. Rather than dispersing a group, social agencies, such as police and juvenile probation departments, may be more interested in steering it into constructive channels, making it healthy and useful.

The actual formation of a crowd may be the culminating or precipitating event in police concern with a group. Because the police objective is to avoid precipitating events, it becomes important for officers to handle crowd situations with good judgment. Good judgment is much more likely if all the pertinent facts are known. Therefore, it is of prime importance that police obtain as much intelligence or information about a group and its composition as possible.

In bygone days when patrolmen walked beats, a good officer knew the people who lived on his beat. He could predict where trouble was likely to occur and who would be involved in it. Often as not, he could prevent an act of violence and avoid the necessity of picking up the pieces afterwards or of making an arrest.

No one would suggest that we give up modern police organization and go back to the officer on the beat per se. However, as we continue to expand and refine our law enforcement techniques and police use of intelligence, we are aware that efficiency may be impersonal. And while people appreciate efficiency, they resent impersonalization; this in itself may cause problems.

Besides ascertaining the duration of a crowd or group, other factors regarding the crowd should be considered if better understanding is to be reached. One of these factors is identification.

Identification. This dimension concerns whether or not a person considers himself a member of a group and/or identifies with it. Identification is a process that occurs within an individual. Nevertheless, groups can be distinguished on the basis of the degree of identification of the members. Other members of a group are frequently aware of one's membership in that group, especially if there is some kind of formal organization, congregation, or interpersonal communication. Strangers are often able to identify members of a group. An example is police, who are readily identified by their uniforms. When a person is easily identified as a member of a given group on the basis of his appearance or behavior, he is said to be highly visible.

The tendency of people to identify with various groups plays an important part in determining their values and their behavior. Their behavior, in turn, may help to identify them as belonging to a particular group. Knowledge that a person identifies with the Black Muslims, the Black Panther Party, or the Ku Klux Klan may be an important piece of informa-discrimination, and hostility; and persons who identify with them may be tion. These groups are based on racial prejudice, social avoidance, active expected to behave in accordance with the group's beliefs.

Polarization. Another dimension of the crowd is polarization. This occurs when members of a group focus their attention toward some object or event. A crowd may be polarized toward a speaker, a movie, or an athletic event, for example.

A group may or may not be polarized. A group of passengers on a commuter train would probably not be; they would be involved in individual pursuits such as reading or talking. But suppose someone fired a gunshot into their car. At this point, in all probability, every passenger in the car would immediately be polarized toward that event.

Polarization is one of the dimensions characterizing the relationship between a leader and his followers. In controlling the behavior of masses of people, police may use the tactic of removing the leader from the group. This will change the pattern of polarization.[5]

Often police manipulate these dimensions in crowd control. The following are examples of this:

1. The use of *bullhorns* for giving orders in an attempt to command the attention of a crowd is essentially an attempt to change the polarization of that crowd.

2. Taking *photographs* of participants in a mob action often makes persons forcibly aware that they are members of a group that is regarded with disapproval. Protective anonymity is lost, and identity with the crowd produces anxiety, causing individuals to withdraw from the group.

3. *Dispersing* a crowd may well physically terminate its duration.

4. Often police *divide* a mob in two, thereby changing its size and converting it into two smaller groups which can be dealt with more easily and effectively.

A close examination of the *acting crowd* is in order, particularly in view of its importance to law enforcement personnel.

---

[5]N. A. Watson, ed., has described the dimensions of a crowd more fully in "Police and Group Behavior," *Police and the Changing Community: Selected Readings* (Washington, D.C.: International Association of Chiefs of Police, 1965), pp. 179–212.

FIGURE 10.1. *Berkeley police officer is attempting to communicate with demonstrators. Prior to any "unlawful assembly arrest," the group must be advised of possible violations. Photo courtesy of the Berkeley Police Department, Berkeley, California.*

THE ACTING CROWD, OR THE HOSTILE OUTBURST: A SOCIOLOGICAL VIEW

Often, hostile outbursts or mob action follows a panic situation. Apparently the important aspect of the panic situation is that people feel there are a limited number of escape routes and these are closing; escape must be made quickly. An audience rushing to the exits when it believes a theater is on fire is an example of a panic situation.

According to Smelser, a hostile outburst usually takes place in the presence of three conditions. These are *a situation of strain, a structurally conducive setting,* and *a means of communication among the persons undergoing the strain.*[6]

In the panic situation cited above, the situation of strain was physical danger. However, many situations of strain are socially institutionalized, such as strains resulting from differences in class, religion, political outlook, or race.

[6]*Theory of Collective Behavior,* pp. 222–69.

If hostilities are to arise from conditions of strain, these conditions must exist in a *structurally conducive setting*. This is a setting in which (a) hostility is permitted, or (b) other responses to strain are prohibited, or (c) both. An example would be in strained racial relations wherein hostility to members of another race is accepted by each race, and there are no means to alleviate the strain, such as by discussion between the two racial groups. This absence of a means of expressing the grievances caused by strain, followed by the group's receiving rumors which intensify its hostile beliefs, is the next phase of the process.

Adequate communication must be available for spreading a hostile belief and for mobilizing for an attack. Individuals who do not understand one another and whose background of experiences differ greatly are not easily molded into a mob. An audience, because it permits rapid communication, common definition of a situation, and face-to-face interaction, has many of the attributes for becoming a mob. These aspects in combination are referred to as *structural conduciveness*. Simply restated, then, the hostile outburst depends upon *strain, the presence of a structurally conducive setting*, and *the means of communicating among the persons who are undergoing strain*.

With the spreading of truths, half-truths, and rumors through a group, the possibility of this information becoming a generalized belief increases. If the group begins to believe the rumors and half-truths, then, given a reason, it may be ready for a hostile outburst. The term for such a reason is a *precipitating cause*. A precipitating cause may justify or confirm existing generalized fears or hatreds. In a racial outburst, for example, the precipitating cause might be a report—true or false—that a person from the other racial group has committed some unwholesome and/or unsavory act.

With this precipitating cause comes the final stage of the outburst, which is a *mobilization for action*. This does not occur, however, unless *structural conduciveness and strain, generalized beliefs*, and *a precipitating cause* are all present.

Considering the stage of mobilization for action calls for an examination of leadership and the organization of the hostile outburst. Leadership may take many forms. It may range from the simple model who may only be the first one to throw a stone in a riot to someone who is highly motivated and who deliberately agitates a group into action through organizations associated with a social or some other type movement. An example of an extreme lack of organization and leadership is the so-called brawl, in which there is no evidence of division of labor or cooperation between individuals involved in the situation. At the other extreme we find the paramilitary units whose members have specialized roles. These units have acted in certain incidents of civil disobedience.

Once a hostile outburst begins and people become aware that there is a crack in the social order that is conducive to the expression of hostility, an interesting phenomenon takes place. A rash of hostile actions appears, many of them motivated by hostilities which are not related to the conditions or strains that gave rise to the initial outburst of hostility. This build-up effect, in which individuals capitalize on the fact that an outburst has occurred, is, in a hostile crowd situation, generally followed by a complaint regarding inappropriate use of force by the police. This fact suggests that such complaints should never intimidate police in their rightful use of authority.

It is often found that a mob will have a number of people who become involved because of the initial strain and/or grievance, but a mob will also have persons who have grievances that are independent of the condition that caused the mob to form. This probably explains why participants in a riot situation may shift their attack from one object to another.

Once behavior has erupted into a hostile outburst such as a riot, social control must be exerted. By reexamining some of the phases in such outbursts, it is possible to see how and at what point a social agency can intercede to try to avoid the riot.

Ideas for Controlling Hostile Outbursts

At the beginning of a build-up of a hostile outburst there is *strain*. This strain may be economic, caused by poverty; interracial, caused by prejudice; or of various natures, caused by any number of situations. It is quite obvious that social agencies can and should intercede in an attempt to alleviate some of this strain.

A *second* factor is a setting that is either *permissive of hostility,* or *prohibits other responses,* or *both.* For this reason persons in the ghetto must be able to make complaints about police brutality to a responsible group that will investigate the complaints. Adequate means for registering discontent with police should be built into the police system. But this should never intimidate police in their rightful use of authority. This is most important, for it has been found that inadequate enforcement of law and order also tends to encourage hostile outbursts.

Social agencies can take action to correct *false beliefs* caused by rumors and half-truths. Constant efforts should be made to sustain a dialogue between the parties in discord and the police. By means of such two-way communication, police have the opportunity of showing up half-truths and rumors for what they actually are and preventing them from crystallizing into generalized beliefs.

In the event that a crowd begins *mobilizing for action*, it may be possible to forestall a hostile outburst by disrupting the organizational process. When there are designated leaders, either personal or of an organizational nature, removing them or rendering their leadership ineffective may result in quelling outburst.

In the last analysis, when a hostile outbreak occurs, the *behavior of social agencies* in the face of the outburst determines how quickly the situation will be resolved. The manner in which force is exercised encourages or discourages further hostility. It has been shown that when authorities issue firm, unyielding, and unbiased decisions in short order, the hostile outburst tends to be dampened.

To this point in the chapter, groups have been viewed in regard to their structure and function. Now it will be of value to view groups as a number of individuals.

THE INDIVIDUAL IN THE GROUP SITUATION: PSYCHOLOGICAL VIEWS

While Gustav LeBon insisted that a crowd had a unique nature distinct from the individuals of which it was composed,[7] Floyd Allport took the other extreme and theorized that there is no real difference in the behavior of individuals in a crowd or when they are isolated. According to Allport, "the individual in the crowd behaves just as he would behave alone, only more so."[8]

This hypothesis holds that the actions of a crowd express the emotional needs, prejudices, and resentments of the members of that crowd. In a crowd individuals may do things they ordinarily would not do, but a crowd does only those things which most of its members would *like* to do. The stimulation of the crowd, coupled with its protection, allows individuals to express hostility they might not be inclined to express in normal circumstances. For example, people often have an impulse to break something; in a riot situation the individual can do this without feeling guilty. To support further Allport's theory, it has been noted that records show that a high proportion of persons arrested during riots have previous arrest and criminal records. Many of these persons were looters, who were taking advantage of the situation.[9]

Mobs constitute a danger to orderly social life because they tend to suppress the selection of rational alternatives in making a decision regarding possible intelligent social policy. The circumstances that excite a crowd or increase its excitement are commonly referred to as *stimuli* by psycholo-

---

[7] LeBon, *The Crowd.*

[8] F. H. Allport, *Social Psychology* (Boston: Houghton Mifflin, 1924), p. 295.

[9] M. E. Wolfgang, "Violence, U.S.A.—Riots and Crime," *Crime and Delinquency* (Oct. 1968), pp. 289–305.

gists.[10] If a stimulus is to affect the crowd, most individuals in the crowd must respond to it. The word "fire" shouted in a crowded public place would be a stimulus. It would tend to arouse a common mass action in the people there. Besides the original stimulus, another may be present. A person observing the responses made by other individuals in a crowd may find that these have become an additional stimulus to him. This accounts for people acting "more so" in a crowd.

There is speculation that most people are not punished but are more or less rewarded for acting with a large group. Supposedly, this begins when children in school are disciplined for stepping out of line while the children who remain in line are not. From childhood on, most people learn to conform to the group and are rewarded for doing so by feeling relaxed because they have no fear of punishment.

Muzafer Sherif, along with other psychologists, believes that when people are in a crowd their perceptions of past experiences and their subsequent behavior is changed by the special social conditions around them.[11] For example, when life becomes difficult and is full of stress and strain, such as during widespread hunger and unbearable living conditions, individuals in a group may view certain social norms differently. Certainly persons who are starving may view the taking of a loaf of bread as something other than theft.

It is probable that most behavioral scientists see a blending of the theory that an individual reacts directly to a stimulus and the theory that he sees a situation differently because of past experience. It is generally felt that an individual learns attitudes, prejudices, and biases, and these affect how a situation is seen by that individual—and thus, how he reacts to the situation. This does not mean that behavioral scientists will not continue to talk about individuals reacting to stimuli. It does mean that they are aware that behavior is very complex.

How Leaders Manipulate Crowds

Psychologists like Miller and Dollard concur with Allport's theory of crowd behavior. They feel that crowd behavior is often surprising because so little is generally known about how individuals really act when they are alone. Often persons conform on the surface, in social circumstances, but they have within them the potential to act antisocially when the right type of stimulus unleashes an antisocial response. Skillful leaders are able frequently to release such antisocial responses.[12]

---

[10]N. E. Miller, and J. Dollard, *Social Learning and Imitation* (New Haven: Yale University Press, 1941), pp. 218–34.

[11]*The Psychology of Social Norms* (New York: Harper & Row, 1966), pp. 67–88.

[12]Miller and Dollard, *Social Learning and Imitation*.

Most people have been trained to follow a leader in certain circumstances. Even the rules of a childhood game are based on this concept. However, people have also been taught to follow the crowd under a different set of circumstances. The example of children made to stay in line in school is an appropriate one.

A leader is able to use these two factors. He generally tends to center attention on himself by standing alone and speaking. Some leaders use repetition and rhythm to stir a crowd to frenzy. Good examples of this can be found in old newsreels which show huge crowds of Nazis responding to Adolf Hitler at party rallies.

Crowd leaders use such tactics to get an "emotional build-up" rising in a crowd. They may use emotionally laden verbal symbols such as "rape," "defense," or any one of a number of racial and/or religious names of a derogatory nature. These words can stir up high emotions in a person, causing him to act in a violent manner.

It has been said that individuals in a crowd do not critically evaluate the leader's use of rhythm and repetition for stimulation. To be critical, one must wait and evaluate a number of alternates in regard to how a situation should be dealt with. In this regard, one means of controlling a crowd and possibly preventing a violent outburst is to introduce a debate with the crowd leader. This debate causes critical evaluation and checks impulsive activity which may take place under the stimulation of repetition and rhythm within the shelter of the crowd.

Crowd Control

We have discussed the fact that when a group of people gets together in a crowd they can be stimulated by the crowd itself to act in a manner that is not typical of their normal behavior. It is obviously in the interests of law enforcement to know the nature of crowds so that they can be controlled or even prevented from forming. Sometimes prevention of potentially dangerous crowd action is effected by declaring martial law and/or by imposing curfew and restrictions against assembly.

Disaster can result from policemen failing to understand crowds and their actions. In ghetto areas, some riotous situations have been touched off when police have made what originally appeared to be routine arrests. Joseph Lohman set forth some ideas regarding how to deal with this kind of situation. They are as follows:

1. The police officer must refrain from impulsive actions; therefore, he must ascertain the facts first.
2. Once the police officer has the facts, he should act quickly. A quick disposition of a matter tends to neutralize the consequences of much interracial hostilities when such emotions are present.

FIGURE 10.2.   *When necessary, an immediate removal of the law violator with a sufficient show of force may neutralize the consequences of much interracial hostility—particularly when such emotions are high. Photo courtesy of the Atlanta Police Department, Atlanta, Georgia.*

3.   A police officer should constantly try to emanate a "fair" and professional attitude. This type of behavior commands the confidence and cooperation of the best elements in a gathering crowd.

4.   If the persons involved in the original incident that the officer was called to investigate are excited and emotionally upset, efforts should be made to separate them from the crowd situation as soon as possible. Such a practice helps prevent the communication of emotions and excitement to the more excitable spectators in the gathering crowd.

5.   Generally speaking, indiscriminate mass arrests have a most undesirable effect on public attitudes toward the police. Mass arrests of this type invariably involve great numbers of innocent people. This magnifies the difficulty since the arrest of innocent bystanders creates the impression of excessive and unbridled use of authority, as well as incompetence.

6.   When unruly crowds gather, it should be possible to mobilize an adequate number of police quickly. A show of force is preferable to a belated use of force. Once an incident gets beyond the control of the police, it can only be brought into control again with a great deal of

difficulty, and the possibility is then quite high of damage to property taking place, coupled with the possibility of the loss of life. A situation should never be permitted to develop wherein control passes from the hands of the police authority to the crowd.[13]

Besides knowing how to handle direct confrontation situations, police should keep other community relations practices in constant operation.

COMMUNITY RELATIONS AND GROUP BEHAVIOR

The police are only one of several resources that may be used in problems of human relations and in relieving the consequences of crowd tension. It is true that police are often accused of aggravating and inciting tension. These accusations are often untrue; however, they probably arise because the police are necessarily constantly involved in incidents involving public order. They will be blamed by a certain segment of the society for what they have done, and they will be blamed by another segment for what they have not done. Police however, can do a great deal toward enlisting the cooperation of responsible elements in the community, thereby bringing about adequate public support in crisis situations.

To get the cooperation of responsible persons in the community, the police must make known to them possible problem situations. A police department is in an unusual position to know when tension may lead to unruly crowd behavior. If each patrolman reports on all incidents that might cause a crowd to gather, a picture of potential reaction can be obtained. Certainly interracial group incidents should be reported.

Incidents nearly always occur in public places. Therefore, schoolteachers, community workers, ministers, transportation employees, housing directors, and social workers will be able to add more information about these situations. Information of this sort can also be obtained from local businessmen, from such people as poolroom operators and tavern owners in particular. Because crowd situations are sometimes set in motion by the activities of juveniles, it is well to keep close tabs on juvenile gangs. Many serious incidents of friction have begun from the predatory activities of such groups.

The reporting of incidents, however, will be of no value unless the information is assimilated and proper steps are taken to alleviate the tension revealed by the reports. One of the proper steps for doing this is to again enlist the cooperation of neighborhood leaders, particularly in ghetto areas. Such individuals might serve as an advisory group. They should participate

[13]*The Police and Minority Groups* (Chicago: Chicago Park District, 1947), pp. 102–107.

at the planning level well before their direct appeals to the people are needed during critical periods.

If, after attempts to resolve the situation have failed, a confrontation does take place between police and a hostile crowd, it should be remembered that excessive use of force is to be avoided. Just enough force should be used to restrain those who need it. This does not mean that adequate numbers of officers should not be called in to try to help quell the disturbance. A large group of police represents a *show* of force which is usually quite different from an excessive *use* of force. Generally speaking, there is no substitute for judicious and impartial action by all police officers. At the time of an incident, tact may well be the ingredient which prevents the situation from getting out of hand.

Our concern with potentially riotous incidents should not be taken to suggest that the role of the police agency in human relations is basically one of riot control. Rather, it is essentially one of preventing such occurrences, for the very foundations of government are involved in the success of the police in minimizing internal strife. The competence and integrity of the police in their ability to guarantee public order is a cornerstone of government. Riots cannot be tolerated by any nation, for once lawful procedures for the solution of conflicts and redress of wrongs are violated or abandoned, the collapse of society is inevitable.[14]

A number of social scientists like J. Skolnick, feel that a civil disorder is an expression of need on the part of the governed and therefore, most energies should be spent in satisfying that need rather than in formulating plans to quell the disturbance. The government's responsibility in the just, speedy, and effective handling of potential situations of civil unrest is a problem with which the police are genuinely concerned.

Skolnick believes that riots are far more structured than many behavior theorists suggest.[15] Based on that contention, he indicates the following regarding the implications of civil disorders:

> An approach that gives equal emphasis to force and reform fails to measure the unanticipated consequences of employing force; and it fails to appreciate the political significance of protest. If American society concentrates on the development of more sophisticated control techniques, it will move itself into a destructive and self-defeating position. A democratic society cannot depend upon force as its recurrent answer to long-standing and legitimate grievances. This nation cannot have it both ways; either it will carry through a firm commitment to

[14]W. T. Gosselt, "Mobbism and Due Process," *Case and Comment*, 74 (Jul.–Aug. 1968), pp. 3–6.

[15]E. Currie, and J. H. Skolnick, "A Critical Note on Conception of Collective Behavior," *Annals of the American Academy of Political and Social Science*, 391 (Sept. 1970), pp. 34–45.

massive and widespread political and social reform or it will develop into a society of garrison cities where order is enforced without due process of law and without the consent of the governed.[16]

SUMMARY

During the past decade the federal government has appointed a number of commissions to investigate into causes of violent behavior, particularly civil disorders. Study of the history of other nations, both past and current, shows that this problem of civil disorder may well be common to mankind in general.

Civil disorders have a number of things in common. With knowledge gained through study, certain patterns and generalized facts about civil disorders emerge and these can be utilized by the government and law enforcement in particular in managing or quelling these occurrences.

Behavioral scientists begin their study of group behavior by separating people en masse into different groupings. Because the main concern of the police is with the grouping called the *crowd*, types of crowds were examined within this chapter. These were the casual crowd, the conventionalized crowd, the expressive crowd, and the acting or aggressive crowd, emphasis on the latter.

The formation of a crowd is usually dependent on a common attention-getting event which generates excitement and sometimes causes a loss of individual self-control. According to the dimensions of such crowd characteristics as size, duration, identification, and polarization, people experience varying degrees of commitment to crowd action. Knowledge of these factors enables law enforcement personnel to handle potentially bad crowd situations.

The acting or aggressive crowd, from a sociological frame of reference, usually grows out of three conditions: a situation of strain, a structurally conducive situation, and a means of communication among the persons undergoing the strain. There is usually a precipitating cause that finally mobilizes the crowd for action. Often a leader can control the crowd by manipulating the generalized feeling of the participants. One good tactic by police is to isolate such a leader from the crowd; Another is to physically divide the crowd to dissipate hostile currents of feeling.

There are various theories about the individual in the crowd situation. Some, such as LeBon, believe that the crowd has a unique nature distinct from the individuals within it. Still others are convinced that the individual in the crowd behaves as he ordinarily would, only more so. At any

[16]J. H. Skolnick, *Task Force Report on Violent Aspects of Protest and Confrontation, The Politics of Protest* (Washington, D.C.: U.S. Government Printing Office, 1969), p. 262.

rate, a crowd environment produces actions on the part of individuals that are not typical of their everyday behavior. Obviously, it is important for law enforcement personnel to understand certain aspects of the crowd, and to seek from community members information about potential crowd causes. This enables them in some cases to prevent crowds from forming and in others to be able to control possibly riotous crowds. A judicious use of force is imperative in crowd control, as is fairness and respect for citizen needs. The function of police in this respect is to maintain public order while making possible the solution of conflicts and the redress of wrongs.

DISCUSSION TOPICS

1. Discuss the idea that different acts of civil disorders have many things in common.

2. List the types of crowds named in this chapter.

3. What does a precipitating incident have to do with a riot?

4. Explain how the characteristics of a crowd may be used by the police in handling a crowd.

5. How does the childhood game of "Follow the leader" condition people to participate in riots?

6. Based on sociological theory, what are some suggestions for dealing with civil disorders?

7. Based on psychological theory, what are some suggestions for handling civil disorders?

ANNOTATED REFERENCES

LeBon, G., *The Crowd: A Study of the Popular Mind.* New York: Viking Press, 1960. One of the first serious treatises on crowd behavior.

Lohman, J. D., *The Police and Minority Groups.* Chicago: Chicago Park District, 1947. This book is almost thirty years old, yet it is still a classic on the subject of civil disorders.

Miller, N. E., and J. Dollard, *Social Learning and Imitation.* New Haven: Yale University Press, 1971. Another classic that applies learning theory to crowd behavior.

Skolnick, J. H., *Task Force Report on Violent Aspects of Protest and Confrontation, The Politics of Protest.* Washington, D.C.: U.S. Government Printing Office, 1969. This report makes a somewhat more liberal interpretation of the value of civil disorders than that of most police agencies. For the serious student of law enforcement, this point of view is an important one to know and understand.

SMELSER, N. J., *Theory of Collective Behavior*. New York: Free Press, 1963. This book, concerned with the behavior of crowds, has particularly pertinent discussions regarding panic situations and the hostile outburst as these relate to human behavior.

The Annals of the American Academy of Political and Social Science, Collective Violence, 391, Sept. 1970. This particular issue is devoted to the theoretical considerations of collective violence.

WATSON, N. A., ed., *Police and The Changing Community: Selected Readings*. Washington, D.C.: International Association of Chiefs of Police, 1965, and New York: New World Foundation, 1965. This contains articles that provide good reference material for the overall subject of police-community relations.

INTERGROUP HUMAN RELATIONS: IMPLICATIONS FOR LAW ENFORCEMENT

11

In Chapter Three we touched upon the fact that as the volume and complexities of laws steadily increase, the proportion of individuals who may be technically defined as criminal also increases. It is doubtful that any adult can claim that he has never violated *some* law—whether it be federal, state, municipal, county, or even military law.

In terms of *enforcing* law, then, it is clear that *some* law rather than *the* law is the reference point of "law enforcement." This being the case, police responsibility must encompass much more than simple "law enforcement." The social changes occurring in the 1960s and early 1970s have greatly expanded police responsibility and influence. In part, the potential of this influence depends upon understanding what *motivates* the groups of people to react to enforcement in the manner that marked the 1960s. This, in turn, suggests better understanding of what motivates groups of people to react to *other groups of people.*

Calling his approach to human relations *transactional analysis,* Eric Berne provided a great deal of insight into social problems relating to law enforcement.[1] He spoke of the rewards that motivate people, and called these rewards *payoffs.* He pointed out that a reward for one person was not necessarily perceived as such by others.

From this point of view, the individual law violator may seem to have no motive, but he may, nevertheless, be receiving a payoff by "proving"

[1] Berne, E. *Games People Play* (New York: Grove Press, 1964).

earlier beliefs—perhaps, for example, about how unfair policemen are (*unfairness* being defined as arrest, etc.). The rioter, in burning down a building, may be motivated by the same payoff principle.[2] In other words, if human beings find a reward in proving their beliefs to be correct, perhaps this is sufficient motivation for them to *provoke* situations that create proof. By provoking situations with racial overtones or by constantly isolating racial issues and situations that require police action, some people may be seeking to prove their beliefs—which may or may not be valid. Of course police officers may also find reward in such proof, in terms of their beliefs that certain individuals are "naturally criminals or troublemakers."

It may well be that influences of this kind determine the degree of respect certain groups in the community hold for police as well as for virtually any other group in the community. And it is to this intergroup aspect of the changing community that this chapter is addressed.

It is impossible to overestimate the significance of intergroup influences on tensions and social change in communities. Underlying the overall law enforcement significance is the practical necessity of recognizing the disproportionately high commitment of police resources to relatively small proportions of the community—particularly high when the intergroup consideration is ignored.

> *Communication with Minority Groups.* A critically important communications problem confronts the police in urban areas with significant minority populations. Those areas have been the scene of civil disorder in recent years, and they frequently require a disproportionately high percentage of police resources. Inhabitants of those areas frequently feel that they have less influence on police enforcement policies and practices than other city residents. Members of minority groups must be convinced that their police service expectations are known and respected by the police. They must be shown that their recommendations are being acted upon.
>
> Many police agencies in cities with large ethnic and racial minority groups have developed programs to insure consideration of the needs of minorities in the development of policies and operational response. Indeed, some police administrators view this as their primary "community relations" effort. These programs have included informal advisory groups and special units within the police agency to work with minority groups in developing channels of communication.
>
> A unique example of police-public communication can be found in the Detroit Police Department's "Buzz the Fuzz" program. The program, which began early in 1971, involves a weekly radio talk show mod-

---

[2]See W. Grier, *Black Rage* (New York: Basic Books, 1967), p. 212. See also Eldridge Cleaver, *Soul on Ice* (New York: McGraw-Hill, 1968), p. 210; J. Cohen, *Burn, Baby, Burn!* (New York: E. P. Dutton & Co., 1967); and R. Conot, *Rivers of Blood* (New York: Bantam Books, 1964), p. 93.

FIGURE 11.1.   A lack of adequate communication between urban American minority groups and the police generated certain frictions which aided in igniting the summer riots. Intensity of the conflict was related to the lack of contact and openness between the disputants. Photo courtesy of the San Francisco Police Department, San Francisco, California.

erated by a local well-known radio personality having an appeal to the city's black community. The panel normally consists of the commissioner of police, an inspector and sergeant from the department's Public Information Office, and two citizen representatives from the chamber of commerce. The panel answers all questions and complaints telephoned in by members of the public.

The panel acts as a referral resource for other city agencies, channels complaints of consumer fraud to the chamber of commerce, and accepts and acts upon complaints of police misconduct. Generally, an answer is provided immediately. If research is required, the answer is delayed until the next show. Cases of substantial police misconduct are referred to the department's Citizen's Complaining Section for investigation; however, weekly progress reports are given until final disposition is announced.

The program, which started out as a 13-week special, has been televised four times and has become a standard means of communication with the community. On occasions, the police commissioner or his representative has gone on the moderator's regular daytime program to dispel rumors or to report on significant crime and other community problems.

Since local conditions dictate the need and type of response, each chief executive should recognize the special problems presented in communicating with minority groups, and strive to develop methods of ensuring that he is in communication with all elements of his community.

Communicating with Non-English Speaking Minorities. Because it is the responsibility of every police agency to provide service uniformly to every person in its jurisdiction, the problem of communicating with substantial portions of the community who speak little or no English must be solved.

Most large police agencies employ officers who speak the most commonly encountered foreign language to answer telephone requests for service. Some agencies maintain files of all officers who speak foreign languages so they may be called upon to interpret calls for service.

San Diego, California, which has a substantial Mexican-American population, teaches Spanish to its police academy, identifies Spanish-speaking police officers on name tags and publishes leaflets describing its police department complaint procedure in both Spanish and English.

The San Jose, California, Police Department explains the police function, the law, and legal procedures on a local radio broadcast in Spanish.

It has been suggested that bilingual officers receive a bonus for maintaining fluency in a foreign language. Linguistic ability should at least be a factor in determining the qualification of a police candidate. In Los Angeles it is considered a compensating factor for candidates who might not otherwise meet a minimum employment requirement, such as height.

While local conditions should dictate if the need exists for a police agency to undertake bilingual programs, as a minimum, every police agency having a substantial non-English speaking minority should ensure that all telephone requests for services can be processed effectively and that agency programs are modified to ensure adequate communication between non-English speaking minority groups and the police agency.[3]

Bearing these considerations in mind, attention is now shifted to intergroup attitudes as opposed to intergroup behavior.

INTERGROUP ATTITUDES VERSUS BEHAVIOR

In discussing various problems relating to psychiatric treatment, Maxwell Jones wrote, "Community attitude studies do not necessarily tell us what people actually do."[4] If this is true in psychiatry, then it is certainly true in law enforcement. Rare is the criminal who does not respect at least some of the laws that he does not break. His attitude toward *those laws* is possibly just as good as the attitudes of noncriminal groups. Embezzlers, for example, may identify with groups that are appalled by violent crimes. Conversely, many assaulters and perhaps rioters may identify with groups that consider the embezzler or the burglar an unwholesome person. The income-tax cheat may well consider himself a member of a group that maintains a generally law-abiding attitude. The reward or payoff that presumably motivates violation of one law may, for any number of reasons, not be rewarding in the violation of other laws. Violation of law, therefore, may not be motivated by "criminal attitude"—particularly if one's *general* attitude tends to correspond with that of a noncriminal group.

To clarify the significance of *attitude,* consideration might be given to those attitudes that seem to correspond with the "noncriminal grouping." Group attitudes that are essentially noncriminal do more than reduce the chances of potential criminals—such attitudes actually form the basis of citizen participation in anticrime programs. In reading the material that follows, consider the potential in two contexts: (1) a group with noncriminal attitudes, and (2) a group attitude that corresponds with the attitude of "criminals."

[3]As appears in *Working Papers for the National Conference on Criminal Justice* Washington, D.C.: U.S. Government Printing Office, Jan. 23–26, 1973, p. P-139–40.

[4]M. Jones, *Social Psychiatry* (Springfield, Ill.: Charles C. Thomas, Publisher, 1962) p. 32.

Every police agency should immediately ensure that there exist within the agency no artificial or arbitrary barriers—cultural or institutional—that discourage qualified individuals from seeking employment or from being employed as police officers.

1. Every police agency should engage in positive efforts to employ ethnic minority group members. When a substantial ethnic minority population resides within the jurisdiction, every police agency should take affirmative action to achieve a ratio of minority group employees in approximate proportion to the makeup of the population.

2. Every police agency seeking to employ members of an ethnic minority group should direct recruitment efforts toward attracting large numbers of minority applicants. In establishing selection standards for recruitment, special abilities such as the ability to speak a foreign language, strength and agility, or any other compensating factor should be taken into consideration in addition to height and weight requirements.

3. Every police agency seeking to employ ethnic minority members should research, develop, and implement specialized minority recruitment methods. These methods should at least include:

   a. Assignment of minority police officers to the specialized recruitment efforts;

   b. Liaison with local minority community leaders to emphasize police sincerity and encourage referral of minority applicants to the police agency;

   c. Recruitment advertising and other material that depicts minority group police personnel performing the police function;

   d. Active cooperation of the minority media as well as the general media in minority recruitment efforts;

   e. Emphasis on the community service aspect of police work; and

   f. Regular, personal contact with the minority applicant from initial application to final determination of employability.

4. Every police chief executive should ensure that hiring, assignment, and promotion policies and practices do not discriminate against minority groups.

5. Every police agency should continually evaluate the effectiveness of specialized minority recruitment methods so that successful methods may be emphasized and unsuccessful ones may be discarded.[5]

Presumably the "noncriminal" attitude emerges as the asset to law enforcement. But *attitude* and *behavior* are not the same thing. Police function on the basis of behavior (or at least potential behavior) rather than on the basis of attitude—attitude being an important but merely causal factor to be considered.

Attitude in this context, then, is certainly less significant than specific

[5]In *Working Papers for the National Conference on Criminals Justice*, p. P-147.

behavior—at least to law enforcement personnel. This raises a question regarding the relationship of attitude and intergroup behavior. And if attitudes in a community are not efficiently correlated with the kinds of behavior which concern law enforcement, a method is necessary to anticipate at least some of the problems between groups before disruptive behavior occurs—a method not dependent on attitude or speculation about attitude.

Perhaps a brief discussion of what the community groups actually are might prove valuable before considering any prediction of behavior on the part of these groups. And some consideration of what the community *is* may be a good starting point.

The Multi-Population Community

One of the accepted sociological definitions of *community* is a "human population living within a geographic area and carying on a common, inter-dependent life."[6] But the depth and breadth of social problems discussed in earlier chapters and elsewhere in this volume could scarcely support the notion of the "human population" enjoying a "common, inter-dependent life." As a matter of fact, the notion that human beings living within a limited geographical area are necessarily just one population group fails to gain support from discussion of the social problems to which this volume is addressed. But if the community has more than one population, and the law enforcement goal is to find a method of anticipating behavior that does not correspond to law-abiding attitudes, then the first step in achieving this goal must be to identify each population.

Although the overriding law enforcement goal of identifying each population has more to do with reducing community tension than with the immediate control of crime, the clear identification of citizen populations offers a great deal of potential in the area of immediate crime control.

> The spectrum of anticrime efforts appropriate for citizens is so wide that almost everyone has many opportunities to promote and pursue crime prevention activities—and on a number of . . . involvement levels. . . . Seizing a fair share of such opportunities need not inconvenience anyone; on the contrary, because of their variety, they are more likely to complement, and constitute an outlet for one's natural interests.
>
> A major category of crime prevention activities pertains to those efforts aimed at what many consider to be the infrastructure of crime: insufficient education, inadequate job skills, unavailable recreation opportunities, and the like. Citizen action in this area constitutes crime prevention in the positive sense of the term. That is, the objective is to fill vacuums in the lives of individuals who might otherwise be drawn

[6]G. Lundberg, C. Schrag, and O. Larsen, *Sociology* (New York: Harper & Row, 1958), p. 128.

dangerously close to the line that separates the legal from the illegal. These kinds of crime prevention activities are brought to bear outside of the criminal justice system and are designed to reduce significantly the need to utilize the sanctions of that system.

Another major category of citizen action encompasses those crime prevention measures that are closely related to the three components of the criminal justice system—police, courts, corrections. In general, these activities seek either to complement the operation of one of the components, as a citizen crime commission might, or to strengthen the component, as probation volunteers might. Efforts in this area constitute crime prevention to the extent that the criminal justice system is thereby improved and thus becomes a more effective crime deterrence.[7]

Identifying populations, then, affords much more than just "anticipating behavior."

A population is a group that might be called any number of things, such as the public, a crowd, mob, gang, etc. What the population is called or the kind of group it is becomes important because this influences both the behavior of the population and the response to the population by other groups, including law enforcement. A population that "gathers" and calls itself (or is called) a gang or a mob may well behave in a different manner than a population labeled "the public," or more simply "a crowd." Care then is needed in defining each population, particularly because the label changes (or should change) when behavior changes.

A particular population may never become a crowd or a mob, simply because the members of this population never gather. But gathering alone does not create a mob or a crowd. Sociologists commonly refer to gatherings of people as plurals, or aggregates (also known as aggregations).[8] *Gathering* simply means being in physical proximity, so a crowd that gathers is an aggregate or plural, temporarily in physical proximity and, of course, without organization. So when members of a population group gather, the *behavior* exhibited is the more significant consideration in determining the label for the population, inasmuch as behavior is frequently the only significant difference in any gathering. For instance, *crowds* have been defined throughout this book in terms of their *behavior*. But they can also be defined in terms of gathering, and in this sense perhaps even a mob might be equated with a crowd.[9] For that matter, even a demonstration might be viewed simply in terms of a gathering. Because, after all, a *crowd* is simply

[7]National Conference on Criminal Justice, "Community Crime Prevention," made possible by Law Enforcement Assistance Administration, January 23–26, 1973 (Washington, D.C.: U.S. Government Printing Office), pp. CC-13–14.

[8]Lundberg, et al., *Sociology*, pp. 382–85.

[9]K. Davis, *Human Society* (New York: The Macmillan Co., 1949), pp. 303–56.

FIGURE 11.2. *A peaceful demonstration and a distinguishing lack of tension is noted among these demonstrators. Police personnel must be able to determine the mood, attitude, and overall demeanor of the demonstrators. Photo courtesy of the Berkeley Police Department, Berkeley, California.*

an unspecified number of persons gathered temporarily in proximity—just as is a demonstration, except for its purposes and *behavior*.

In order to move toward an understanding of the kind of population to be considered in this chapter, let us consider the gang, inasmuch as it does more than gather, regardless of its *behavior* after gathering. And unlike other groups, the gang is usually the same population each time it gathers. It is this sameness that permits law enforcement to examine not only the *behavior* of the gang but predictable and controllable influences on this behavior as well. A gang, like a crowd or a mob, is a *group*, but it is a group that is distinguished from other groups in terms of sameness. This sameness is the focus of this chapter because of its relevance to law enforcement on a *continuing basis*.[10]

Sameness in a group on a continuing basis suggests still another sociological label—in this case, the *category*. The gang group is a category because each member of the group is a gang member, whereas each member of a crowd may or may not be a crowd member. The category of gang mem-

[10]See J. Toro-Calder, C. Cedeno, and W. Reckless, "A Comparative Study of Puerto Rican Attitudes toward the Legal System Dealing with Crime," *Journal of Criminal Law, Criminology and Police Science*, 59, No. 4 (Dec. 1968), pp. 536–41.

FIGURE 11.3. *Black Panther Party demonstrating in front of the Federal Building in San Francisco, California, May 1968. Photo courtesy of the San Francisco Police Department, San Francisco, California.*

ber suggests a sameness in the group—having a characteristic in common—just as does the category of Anglo-Saxon, Negro, Puerto Rican, etc. But unlike the category of gang member, there is no requisite that the categories of Anglo-Saxons, Negroes, or Puerto Ricans "gather" in order to be a category. Categories, then, are the community population groups between which stress may occur—stress that forewarns of violence between community groups. Some consideration of the sizes of categories may be helpful here.

The Size of Community Populations

The size of a community population group or category refers, of course, to the number of persons in the group. But if the concept of multiple populations in the community is accepted, then size also refers to *proportion*—the relative size of a population as compared with other population groups in the community. Moreover, consideration of the size of a population group implies enough of the sameness just discussed to classify the group a category. Categories of people in the community that outnumber other categories of people are *majority groups*. Categories that are outnumbered by others then are *minority groups* and are referred to as such throughout this volume. Stress and tension between these different-sized groups is the focus of this chapter.

Emphasis on stress and tension between different-sized groups may well create a common ground on which two distinctly different police administrative philosophies can merge, as is indicated in the following quotation:

> At the outset, identifying the role of the chief of police in the community seemed a rather simple task. I would merely reflect on long-held convictions, reduce them to the simple truths I knew them to be, and write them all down. I would say things such as, "maintain a meaningful dialogue with (a) youth, (b) their parents, (c) the schools, (d) merchants, (e) everybody," and "relate meaningfully to (a) the community, (b) neighboring communities, (c) the state, (d) the nation —everybody."
>
> After awhile it got pretty bad and I began to realize that the role of one in public service, like a role in a play, cannot be defined by merely setting down a list of tasks. It must be explored to be understood.
>
> Two kinds of people undertake to define roles: those who speak from the authority of their experience, and those, like myself, who speak from the subjective analysis of their observations. In the first instances, the audience will usually react without suspicion to the pronouncements of the expert. The novice, however, will be shown no such deference. He must prove his contentions, and this is as it should be.[11]

The acknowledgment that both approaches must incorporate the goal of reducing tension between different-sized populations affords a common basis on which law enforcement personnel can approach the changing community on a uniform basis. In the context of such common ground, the discussion is now directed toward the goals of groups that may generate stress and tension.

GROUP GOALS AND INTERGROUP RELATIONS

Though the relationship between majority and minority groups is of vital concern, specific consideration of the minority group is necessary before examining the intergroup relationship in terms of potential stress.

With the obvious exception of the ruling class, the position of minority groups throughout history has been far less favorable than that of majority groups. In more recent times, however, there have been varying degrees of interest in human rights, pertaining to both the majority and minority categories. In various treaties following World War II, this interest really became evident. The ruthless, wholesale slaughter of millions of members of certain minority groups by the Nazis no doubt motivated many

[11]Kenneth M. Cable, "The Chief and the Community," *The Police Chief*, 38, No. 3 (Mar. 1971), p. 24.

of the demands for human rights voiced at the first meeting of the United Nations in San Francisco in 1945. On December 10, 1948, at the meeting of the UN General Assembly in Paris, a declaration was unanimously adopted that proclaimed to be "a common standard of achievement for all peoples." This standard would "strive to promote respect for rights and freedoms." Although the declaration was geared to the international scene, it is noteworthy that it nevertheless implied universal endorsement of the constitutionally guaranteed "rights and freedoms" in America. Many envisioned this declaration as the threshold of an enlightened era of increasing tolerance. But far from ushering in such an era, this historic declaration was made during the early stages of perhaps the greatest unrest America has ever witnessed between majority and minority groups.

Intergroup Human Relations

Certainly there is little reason to believe that the United Nations declaration itself caused unrest between groups. But it may well be that the same worldwide concern with individual dignity was the basis for both the initiative of the UN and the increasing militancy of various minority groups. Whether they are related or not, however, at least some American minority-group members have done more to "promote . . . rights and freedoms" than has the UN, which declared this intent in 1948. Although some of the behavior of certain members of the minorities may have actually slowed development of "respect," thereby increasing the stress between groups there can be little doubt that the period since World War II has been marked by a definite movement toward greater individual freedom and human dignity. The primary motive for seeking the political and economic power needed to influence one's own destiny is probably to gain the dignity proclaimed by the United Nations as a human right.

To the degree that police practices before the emerging era of individual dignity may have mitigated the dignity of individuals, to that same degree must there be changes made. Moreover, in an era of general social change, policing must change to correspond to the ever-shifting intergroup and interracial patterns. But such change demands full-scale effort.

Change in American policing will not occur unless and until large numbers of concerned citizens from all enclaves of the community, socially aware police and criminal justice personnel, sensitive government legislators and administrators begin to address the real issues, rather than dealing with abstractions and procedural minutiae. It is correct to say that "we the people" must sit down as members of one family and hear each other. If we cannot do this, we are doomed to increasing violence in our communities, with police playing a central role.

In a viable democracy, concepts such as "Power to the People," and "To Protect and to Serve" must be more than mere rhetoric.[12]

The question then becomes, Why cannot achievement of such a laudable goal serve as a positive payoff or reward in the context of the discussion at the beginning of this chapter? Why, indeed, it might be asked, should tension arise between groups in the community when all seek merely to control or influence their own destiny? Law enforcement must first understand tension between groups as a source of disruptive behavior. Such understanding is the source of a remedy for stresses and tensions emerging from many groups pursuing a goal—even a laudable goal.

Goals and Conflict

Individual freedom, it has been said, "ends at the end of the other fellow's nose." In terms of various community groups having the mutual goal of individual freedom, the end might instead be "the other group's dignity." That is, the individual cannot be "free" to strike the other fellow's nose, nor can one group be "free" to deprive the other group of dignity. It follows then that there must be restrictions on the goal of individual freedom—at least if dignity is to be part of the goal of freedom. The freedom to strike the other fellow's nose (or to deprive the other group of dignity) is not, and cannot be dignified. Freedom to seek control over one's destiny in such diversified areas as education, economics, and personal respect must by necessity be *restricted freedom*—perhaps, the most freedom possible. When intergroup tension, or conflict, occurs between the majority and minority, with both proclaiming the mutual goal of freedom, it is most often traceable to the failure of either or both groups to recognize the restrictions on their own freedom. The first step in bringing these restrictions into focus is *meaningful dialogue* between the groups.[13]

Meaningful Dialogue

Bringing about meaningful dialogue between groups probably begins with meaningful dialogue between police and the community. As will be noted in the next chapter, this at times is the most difficult of law enforcement tasks. Nevertheless, it remains a vital need in *successful* law enforcement.

All law enforcement agencies have a need for improved police-community relations. ... One practical way of stimulating supervisory

[12]A. C. Germann, "Changing the Police—The Impossible Dream," *Journal of Criminal Law, Criminology and Police Science*, 62, No. 3 (Sept. 1971), p. 421.

[13]S. Coppersmith, *The Antecedents of Self-Esteem* (San Francisco, Cal.: W. H. Freeman, 1967), p. 264.

concern about police-community relations is to give this aspect of police work greater emphasis in evaluation for promotion.

Every law enforcement officer makes good or bad police-community relations in day-to-day contacts with the public. Therefore, even though an agency may create a specialized community relations unit, police officials must stress that community relations are the concern of all police personnel and that professional performance of duties commands public respect.[14]

Someone once defined police relations with the public as "the sum total of all contacts, good or bad, between the police and the public." Undoubtedly, this is a true statement, but one which raises important questions for us to consider.

Many police departments have established commissions to deal with the important task of improving channels of communication between the law enforcement agency and the public it serves. Speaker bureaus, press conferences, community meetings, and neighborhood and store-front offices have done much to inform citizens of the role of the police and the problems of law enforcement. But these innovations can only serve as instruments of the total public relations program. A plan should involve, directly or indirectly, every citizen and every police officer.

Organizational programs are excellent, but, by their very nature, they affect a limited number of citizens. Positive contacts by police administrators are also necessarily confined to the number of individuals contacted. A truly productive and worthwhile program of influencing public opinion must involve every member of the organization. And each officer must know that he is involved. The program must be one of *positive communications*, covering a variety of types, areas, and situations, to achieve the desired goals.[15]

Communication, then, is indeed a significant segment of meaningful dialogue, many considering communication to be of *immediate* significance; as is indicated in the following quote:

Every police agency should immediately establish programs to develop and improve the interpersonal communications skills of all officers. These skills are essential to the productive exchange of information and opinion between the police, other elements of the criminal justice system, and the public; their use assists officers to perform their task more effectively.

1. Where appropriate, an outside consultant should be used to advise regarding program methodology, to develop material, to train sworn

[14]Lloyd G. Sealy, "A Police-Community Relations Program," *FBI Law Enforcement Bulletin*, 37, No. 7 (July 1968), p. 8.

[15]Col. Jacob W. Schott, "The Policeman and His Public," *FBI Law Enforcement Bulletin*, 38, No. 2 (Feb. 1969), pp. 17–18.

officers as instructors and discussion leaders, and to participate to the greatest extent possible in both the presentation of the program and its evaluation.

2. Every recruit training program should include instruction in interpersonal communications and should make appropriate use of programmed instruction as a supplement to other training.

3. Every police agency should develop programs such as workshops and seminars which bring officers, personnel from other elements of the criminal justice system, and the public together to discuss the role of the police and participants' attitudes toward that role.[16]

Two-way communication, or meaningful dialogue, implies a great deal more than points of view. Two-way communication, particularly when geared to clarifying certain restrictions on the freedoms of the majority and minority, must first consider those limitations that exist—particularly because frustrations resulting from them have so often exploded into violent outbursts in recent times. Most of these already existing restrictions have been discussed elsewhere in this text in terms of bias and prejudice; but a more subtle, yet nevertheless equally significant, restriction needs clarification, perhaps under the title of motivation.[17]

Motivation is restrictive through its absence. Earlier chapters referred to the Puritan Ethic, which holds work of any kind to be sacred. So ingrained in the American cultural pattern is this concept of work for work's sake that the Industrial Revolution failed to dislodge it, in spite of virtually removing the farm as a source of almost guaranteed work.

Dialogue between the majority and the minority must conceive of the lack of motivation as being equally restrictive as bias and prejudice because it comprises the *basis* of much existing bias and prejudice.

The majority group is from what sociologists like to call the middle class. This group values steady employment if for no other reason than that most of the "material prizes" that are culturally valued are thought to be accessible only through work. Far more important, however, is the virtual certainty that when a middle-class child reaches work age, he will be in the position of being limited only by his own talent and initiative. Of course, such an expectation does not apply to the children in certain minority groups.[18] The very educational process may indeed support the implication that the expectation of work is inappropriate to many minority-group mem-

---

[16]As appears in *Working Papers for the National Conference on Criminal Justice,* p. P-154.

[17]See B. Berelson and G. Steiner, *Human Behavior* (New York: Harcourt, Brace & World, 1964), p. 668.

[18]M. Drimmer, ed., *Black History* (Garden City, N.Y.: Doubleday, 1967), p. 530. See also S. Bronz, *Roots of Negro Racial Consciousness* (New York: Libra Publications, 1964), p. 93.

bers, although in a far more subtle manner in some areas than in others.[19]

Whenever motivation is examined, the significance of expectations emerges. Two-way communication, dependent as it is on each group's *expecting* to hear and be heard, also isolates the significance of expectations. Put another way, a group that does not *expect* to be heard or to hear is not likely to feel motivated to attempt meaningful dialogue, thereby preventing two-way communication. But more than the motive to attempt communication is lost when a *minority* group fails to develop the *expectation* that cultural rewards are as available for it as for the majority. Lost along with the motives to *try* is confidence in government.

When confidence in the government is lost, *all* government services suffer, not just police. Police, however, bear the brunt of most of the problems when loss of confidence is severe. Nevertheless, all are concerned (or should be) when confidence in government dwindles. Moreover, all programs of all concerned are (or should be) involved. This is actually the "secondary value" of community relations for *any* program. Consider, for example, the following rationale for public relations in the area of delinquency prevention—but consider the rationale in terms of its potential to *also restore confidence in government*:

> The need for sound public relations in all social-action programs involving the cooperation of groups as well as of individuals is self-evident; police delinquency-prevention programs are no exception. Many individuals and groups must come to mutual understanding and cooperate if the program is to be successful. There are always "blind spots" in thinking, fixed attitudes, resistances, prejudices, and other barriers to communication that must be considered.[20]

Removing these blind spots for any one program bears directly upon similar blind spots regarding confidence in government. This in turn bears on the expectation of cultural rewards for a minority group.

Some consideration might be given at this point to the possible manner in which expectations are developed, or not developed, and the alternative expectations that may occur.

FAMILY CRISIS AND EXPECTATIONS

The following chapter will explore some of the program implications of police efforts to include *family crisis intervention* in community relations for

---

[19]L. Harlan, *Separate and Unequal* (Chapel Hill: University of North Carolina Press, 1968), p. 275; and J. Conant, *Slums and Suburbs* (New York: McGraw-Hill, 1961), p. 147.

[20]A. F. Brandstatter and James J. Brennan, "Delinquency Prevention," in W. Amos and C. Welford, eds., *Delinquency Theory and Practice* (Englewood Cliffs, N.J.: Prentice-Hall, Inc., 1967), p. 204.

law enforcement. "Family crisis" means just that—a *crisis* within a family. "Intervention," insofar as police are concerned, concerns those police activities brought to bear on either resolving the crisis or referring the family to such help, or both.

In terms of the discussion of expectations, such police programming is (or could be) extremely significant. In terms of these expectations as discussed thus far, consider the following article by Myron Katz relating to family crisis training:

FAMILY CRISIS TRAINING: UPGRADING THE POLICE WHILE BUILDING A BRIDGE TO THE MINORITY COMMUNITY[21]

The need for considerable change in police policy and practices has been discussed and documented. The report submitted by *The National Advisory Commission on Civil Disorders*[22] concluded with the quotation from Dr. Kenneth B. Clark, recent past president of the American Psychological Association and an expert on ghetto psychology, which is reiterated here in an attempt to develop a framework of this paper:

> I read that report ... of the 1919 riot in Chicago, and it is as if I were reading the report of the Investigating Committee on the Harlem riot of '35, the report of the Investigating Committee on the Harlem riot of '43, and the report of the McCone Commission on the Watts riot. I must again in candor say ... it is a kind of Alice in Wonderland— with the same moving picture reshown over and over again, the same analysis, the same recommendations, and the same inaction.

The complaints from the minority community are heard in a resounding way through the mass media in their coverage of specific incidents that demonstrate the conflict that exists between members of that community and the police. As a consequence, active attempts have been made to bridge the gap between the minorities and the police. "Community relations" programs (e.g., storefronts, rap sessions, T-groups, lectures by community relations specialists in the schools) have begun to take on the aura of a panacea for coping with growing urban stress. Although it is clear that these approaches for increasing the exposure between community members and the police in a controlled and focused manner can be fruitful, it is also the case that one impulsive act by one uniformed patrolman can destroy the good will that is generated by community relations programs. More often than not "community relations" is perceived as "public

---

[21]This section adopted from M. Katz, "Family Crisis Training: Upgrading the Police while Building a Bridge to the Minority Community," *Journal of Police Science and Administration*, 1, No. 1 (1973), pp. 30–35 (Courtesy of the Publisher).

[22]*Report on the National Advisory Commission on Civil Disorders* (1968).

relations," and as a con game by the community whose members cannot see the relationship between the activities of the community relations specialist and those of the patrolmen on the street, who are, according to members of the minority community, enforcing laws differentially for the majority and minority communities, engaging in harassment tactics, and not responding as quickly to complaints in the black and Spanish-speaking communities as they do for whites.

Experimental models have been proposed that modify the more traditional organization structure in policing. Angell[23] has proposed a team policing model that appears to deal effectively with the realities of intraorganizational problems of job dissatisfaction, poor communication, and control that currently exist in most police organizations. The orientation of a community-based police department, responding to the pressures that exist within the community and developing procedures for handling problems specifically for the local district, offers hope in bridging the gap between the police and the policed.

There still exists the need to attack the problem at the individual street officer level. Rokeach, Miller and Snyder[24] have identified significant differences between police personnel and members of the majority and minority populations with regard to basic values that relate to conservatism and maintaining the status quo. The research indicates that police personnel put a far heavier value upon dealing with people in an impersonal manner, relying heavily upon obedience and self-control. Little emphasis is placed upon leniency, tolerance and spontaneity. It is suggested by Rokeach et al. that police personnel have significantly different values than most Americans, and especially Americans who happen to be black. Although there can be little doubt that functioning as a policeman on the street over the years changes a man, Rokeach's research supports the notion that many of these differences between the police and the general population exist prior to entry into police work.

The reliance upon control and obedience, both in an internal value system and in departmental policy and training procedures, do not coincide with the demands of the street policeman's job on the street. He is asked to respond, on his own much of the time, to a constantly changing environment calling for flexibility and creativity in the resolution of conflict situations. A framework of control and rigid obedience will not only not serve him as well as innovative use of his skills and abilities, but it is likely to force confrontations between himself and people in the community who are not responding to the same values and pressures.

[23]J. Angell, "Toward an Alternative to the Classic Police Organizational Arrangements: A Democratic Model," *Criminology* (Aug./Nov. 1971).

[24]M. Rokeach, M. Miller, and J. Snyder, "Value Gap between Police and Policed," *Journal of Social Issues*, 27, 2 (1971).

Different value systems appear to translate into behavior relating to the way in which segments of society perceive the police and the way in which various subgroups should be treated by the police. Westley[25] discusses a continuum relating to the degree of respect that various groups have for the police and the corresponding way in which police personnel treat members of these groups. The points on the continuum are: children; the "better class of people"; the slum dwellers; the Negroes; and criminals. Although there is not necessarily a direct relationship between attitudes and behavior change, there is sufficient evidence that each affects the other. Considering the traditional reward systems and promotional practices that exist in most departments, there is little to generate change on the part of the individual patrolman in the direction of bridging the gap with the minority community. Unless it can be demonstrated that change will make him more effective on the job; lead to promotion or transfer into a high status position; or make his job easier, there is little reason for patrolmen to respond differently to minority group members or to take seriously new techniques that move the police toward a more realistic weighting of the service functions inherent in the maintenance of order.

Bard and Berkowitz[26] formulated a viable model for training a group of selected patrolmen in New York City to function as mental health paraprofessionals in coping with the difficult problem of family crisis intervention. In the context of a team policing program designed to train patrolmen in a "generalist-specialist" orientation, Barocas and Katz[27] generalized from the model to deal with community disputes, youth problems, as well as family crises.

Approaches emphasize that assistance offered during a crisis situation and the constructive resolution of interpersonal conflict provide the police with an opportunity to demonstrate honest concern toward minority group members. Similarly, the potential for change is greatly enhanced as a result of conflict when the disputants' defenses are down. Assistance, with an eye toward resolution, can frequently provide a far more effective outcome than the traditional approaches of arrest, temporary separation, or playing the authoritarian role to prevent violence and avoid personal attack (which often comes once the authoritarian role is assumed).

Recognizing the opportunity for upgrading his department in Lowell, Massachusetts, the late Chief Peter Guduras received funding from the Governor's Committee on Law Enforcement to develop a family crisis unit.

[25]W. A. Westley, *Violence and the Police: A Sociological Study of Law, Custom and Morality* (1971).

[26]M. Bard and B. Berkowitz, "Training Police as Specialists in Family Crisis Intervention," *Community Mental Health Journal* (Winter 1967).

[27]H. Barocas and M. Katz, "Dayton's Pilot Training Program in Crisis Prevention," *The Police Chief* (July 1971).

The rationale for concentrating upon family crisis was:

1. Police are currently engaged in a number of service functions and mental health activities with insufficient technical and attitudinal training.

2. The family dispute is one of the most common services with which the police have to deal.

3. Family conflict situations are characterized by high recidivism primarily because the traditional methods of law enforcement can, at best, only end the immediate conflict situation without doing anything to remedy the underlying factors contributing to conflict within the family.

4. It represents a situation in which the upgraded patrolman has an opportunity to provide direct assistance to non-criminal persons in distress.

5. There is no way in which sophisticated law enforcement equipment can aid in the handling of a family conflict. The patrolman has to depend solely on his own powers and inner resources.

6. Increased success in handling family disturbances, valuable in itself, improves the image of police in the eyes of the community members.

7. Because of the high degree of recidivism, the difficulty of attaining a clear-cut solution and the hostility often directed at the patrolman, family crisis intervention is one of the most frustrating of all police experiences. It is critical to deal with this frustration and the anger or apathy to which it will inevitably lead.

8. Family crisis intervention requires a wide variety of new knowledge, skill, and attitudes which are transferrable to many other police-community interactions and lead to a general upgrading of police capability.

The program in Lowell was designed to train ten experienced officers in knowledge, skills and attitudes necessary for effective family crisis intervention. All held the rank of patrolman except for one lieutenant. The lieutenant's role was primarily that of observer, administrative supervisor and liaison with the Chief's office.

Theoretically, the initial thrust should have been to concentrate upon attitude change. However, based upon experiences in previous crisis management programs, it was decided to focus first upon the problem of imparting skills and knowledge. In practice, attitude change appears to come last—if at all. It comes from within, after a good deal of introspection and insight. It was felt that attitude change would be more likely to occur after successful experiences using the new techniques and skills occurred.

For this reason training had to have the following characteristics:

1. Intensive—involving many different experiences that had a high degree of initial personal impact.

2. Extensive—lasting over a long period of time, providing reinforcement and repetition.

3. Based upon the practical experiences of the patrolmen and trainers.

4. High degree of learner participation (as opposed to passive note taking or listening to lecturers).

5. Small number of participants to maximize involvement.

To meet the needs for intensive and extensive training, the program was divided into two segments: Phase 1, the "input" phase, consisted of eight days of varied experiences, all calling for active responding on the part of participants, and all designed to cover the basic knowledge and skill areas needed in effective family crisis intervention. Emphasis was on:

1. Tactics to ensure physical safety of patrolmen and disputants.
2. Interviewing skills, including the importance of verbal and non-verbal cues in communication.
3. Factors that keep a family in a state of balance and that which causes an upset of the balance
4. Basic principles of human behavior with emphasis upon special problem areas such as alcoholism, depression, and suicide.
5. Availability within the community of social service agencies to whom referral could be made.
6. Self-insight.

Presentation by Trainers

The presentations were designed to bear little resemblance to the traditional lecture method. Experience with police in other cities and with many other training populations has shown that the lecture method is rarely effective in terms of holding attention and promoting retention of the material. Two trainers made each presentation. During the presentation both trainers moderated the discussion. The advantages of using two leaders simultaneously are:

1. While one is presenting the material, the other is free to gauge reactions, spot signs of emotional resistance, and obtain other important feedback.
2. Both trainers have a common core of shared expertise, but each brings a somewhat different background and perspective to the discussion.
3. Reduction in pressure upon the trainers and resultant increase in the effectiveness of each person.

Films

Films were used to serve as input material, to highlight important points, and to serve as a basis for discussion.

Interaction with Social Agency Personnel

Each participant in the program spent a day in a social agency, talking with the staff, meeting agency clients, and observing the functioning of the agency. Each patrolman was to report back to the group of fellow officers regarding his experiences and the strengths and weaknesses of the agency and its personnel. Finally, the entire group of patrolmen spent several hours interacting with the key agency personnel to exchange views and to grease the lines of communication in preparation for the time when the unit would be on the street referring disputants to agencies and calling upon agency personnel for assistance.

Intervention Scenarios

Alternatives to arrest, conflict psychology, and understanding one's own motivations are best handled in action framework in which two-man teams of patrolmen attempt to solve the problems of family crisis with their peers—observing and evaluating the solutions. Role-playing, using professional actors, video-tape feedback, and group discussion between actors and participating patrolmen incorporate the necessary realism and group pressure to ensure an effective training experience. It gave each participant an opportunity to practice his intervention style, interviewing, and counseling, and to pay particular attention to the safety precautions under the watchful eyes of his peers and the video-tape.

In Phase 2, the "follow-up" phase, which began immediately after the patrolmen were in uniform back on the street, the trainer met with the participants an average of five hours each week, every other week, over a 26-week period.

Approximately two hours were spent meeting with the entire group

— Relating the street experiences of the participants to the input training they had received.

— Sharing information on problem families and comparing intervention styles and experiences.

— Examining the underlying attitudes of the participants in an attempt to demonstrate how each patrolman's motivations and expectations can positively or negatively influence his skill in crisis intervention.

The trainer spent about one hour with each three-man team discussing the interactions of the team members in relation to the details of the success and failures in handling family disturbances and other calls.

An unusual and highly productive feature of the "follow-up" phase of the program was the practice of having the trainer ride with each team and enter in on interventions. It enabled the trainer to get first-hand knowledge of the problems, to observe the intervention styles of participants and offer constructive criticism. It gave the team members an opportunity to observe the trainer's strategy and style in handling crisis situations.

Observations and Recommendations

1. Support and reinforcement from command personnel is essential to the success of upgrading any experimental program that potentiates change.

Command should be included in the initial planning of the "change" program. There is a tendency to react to a new unit in the police system as if it were an organ transplant. The antibodies within the system react strongly to reject the new unit.

2. It is felt here that specialists in crisis intervention are only a stopgap procedure and that training in this area should serve as a foundation for upgrading *all* departmental personnel in understanding and coping with urban conflict.

Initially, however, work in the area has to raise questions regarding the value of such work and its relation to reward and promotion within the system. If a patrolman arrests a burglar and secures a conviction, his performance does not go unnoticed. Similarly, if a family crisis unit is able to avoid crowding the courts with additional arrests, to prevent violence, to attain a lowered recidivism rate, or to give emergency assistance to a person or family that could not have been obtained elsewhere, they deserve appropriate reward and recognition within the department.

3. Crisis training should be built into basic recruit police training and in-service training programs. The experience in Lowell demonstrated that although the incidence of family calls was low, the family crisis unit was called upon (by command officers who favored the program) to handle conflict situations that were quite unrelated to family crisis such as: coping with the emotionally disturbed; talking down suicide attempts; working with young people in conflict. The skills and attitudes learned can be generalized to other areas of police work.

4. The focused small group, interactional (as opposed to lecture) style of training should be blended into recruit and in-service training. The problems that street personnel are responding to require innovative, flexible behavior styles that are not learned in a highly regimented, authoritarian training atmosphere. Understanding the dynamics of interpersonal experiences, attitudes, and behavior of the street patrolman, demand a training environment in which patrolmen can discuss, in a focused and spontaneous way, their expectations and frustrations of their street experiences. The model for crisis training is a dynamic one that changes from one program to the next and has been altered in responding to the demands of each training situation. Although the changes make evaluation more difficult, the insights that evolve from this approach are contributing to preventative social intervention in coping with the urban crush.

Beyond the "preventive social intervention" cited above is the crucially significant leadership role in shaping *expectations* as discussed earlier—critically important if for no other reason than acknowledging the *differences* in various groups in terms of the difficulty in gaining influence. Police activities in the area of family crisis may indeed serve as the *only* "visible" evidence that government is sensitive to either *expectations* or to the differing levels of difficulty in bringing group expectations to bear on government.

Within the context of such variations, attention is now focused upon the influence on expectations of interracial human relations.

INTERRACIAL HUMAN RELATIONS

Minority to Majority—Easier for Some

As noted elsewhere in this volume, membership in a minority group is sometimes difficult to determine—at least by persons outside the group. Intergroup relations often function without knowledge or concern about the racial background of the members.

Earlier in American history, any number of European immigrant groups were minorities and, as such, suffered many of the disadvantages noted earlier. But unlike racial minority groups, minorities from Europe have traditionally been encouraged to *expect* that a single generation's "turnover" would remove the language barrier that clearly set them apart from the majority. These minorities were also encouraged to expect even more; in a single generation the typical European minority group could reasonably expect that they would acquire the majority group's clothing styles, living habits, and social skills, along with its language.

Being able to *expect* such a dramatic loss of minority identity may well have motivated the incredible speed with which many immigrant groups undertook, on their own, the loss of their minority identity—and did, in fact, lose it. Frequently enriched with occupational skills from the old country, most Europeans have taken a comparatively short time to "join" the majority. And once joined, there are methods of identifying the minority background of the European immigrant. But the *race* of these immigrant minorities is Caucasian, the race of the *majority*.

Joining by Degrees

Many American minorities, however, are identifiable by racial characteristics. These minorities often do not *expect* to join the majority to the same level or degree as do those minorities identifiable only by language and dress. Indeed, in many respects, acquiring the social behavior, the dress, and the language habits of the majority often tends to draw attention to the minority stereotype—more often than not, a degrading and undignified stereotype.

The term *interracial human relations*, then, acknowledges a great deal more than the inherent frustration of membership in a "relegated minority." It goes far beyond acknowledging the despair that accompanies generation after generation witnessing the elevation of nearly all relegated minorities but theirs, and a system that includes additional severe socioeconomic penalties for those already penalized in terms of dignity. To be meaningful, then, interracial human relations must avow the *right* of every human being to be respected as a human being. Moreover, this respect must flow from the belief that *all* human beings are of the highest form of life, and that only the *behavior* of people can be called good or bad. Bad behavior is always subject to modification in proportion to the degree of human dignity accorded.

In this sense, interracial human relations differ very little from intergroup relations. After all, both are intergroup human relations. But a sensitivity to all the problems affecting intergroup relations is only the beginning of good interracial human relations. With interracial groups comes a sense of urgency, following the recognition that time alone did not—and cannot—resolve problems that it has resolved for other intergroup relations. Time, on the contrary, has amplified racial problems, and as has been expressed throughout this text, time appears to be running out.

SUMMARY

This chapter began with an assertion that the police function has been conceived of in terms of either apprehending criminals or in some other way directly responding to crime. Complexities in modern law have done little to modify this conception of enforcement, in spite of an ever-increasing proportion of persons formerly not considered "criminal" who may now be so defined. There is a need for a vast broadening of the police role beyond crime—to the point at which crime *itself* is controlled while disruptive community influences are also controlled (or at least anticipated). Broadening the police role in this manner was proposed in this chapter in terms of Berne's theory of behavior—in which transactional analysis is a key concept. According to this theory, an especially workable one in relation to law enforcement concern, behavior "proves" one's beliefs, which are always significant to the believer whether they are valid or not.

Attitudes of a group may be to some degree law-abiding, even when certain laws are collectively violated by the group membership. Even those defined as criminals retain a quasi-respectful attitude toward *certain* laws. Having a law-abiding attitude is thus shown to be weakened as a predictor of general law-abiding behavior.

The concept of a community was discussed in this chapter in terms of geographical area and, more importantly, in terms of the community's various populations. It is vital for law enforcement personnel to be aware of the various kinds of intergroup relationships in order to actively seek the reduction of stress between varying populations when such stress is in evidence.

In discussing law enforcement's interest in friction between population groups, this chapter distinguished between crowds, mobs, gangs, plurals, aggregates, and demonstrations. Group activity on a *continuing basis* with a category of membership, such as race, is helpful in identifying population groups between which stress may occur.

Stress between population groups relates to rights, freedoms, and dignity; the absence of these in any group lessens the possibility of community cohesion. Achieving freedom can bring about conflict when such freedom is either gained or maintained at the expense of another's freedom or dignity. This, in turn, implies certain restrictions on the freedom of many to insure the freedom and dignity of all.

Meaningful dialogue resulting from two-way communication is the prime ingredient of all human relations. Human motivation is related to this dialogue, and the lack of it. Motivation develops only when dialogue permits certain expectations to be realized.

The racial identity of some minority-group members keeps them in a permanent minority-group status. This permanence contrasts with the relative ease with which various Caucasian minority groups have lost such status by "joining" the population majority within a few generations.

DISCUSSION TOPICS

1. Elaborate on the implications of what this chapter noted as a probability that virtually *all* adults violate some law.

2. Relate Berne's concept of *reward* ("payoff") to group behavior.

3. Discuss the expansion of the police role beyond that of direct response to law violation.

4. Discuss the relationship between law violation, beliefs, and motivation. Between beliefs and the "proving" of beliefs.

5. How can social problems divide the community's population?

6. How do racially identifiable minority groups differ significantly from minority groups in general?

7. Discuss the community in terms of "joining" the majority population group. In terms of criteria for distinguishing between the community's population groups. In terms of stress between population groups.

8. Discuss two-way communication, stress, and population groups in terms of restrictions on freedom. In terms of dignity.

ANNOTATED REFERENCES

BRONZ, S., *Roots of Negro Racial Consciousness*. New York: Libra Publications, 1964. This book describes the contrasts between the typical stereotyped Negro background and that of the majority group.

CABLE, KENNETH M., "The Chief and The Community," *The Police Chief*, 38, No. 3 (March 1971). This provides excellent reading about law enforcement administration as it relates to the community.

COFFEY, ALAN R., *Criminal Justice Administration: A Management Systems Approach.* Englewood Cliffs, N.J.: Prentice-Hall, Inc., 1974. Chapter Ten covers police administration and Chapter Fifteen concerns certain community political influences, both bearing directly upon the administrative implications of law enforcement program efforts to cope with community problems.

CONANT, J., *Slums and Suburbs,* New York: McGraw-Hill, 1961. This provides an excellent perception of the depth of cultural institutions impinging on minority groups.

DRIMMER, M., ed., *Black History.* Garden City, N.Y.: Doubleday, 1967. Like Bronz's book, this book discusses the American Negro's historical background.

GERMANN, A. C., "Changing the Police—The Impossible Dream," *Journal of Criminal Law, Criminology and Police Science,* 62, No. 3 (Sept. 1971). Excellent coverage of the title subject in the same context as this chapter.

HARLAN, L., *Separate and Unequal.* Chapel Hill: University of North Carolina Press, 1968. This volume discusses the inequities in the minority-group treatment in America.

COMMUNITY RELATIONS PROGRAMMING

12

The past two decades have witnessed not only massive social changes but also an ever-increasing sensitivity among police to the shifting role of law enforcement. Particularly in recent years, dramatic changes have demonstrated the impact of the changing police role—changes such as law enforcement agencies creating full-scale units to deal with what has become known as "community relations."

Though there is wide range of approaches to community relations programming, all such programs have in common the goal of answering this question: *What must be done to promote the understanding and use of social influences to encourage voluntary law observance?*

Of course this question has profound implications for all police functions. But as an example of these implications, further discussion of *family crisis intervention* may help clarify at least part of the approach to answering this question. First, consider these remarks on "crisis."

> Crises are a part of living. If one takes their broad definition, they are a frequent and desirable part of the human growth process. Some learning takes place in a relatively calm and evolutionary way, but some learning takes place, inevitably, in a tumultuous way. If everything we learned came to us slowly, gradually, and calmly, the sum total of what we learn would be far less than optimum. Spurts in learning take place most often in states of heightened excitability and unsettlement.
>
> As help-givers we need to know *whether* and *when* to intervene in

other people's crises. It is not so simple a matter as it may be assumed to be. We cannot decide that whether to intervene should be determined by whether we are asked for help or not; nor can we comfortably decide *when* to intervene by when we are asked. Sometimes we are not asked at all, yet intervention could prevent destructive consequences. Sometimes we are asked too late and at still other times we are asked too early. Sometimes we are asked for help when help is not necessary. So we must have other criteria for whether and when to try to help. A simple framework for classifying crises along this dimension would be as follows:

1. Crises in which help is contraindicated—those in which help should positively not be given.
2. Crises in which help *may* be given but is not really needed.
3. Crises in which help *is needed* if the best solutions are to be found to the problems confronting a person.
4. Crises in which help is mandatory to avert disaster.[1]

POLICE FAMILY CRISIS INTERVENTION

It must be reemphasized that police intervention into family crises is only one of many examples that could be used to clarify police-community relations. But it serves as a good example because very few police officers are unaware of the high proportion of family fights in the typical police patrol function and the community relations implications. Moreover, the potential for violence and possible bodily harm inherent in family fight situations clearly establish domestic difficulties as a continuing police problem—a problem that requires continual attention in most jurisdictions. Beyond the immediate problem, however, is the overall community relations potential in providing effective aid to families experiencing problems—a potential to begin *promoting social influences to encourage voluntary law observance.*

Police understanding and use of family crisis intervention as a tool in encouraging positive attitudes toward law and the enforcers of society's laws is of paramount importance. It is vital, therefore, that all peace officers have some understanding of family crisis intervention.

Attempting to distinguish between "intervention" by police and "intrusion" by police is, in many ways, meaningless. The virtual ease with which it can be established that *all* police control of human behavior constitutes *intrusion* underpins the contention that police "intervention" into family strife *is* "intrusion." In other words, the term "intervention" is simply "intrusion" by another name *because* police are seeking to

[1]D. A. Schwartz, *Crisis: Concepts and Intervention*, speech delivered at University of California, Santa Cruz, Mar. 15, 1968, pp. 6–7.

control human behavior. This intent to *control*, whether or not the control is welcome, can serve as a persuasive argument for calling police efforts to intervene in family strife "family-crisis-intrusion" instead of "family-crisis-intervention."

But while it remains true that *any* police effort to control human behavior *is* intrusion, it is also true that there is an extremely wide variation in both nature of such police effort, and the intended outcome of such police effort. This wide variation appears to more than justify distinguishing between *intruding* for the purposes of enforcing law, and *intervening* to prevent law violation. In short, the distinction between police "intrusion" and police "intervention" is a matter of the intent to "enforce law" as opposed to the intent to "prevent law violation."

This distinction, however, loses a great deal of significance in many, if not most, of the family disturbances in which police involvement is *perceived* as *intrusion*, regardless of police intentions. This reality suggests emphasis upon the recognition that even the most sensitive *intervention* on the part of police tends to come across as *intrusion*. Such emphasis also permits easier recognition of the *risks* involved in police efforts to intervene in family strife—that how police are perceived may be far more significant than the police intentions. In other words, understanding the *risks* involved in police contact with family strife suggests emphasis upon the intruding nature of *all* police effort to control human behavior, with only secondary emphasis upon police intentions.

Recognizing the intruding nature of police involvement in family strife also affords a basis for defining the actual nature of police risks during such intrusion—intrusion into crisis defined as "one or more family members unable to cope with stress." The first dimension of this general nature has to do with the *reaction* to intrusion—a reaction that might be thought of as we-versus-they.[2]

TRAINING POLICE IN FAMILY CRISIS INTERVENTION[3]

Why do police officers find themselves spending a significant proportion of their on-duty time dealing with families in conflict? On the surface, the reason is that no one else takes the responsibility for mediating family disputes. This *no-one-else* explanation is admittedly a superficial one as it stands, but becomes meaningful with reference to the fact that in less complex societies—or at least in some societies unlike current American society

---

[2]Alan R. Coffey, *Police Intervention Into Family Crisis* (Santa Cruz: Davis, 1974), p. 30.

[3]This section adopted from J. M. Driscoll, R. H. Meyer, and C. F. Schanie, "Training Police in Family Crisis Intervention," *Journal of Applied Behavioral Science,* 9, No. 1 (1973), 62–82. (Courtesy of the publisher).

—family conflict is handled by the extended family or senior members of the kinship system. Parents, close relatives, kinship elders, or some other respected or legitimate insider mediates with authority, with the interest of the family and its immediate social extensions in mind.

In modern America, however, social mobility has placed most nuclear families in geographical settings distant from parents, relatives, or even neighbors who could be counted on to mediate a dispute fairly or to regulate unacceptable behavior on the part of one or both marital partners. Consequently, when a nuclear family in such social isolation has exhausted its internal resources and methods for handling conflict, its members often have no place to turn but to public arbitration.

This isolation is aggravated by certain facts: the mental health system in most communities is not responsive to this type of problems, it is seldom available round-the-clock on short notice, and many family conflicts involve violence. All this sets the problem squarely on the shoulders of the police.

The police are the only agents of society licensed to use counter-force against citizens prior to litigation (see Bittner, 1970). Since scores of family crises require the use of counter-force to prevent or offset violence, the problem of domestic trouble can legitimately be placed within their domain—at least in part. Ignoring the potential for violence in domestic disputes would be foolhardy: most homicides and assaults occur among family members or persons closely related to one another (Wolfgang, 1958; Federal Bureau of Investigation, 1970).

Additionally, since effective social control is dependent on the range of outcomes available to the controlling agent and his ability to use them, most will concede that the policeman is in an enviable position in this respect. It is also true that a police officer is a legally constituted authority of the entire community and, as such, possesses different stimulus properties than the mental health agent or the social worker. In his legitimately constituted role, a police officer may be perceived as a legitimate intervention agent more often than a mental health worker would be under the circumstances of most family crises. He is representative of the community as a whole, has that community's backing, and is powerful in terms of the action alternatives available to him. Disputants are therefore compelled to accept an officer's presence in the crisis as a sanctioned agent of society.

Most important, perhaps, is the fact that the police officer usually arrives at the point of crisis in family conflicts. Caplan and Grunebaum (1967) have noted that the turmoil in which crisis-plagued individuals find themselves often makes them particularly pliable. Characteristically, such persons realize that they have exhausted their repertoire of coping behavior and are no longer capable of handling the situation. They are therefore more susceptible to influence that might lead them to more adaptive behavior.

The Effectiveness of Training

Unfortunately, the reasonable expectation that police responsibility for dealing with domestic trouble be met with some degree of competency is usually not satisfied. Few police officers have the behavioral science training necessary for an effective family crisis intervention. Bard (1970) has suggested recently, however, that such competency can be gained in a relatively short time within the context of an intensive and specialized training program; this possibility is certainly worth serious attention.

On the other hand, caution must be exercised, since several considerations suggest that training in family crisis intervention might not be accepted by police officers—and, if accepted, might not prove effective. Several major forces might militate against the development of a potential for effective handling of domestic trouble. For instance, most police systems currently reject family trouble as a legitimate aspect of policing, place low priority upon it, and fail to reward activities so directed. As a consequence, the begrudging police response to a family in conflict is usually either legalistic ("Take a warrant, lady") or coercive ("If we have to come back again, we'll lock you all up"). Moreover, the educational level of most police forces is not particularly high, and there is a traditional distaste for service functions, along with an almost single-minded orientation toward crime control.

Evaluating the New York Project

Thus, prudence would dictate that evidence on the effectiveness of police training in crisis intervention be amassed before investing substantial money or manpower in such training. The initial project in family crisis training for police was designed and conducted in New York City by Dr. Morton Bard (1970). Unfortunately, it provides, at best, equivocal support for the efficacy of such training. However, serious problems in the study, stemming from Bard's evaluation strategy, appear primarily responsible for the failure to obtain convincing evidence in favor of the training program. Since the goal of our project was a different evaluation strategy, we present here a brief review of the New York project.

The New York project focused on six evaluative criteria, with expectations for each as to the direction of change. It was hypothesized that, in comparison with a control precinct, in a demonstration precinct of trained patrolmen: (1) the number of family disturbance complaints would decrease; (2) the number of repeat interventions for trained officers would decrease (as a function of problem resolution); (3) homicides would be reduced; (4) homicides among family members would decrease; (5) assaults would decrease; and (6) injuries to policemen would be reduced.

Disturbingly, results on four of these six criteria in the evaluation of the New York project were *opposite* to expectation. There were three times more disturbance complaints in the demonstration precinct than in the control precinct; more repeat cases; an increase of three and one-half per cent in the number of homicides in the control precinct; and an increase in family homicides in the demonstration precinct as compared with no change in the control. Fortunately, fewer assaults were found in the demonstration precinct than the control precinct; and no trained officer was injured, while two members of the regular force in the demonstration precinct and one officer in the control precinct sustained injuries in family disputes.

All in all, the results of the New York project permit little confidence to be placed in the type of training devised by Bard to help police officers deal effectively with family disturbances. Had the number of family disturbance calls been fewer, and had homicides decreased in the demonstration precinct, the logic of the experimental design would have permitted the conclusion that the project was responsible for these positive effects. But since family disturbance calls increased and homicides were greater in the demonstration precinct than in the control, the conclusions that the project was responsible for these negative effects is equally valid.

The only recourse from this conclusion is the existence of confounding variables extraneous in the experimental design. Bard (1970) argues that differences in reporting between the Family Crisis Intervention Unit (FCIU) officers and untrained control officers account for the differences found in the number of disturbance complaints and the number of repeat interventions. This is perhaps an acceptable explanation (knowing the aversion of most police officers to completing written reports). As an explanation of the greater number of domestic trouble calls in the demonstration precinct, Bard (1970) also suggests that "... the availability of a more effective police service in this connection may have resulted in greater and more effective community utilization of the FCIU."

It is somewhat more difficult to explain the increases in both general and family homicides found in the New York project, and Bard's (1970) conclusion that "... the operation of the FCIU failed to effect any change in overall homicide incidence in the demonstration area" is patently erroneous, given the logic of the design of the evaluation, within which an increase in homicides must be considered a probable effect of the experimental treatment. Furthermore, in the case of homicide statistics, differential reporting cannot be suggested as a plausible external confounding factor, since homicide statistics were collected independently of the project, in the usual manner of the New York City Police Department. Thus, either the effects must be accepted as due to the project or a reasonable argument must be made that it is extremely unlikely that such effects could emerge from the project and that other extraneous factors were responsible for them.

Using Crime Statistics in Evaluation. One possible extraneous consideration is that the New York Project was run during the summer of 1967 —a time of notable black unrest. The increase in homicides *may* have been a reflection of heightened tensions in the black community. The difference between the demonstration and the control precinct, then, might be more a function of the unfortunate fact that the demonstration precinct was almost totally black and the control precinct largely Puerto Rican. There is no evidence to support this argument, however, and it rests on a chain of possible intervening variables too long to warrant its casual acceptance.

This set of design problems, however, did prevent the sort of direct and unconfounded evaluation deserved by a training program as creative and promising as that devised by Bard. While the reduction of crime incidence is obviously a worthy goal, the problems inherent in the use of crime statistics as indices of success of a police training project invite near-certain failure. Two major problems encountered by Bard seem to have been differential reporting and the operation of variables extraneous to the project that may have been more powerful than the effects of the project itself. Relatedly, there is usually considerable cross-district variation in crime statistics, which make them unreliable for assessment of all but very large projects.

An Alternative Evaluation Approach: Louisville

The Louisville project was accordingly conducted to evaluate the Bard model of crisis intervention training for police by using an evaluation stategy that focused directly on the efficacy of the intervention. In this manner, the problems associated with crime statistics can be avoided and evaluation can be made directly at the point of program impact, the most probable focus of unconfounded effects—the crisis situation itself.

Using Psychosocial Criteria. If training is effective in helping officers conduct efficient and effective family crisis interventions, several consequences pertaining to the intervention itself should ensue. In general, citizens could be expected to respond to police intervention more favorably along several psychosocial dimensions. In particular, it was predicted that citizens dealt with by trained officers would report higher levels of rapport between themselves and the officers, a greater involvement on the part of the officer, a greater level of success in working with the problem, more satisfaction with the way the situation was handled, an increased regard for police, and a greater acceptance of police in similar circumstances.

Trained officers could be expected to report changes along several dimensions related to their experience in interventions: an increased understanding of the problems with which they are dealing; an increase in the acceptance of them by citizens; a greater receptivity to their suggestions; a decrease in the necessity for force; and increase in their effectiveness in dealing with domestic trouble; and an overall favorability toward the new techniques and the training program.

Each of these conceptual dimensions was operationalized by a question put to either citizens or participating officers. Results for questions put to citizens were analyzed for statistically significant differences between responses of citizens dealt with by trained and untrained officers. Results for questions put to officers were dealt with descriptively as self-reported differences between experiences before and after training.

The Louisville Training Model

The Bard training model was followed as closely as possible, given local conditions, such as the makeup of the training staff and orientation of available expert contributors.

Theory. One major difference produced by these local conditions was in the theoretical underpinnings of the project. Although the training schedules of the New York and Louisville projects (see Bard, 1970; Driscoll, Meyer, & Schanie, 1971) appear very similar, the explanatory concepts behind topics presented and the procedures employed were quite different. The New York project contained elements suggestive of sensitivity training, and relied to some extent on psychodynamic concepts for its theoretical base. An explicit effort to change the police officers as persons, both dispositionally and affectively, was made, and a good deal of attention was paid to self-examination and awareness. Intervention procedures were based to a considerable extent on assumptions about personal and interpersonal dynamics underlying the crisis situation.

In contrast, the theoretical basis of the Louisville project was that of contemporary experimental social psychology, combined with a behavior modification approach to intervention. Within social psychology, basic social learning and imitation principles were used for the understanding of behavior and of its etiology, while exchange theory (Thibaut & Kelley, 1959) provided the context for analyzing interpersonal relations. Behavior modification principles (Wolpe, Salter, & Reyna, 1964) were used largely as the basis for intervention techniques and actions directed at a solution to problems encountered.

One immediately obvious benefit of the theoretical orientation of the Louisville project was that the release from demands on the police officers to achieve personal change yielded an immediate gain in rapport. When the officers saw that they were not to be tested, probed, or submitted to criticism for personal attitudes, beliefs, or values, they soon accepted the staff and approached training with some measure of trust and enthusiasm. Philosophically, the orientation was one in which educators and police officers were mutually involved in changing policing techniques; officers brought their expertise in police matters, and training staff offered their expertise as educators and behavioral scientists.

Throughout the course of training, the emphasis on intervention skills and techniques emerged as the dominant concern. The training philosophy became, in the main: provide the techniques, provide an opportunity for their practice under conditions of diminishing supervision, and count on their application in the field.

Selection. Police officers were recruited by superiors within the Louisville Division of Police, who provided an initial group of 13 volunteers. Each of these men was interviewed, and 12 were judged acceptable for the project.

The extent to which the police officers in the Louisville project were selected is an important issue, since it forms a potential point of comparison with the New York project, which used highly selected men. Accordingly, some basic data on crisis unit officers were compared with data from a nominal group formed by a random selection of 12 patrolmen from the Louisville force. Men of the crisis unit were on the average 33 years of age, some 4.4 years younger than the average of the nominal group, and had 5.6 years less experience on the force.[4] However, if crisis unit officers and officers of the nominal group are ordered by age, 8 of the 12 men of the crisis unit can be paired with a nominal group counterpart within three years of age, either younger or older. Nearly the same holds true for date-joined-the-force; half of the men from the crisis unit and nominal group can be paired in experience within one year. In contrast, Bard (1970) decided to limit the New York project to volunteers ". . . with at least 3 years, but no more than 10 years, of service." Eighteen men were selected from 42 volunteers in the New York project. At the very least, a comparison of selection procedures suggests that officers in the Louisville project were less subject to volunteer bias and somewhat more representative of policemen in general. However, some selection obviously operated on the Louisville sample, and whatever conclusions are made possible by our results hold strictly and only for policemen selected in a comparable manner.

In the formation of teams, the staff police to involve police officers in decisions about the program led to the officer's rejection of the staff's pro-

[4]Comparison of selected with unselected officers on attitudinal and value dimensions was precluded by the decision not to test officers. This decision was made within the context of the philosophy of the project, which stressed that officers were not to be treated as subjects but as equals engaged in the joint enterprise (with the academic staff) of developing techniques and skills in family crisis intervention.

posed sociometric techniques in favor of choosing partner assignments for themselves. This wish was stated strongly and with unanimity, and was accepted by the training staff. Officers were thus left free to work out their own partnerships and to report them to the staff at the end of the day. No complaints were made to the staff and no partners separated before the end of the evaluation.

Training.   Intensive training consisted of five to seven hours of activities each weekday for a five-week period.

Presentations, Readings, and Films.   Presentations with discussions were intended to provide officers with information basic to the understanding of problems in family crisis and with the background needed for application of the techniques to be taught. Officers received presentations on the role of the police in family disputes, new concepts of police work, causes of behavior, effects of early experience, changing behavior, children in families, family structure and interactions, and alcohol and drug abuse (see Bard, 1970; Driscoll, Meyer, & Schanie, 1971).

Contributors were told of the intent of the program and left free to direct their comments in any way they, as experts, felt was most appropriate.

Review, extension, and integration of the above material took place in discussions after each presentation, in training groups, in morning feedback sessions, and in informal contact between officers and staff. Readings and films were used to supplement and extend the presentations, while simultaneously providing the implicit support gained through the use of multiple media.

Field Trips.   Two agency field trips were arranged to take place at opportune times in the intensive training program, with an eye toward impressing upon the officers the importance of community agencies. At this time, a condensed listing of referral agencies and a supply of referral slips were given officers; these were to be carried with them at all times when on duty.

Simulations.   In changing longstanding practices, such as those used over the years by police officers in handling family trouble, lecture techniques can be anticipated to have only limited impact. Most psychologists would agree that to consolidate such learning the person must actually execute the new behavior and find it successful. For this general reason, and because of Bard's strong recommendation, simulated family crisis interventions were included as a major aspect of the training programs. In contrast to the format of the New York project, which provided partially written scripts, a decision to work with groups of actors for new, more creative simulations was made.

A week or so before each simulation, the project staff worked with actors to decide upon the main story line in terms of the requirements of good stage production and systematic psychology. These sessions resulted most often in a significant extension of the initial plan, given input from the actors and ideas generated by them while they played out the basic scene. (A basic scene was played out prior to each "intervention" as a sort of warm-up). This scene changed a little each time it was played, since a script was never used, but its main themes remained essentially the same. However, once the team of officers arrived, scenes took unpredictable turns, since actors were instructed again and again to respond to the officers from the viewpoint of the role being played.

More simulations were included in the Louisville project than were used previously. In the New York project, each team of officers was involved in one simulated intervention and observed other teams six times. Three different plays were seen: the one in which each officer intervened and two in which other officers intervened. In the Louisville project, each officer intervened in three simulations and observed, on the average, seventeen others, involving three different plays. Each team of officers handled each simulation, then went behind a one-way mirror to observe their colleagues handling the same situation. Officers were scheduled so that they did not observe before they "intervened."

The last two simulations represented an innovation; officers in the project helped devise simulations for their colleagues. In retrospect this seems to be an excellent practice and is strongly recommended.

Feedback Sessions: Conference with Actors and Video Replay. Following the format of the New York project, feedback sessions were provided. On the day after the simulation, selected actors were asked to meet with policemen and to comment on their reactions to the officers. Another innovation was a videotape replay of each intervention. Replay was controlled by the trainer, who replayed segments so that officers, actors, and psychologist-trainers could comment on whatever occurred that could be used for learning purposes.

Simulations, supplemented by actor conferences and videotape feedback (in particular), proved, we believe, to be the most effective and stimulating aspect of the entire intensive training program.

Field Interventions and Reports. In addition to videotape feedback, the Louisville project was also able to add field interventions to the basic design of the New York project. These were possible because the Louisville Division of Police has the enlightened policy that qualified persons interested in seeing police work can, with proper arrangements, ride in patrol cars with beat officers. Under this provision, field interventions were made by each team of police officers in the company of a staff member. On these interventions, teams were permitted to roam freely and to answer family dispute calls. Each team answered at least one call and several answered two in the one evening. On the following day, the staff member worked with the officers, who later reported on their field interventions to the entire unit.

Reports on field interventions proved valuable in two ways: they provided an opportunity for officers to convince one another that they could make effective crisis interventions in the field under actual conditions, and provided a format for the training groups in the operational phase of the project.

Training Groups. Training groups were the main source of flexibility, informal discussion, and opportunity to deal with feelings, uncertainties, and other personal matters in the program. Two permanent training groups operated throughout the course of the intensive training program, each with the same six officers, graduate assistant, and group leader. As might be expected, each group performed somewhat different functions for the persons in them. Following training, groups were kept intact with the same graduate assistant and membership. Groups met once every two weeks for the first two months of the operational phase of the project and once a month thereafter. The purposes of the groups during the operational phase of the project were multifold, but the major amount of time was spent in what might best be called case conferences.

Field Operation and Evaluation Procedure

As indicated earlier, assessment of the effectiveness of crisis intervention training for police in terms of crime statistics seems the obvious evaluation technique. However, crime statistics have many shortcomings which make them inappropriate for evaluation of a project such as this. The two most serious are their sizable natural variation within samples no larger than police districts and their susceptibility to extraneous influence. For this reason as well as others, evaluation efforts were directed to the effectiveness of the crisis interventions themselves.

The option of evaluating at the point of the crisis intervention, though perhaps not as immediately compelling as a focus on crime statistics, is not an intrinsically undesirable one: most persons, we believe, would agree that direct demonstration of effective crisis intervention by police would be a most significant step. To this end, a structured Client Telephone Questionnaire was designed to assess the reaction of citizens to several dimensions of an effective crisis intervention and to compare the effectiveness of trained with untrained officers. In addition to the Client Telephone Questionnaire, an effort was made to gauge the reactions of the participating officers to the novel intervention procedures with an Officer Participant Questionnaire.

Late in July of 1970, following the completion of the five weeks of intervention training, formal operation of the six 2-man crisis teams was initiated. Trained officers were given regular assignments, consistent with the understanding that training in family crisis intervention was intended not to produce police specialists but to make the general patrolman more adept at a task he was already performing as a general patrolman. Two of the six teams were assigned to each of the three 8-hour shifts, so that at any given time of the day there were two crisis intervention teams on duty in the eight-beat district. This arrangement was maintained from late July through December of 1970 to allow for the data collection. During this period, radio dispatchers assigned domestic trouble calls in any part of the district to trained intervention teams whenever possible.

When this was not possible (as when crisis officers were busy with regular beat duties), the call was assigned to another patrol in the district manned by two untrained officers. This provided a systematic assignment of domestic cases to trained and untrained officers for subsequent evaluation follow-up in the form of the Client Telephone Questionnaire.

Over the data collection period, 421 domestic trouble runs were made in the third district by all officers, and of these runs, 129, or 31 per cent, were made by trained officers (who constituted 25 per cent of the officer teams on duty).[5]

The Client Telephone Questionnaire. Six evaluative questions were included on the Client Telephone Questionnaire, each designed to assess a particular dimension relevant to the effectiveness of the intervention. These dimensions were:

Rapport—Question 1: How friendly would you say that officers were? Would you say that:

A. They were friendly like a stranger in the street.
B. They were friendly like a neighbor.
C. They were friendly like a big brother or sister.

Involvement—Question 2: How hard do you think the officers tried to help you with the problem that brought them? Would you say that:

A. They tried very hard to help.
B. They tried a little to help, but not much.
C. They didn't try to help at all.

Perceived Success—Question 3: How helpful did you feel the policemen were in settling your problem? Would you say that:

A. They were very helpful.
B. They were a little helpful, but not much.
C. They were not helpful at all.

---

[5]Comparisons of arrest rates and other crime statistics for trained and untrained officers was not made because of the problems associated with such indices discussed in the introduction of this paper.

Satisfaction—Question 4: How happy were you with the way the police-men handled the situation? Would you say that:

A. You were happy with the way they handled the situation.
B. You think they handled it okay.
C. You were unhappy with the way they handled it.

Regard—Question 5: Did the way these police officers acted in your home change your opinion of police?

YES   NO

If yes, do you think:
More of the police?   Less of the police?

Acceptance—Question 6: Now that the police have visited your home, would you be more likely, less likely, or about as likely as before to call them back if you needed them?

A. More likely to call them.
B. Less likely to call them.
C. About as likely as before.

Three questions not related directly to the impact of the intervention but of use in other ways were posed: one as to whether a referral was made, a second on whether the agency was visited, and a third asking if the police had made a previous visit for a similar problem.

A procedure of interviewing the first adult of the household arriving at the phone was deliberately adopted over a theoretically more desirable equal-sex sampling procedure. This was done out of concern for its potential for exacerbating conflict in the home (by perhaps implying to the spouse who happened to answer the phone that the other's opinion was preferred). Three householders seen by the untrained group and one seen by the trained group admitted at this point in the interview that the police had been to their home but refused to talk to the interviewer. After elimination of these cases, the number of completed interviews with householders seen by the untrained and trained groups was 26 and 29, respectively.

One question which might be reasonably posed is the extent to which the asystematic (but not random) sampling procedure and the necessity of telephone contact produced like samples for the two groups. One available indicator of similarity was average family income. Average family incomes for the census tracts into which the households fell were determined from the 1960 United States Census. The median, mode, and means of these incomes were then computed for each group. Median and mode for both samples were exactly equal at a value of $7,052. The mean for the households seen by the untrained group was $6,689; for those seen by the trained group, $6,625, or $64.00 less. On this basis the groups appear comparable.

The Officer Participant Questionnaire. The 12 participating officers were mailed the Officer Participant Questionnaire four months after formal operation of the crisis intervention units began, with instructions to return it anonymously. Five items on this questionnaire concerned the officer's perception of the amount of change on several dimensions indicative of his handling of domestic trouble calls after, as compared with before, training. The issue of participant overall favorability toward the program was examined by a sixth question. All questions were stated in a form allowing for both positive or negative change. Most questions were followed by a seven-point scale with a center position labeled *no change*, the extreme left position labeled *a great deal. . .* or *much more,. . .* and the extreme right position labeled *much less* or *a great deal less. . . .*

The six dimensions assessed and their respective questions were:

Understanding—Question 1: How much better or worse do you feel you understand the nature of family crisis as a result of your training?

Acceptance—Question 2: How much more or less welcome is your presence in the homes of disputants as a result of your training?

Receptivity—Question 3: How much more or less receptive do the disputants seem to be to what you have to say in family crisis interventions as a result of your training?

Force Reduction—Question 4: How much more or less force have you found necessary to employ in handling family crisis as a result of your training?

Effectiveness—Question 5: How much more or less effective are you in handling family crises as a result of your training?

Overall Favorability—Question 6: What type of recommendation would you give a fellow officer if he asked for your opinion concerning whether or not he should participate in a crisis intervention training of this sort?

Results and Discussion

Either the Client Telephone Questionnaire or the Officer Participant Questionnaire alone would have provided rather tenuous support for crisis intervention training of police officers. However, the two questionnaires complement one another and offer cross-validation of their findings. Their results will be discussed together.

The results from both evaluation instruments provide reasonable support for the proposition that trained policemen managed to resolve the immediate conflict in the crisis situation more adequately than did untrained policemen (see Table 1). The Officer Participant Questionnaire showed strong changes in the direction of improved understanding of interpersonal conflict (q. 1), plus enhanced acceptance of officers by clients (q. 2), greater receptivity to suggestions (q. 3), less need of force (q. 4), and increased overall effectiveness (q. 5). The Client Telephone Questionnaire showed statistically significant effects in trained officer's rapport with client's (q. 1),

TABLE 12.1. Frequencies of Choice of Response Categories on the Client Telephone Questionnaire and Officer Participant Questionnaire

	Client Telephone Questionnaire						
Question	Trained (N = 29)			Untrained (N = 26)			Sig.*
	Neg.	Neut.	Pos.	Neg.	Neut.	Pos.	
1. Rapport	1	17	11	8	17	1	p < .01
2. Involvement	1	5	23	3	11	12	p < .05
3. Perceived Success	5	6	18	3	10	13	n.s.
4. Satisfaction	1	5	23	3	14	9	p < .01
5. Regard		19	10		25	1	p < .02
6. Acceptance	3	11	15		14	12	n.s.

	Officer Participant Questionnaire (N = 12)						
Question and Scale Positions	Negative or Negative Change			Neutral or No Change			Positive or Positive Change
	1	2	3	4	5	6	7
1. Understanding					1		11
2. Acceptance				1	2	5	4
3. Receptivity				1	1	6	4
4. Force Reduction				2	1	5	4
5. Effectiveness					1	2	9
6. Overall Favorability					1		11

*By chi-square analysis. Low-frequency categories collapsed where necessary and possible.

perceived involvement in the problem with accompanying efforts to help (q. 2), overall satisfaction with the intervention (q. 4), and increased regard for the police (q. 5).

Any one specific effect listed here might easily be questioned, but the consensus that is apparent between officers and clients on the different dimensions involved in dealing with family crisis argues persuasively that trained officers injected themselves into the crisis situation more satisfactorily and managed a de-escalation of the conflict more effectively than did untrained officers.

The above findings recommend crisis intervention training generally, with results in the change in use of force (q. 4, officers) and opinion of police (q. 5, clients) perhaps of particular interest to police administrators. Police administrators might, however, be even more inclined to consider the results for question 6 of the Officer Participant Questionnaire, which showed that trained officers, four months into the operational phase of the project, reported that they would strongly recommend the training to a colleague.

Two questions from the Client Telephone Questionnaire failed to show statistically significant differences and thus leave two issues largely un-determined: question 3, "How helpful do you feel the policemen were in settling your problem?" and question 6, which asked about the likelihood of calling the police again. Apparently question 3 suffers from an unfortu-nate choice of words; the intention of the question was to ask about the resolution of the immediate crisis, but the term, "your problem," appears to direct attention to long standing difficulties. In this light, it is not too surprising to find that trained officers failed to out-perform their colleagues, since the problems with which they were dealing were, for the most part, notably intransigent (half the cases with which officers dealt were repeaters); i.e., the police had previously been to the home for similar reasons. If it is accepted that question 3 inappropriately directed attention to the solution of more severe problems than the policemen could be expected to deal with in the 20 or 30 minutes usual for an intervention, then the satisfaction question, which showed results favorable to trained officers, stands alone as the best indicator of success in resolving the immediate crisis.

Comparison of Findings: Louisville and New York

The issue of long-term problem resolution and aid is not completely unanswered, however, since officers were able to make referrals to agencies which provide help with such problems. Of the 21 referrals made by trained officers in the Louisville project, three persons (7 per cent) reported that they went to an agency. Unfortunately, frequencies are too low here to rely heavily on this estimate of referral rate; this is one shortcoming of the current evaluation in its focus on crisis interventions rather than on out-comes. However, the New York project was outcome-directed; and on sev-eral issues, such as referral rates, the New York and Louisville projects particularly complement one another. Of the 719 families referred to a social agency in New York, it could be verified that 69 (9.6 per cent) took advantage of the referral and contacted the agency. Though the referral rate for both projects is quite low (it appears to lie somewhere within 7 to 10 per cent), it is obvious that some persons received help who would other-wise have remained unaided.[6]

---

[6]Referral rates for untrained policemen are unavailable. Such rates were not obtained because of the relative certainty that they are at or near zero, except for referrals to family court.

A second area of complementarity of findings between the New York and Louisville projects is the issue of call-backs and increased utilization of police in domestic disturbances. Here, the New York finding that FCIU officers made more repeat calls combines with the positive findings from the Louisville project (such as greater regard for and satisfaction with the police) to make it at least likely that the program enhances the police function in a community by affecting variables one would expect to be positively associated with the voluntary use of police in family quarrels. Thus, the failure to obtain significant differences on the call-back question (q. 6 of the Client Telephone Questionnaire) in the Louisville project appears to be out of line with both actual call-back data obtained by Bard and with the implication of reports by citizens of increased satisfaction with the police obtained in this present evaluation. Many reasons (such as the unwillingness of people to admit the possibility of calling police again for a similar problem) might be advanced for the failure of question 6 to show the expected results, but none can be substantiated from available data. Thus, the actual call-back results of the New York study should be taken as the best indicator of willingness to recall trained police, with the possible realization that people might not be willing to state a possibility before the fact.

A third area of comparison between the New York and Louisville projects concerns the issue of force and violence. In the New York project, no FCIU officer was injured, while three untrained patrolmen in the area were injured on domestic trouble calls. These frequencies are too small for statistical tests, so additional support is desirable. Such support seems to be provided by the officers' reports in the Louisville project that they required less force in handling domestic conflicts after training than before. Thus a benefit of crisis intervention training appears to be that it provides officers alternatives to force, which in turn reduce their own liability to injury.

The final comparative point is that results of the Louisville project make it somewhat less likely that the increases in homicides found in the New York project were due to the application of crisis intervention techniques in domestic trouble situations. If trained policemen were inadvertently exacerbating domestic conflict, negative consequences might be understood. If, on the other hand, trained policemen are responded to positively by citizens, as shown in the evaluation of the Louisville project, it is unlikely that they are contributing to conflict, or to increases in violence.

Thus, results from the Louisville project's evaluation showing effects such as increased friendliness, satisfaction, and appreciation of the officers favor the argument that whatever the cause of the increased incidence of assaults and homicides in the New York project, it is unlikely that FCIU officers contributed to conflict and violence through their crisis interventions. Interventions which produce high levels of positive psychosocial reaction are unlikely to leave a residual for violence.

Adaptations for Future Training

These comparisons assume that the differences between the two programs are not so substantial as to preclude meaningful comparison. Such differences can also serve as a source of information relative to future applications, and to answering the general question about any program: is it transferable—can others apply the same procedures and expect comparable outcomes?

The success of the Louisville project, modeled after the New York project, argues that crisis intervention training for police can be generally applied. Indeed, the program appears to be robust, since it can tolerate a number of significant deviations from the initial plan. Some deviations made successfully in the Louisville project are instructive:

1. Police personnel in the New York project were highly selected, whereas in the Louisville project little selection beyond the recruitment of superiors was possible. Given the success of the Louisville project, it follows that highly selected police officers are not a prerequisite, and the program can be applied to larger groups without major revision based on the qualities of the police personnel.

2. The theoretical point of view of the New York project was generally analytic, compared to the more behaviorally oriented Louisville staff. At the least, such differences in theoretical orientation do not seem crucial to the success of the project.

3. The Louisville project placed considerably more emphasis on simulations, on videotaping, and on field intervention practice. There is no way to know from the data available whether this difference, combined with the theoretical difference, accounted for success.

4. The target population in the New York project was almost exclusively black, while in the Louisville project the target population was over 90 per cent white. These differences seemed unimportant in the training, save for requiring a few special presentations on special aspects of the target population. Whether they influenced project success is not known.

Many other differences can probably be tolerated in any new application of crisis intervention training for police. However, some problems encountered in the present project point to a few areas where laxness may seriously restrict the effectiveness of the program. One of these is the support of immediate superiors. Support for the Louisville program came from the top command of the Police Department, and the officers in the program soon became advocates of crisis training. However, command personnel at the level of sergeant, lieutenant, and captain proved indifferent, at best, and hostile at worst. The New York FCIU officers were subject to ridicule at times from untrained officers, which was felt as particularly harsh in the absence of active support from immediate superiors. However, the most serious obstacle was pressure from sergeants against investing time and effort in domestic cases. Bard (1970) avoided many of these problems by a program of conferences with all personnel indirectly involved with the project. This procedure is strongly to be recommended. However, we even more strongly recommend a procedure in which an autonomous subsystem is selected, and everyone within that subsystem (say, a precinct) receives the training program. This, in effect, isolates the trained personnel from counterinfluences from the larger organization.

Another shortcoming shared by the New York and Louisville projects was inadequacy of the service agency liaison. In both projects, for instance, agencies indifferent to the extent that agency referrals could not be traced. This is a particularly insidious problem. Surface cooperation is often easily obtained from colleagues working in agencies, but the day-to-day demands upon staff in these agencies seem so pressing that they invariably neglect their participation in the project. Closer liaison with social agencies is one answer, but an established Crisis Center with an adequate referral and follow-up service is strongly recommended.

Given the precautions stated above, there appears to be reasonable assurance that the Bard model of crisis intervention training, with some adaptation, can produce more satisfactory and effective family crisis interventions by police officers.

Coping with some (perhaps all) of the difficulties noted in the above study does not *necessarily* pose major police problems. For example, when it is not practical to provide police training in the area of family crisis intervention, compiling a "directory" of locally available family counselors and therapists is an appropriate alternative. Indeed, in the context of community relations, such a directory can be prepared in a manner that literally encompasses all available social services to which community relations programming might relate. In this regard, see Appendix D in this volume.

"Synthesizing" the police activities in family crisis intervention with other community relations programs to be discussed in this chapter can take many forms—perhaps even relate directly to enforcement operations through a "modified-diversion" approach.

A pioneering effort in preventive corrections has been operational for the past two years to alleviate overloading of law enforcement, prosecution and the courts with non-violent misdemeanants.

The Social Service Project is a three-year University action-research project funded by the Illinois Law Enforcement Commission, the City of Wheaton, and the Village of Niles, Illinois.

The purpose of the Project, which places a social service unit in a community police department, is to determine if non-violent misdemeanant offenders—juveniles (their families) and adults—whose offenses are minor, can be handled at far less expense than by traditional handling in the criminal justice system. Speedy social assessment and early treatment intervention at the point of police contact, and before prosecution, is provided, with police, legal, medical and psychiatric consultation inputs as needed. It is believed that by providing needed services as early as possible, continued overloading of the system can be alleviated.

The Wheaton unit has been operational since June 4, 1970, while the Niles unit began offering services on May 4, 1971.

Individuals receiving services by the Social Service Units are referred by police officers. As of July 1, 1972, at the Wheaton Unit we have given service to 298 cases, at the Niles Unit service has been given to 174 cases. Currently, the Wheaton Unit has an active caseload of 93, while Niles has 50. It is significant to note that 42% of the people come voluntarily without arrest or official police disposition. Besides the actual client, significant family members and friends are also seen, so that the service is family-centered. The most usual offenses among juveniles are runaways, theft and possession of marijuana. Adult clients have been referred largely because of marital and emotional problems, which sometimes are masked by the violation which brings them to the attention of the law enforcement officer. At Wheaton, approximately one-half of the clients are adults, while at Niles, adults make up one-third of the caseload. Relatives of clients also receive services and sometimes have as many sessions with the social worker as the primary client.

A deferred prosecution plan has been developed with State's Attorney Hopf of DuPage County for selected adults in the Wheaton and DuPage area. These are largely young people whose offenses are minor and who could benefit from social and psychological services at low risk to the community. Individuals selected for this program agree to cooperate in receiving social services for a period of time not to exceed 18 months, and abide by the agreed conditions.

A similar program of pretrial diversion is available in Niles upon referral by a judge.

The typical question usually considered by the police officers before referring someone to the Unit would be, "Is there indication of social disharmony within the individual or his family?" In other words, are there social or emotional problems which have contributed to the legal problem which have brought the individual to the attention of the police?

The Social Service Units are prepared to offer four types of services:

1. Social assessments to law enforcement and the citizen;
2. Crisis intervention at critical times, immediate service 24 hours a day;

3. Direct social treatment (individual, marital, family, and group service); and

4. Referral to community agencies.

Each unit has relationships with most of the social welfare agencies within the area served, including mental health clinics, psychiatrists, physicians, vocational training centers, employment centers, public aid, schools, and the like.

The units provide consultation to the police on social problems and are available to citizens of the City of Wheaton and the Village of Niles upon referral by a police officer.

In summary, this is the first project of its type located in a police department and an integral unit of the law enforcement team. Professional social work services are available at the earliest possible point— at the point of arrest or before arrest—in an effort to deter further entry into the system. Quality services are provided to the citizens of Wheaton and Niles who need it, want it, and can benefit from it. Most of the clients keep their appointments and we have not seen the resistance that is typical of people who have gone further into the criminal justice system.

The most important piece of data about the project is that it works. Police and social workers can work together to provide needed services to the community.[7]

Against this background of approaches to police-community relations through family crisis intervention, attention is returned to the question that establishes the context for *all* community relations programs: *what must be done to promote the understanding and use of social influences to encourage voluntary law observance?*

It should be noted in the literature of criminology that certain influences either encourage or discourage crime. These influences are necessarily of concern to police and the police effort to insure conformity to society's rules and regulations.

One such influence is the manner in which enforcing rules, or law enforcement, is perceived by the public. Another related influence is the manner in which the children in a society are raised. Resentment of law enforcement learned as a child influences adult behavior. The conditions and tensions discussed throughout this text contribute to an absence of childhood respect for law enforcement. But of even greater significance is unfortunate childhood experiences with law enforcement personnel. The pressing need to deal with the lasting detriments of unfortunate childhood experience is an integral part of community relations programming—a part

[7]H. Treger, "The Police-Social Work Team: A New Model for Community Service," *Law and Order* (Mar. 1973), pp. 41–64.

that might be called *human relations* in order to stress the fundamental nature of this segment of the program.

HUMAN RELATIONS AND COMMUNITY RELATIONS PROGRAMS

As noted earlier in this volume, human relations has been defined in terms of the goal of "police participation in any activity that seeks law observance through respect rather than enforcement."

Police interest in human relations, of course is in behavior that requires police action. Any such behaviors, whether or not the causes are known (i.e., childhood experience, poverty, neglect, etc.), should be examined in relation to the *influences* on which police can have impact. For it is these influences that usually relate to the problems most susceptible to *prevention* rather than "cure." Successful community relations programs deal with these influences as they relate to behavior, and the *human relations* segment of these programs seeks to facilitate a community attitude of accepting this police role (the police image). The citizen who is convinced that police are brutal is reluctant to participate in the broader community

FIGURE 12.1,   *Courtesy Los Angeles Police Department, Los Angeles, Cal.*

FIGURE 12.2   *Police line supervisor discusses law enforcement code of ethics with officer under his supervision. Courtesy Anaheim Police Department, Anaheim, Cal.*

relations program. And the *validity* of the belief matters less than the *strength* of the belief.

Personnel selection, training, and supervision that adhere strictly to an ethical code usually insure public respect of law enforcement officers. Strict adherence will help eliminate corrupt practices and cut down on those in the marginal, gray area as well. And, of more importance, men striving to follow the ideal should become better human beings and therefore better officers.

But in spite of high ethical standards and conscientious performance of duty by police, certain members of the community often require further persuasion, or "selling," to change the bad police image they have. The news media can frequently have a significant impact on this segment of the community.

Unfortunate is the department that functions in a community in which the typical citizen expects law enforcement to completely eliminate crime and safety problems. Equally unfortunate is a community that expects absolutely nothing from law enforcement insofar as crime and safety are concerned.[8] But public opinion usually has an effect that causes citizens to expect something between these two extremes, and the news media is frequently instrumental in determining where it settles.

One of the more difficult tasks of a community relations program is to evaluate public opinion precisely enough to determine with accuracy the degree of public *support* police enjoy at a given time. In recent years, considerable evidence has emerged that public support of law enforcement changes as rapidly with respect to "classical" crime as with community unrest and civil disobedience. Perhaps the beginnings of this trend began to be obvious when a widely publicized tragedy occurred in the Queens section of New York. During early morning hours, a 28-year-old woman named Kitty Genovese was attacked three times over a span of forty minutes by a knife-wielding assailant. No fewer than thirty-eight persons heard her scream for help or actually witnessed the attacks. Yet not one of them telephoned the police or went to the aid of the victim. Finally, after nearly forty minutes, a 70-year-old woman living in the neighborhood called the police. A squad was at the scene two minutes later, but by that time Miss Genovese was dead.

Rather than producing answers, attempts to judge public opinion raise the further question of whether or not the news media *reflect* opinion or *create* it. This question is of particular concern in cities where the news media consistently headline crime, giving the impression of a higher crime rate than is actually the case. The news media, of course, argue that the public is entitled to all possible information on crime and other social problems. The ensuing compromises are traditionally resolved in favor of the news media. Assigning priority to the types of problems that are of most concern to the public, nevertheless, is the task of community relations programs in police departments.[9] Of course, any such program must take into account the long-range consequence of removing line officers from "nearly jelled" stakeouts, from patrols in "recently quieted" areas, from "barely adequate" traffic programs, and so on. The policy of "stripping" all services to satisfy a single, and possibly, temporary need in no way serves the community's long-range interest. And yet a crucial variable in any community relations program is evidence that the police are responsive to public opinion.

Perhaps further clarification of what is meant by *community relations* would permit greater understanding of this need to demonstrate police responsiveness to public opinion.

[8]O. H. Ibele, "Law Enforcement and the Permissive Society," *Police* (Sept.–Oct. 1965), p. 15.

[9]O. W. Wilson, "Police Authority in a Free Society," *Criminal Law, Criminology and Police Science*, 54, No. 2 (June 1963), p. 175.

The term "police-community relations" has been used so frequently in recent years that it is almost a cliché to police officers. Yet the establishment of a good working relationship between the police and the public is an essential part of law enforcement. Every policeman must recognize that he is a public servant who has sworn to protect the entire community and every segment of it. The community relations effort is not the responsibility merely of a special unit of police departments, but it is the obligation of every policeman and affects every phase of police work. The necessity for a strong rapport between the police and the citizenry must be understood by every police officer.[10]

The very process of building a strong rapport between police and the citizenry establishes overwhelming evidence of police responsiveness. Far beyond the immediate value of such evidence is the long-range benefit to law enforcement for a supportive citizenry. *Citizen participation* programs emerge as distinct possibilities. And lest the impression be gained that citizen participation is not of great significance, consider the following as only one of many possibilities:

An important group of police-related citizen efforts pertains to *reporting crime*. Not only can citizens assume this responsibility as individuals but also as members of a collective effort promoting increased crime reporting by the public.

In cooperation with law enforcement agencies, many citizen organizations sponsor special area-wide campaigns to educate and motivate the public to report (1) crimes in the process of being committed, (2) information that would help police solve crimes, and (3) persons and events considered suspicious. Various names have been attached to such campaigns, such as *crime check*, crime alert, chec-mate, citizen alert, chec, crime stop, project alert, home alert, and the like.

Another crime-reporting activity often called *community radio watch*, involves business firms whose vehicles are equipped with two-way radios. When drivers spot an emergency—crime, fire or accident—they report it to their dispatchers, who contact the police or other appropriate agencies.

Still another variety of crime-reporting activity is informer-oriented. An organization posts a sizable reward for information leading to the arrest and conviction of lawbreakers. A special phone number is publicized and callers need not reveal their names; a code number is supplied each caller and his or her anonymity is preserved. Sometimes such programs are called *Project TIP* (Turn in a Pusher or Turn in a Punk) or *Secret Witness*.

[10]Hon. Earl F. Morris, "The Police and the Community: A Lawyer's View," *FBI Law Enforcement Bulletin*, 37, No. 5 (May 1968), p. 4.

Frequently, crime-reporting campaigns also entail attempts to inform citizens about the basic steps available to increase *protection of home, person and property*. Emphasized are proper locks for conventional exterior doors, sliding glass doors, garage doors and windows, sash windows, and basement windows. The security implications of fences, shrubbery, yard appearance and lighting are also stressed. . . .

Other measures and programs designed to protect family and belongings employ a neighborhood approach. Some blocks utilize *House Watch Contracts*, which are signed agreements (no legal effect, though) whereby one neighbor agrees to keep an eye on another's home during certain hours. The "contract" also specifies that crimes or suspicious activities will be promptly reported to police.[11]

Of course such impressive practical help from the citizenry is not the primary purpose of community relations programming.

The basic reason for police-community relations activity is to effect a continuous level of cooperation and understanding between the police and the community. It would be naive to state that in the past there has been an adequate level of cooperation and understanding between the police and the public. From the beginning of recorded time, history tells us of conflict between those with authority and the people. No doubt when the policeman worked on the street and lived in the area where he was accepted as part of the neighborhood, and when society in general was less apathetic, the ability to communicate was in fact much greater than now.[12]

The *primary* purpose of community relations programming is restoration of some of these advantages from bygone days—days in which police work demanded far less mobility. Nevertheless, many advantages accrue to community relations programming in terms of *direct law enforcement*, along with the indirect advantages referred to throughout this volume.

Returning to the need for evidence that police *are* responsive to public opinion and are thereby worthy of respect, attention is now focused upon one of the core difficulties involved—rewarding false beliefs.

Rewarding False Beliefs

Community relations programs that seek to promote or sell respect for police goals must take into consideration the apparent reasons for disrespect of law enforcement. It seems reasonable to assume that a person

---

[11]National Conference on Criminal Justice, "Community Crime Prevention," made possible by Law Enforcement Assistance Administration, January 23–26, 1973 (Washington, D.C.: U.S. Government Printing Office), pp. CC-23-24.

[12]Maj. Nolen W. Freeman, "Building a Better Public Image," *FBI Law Enforcement Bulletin*, 40, No. 2 (Feb. 1971), p. 16.

FIGURE 12.3. As a practical matter, the validity of police brutality may matter less than the strength of the belief that such does occur. Individuals usually function on the basis of what is believed regardless of the validity of the belief. Therefore, before programs geared to alleviate combinations of community problems can prove effective, establishment of a community's attitude toward police (or the police image) is of crucial importance. Photo courtesy of the San Francisco Police Department.

brutally mishandled by one policeman may have difficulty in conceding how helpful most policemen really are. This possibility alone should afford a most convincing argument for eliminating force wherever possible. Behavioral scientists believe that a kind of "selective perception" sets in which causes an unjustly abused individual to look for and "see" only those incidents that prove what he then believes to be true—in terms of our concern, seeing police as brutal. Years and years of looking for and seeing such incidents, combined with reassurances from others doing the same thing, of course, creates such an individual's undesirable image of police.

Recall that in the preceding chapter transactional analysis was offered as one explanation of people's conduct. Devised by psychiatrist Eric Berne,[13] it describes the reasons people behave as they do in terms of rewards or payoffs. From this point of view, the individual law violator might be able to "prove" a belief that police are brutal simply by behaving in a manner that requires police to use force. People could use techniques similar to this to "prove" police to be racially prejudiced, etc. In these incidents the "proof" is rewarding in terms of confidence gained in one's judgment and one's beliefs, whether these beliefs are valid or not. Of course, a policeman who believes that someone is criminally inclined may also be rewarded if this judgment is "proved" correct. However, most crime and behavior requiring police attention may not be motivated in this manner. And yet influence of this sort may determine how much respect for police is held by community groups.

To whatever degree respect for law enforcement goals affects voluntary law observance, community relations programs are completely justified. Understanding this justification is one thing, nevertheless, whereas implementing effective programs may prove quite another matter.

Indeed, implementing *effective* community relations programs usually proves to be quite difficult. Seasoned police officers in many instances are somewhat skeptical about the legitimacy of police involvement in social matters. Many other officers are cynical about the successful prospects of such programs. Many militants declare downright conviction that such programs are, at best, insincere efforts to avoid such controls as citizens' review boards. Many politicians prove far more willing to declare the rightness of community relations than to actually support police efforts to this end. Many press reporters are far more sensitive to seeming failures of police efforts than to the less dramatic methodical successes. And perhaps above all else, many citizens could not care less. These problems are real—painfully real—but not insurmountable.

And in terms of community relations being a literal prerequisite for police success, there really is no choice for the *effective* police organization.

---

[13]*Games People Play* (New York: Grove Press, 1964).

The lessons of the 1960s and early 1970s need not be repeated—indeed cannot be repeated if police are to cope successfully with the law enforcement mission. With this in mind, attention is now turned to community relations programming.

COMMUNITY RELATIONS AS A CONCEPT

We have referred in Chapter Seven to the fact that certain methods of effecting close relationships with the community are both uncomplicated and effective. Of course *needs* vary from one jurisdiction to another and so do the actual activities of programs. Nevertheless, police community relations often have much in common, even when different methods are utilized.

The community itself traditionally approaches problems, particularly social problems, through some kind of council. Councils usually function to coordinate the activities of groups or social agencies which would

FIGURE 12.4.   *Anaheim police officer discusses the role of police traffic officers with school children. Courtesy Anaheim Police Department, Anaheim, Cal.*

FIGURE 12.5. *Anaheim police officer explains and demonstrates the use of standard police equipment to school children of the community as a part of the agency's community relations program. Courtesy Anaheim Police Department, Anaheim, Cal.*

otherwise operate on the philosophy that they "exist to provide distinct services to groups able to accept them...."[14] A variety of opinions exist regarding how involved the coordinating of broad community problems outside specific neighborhoods should become. But the central idea, nevertheless, of bringing the combined forces of various agencies to bear on defined problems remains.[15] During an era in which a bad police image increasingly stimulates consideration of *civilian* police review panels,[16] law enforcement can scarcely ignore the implementing of community relations programs. Until recently there appeared to be something less than a conspicuous national trend toward police-community relations programs.

To date, the police have rarely sought civilian assistance—least of all in those areas where the forces of the law have been hardest pressed.

[14]H. H. Stroup, *Community Welfare Organization* (New York: Harper & Row, 1952), p. 305.

[15]A. Dunham, *Community Welfare Organization* (New York: Thomas Y. Crowell, 1962), p. 31.

[16]A. Germann, F. Day, and R. Gallati, *Introduction to Law Enforcement* (Springfield, Ill.: Charles C. Thomas, Publisher, 1962), pp. 187, 188.

Yet the great majority of residents in these areas, just as in others, are law-abiding. Thus, chances of obtaining citizen support for genuine efforts to curb crime are much better in such neighborhoods than people generally realize. Roy Wilkins, Executive Director of the National Association for the Advancement of Colored People, recently emphasized the Negro community's increasing willingness to support vigorous law enforcement:

Negro law violators enjoyed a sort of racial brotherhood status, not because all other Negroes were criminally inclined, but because black men have had such a hard way to go that other black men nearly always give them a break against the law officers. The real news is that a part of the Negro community is now ready to blow the whistle on the robbers, muggers and knife men. It still works in many places but apparently the days of the black-skinned distress signals are numbered. Crime control becomes a real possibility as soon as law-abiding Negro citizens, always in the vast majority, take an active rather than passive role against crime and criminals.[17]

Loss of faith in the law enforcement establishment is increasingly manifested among the citizenry, especially minority group members, by increases in crime rates and riots; community indifference; charges of police prejudice, brutality, and disrespect for citizens; and complaints of lack of police protection.

On the other side, police officers frequently appear to have lost faith in the country's leaders and the public. They charge that they are subjected to strong political pressures and undue restraints, are held accountable for most social ills, are accorded low status and respect by the community, have little opportunity for redress of grievances, and must perform a tremendously complex job under conditions which, at best, are frustrating.

The escalation of antagonisms between police and citizens in certain sections of society has tended to induce the formation of two separate and distinct groups who communicate with and understand each other minimally, if at all.

These are harsh statements. To be sure, it must be recognized that the problem is complicated by inadequacies in housing, welfare, education and employment. Yet, the magnification of these "opposing forces" is, in considerable part, a cause of the problem described. It threatens to undermine the basis of support from more temperate, sensitive, and rational people who constitute the essential communication links through which we can reclaim the middle ground necessary for the de-escalation of antagonisms and the resolution of differences.[18]

[17]G. Edwards, *The Police on the Urban Frontier*, Bulletin No. 9 (New York: Institute of Human Relations, 1968), pp. 77–78.

[18]T. Eisenberg, A. Glickman, and R. Rosen, "Action for Change in Police-Community Behaviors," *Crime and Delinquency*, 15, No. 3 (July 1969), p. 394.

FIGURE 12.6.   Carnival-like atmosphere of the Stanford Research Institute Protest (May 17, 1969) subsequently ended abruptly as police were forced to use tear gas to control demonstrators. Photo courtesy of the San Jose Mercury, Staff photographer, Al Magazu.

Of course the gradual perspective emerging through review of the 1960s and first half of the 1970s mitigates many of these regrettably accurate observations. *But it would be grossly inaccurate to conclude that such observations were no longer relevant.*

Regardless of their discomfort while reading such harsh observations about the law enforcement scene, few, if any, professional policemen would deny that they contain at least a degree of validity. Indeed, some professionals interpret the mounting difficulties facing urban police organizations as clear evidence that such indictments are not only true but that they leave the police no choice but to embark on corrective programs in anticipation of an "escalation of antagonisms between police and citizens.[19]

Early clarification of the many facets of such programming were reflected in some of the literature of the 1960s.[20] Still more clarification emerged in the early "handouts" used by progressive police organizations in the late 1960s—for example, the following is part of a slide presentation given to schools in Santa Clara County:

[19]M. E. Leary, "The Trouble with Troubleshooting," *The Atlantic Monthly Special Police Supplement,* 223, No. 3 (Mar. 1969), pp. 94–99.

[20]See for example, Nelson A. Watson, *The Fringes of Police-Community Relations,* material from the Police Administrators' Conference, Indiana Medical Center, June 29, 1966.

The basic purpose of these talks is to develop a more positive relationship between the young people of the community and the police, and to foster a greater degree of social consciousness on the part of these young people. Rather than dealing simply in what the law is and how it affects young people, which tends very often to be somewhat sterile, we draw more on motivating good behavior in general. We attempt to define a role for the vast majority of young people who do not get into trouble but at the same time exert little influence, if any, on those that do. This represents the first phase of the presentation.

The second phase of the presentation is devoted to a colored slide program showing Juvenile Hall, the ranches and a Youth Authority institution. What we are striving to do is to take the glamour away from young people who go to these facilities. Very often they come back to school and become leaders because the rest of the young people think that this is some sort of achievement after listening to the stories fabricated by these individuals. Also, we found that most of the questions by students previously were directed to the nature of these facilities, and the slides provide the closest thing to a guided tour.

The third phase of the program is devoted to answering any questions that the students might have. The interaction hopefully develops the

FIGURE 12.7. *It is incumbent upon police agencies to develop community relations programs relevant to the youths in their community.* Courtesy Los Angeles Police Department, Los Angeles, Cal.

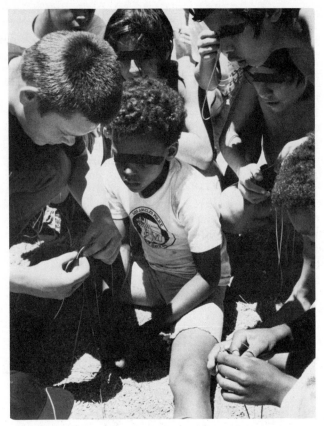

FIGURE 12.8. *Summer camp. Courtesy Los Angeles Police Department, Los Angeles, Cal.*

positive nature of the contact between the students and someone who represents the police department. It is with this in mind that we desire to keep presentations at the classroom level to develop the highest degree of communication and interaction.

This handout was presented to teachers prior to addresses at schools by officers assigned to the community relations unit of the San Jose (California) Police Department. Although it deals primarily with improving youths' image of the police, it seems reasonable to assume that this activity might gain the respect of the community at large. Even citizens completely satisfied with conventional police services are likely to respond favorably to programs of this type.

Other approaches during the late 1960s emerged in the area of specific efforts to improve police image among groups ordinarily resentful of law enforcement. In this regard, consider the following:

Mr. Nat Shaffer, Council of Community Services
431 Sixth Street
Richmond, California

Subject: Relation of Police-Community Relation Aids to Police-Youth
Discussion Group Program

Dear Sir:

There has been exhibited throughout the nation a dislike, distrust, and in some cases, hatred of police by a large segment of our Negro citizens. The City of Richmond with one-fouth of the population Negro falls into the national pattern. I shall not attempt to go into the "whys" of this situation at this time. I would rather accept this situation as a fact and seek solutions.

It is my strong conviction that in today's society we must attempt to reach the youth with a concentrated effort to establish more meaningful lines of communication between them and the police, in particular with Negro youth. We must try to bring about a better understanding, a deeper appreciation for one another and our problems.

We have in the City of Richmond taken steps to reach the Negro youth through a series of police-youth discussion groups. Our method of setting up such groups is quite simple. Take a small geographical area of the city, seek out the youth who have exhibited antisocial behavior, get them to a meeting with selected police officers. At such meetings the youth are encouraged to speak their minds regardless of how hard it is on the police. On the other hand, the police are to answer all questions, avoiding none. They explain their responsibility, the law and the policy with which the police must govern themselves. I hasten to add that such a meeting is not attempted on the basis that all ills or misunderstandings will be cleared away at a single meeting or a dozen meetings. However, we have, through discussion groups, brought about far more understanding between these two forces. This is demonstrated by lessening of crimes committed by those youth who have participated and by many, having been school dropouts, having returned to school.

Much of the success of the police-youth discussion groups can be attributed to the work and dedication of the five police community relations aids. It is they who go out into the community and invite the youth to the group meeting. They pick them up at their homes (or wherever they can be located), bring them to the meetings and take them home at the close. Further, the personal contacts with the youth in their homes oftentimes bridges the gaps of communication, counsels both the youth and their parents.

At the present time, the Richmond police have conducted two 12-week police-youth discussion groups within the Negro community. Just during the past two weeks, three new discussion groups have been formed. We cannot at this time even offer a guess as to the number of groups that might form within the next six months. Regardless of the number now or in the future, we can see the police-community relations aids as a very important part of a program that shall have a present and lasting value to those in the various groups, their families and the community.

Very truly yours,

C. E. Brown

Chief of Police

It might be noted that although youth was the primary subject of this community relations project, the entire community stood to gain by it from the start.

A United Press International Syndicated release on February 23, 1969, brought national recognition to how sophisticated the process of community relations was even before the "serious studies" of the early 1970s. Published under the byline of Paul Lowenberg, the UPI release elaborated what was then called Watts Rumor Control Center.

The release acquainted the public with the twofold problem of escalating antagonism through unfounded rumor, accompanied by escalating antagonism through actions and reactions based upon rumors. Far more important, however, national press coverage of this type of community relations brought home the widening scope of police responsibilities.

In July of the same year, *Crime and Delinquency* carried the Eisenberg-Glickman-Foster article "Action For Change in Police-Community Behaviors.'" Going far beyond the mere concession that the scope of police role was widening, this article effectively clarified many of the methods and approaches necessary for police to accept new responsibilities. Moreover, the article even provided police with criteria for evaluating police effectiveness:

1. Changes in police and citizen attitudes
2. Changes in behavioral information, including crime statistics, police agency or precinct effectiveness, and citizen and community behavior
3. Nature of responses and opinions of policemen and citizens who have participated in the training program
4. Mass media indicators, including radio and television news reports, press clippings, etc.

The overwhelming need for the assessment of community relations programming is customarily justified in terms of either research designs or of the often-cited ramifications of civilian review boards for police. An occasionally overlooked but equally compelling justification for methods of estimating the effectiveness of such programming rests in the sociological concept of *power*. To whatever degree power breeds discontent, to that same degree must police seek to establish *trust* in those perceiving police *power*.[21] This is by no means an easy task. On the one hand, the *enforcement*

---

[21]W. A. Gamson, *Power and Discontent* (Homewood, Ill.: Dorsey Press, 1968).

of law *requires* certain powers. On the other hand, power often breeds distrust—and distrust ultimately leads to violence in many cases. The varied contradictions of this paradox confront every police officer every time he works a shift. But awareness of the problem is not new. As early as 1966, the police-community relations literature was exploring citizen trust and confidence in terms of police finding that "fear of becoming involved is a major factor in the reluctance of citizens to communicate with police."[22] Awareness of this fear of police power—the power to involve citizens excessively in even the crimes they might report—has been one target of all the more enlightened police-community relations programs. In isolating citizens' fear of police as a prime target for "PCR" programming, it is often possible to systematically erode the distrust of even the most militant groups. And as distrust is replaced by trust, it becomees possible to bridge the often tremendous gap between police power and citizen support. Citizen support is vitally needed by law enforcement in a changing community.

Public Support

Because of the impossibility of taking citizen respect and contentment for granted,[23] and because of the need to persuade at least part of the community that a bad police image is inappropriate, there is indeed a tremendous task faced by those concerned with community relations. The task is as complicated as it is tremendous.

Among the many police agencies currently involved in or undertaking community relations programs, few, if any, could honestly claim success without at least some help from community leaders. Leaders—whether mayors, presidents of a PTA, neighborhood organization directors, heads of service clubs, clergymen, or some combination of these—either directly assist or influence others to assist in most successful police-sponsored programs. In many instances, gaining this type of support is relatively easy—merely a matter of showing a need. The difficulty then is often not whether community programs can be undertaken by police, but rather *who* the programs influence and *how* they do so. Included in this particular concern are all of the influences and considerations presented throughout this volume. Specifically, however, the determination of *who* is influential assumes an incorporation of intergroup relationships in terms of community tension. In other words, those who initiate and carry out relations programs examine not only influences upon certain groups but also the *impact* that one group has upon another group. Only then can determination of *how* such influence occurs

---

[22]*Police and Community Relations Newsletter*, National Center on Police and Community Relations, Michigan State University, Michigan, Nov. 1966.

[23]*Crime and Law Enforcement, A Special Analysis*, College Debate Series No. 16 (Washington, D.C.: The American Institute of Public Policy Research, 1965), p. 81.

avoid the police-community difficulties of the 1960s and first half of the 1970s.

This, then, is the nature of public support being sought—support that favorably influences not only the law enforcement group but also the community's "intergroup." Within the context of this definition, consideration can now be given the definition of "success."

Success

If the term *public support* simply involved a majority of citizens, most police-sponsored community programs would enjoy the success of public support. If, however, it includes the support of all minority groups and neighborhoods that pose the greatest problems, then many "successful" programs fall short of the police goal of gaining public support.

This indictment must be examined in the light of payoffs or rewards discussed earlier. If the law violator finds a reward in "proving" that police hate because they arrest (even if the arrest has to be provoked), then rewards might also be possible if police can prove that they sponsor programs only for those they do not hate and do not want to arrest. And in the case of misbehaving until confirming the belief that police hate enough to arrest, the "proof" that police-sponsored programs are meant for someone else may merely be a matter of not showing interest or of actually disrupting the program until police patience and tolerance are exhausted—thereby supplying the desired "proof."

The subtleness of such a process, of course, is often such that it is barely discernible even when effort is exerted to detect its presence. But the presence of this process is not the point—it is the *results* (or at least the potential results) of "proving" police programs are for "someone else" that is of great concern. When such negative results occur, there is, in effect, virtual destruction of any possibility of bringing about full citizen support.

Here, then, is the frequently overlooked dilemma in community relations programming. If, as recommended earlier in this chapter, police seek to understand what efforts are needed to remedy a bad image, they are likely to recruit the aid of community leaders in whatever human relations programming they undertake. Such aid is a virtual requisite to successful program promotion. But if the groups for whom the image change is designed prefer to view community leaders as police collaborators rather than real leaders, then much reward accrues to "proving" the program is for *someone else* (simply by forcing police rejection).

The solution to this problem varies greatly depending on the unique characteristics and social resources of the community. But in communities in which respect for law enforcement has deteriorated for a segment of the population, efforts are almost invariably needed to insure these people that program planning and operation involves leaders from both their segment and the community at large. However, even in a police agency sensitive to the ways a bad image is reinforced, it is anything but easy to combine the often divergent views of leadership from both areas of the community. This difficulty is singularly hard to overcome when years of resentment between the segments have fostered a belief that "the other guy cannot be trusted." This again points up the need for establishing *trust* as a prime goal in all community relations programming.

But easy or not, a systematic effort invariably proves justified in its strengthening of respect for law enforcement. And because this respect can contribute to law enforcement goals even beyond preventing crime, using the principles of human relations to promote it is not only appropriate, but imperative.

A brief comment on various randomly selected community relations efforts might be useful at this point.

THE PROGRAMS OF COMMUNITY RELATIONS

Even in the 1960s, there was strong evidence that the press was moving some of the focus off the sensationalized violence of that decade and toward programmed efforts by police in the area of community relations. An example of this shifting emphasis was a Sunday Supplement article written by Robert deRoos for the *San Francisco Examiner and Chronicle* (July 15, 1969). Among many other cogent comments, there was a section called "Required Reading for Police Officers"—this section commented that

> the idea of police as we know them is relatively new, I was surprised to learn. In the 1820's in England there had been no police at all for many years. And when the Metropolitan Police came into being in 1829, almost everyone was against the idea. . . . The article went on to tell of early policemen being assaulted and sometimes kicked to death on the pavements. . . . and in court, facing shameful hostility from counsels, juries and judges.

Even at the time the deRoos article was written, it was clear that improvement in police-community relations was not an invention of the twentieth century. And yet, as pointed out throughout this text, systematic efforts to establish community relations programming is indeed relatively new. On October 14, 1966, the New York City Police Department issued Standard Operating Procedure No. 8 as "a guide for commanding officers in developing and operating precinct community councils." Although this was scarcely the first effort by New York City Police to initiate community relations programs, Section 1.0 nevertheless launches its instructions to commanding officers in this manner: "The primary objective of the department's community relations program is to emphasize the mutual interdependence of the police department and the community-at-large in the maintenance of law and order and in the prevention of crime; to develop mutual respect and understanding between police and the people they serve; to promote an atmosphere conducive to the greater public cooperation and, as a consequence, greater police effectiveness." On the other side of the country, the San Francisco Police Department issued a circular entitled "Community Relations Unit," which begins with the statment: "The San Francisco Police Department's community relations unit was established by a directive from the police commission. The directive was in the form of a permanent order. The police-community relations unit began with a lieutenant, two sergeants and ten patrolmen."

Such examples from large, medium, and small police departments have grown in recent years to the point that *community relations* as a concept has become standard in American law enforcement. And just as the concept has grown, so also has there been growth in the sophistication and effectiveness of police in *applying* community relations functions to the community's problems.

In a sense, this entire volume has been geared to the further enrichment and the continued success of police-community relations—which is, after all, *human relations* for law enforcement in the changing community.

SUMMARY

As the final chapter of this text, Chapter Twelve examined the concept of police organization programming to anticipate and to deal with community problems discussed in preceding chapters. This text began with two chapters which described the nature and scope of community problems relating to police. In the chapters that followed, the implications of social problems were considered in terms of constitutional government, police image, and racial prejudice. Increasingly concerned with the concrete and the specific, the text moved toward the concept of community relations programming as social change and its accompanying problems were discussed. Finally, in the two chapters immediately preceding this, the implications of group behavior were examined in the context of behavior per se, and then in terms of racial consideration.

This chapter concludes the text by considering both the nature of community relations programs and the purpose of such programming. In this context, influences on behavior were presented as *forces*, and forces were related to the power to encourage voluntary conformity to law. *Human relations* was cast as the instrument through which respect for police might be sought, and respect for police was cast as a prime requisite for voluntary (rather than enforced) observance of the law. The attitudes, ethics, and conduct of police were presented as the essential ingredients of human relations efforts to gain needed public support.

The basis for both founded and unfounded beliefs about police were reviewed in terms of ways in which an unfavorable police image is perpetuated, and in ways in which community support for police is lost. Programming for community support of police goals was discussed first as a pressing need. The value and potential of such support were presented. This was followed by a review of various facets of community relations programs, presented through examples reflecting the universal necessity for public support and the variations in specific local needs.

Success in community relations programming often depends on general community support, but establishing majority support in some instances poses a great dilemma by producing minority rejection—rejection among the very persons to whom community relations programming is essentially addressed. There are many ways in which law enforcement personnel and community leaders can systematically meet this dilemma. But a thorough knowledge of social change, a dedication to democratic principles, and development of public support are absolute requisites in encouraging the use of social influences to encourage voluntary law observance and justice for all. In the final analysis, *if it is what people do rather than what people are that causes problems, then some misery is optional and can indeed be prevented.*

DISCUSSION TOPICS

1. Elaborate the implications of the opening remarks of this chapter with regard to an expanding police role.

2. Discuss the question presented early in the chapter: What can be done to promote the understanding and use of social influence to encourage voluntary law observance?

3. Discuss societal influences on the causes of human behavior. On police activities.

4. Relate human relations to police programs for community relations.

5. Discuss police image and public support.

6. Discuss police ethics and police image.

7. Relate the concept of rewarding false belief, as discussed in this chapter to community relations.

8. What do the various existing community relations programs cited have in common? How do they differ?

9. What is the dilemma in seeking successful public support for community relations programs?

ANNOTATED REFERENCES

ANDELSON, W., ed., *The Age of Protest*. Pacific Palisades, Cal.: Goodyear Publishing Co., 1969. This book provides an excellent collection of writings which provide a background for examining the cross-cultural ramifications of organized demonstrations and protests affording the scientifically minded the peripheral advantage of analytical objectivity with concern for political ideology.

BAYLEY, D. H., AND H. MENDELSOHN, *Minorities and the Police: Confrontation in America*. New York: The Free Press, 1968. Chapter 8 examines the subject of the title in terms of improving police-community relations.

COFFEY, ALAN R., *Police—Intervention Into Family Crisis*. Santa Cruz: Davis Publishing, 1974. Comprehensive presentation of title subject.

————, *Prevention of Crime and Delinquency*. Englewood Cliffs, Inc., N.J.: Prentice-Hall, 1975. Presents systems-approach to relating police community functions to the *prevention* of crime.

————, *Criminal Justice Administration: A Management Systems Approach*. Englewood Cliffs, N.J.: Prentice-Hall, Inc., 1974. A comprehensive elaboration of managerial considerations involved in all criminal justice program efforts.

ELDEFONSO, EDWARD, ed., *Readings in Criminal Justice*. New York: Glencoe Press, 1973. Part V is particularly relevant to this chapter in terms of police-community relations.

MARX, J., *Officer, Tell Your Story: A Guide to Police Public Relations*. Springfield, Ill., Charles C. Thomas, 1969. In reviewing the need for public support of police goals, this book deals with the attitudes and procedures of police agencies in the context of community relations programming.

MOMBOISSE, R., *Community Relations and Riot Prevention*. Springfield, Ill.: Charles C. Thomas, 1969. The theme of this text is that *the only effective way to control a riot is to prevent it*. This theme is reviewed in the context of community relations programming.

The footnotes of this chapter are also recommended to the reader as in-depth embellishment of the concept reviewed.

APPENDIX A
Major American Disorders

MAJOR AMERICAN DISORDERS*

1765	Stamp Act Riots in Boston and New York
1771	The Regulators
1772	Burning of the *Gaspee*
1774	Resistance to the Boston Port Bill
1784	Revolt against North Carolina
1786	Shays' Rebellion
1788	Doctors' Riot, or Anti-Dissection Riot
1794	Whiskey Rebellion in Pennsylvania
1795	Demonstrations against the Jay Treaty
1798	Virginia and Kentucky Resolutions
1799	Fries Rebellion
1832	Tariff Nullification
1842	Dorr Rebellion
1844	Anti-Catholic Riots in Philadelphia
1849	Astor Place Riot in New York City—31 killed, 150 wounded, 86 arrested
1851	San Francisco Committee of Vigilance
1854	Struggle in Kansas over slavery

*Adopted from V. G. Strecher, *The Environment of Law Enforcement: A Community Relations Guide* (Englewood Cliffs, N.J.: Prentice-Hall, Essentials of Law Enforcement Series, 1971), pp. 35–49. By Permission of the Publisher.

1855	German Tavern-Keepers' Revolt in Chicago—many killed, hundreds wounded by gunfire
1863	Conscription Riots in Boston and New York City—many killed, hundreds injured
1871	Anti-Chinese Riot in Los Angeles—23 Chinese killed (18 in one afternoon)
1871	Orange Riots in New York City—33 killed, 91 wounded
1877	Great labor strikes in West Virginia, and Pittsburgh, Pa.— in two days, 16 soldiers and 50 strikers killed; 125 locomotives, 2000 freight cars and a depot burned and destroyed; many killed and wounded in Chicago
1913	Ludlow Massacre—more than 50 killed
1919	Chicago Race Riot—38 killed, 537 injured
1921	Tulsa Race Riot—30 killed, several hundred injured
1943	Detroit Race Riot—34 killed, 700 injured
1964	Race riots in New York City, Rochester, Philadelphia, Jersey City, Paterson, Elizabeth, and Chicago—6 killed, 952 injured
1965	Los Angeles (Watts) Race Riot—36 killed, 895 injured

Boston—1765

INCIDENT: Stamp Act Riots[1]

YEAR: 1765

LOCATION: Boston (Concurrent location: other colonies; less destructive riots)

PROTAGONISTS: British government vs. Sons of Liberty

GENERATIONAL ISSUES: Presence of British troops in the colonies; oppressiveness of colonial government

TRANSIENT ISSUES: Sons of Liberty movement; tactless commands of the government

PRECIPITANT: Appointment of Stamp Distributor; organized agitation by the Sons of Liberty; a hanging in effigy from the "Liberty Tree"

POLICE INVOLVEMENT: Chief Justice and Sheriff of Suffolk County were stoned when they attempted to persuade a mob to disperse. The mob destroyed the home of the newly appointed Stamp Distributor. On another day a law officer read the riot act to a mob forming under the Liberty Tree. This mob left to destroy the office of the Vice Admiralty Court, where they burned all records, and also the new home of the Comptroller

[1]W. A. Heaps, *Riots, U.S.A., 1765–1965* (New York: Seabury Press, 1966), pp. 9–18.

of Customs; here they "enjoyed the contents of his wine cellar."[2] Later that day the mob completely demolished the mansion of the Chief Justice. He had opposed the Stamp Act but as noted above, had previously sought to dissuade the mob from violence. At least 11 violent disorders occurred in this general pattern.

DISPOSITION: The Stamp Act was never enforced; it was repealed in 1766. Six or seven arrestees were released by the rioters, "who had forced the jailer to give up the keys."[3]

New York—1788

INCIDENT: Doctors' Riot,[4] or Anti-Dissection Riot

YEAR: 1788

LOCATION: New York City

PROTAGONISTS: Medical students and faculty of the New York Hospital vs. neighborhood workmen

GENERATIONAL ISSUES: No legitimate means of obtaining human bodies for medical studies. Growth of medical science, development of scientific method in medical education

TRANSIENT ISSUES: Medical students stole bodies, at first from the potter's field and Negro graves, later from a church graveyard. Newspapers criticized the activity, and public anger grew.

PRECIPITANT: A curious boy, peeking into the dissection class, was chased off by a student who held up a human arm, telling the boy it was his mother's. By grisly coincidence, the boy's mother had recently died; her husband discovered that her grave had been opened and the body removed. He gathered a mob of more than 1,000 and demolished much of the medical school. Parts of human bodies were paraded by rioters to recruit a larger mob, which now included "sailors, loafers, criminals and motley mischief-makers."[5]

POLICE INVOLVEMENT: Sheriff, accompanied by the mayor, rescued four medical students in the intial incident. Lacking suf-

[2]Ibid., p. 14.
[3]Ibid., p. 16.
[4]Ibid., pp. 19–29.
[5]Ibid., p. 22.

ficient officers and unable to disperse a mob surrounding the hospital-medical school, the sheriff organized an 18-man military detachment and marched on the crowd. The mob mocked them and threw dirt and stones at them. The force withdrew and then returned, whereupon the mob smashed their muskets, chased off the troops, and stormed the jail, where the doctors had taken refuge. There followed ten additional confrontations of mobs (now numbering some 5,000) and military units. At least seven persons were killed and nine seriously injured. Most injuries were not recorded. The militia finally used armed force to quell the major disorder.

DISPOSITION: Grand Jury recommendations for penalizing doctors and students were dropped by the court. Hospital authorities dismissed from the staff those doctors and students who had been in the dissecting room when the precipitating incident occurred, and fined each offender $20. A law was enacted to supply a limited number of cadavers for medical education.

Philadelphia—1844

INCIDENT: Anti-Catholic Riots[6]

YEAR: 1844

LOCATION: Philadelphia (Concurrent locations: many other cities during the 1840s and under the Know-Nothing movement of the 1850s)

PROTAGONISTS: American Republicans (Nativists) vs. Irish Catholic immigrants

GENERATIONAL ISSUES: Religious intolerance based on belief "that the loyalty of Irish immigrants would be owed to Rome and the Pope rather than to their new country and that cheap Irish labor would lower American standard of living.[7]

TRANSIENT ISSUES: Bishop asked school board to excuse Catholic children from reading King James version of the Bible so that they could be instructed in the Catholic translation. Nativists attacked this request (approved by the board) as a move to take the Bible out of the classroom.

[6]Ibid., pp. 30–38.
[7]Ibid., pp. 30–38.

PRECIPITANT: Huge gathering of Nativists in the middle of the Irish section of the city. A fight started and moved into the street. Guns were fired from buildings into the crowd by Irish residents. Nativists fought back with bricks; one of them was killed and many wounded.

POLICE INVOLVEMENT: First the militia, then the citizen police and a sheriff's posse intervened in the three major pitched battles between the Irish and Nativists. The mob fired cannon into the military force and sniped from upper-story windows and rooftops. Nativist rioters engaged military and police units in pitched battles. Twenty to twenty-four were killed, more than a hundred seriously injured. One arrest.

DISPOSITION: Two Grand Jury hearings blamed the Catholics for the riot, citing their efforts to exclude the Bible from public schools.[8]

New York—1849

INCIDENT: Astor Place Riot[9]

YEAR: 1849

LOCATION: New York City

PROTAGONISTS: Anti-British theatre patrons vs. English actor McReady and Astor Place Opera House

GENERATIONAL ISSUES: Anti-British feeling generated over a long period by critical articles written about America by British travelers. Native American movement generated national hatreds.

TRANSIENT ISSUES: National feelings focused on the prime British actor and the prime American actor of the time; each was treated rudely in the other's land. A downward spiral to violence occurred in the United States.

PRECIPITANT: A McReady performance of Macbeth at the Astor Place Opera House was greeted with "Down with the English hog!" and then continual catcalling; a shower of pennies, fruit, and finally chairs. The following night McReady was persuaded by 48 leading citizens to appear again. Nativists circulated handbills citing a (fictitious) threat to McReady's detractors by British seamen then in port. Nativists attended

[8]Ibid., p. 38.
[9]Ibid., pp. 39–60.

the performance to disrupt it. Audience included 1,800 men and 6 women. Police removed the riotous 10 percent of the audience. Nativists rioted outside the theatre, where a great crowd had gathered through curiosity. Many windows were broken, and stones hit the audience. The outside mob was swelled by ruffians. Police and infantry fought the mob without gunfire for some time, but they sustained many serious injuries from paving blocks and bricks. Then a pistol shot from a rioter hit a troop commander; an unsuccessful bayonet charge was ordered, warning shots were fired, and finally, three volleys were fired into the mob. Despite many deaths and injuries, the mob continued the fight until two cannon were loaded with grapeshot and aimed; the rioters then dispersed. Thirty-one were killed, 150 seriously injured, and 86 arrested.

DISPOSITION: A Nativist resolution censured the police and military for their "barbarous treatment of peace-loving citizens." A coroner's jury found police and military action justified. Ten rioters were finally tried, found guilty, and sentenced to varying jail terms. "Before the Astor Place Riot it was the legal opinion that no one could be prosecuted for a riot, as it was presumed to be "the natural effect of political passion." Judge Daly's charge completely reversed this concept, and prosecution for rioting became accepted under American law.[10]

Chicago—1855

INCIDENT: German Tavern-Keepers' Revolt[11]
YEAR: 1855
LOCATION: Chicago
PROTAGONISTS: Native American, Know-Nothing political party vs. German immigrants and tavern-keepers of the North Side
GENERATIONAL ISSUES: Election of Native American mayor and his commitment to suppress immigrants and drive them out of business. Nativist reaction to great migrations from

[10]Ibid., p. 49.
[11]Flinn, *History of the Chicago Police*, pp. 72–79.

the British Isles and Germany during the 1830s and 1840s.

TRANSIENT ISSUES: Nativist-inspired high liquor license fees, which would have driven out of business the hundreds of small beer dealers of Chicago, nearly all of whom were German immigrants.

PRECIPITANT: The arrest of more than 200 German saloon-keepers for violation of a previously unenforced Sunday closing law. A test-case criminal trial was disturbed by a demonstration of 500 Germans and a counterdemonstration at Clark and Randolph Streets.

POLICE INVOLVEMENT: Captain Nichols, who headed the police department, cleared the streets and dispersed the mob upon orders from the mayor. A few men who resisted were arrested and taken into custody. That night, North Side Germans decided to cross the river and "rescue the prisoners. The rioters armed themselves with shotguns, rifles, pistols, clubs, knives, and every species of weapon. . . .[12] The spirit of revolt was heightened by rumor of a "raid" and by speeches exhorting immigrants to revolt against impending "slavery." "... the bridge opened, and the rioters swarmed across, only to be met by a solid body of policemen. . . . A collision was expected, and it came. Cries of 'Shoot the Police,' 'Pick out the stars,' rose from the mob, accompanied by the cracking of guns and pistols. The police replied without waiting for orders, and for several minutes there was a hot engagement in the vicinity of the Sherman House. A German, whose name is lost, levelled a double-barrelled shotgun at Officer Hunt and blew off his left arm. Sheriff Andrews . . . ordered a young man named Frazer . . . to return the fire. He did so, shooting the German dead. A large number were wounded on both sides, and several mysterious funerals occurred on the North Side within the next few days. . . .[13]

DISPOSITION: Sixty prisoners were added to those already being held, and the mayor ordered two military companies to protect the Court House with their artillery. But the riot was over, and "nearly all the cases against the imprisoned rioters were dismissed. . . ."[14]

[12]Ibid., pp. 75–77.
[13]Ibid., p. 78.
[14]Ibid., p. 37.

Boston—1863

INCIDENT: Conscription Riot[15]

YEAR: 1863

LOCATION: Boston (Concurrent location: New York City, two days before)

PROTAGONISTS: Citizens opposed to lottery-type draft vs. Provost Marshal's serving draft notices in Boston

TRANSIENT ISSUES: General opposition to the conscription, "as unconstitutional, unjust, and oppressive,. . ."[16] especially the provision that a man was entitled to exemption if he paid a $300 fee or furnished a substitute. Hourly newspaper specials on the New York conscription riot.

PRECIPITANT: A woman attacked two marshals, whom she mistakenly thought had come to take her husband into the army. She was joined by neighbors, passersby, and finally the entire crowd watching the draft lottery became involved.

POLICE INVOLVEMENT: Several policemen were attracted to the disorder and beaten by the crowd; more were sent in with the same results. The rioters then surrounded one of the police stations and were seen to be armed. That night several armed mobs moved about the city, largely beating strangers, police, and members of the military forces. There was window smashing and looting in the commercial districts, and several cases of arson occurred. At least eight were killed, many were seriously injured, and approximately a dozen persons were arrested.

DISPOSITION: Then, as now, there were serious questions about the causes. The police historian reported: "Whether the Conscription Riot . . . was the result of regular and extensive organization, reaching far beyond the limits of our own city or State, for the purpose of aiding the Rebellion, or whether it was only composed of a combination of men limited within the bounds of Boston and the surburban towns, or whether it was only a spontaneous outbreak, which is at any time liable to happen in all thickly populated places, is a

[15]Edward H. Savage, *Police Records and Recollections* (Boston: John P. Dale and Co., 1873), pp. 347–70.

[16]Ibid., p. 349.

question not well understood."[17] No arrests or prosecutions are recorded.

Los Angeles—1871

INCIDENT: Anti-Chinese Riot[18]
YEAR: 1871
LOCATION: Los Angeles (Concurrent locations: San Francisco, 1877; Denver, 1880; Wyoming, 1885)
PROTAGONISTS: White residents vs. Chinese community
GENERATIONAL ISSUES: A shortage of manpower in the mining and railroad industries inspired the importation of shiploads of indentured coolies. Even though profits increased for company owners, there was a reduction of wages for whites; racial prejudice followed.
TRANSIENT ISSUES: To avoid payment of the bride-price, a young man from one tong [a Chinese family society or organization] married a girl owned by a rival tong in a civil ceremony. Tong warfare ensued among the Chinese of Los Angeles. There was some gunfire between the rival clans.
PRECIPITANT: A policeman, one of the six-man Los Angeles force, intervened in an intertong exchange of gunfire and was wounded. Soon after, a rancher assisting another policeman was fatally wounded. A large crowd (at least 10 percent of Los Angeles' population of 6,000) gathered at the false report that Chinese were "killing whites wholesale."
POLICE INVOLVEMENT: The marshal deputized guards, and surrounded the large building-courtyard in which most of the city's Chinese lived. A lynching occurred shortly afterward, and the mob shot 18 Chinese during the afternoon and hung their bodies in various places in the town. Others were hanged outright, many were mutilated. The police assisted in securing many Chinese in the jailhouse, even though some of the policemen were found to have participated in the shootings, and others were intimidated and prevented from interfering with lynching parties. Twenty-three Chinese are known to have been killed. $30,000 was looted from Chinese quarters.

[17]Ibid., pp. 368–69.
[18]Heaps, *Riots*, pp. 61–71.

DISPOSITION: Arrests were variously reported at 30, 39, and 150. Ten men were brought to trial for the killing of a Chinese physician; eight were found guilty and given sentences of two to six years. A year later, the California Supreme Court reversed the verdict, stating that the indictment charged only the killing of the Chinese, not murder.

New York—1871

INCIDENT: Orange Riots[19]
YEAR: 1871
LOCATION: New York City
PROTAGONISTS: The Orange Societies vs. the "green" (Catholic) Irish
HISTORICAL ISSUES: Two-hundred year quarrel between Orange-Protestant Irishmen and Catholic Irishmen, carried over from Ireland to New York
TRANSIENT ISSUES: Orangemen applied for a parade permit to celebrate an anniversary date of William of Orange, first Protestant monarch of Ireland. Permit at first refused on public safety grounds, later issued.
PRECIPITANT: During the parade along a route lined by hostile Irish Catholics, a shot was fired from a window.
POLICE INVOLVEMENT: Police, in addition to a military regiment, were accompanying the Orangemen in large numbers. When the shot was fired from the window, without awaiting orders, the regiment fired into the crowd. Their first volley killed policemen as well as bystanders. Thirty-three were killed and 91 seriously injured.
DISPOSITION: Much indignation was expressed at the action of the troops for firing without waiting for order, and firing so wildly as to wound and kill some of their own men.[20]

[19]Augustine E. Costello, *Our Police Protectors* (New York: Police Pension Fund, 1885), pp. 244–48.
[20]Ibid., p. 246.

APPENDIX B
Equal Opportunity Guidelines

On March 9, 1973, the Law Enforcement Assistance Administration of the Department of Justice (LEAA) promulgated equal employment opportunity guidelines (28 CFR 42.301, et seq., Subpart E). The second paragraph of those guidelines reads as follows:

> In accordance with the spirit of the public policy set forth in 5 U.S.C. 553, interested persons may submit written comments, suggestions, data or arguments to the Administrator, Law Enforcement Assistance Administration, U.S. Department of Justice, Washington, D.C., 20530, Attention: Office of Civil Rights Compliance, within 45 days of the publication of the guidelines contained in this part. Material thus submitted will be evaluated and acted upon in the same manner as if this document were a proposal. Until such time as further changes are made, however, Part 42, Subpart E as set forth herein shall remain in effect, thus permitting the public business to proceed more expeditiously.

In accordance with the preceding paragraph, written comments, suggestions, data or arguments, have been received by the Administrator of the Law Enforcement Assistance Administration. Material submitted has been evaluated and changes deemed by LEAA to be appropriate have been incorporated into revised equal employment opportunity guidelines, the text of which follows.

By virtue of the authority vested in it by 5 U.S.C. 301, and section 501 of the Omnibus Crime Control and Safe Streets Act of 1968, Pub. L. 90–351, 82 Stat. 197, as amended, the Law Enforcement Assistance Administration hereby issues Title 28, Chapter 1, Subpart E, of Part 42 of the code of Federal Regulations. In that the material contained herein is a matter relating to the grant program of the Law Enforcement Assistance Administration, the relevant provisions of the Administrative Procedure Act (5 U.S.C. 553) requiring notice of proposed rulemaking, opportunity for public participation, and delay in effective date are inapplicable.

Subpart E—Equal Employment Opportunity Guidelines

Sec.

42.301   Purpose.

42.302   Application.

42.303   Evaluation of employment opportunities.

42.304   Written Equal Employment Opportunity Program.

42.305   Recordkeeping and certification.

42.306   Guidelines.

42.307   Obligations of recipients.

42.308   Noncompliance.

AUTHORITY: 5 U.S.C. sec. 501 of the Omnibus Crime Control and Safe Streets Act of 1968, Pub. L. 90–351, 82 Stat. 197, as amended.

42.301   Purpose

(a) The experience of the Law Enforcement Assistance Administration in implementing its responsibilities under the Omnibus Crime Control and Safe Streets Act of 1968, as amended, (Pub. L. 90–351, 82 Stat. 197; Pub. L. 91–644, 84 Stat. 1881) has demonstrated that the full and equal participation of women and minority individuals in employment opportunities in the criminal justice system is a necessary component to the Safe Streets Act's program to reduce crime and delinquency in the United States.

(b) Pursuant to the authority of the Safe Streets Act and the equal employment opportunity regulations of the LEAA relating to LEAA-assisted programs and activities (28 CFR 42.201, et seq., Subpart D), the following Equal Employment Opportunity Guidelines are established.

42.302   Application

(a) As used in these guidelines "Recipient" means any state, political subdivision of any state, combination of such states or subdivisions, or any department, agency or instrumentality of any of the foregoing receiving Federal financial assistance from LEAA, directly or through another recipient, or with respect to whom an assurance of civil rights compliance given as a condition of the earlier receipt of assistance is still in effect.

(b) The obligation of a recipient to formulate, implement, and maintain part, extends to state and local police agencies, correctional agencies, criman equal employment opportunity program, in accordance with this Subinal court systems, probation and parole agencies, and similar agencies responsible for the reduction and control of crime and delinquency.

(c) Assignments of compliance responsibility for Title VI of the Civil Rights Act of 1964 have been made by the Department of Justice to the Department of Health, Education and Welfare, covering educational institutions and general hospital or medical facilities. Similarly, the Department of Labor, in pursuance of its authority under Executive Orders 11246 and 11375, has assigned responsibility for monitoring equal employment opportunity under government contracts with medical and educational institutions, and non-profit organizations, to the Department of Health, Education and Welfare. Accordingly, monitoring responsibility in compliance matters in agencies of the kind mentioned in this paragraph rests with the Department of Health, Education and Welfare, and agencies of this kind are exempt from the provisions of this subpart, and are not responsible for the development of equal employment opportunity programs in accordance herewith.

(d) Each recipient of LEAA assistance within the Criminal justice system which has 50 or more employees and which has received grants or subgrants of $25,000 or more pursuant to and since the enactment of the Safe Streets Act of 1968, as amended, and which has a service population with a minority representation of 3 percent or more, is required to formulate, implement and maintain an Equal Employment Opportunity Program relating to employment practices affecting minority persons and women within 120 days after either the promulgation of these amended guidelines, or the initial application for assistance is approved, whichever is sooner. Where a recipient has 50 or more employees, and has received grants or subgrants of $25,000 or more, and has a service population with a minority representation of less than 3 percent, such recipient is required to formulate, implement, and maintain an equal employment opportunity program relating to employment practices affecting women. For a definition of "employment practices" within the meaning of this paragraph, see 42.202(b)

(e) "Minority persons" shall include persons who are Negro, Oriental, American-Indian, or Spanish-surnamed Americans. "Spanish-surnamed Americans" means those of Latin American, Cuban, Mexican, Puerto Rican or Spanish origin. In Alaska, Eskimos and Aleuts should be included as "American Indians."

(f) For the purpose of these guidelines, the relevant "service population" shall be determined as follows:

(1) For adult and juvenile correctional institutions, facilities and programs including probation and parole programs, the "service population" shall be the inmate or client population serviced by the institution, facility, or program during the preceding fiscal year.

(2) For all other recipient agencies (e.g., police and courts), the "service population" shall be the State population for state agencies, the county population for county agencies, and the municipal population for municipal agencies.

(g) "Fiscal year" means the twelve calendar months beginning July 1, and ending June 30, of the following calendar year. A fiscal year is designated by the calendar year in which it ends.

42.303   Evaluation of Employment Opportunities

(a) A necessary prerequisite to the development and implementation of a satisfactory Equal Employment Opportunity Program is the identification and analysis of any problem areas inherent in the utilization or participation of minorities and women in all of the recipient's employment phases (e.g., recruitment, selection, and promotion) and the evaluation of employment opportunities for minorities and women.

(b) In many cases an effective Equal Employment Opportunity Program may only be accomplished where the program is coordinated by the recipient agency with the cognizant Civil Service Commission or similar agency responsible by law, in whole or in part, for the recruitment and selection of entrance candidates and selection of candidates for promotion.

(c) In making the evaluation of employment opportunities, the recipient shall conduct such analysis separately for minorities and women. However, all racial and ethnic data collected to perform an evaluation pursuant to the requirements of this section should be cross classified by sex to ascertain the extent to which minority women or minority men may be underutilized. The evaluation should include but not necessarily be limited to the following factors:

(1) An analysis of present representation of women and minority persons in all job categories:

(2) An analysis of all recruitment and employment selection procedures for the preceding fiscal year, including such things as position description, application forms, recruitment methods and sources, interview procedures, test administration and test validity, educational prerequisites, referral procedures and final selection methods, to insure

that equal employment opportunity is being afforded in all job categories;

(3) An analysis of seniority practices and provisions, upgrading and promotion procedures, transfer procedures (internal or vertical), and formal and informal training programs during the preceding fiscal year, in order to insure that equal employment opportunity is being afforded;

(4) A reasonable assessment to determine whether minority employment is inhibited by external factors such as the lack of access to suitable housing in the geographical area served by a certain facility or the lack of suitable transportation (public or private) to the workplace.

42.304   Written Equal Employment Opportunity Program

Each recipient's Equal Employment Opportunity Program shall be in writing and shall include:

(a) A job classification table or chart which clearly indicates for each job classification or assignment the number of employees within each respective job category classified by race, sex and national origin (include for example Spanish-surnamed, Oriental, and American Indian). Also principal duties and rates of pay should be clearly indicated for each job classification. Where auxiliary duties are assigned or more than one rate of pay applies because of length of time in the job or other factors, a special notation should be made. Where the recipient operates more than one shift or assigns employees within each shift to varying locations, as in law enforcement agencies, the number by race, sex and national origin on each shift and in each location should be identified. When relevant, the recipient should indicate the racial/ethnic mix of the geographic area of assignments by the inclusion of minority population and percentage statistics.

(b) The number of disciplinary actions taken against employees by race, sex, and national origin within the preceding fiscal year, the number and types of sanctions imposed (suspension indefinitely, suspension for a term, loss of pay, written reprimand, oral reprimand, other) against individuals by race, sex and national origin.

(c) The number of individuals by race, sex and national origin (if available) applying for employment within the preceding fiscal year and the number by race, sex and national origin (if available) of those applicants who were offered employment and those who were actually hired. If such data is unavailable, the recipient should institute a system for the collection of such data.

(d) The number of employees in each job category by race, sex, and national origin who made application for promotion or transfer within the preceding fiscal year and the number in each job category by race, sex, and national origin who were promoted or transferred.

(e) The number of employees by race, sex, and national origin who were terminated within the preceding fiscal year, identifying by race, sex and national origin which were voluntary and involuntary terminations.

(f) Available community and area labor characteristics within the relevant geographical area including total population, workforce and existing unemployment by race, sex and national origin. Such data may be obtained from the Bureau of Labor Statistics, Washington, D.C., state and local employment services, or other reliable sources. Recipients should identify the sources of the data used.

(g) A detailed narrative statement setting forth the recipient's existing employment policies and practices as defined in 42.202(b). Thus, for example, where testing is used in the employment selection process, it is not sufficient for the recipient to simply note the fact. The recipient should identify the test, describe the procedures followed in administering and scoring the test, state what weight is given to test scores, how a cutoff score is established and whether the test has been validated to predict or measure job performance and, if so, a detailed description of the validation study. Similarly detailed responses are required with respect to other employment policies, procedures, and practices used by the applicant.

(1) The statement should include the recipient's detailed analysis of existing employment policies, procedures, and practices as they relate to employment of minorities and women, (see 42.303) and, where improvements are necessary, the statement should set forth in detail the specific steps the recipient will take for the achievement of full and equal employment opportunity. For example, the Equal Employment Opportunity Commission, in carrying out its responsibilities in ensuring compliance with Title VII has published Guidelines on Employee Selection Procedures (29 CFR Part 1607) which among other things, proscribes the use of employee selection practices, procedures and devices (such as tests, minimum educational levels, oral interviews and the like) which have not been shown by the user thereof to be related to job performance and where the use of such an unvalidated selection device tends to disqualify a disproportionate number of minority individuals or women for employment. The EEOC Guidelines set out appropriate procedures to assist in establishing and maintaining equal employment opportunities. Recipients of LEAA assistance using selection procedures which are not in conformity with the EEOC Guidelines shall set forth the specific areas of nonconformity, the reasons which may explain any such nonconformity, and, if necessary, the steps the recipient agency will take to correct any existing deficiency.

(2) The recipient should also set forth a program for recruitment of minority persons based on an informed judgment of what is necessary to attract minority applications including, but not necessarily limited to, dissemination of posters, use of advertising media patronized by minorities, minority group contacts and community relations programs. As appropriate, recipients may wish to refer to recruitment techniques suggested in Revised Order No. 4 of the Office of Federal Contract Compliance, U.S. Department of Labor, found at 41 CFR 60–2.24(e).

(h) Plan for dissemination of the applicant's Equal Employment Opportunity Program to all personnel, applicants and the general public. As appropriate, recipients may wish to refer to the recommendations for dissemination of policy suggested in Revised Order No. 4 of the Office of Federal Contract Compliance, U.S. Department of Labor, found at 41 CFR 60–2.21.

(i) Designation of specified personnel to implement and maintain adherence to the Equal Employment Opportunity Program and a description of their specific responsibilities suggested in Revised Order No. 4 of the Office of Federal Contract Compliance, U.S. Department of Labor, found at 41 CFR 60–2.22.

42.305 Recordkeeping and Certification

The Equal Employment Opportunity Program and all records used in its preparation shall be kept on file and retained by each recipient covered by these guidelines for subsequent audit or review by responsible personnel of the cognizant state planning agency or the LEAA. Prior to the authorization to fund new or continuing programs under the Omnibus Crime Control and Safe Streets Act of 1968, the recipient shall file a certificate with the cognizant state planning agency or LEAA regional office stating that the equal employment opportunity program is on file with the recipient. The form of the certification shall be as follows:

I, _____ (person filing the application) certify that the _____ _____(criminal justice agency) has formulated an equal employment opportunity program in accordance with 28 CFR 42.301, et seq., Subpart E, and that it is on file in the _____ (name of office) _____ (address), _____ (title), for review or audit by officials of the cognizant state planning agency or the Law Enforcement Assistance Administration, as required by relevant laws and regulations.

The criminal justice agency created by the Governor to implement the Safe Streets Act within each state shall certify that it requires, as a condition of the recipient of block grant funds, that recipients from it have executed an Equal Employment Opportunity Program in accordance with this subpart, or that, in conformity with the terms and conditions of this regulation no equal employment opportunity programs are required to be filed by that jurisdiction.

42.306   Guidelines

(a) Recipient agencies are expected to conduct a continuing program of self-evaluation to ascertain whether any of their recruitment, employee selection or promotional policies (or lack thereof) directly or indirectly have the effect of denying equal employment opportunities to minority individuals and women.

(b) Post award compliance reviews of recipient agencies will be scheduled by LEAA, giving priority to any recipient agencies which have a significant disparity between the percentage of minority persons in the service population and the percentage of minority employees in the agency. Equal employment program modification may be suggested by LEAA the appropriates of improved selection procedures and policies. Accordingly, any recipient agencies falling within this category are encouraged to develop recruitment, hiring or promotional guidelines under their equal employment opportunity program which will correct, in a timely manner, any identifiable employment impediments which may have contributed to the existing disparities.

(c) A significant disparity between minority representation in the service population and the minority representation in the agency workforce may be deemed to exist if the percentage of a minority group in the employment of the agency is not at least seventy (70) percent of the percentage of that minority in the service population.

42.307   Obligations of Recipients

The obligation of those recipients subject to these Guidelines for the maintenance of an Equal Employment Opportunity Program shall continue for the period during which the LEAA assistance is extended to a recipient or for the period during which a comprehensive law enforcement plan filed pursuant to the Safe Streets Act is in effect within the State, whichever is longer, unless the assurances of compliance, filed by a recipient in accordance with 42.204(a)(2), specify a different period.

42.308   Noncompliance

Failure to implement and maintain an Equal Employment Opportunity Program as required by these Guidelines shall subject recipient of LEAA assistance to the sanctions prescribed by the Safe Streets Act and the equal employment opportunity regulations of the Department of Justice (Sec 42 U.S.C. 3757 and 42.206).

Effective date—This Guideline shall become effective on

August 31, 1973.

Dated August 24, 1973.

DONALD E. SANTARELLI

Administrator, Law Enforcement

Assistance Administration

[FR Doc. 73–18555 Filed 8–30–73;8:45 AM]

APPENDIX C
A Checklist for Police Administrators to Establish Effective Means of Dealing with Community Tensions and Civil Disturbances*

I. *FACTORS CONTRIBUTING TO COMMUNITY TENSIONS AND CIVIL DISTURBANCES*
   A. Social Factors
      1. Racial or minority group injustices, whether real or imagined, create an atmosphere of distrust and fear.
      2. Religious differences can often create schisms in the community just as serious as racial differences.
      3. Normal community activities, involving crowds, could deteriorate into serious disorder under certain conditions (e.g., large crowds outside, hot weather, an "incident").
      4. Existence of a matriarchal society prevalent in Negro areas can present unusual problems to police and the larger community.
      5. Adult attitudes towards conduct of young people, teen-agers, etc., may vary due to different cultural values and attitudes. These may be in conflict with the norms of the community.
   B. Economic Factors
      1. Extreme poverty can breed crime and perpetuate barriers to social advancement.
      2. Unemployment and/or unfair hiring practices tend to confirm for minority group persons that they are facing a "stacked deck" in their efforts to improve their lot.

*Taken from California Commission on Peace Officers Standards Training Post (CONDENSED).

350

3. Poor housing conditions and discrimination in the sale of real estate create dislike for the "power structure," and the policeman who symbolizes the establishment.
4. Affluence of large parts of the community create unawareness and insensitivity so that no desire to cope with "minority group" problems exists.

C. Political Factors
   1. Power struggles:
      a. Efforts by the majority, legal and otherwise, to maintain the status quo.
      b. Efforts, legal and otherwise, by minority groups to upset the balance of power; to share, dominate, or alter the political system.

D. Absence or Failure of Constituted Authority
   1. Failure of law enforcement to act:
      a. In a crowd or arrest situation, due to indecision, or lack of appropriate laws.
      b. In certain situations due to a lack of manpower, or inadequately trained manpower.
      c. Because of a fear of adverse public reaction.
   2. Absence of law enforcement:
      a. Serves as a contributing factor to disorder because members of the crowd (or mob) feel they can act with impunity.
      b. Some in minority group areas feel they are not receiving adequate police services.

E. General Factors
   1. Minority group struggles for full enjoyment of civil rights.
   2. Inequitable law enforcement, real or imagined, toward minority groups.
      a. Demonstrated bias or prejudice on the part of police.
      b. A feeling in some areas that they are "overpoliced."
   3. Lack of meaningful communication between police and the minority community.
   4. Stereotyping:
      a. Of minorities by police and other city officials.
      b. Of police and city officials by minorities and the larger community.
   5. Rumors and sensationalism:
      a. Inflammatory statements and stories based upon distortions and/or half-truths.
      b. May be originated by police, city officials, minority groups, religious and lay groups, news media.

6. Absence of organization and leadership among the masses of minority group members.
   a. Self-proclaimed leaders much in evidence.
   b. Leaders selected by the white majority to represent the minority much in evidence.
   c. General lack of opposition among the minorities against the radical elements (tacit approval).
   d. No real leadership for the minority community.
7. General public apathy towards the issue of civil rights and impartial law enforcement.
8. Outsiders who capitalize on local problems as a means of promoting their own goals.

II. *WARNING SIGNS OF COMMUNITY TENSIONS*
   A. Early Manifestations
      1. A greater frequency of resisting arrest in certain areas. Gathering of crowds when arrests are made.
      2. An increase in charges of alleged police brutality, an increased distrust or resentment of law enforcement.
      3. A rising volume in the number of incidents of violence, or threats of violence.
      4. Increasing rumors and statements of dissatisfaction, public name-calling and other attempts at provocation.
      5. The appearance of "hate" literature, threatening or derogatory signs, leaflets, pamphlets.
      6. A stepping-up of gang activity, characterized by anti-social activity on the part of minority group members; acts of vandalism and malicious mischief, particularly on public property.
      7. Progressively overt attacks upon constituted authority through:
         a. Protest meetings.
         b. Speeches and literature.
         c. Sit-ins, lie-ins, etc., in commercial and public buildings.
         d. Disruption of and interference with police activities.
      8. Apprehension or fear on the part of police officers.

III. *POLICY RE COMMUNITY TENSIONS AND CIVIL DISTURBANCES*

It is the department head's responsibility to formulate sound policies that will serve as guidelines to members of his agency in their contacts with the public. It is suggested that thoughtful consideration be given to the following areas of police policy:

   A. Administrative Policy
      1. This involves a stated position on the issues of police-community relations, human relations, and civil disturbances. This position would recognize the right of peaceful demonstration,

and at the same time point out the responsibilities of those who demonstrate. It should contain a pledge of fair and impartial enforcement for all members of the community.

2. Policy statements should be reduced to writing.
3. Obtain concurrence of other city officials.
4. Provide appropriate dissemination through:
    a. News media.
    b. Departmental orders.
    c. Staff meetings
    (Releases to the public would consist of a statement of general principles. Material distributed to the department would be specific and detailed.)
5. Policy Inspection
   There should be an affirmative answer to each of the following questions:
    a. Is middle management selling it?
    b. Does everyone understand it?
    c. Are they demonstrating that they believe in it, and are following policy?
    d. Is someone officially designated to make such inspections and report back to the chief?

B. Organizational Policy
1. Considerations:
    a. The size of the department and the magnitude of the problem will determine whether community relations will be an assignment for one individual, or a special unit should be formed.
    b. The person or unit should operate in a staff capacity, and should report directly to the chief.
    c. A summary of collected intelligence should be furnished the department head on a regular basis for review and analysis.
2. Special operations dealing with civil disturbances.
    a. The field commander (designated in advance) will be in complete charge.
    b. A second-in-command and an alternate should be chosen to provide 24-hour continuity.
    c. In the event of a major disturbance, the field commander would relieve the district and/or shift commander, and would assume charge.
    d. The field commander, subject to the approval of the chief of police, would have authority to mobilize and request mutual aid.

e. The field commander would maintain liaison for legal advice in the field with the District Attorney.

f. The field commander would be responsible for public information releases.

C. Operational Policy for Disturbances

1. Personnel:

a. All personnel would be required to "report in," upon hearing announcements on radio or TV, or upon notification to their residence.

b. An adequate supervisory ratio should be maintained.

c. Training and re-training should be continuous.

d. Assignment of men should be commensurate with the size and seriousness of the situation.

e. Overtime limitations should be kept in mind in routine operations.

2. The Field Commander:

a. He should specify the geographical area that contains the problem and then assume complete charge of that area.

b. Headquarters and communications should be advised of the perimeter established.

c. The community relations unit and headquarters will act in a staff capacity to the field commander.

3. External Relations:

a. Policy should be pre-established that would clarify the involvement of other city departments' personnel, as well as outside law enforcement agencies.

b. The public should be kept informed but steps should be taken to keep curiosity-seekers out of the area.

4. Use of Force:

a. The use of force, particularly individual combat, should be avoided. There must be a great deal of restraint on the part of police, and when action is taken it should be by units, not individual officers.

b. Chemicals, such as smoke or tear gas, should be used only when authorized by the field commander. When it is used, there should be a more than adequate supply available at the designated location in the field. Provisions should be made for escape routes for the crowd and first aid for rioters, when requested.

c. Dogs frequently create a negative reaction in crowds when they are used for crowd control and/or arrest They should be used only in extreme situations.

d. The use of firearms should be avoided and the practice of firing "warning shots" is not advised. The use of firearms should be considered as a last resort, and then only when necessary to protect the lives of citizens and officers.

e. Insulting language is often construed as a form of "harassment" and "brutality." Care should be given to avoiding terms and names that would antagonize the group being dealt with.

  (1) Officers should expect to receive abusive language and should avoid being baited into making imprudent remarks and/or arrests.

5. News Media:

a. A public information officer should be part of the field command staff. He should have a counterpart at headquarters (in disturbances of major proportions) to whom he will feed information as it becomes available.

b. The P.I.O. should arrange for a specific schedule for press releases and a point of dissemination. He should not deviate from this procedure unless a major event occurs.

c. The P.I.O. should act as a "buffer" between the press and the field commander, so that the commander can devote maximum time and attention to the problem.

d. Reasonable limitations should be set for the press re-entry into high hazard areas. Contacts by the press with police personnel in the field, in the form of personal interviews, should be minimized. Efforts should be made to confine such interviews to the command post area, and with the approval of the officer in charge.

e. News media representatives should be required to produce bona fide credentials in order to enter the area. In major disturbances consideration could be given to the issuance of special press cards by the P.I.O.

6. Arrests:

a. When demonstrations are known in advance, meetings should be held with the head of the organization against whom the demonstration would take place, and his counsel. Policy should be agreed upon as to what point arrest would be in order, and that the firm or organization would be willing to prosecute.

b. Similar meetings should be held with the leaders of the demonstrating groups. Ground rules should be formulated that both the demonstrators and police understand.

        c. Whenever possible it should be decided in advance whether physical arrests and the bail procedure would be used, or whether arrestees could simply be released on citation or summons following the booking.

        d. Alternatives should be decided upon to handle prisoners in the event custodial facilities are saturated.

    7. Emergency Funding:

        a. Certain staff members should be authorized to sign emergency requisitions.

        b. These requisitions could be for food, lumber, gasoline, vehicle parts or repair, guns, ammunition, etc.

        c. Major purchases should be with the knowledge and approval of the logistical commander, and normally through his office.

IV. PREVENTION—THE KEY TO COPING WITH COMMUNITY TENSIONS

Experience of many law enforcement agencies indicates that most civil disturbances can be prevented, or if not prevented, their negative effects can be minimized. One of the best prevention tools is the reputation of an agency in terms of fair, impartial, and efficient law enforcement, and the knowledge that the agency possesses an interest in and knowledge of the problems of the community.

The following factors have been shown to be important in the development and maintenance of a good prevention program:

  A. The Selection Process

    1. Recruiting standards at the entrance level should stress the selection of intelligent and stable individuals who react well under stress. It is most desirable to select persons:

        a. Who are able to deal effectively both in group and individual relationships.

        b. Who possess a background that helps equip them to deal with a variety of people, and changing social, cultural, and political conditions.

    2. An inventory of existing staff should be made to identify those individuals who can be assigned to important posts in sensitive areas.

  B. Training and its Role in Prevention

    1. The benefits of good training should be stressed to individual officers.

    2. Basic concepts of community relations should be covered at the recruit level. In-depth training should be administered at the in-service and re-training levels.

3. Legal training, in addition to its normal implications, should include study of laws specifically relating to community problems and disturbances. This would include:
   a. Local and county ordinances
   b. State and Federal statutes
   c. Other laws governing public assembly, constitutional rights, etc.
4. Field tactics and techniques of self-defense should be taught as part of the continuing curriculum.
   a. Basic training should be on a department-wide basis, with provisions for periodic re-training.
   b. Special and intensive training of a continuous nature should be provided to crowd control units.
5. Decision-making is difficult at all levels. An effective exercise of this skill can be developed through role-playing in problem solving sessions wherein individuals must evaluate situations and decide on courses of action.
6. Department policies and procedures are subject to change. There should be particular emphasis on keeping all personnel aware of changes or modifications relative to:
   a. Court decisions
   b. Community relations programs
   c. Standards of conduct for officers
   d. Collecting and reporting intelligence
   e. Coping with disturbances
   f. Post-disturbance recovery
7. In order to have an effective liaison with the community, there must be good two-way communication. This can often be facilitated through training in:
   a. Understanding minority group cultures and their problems.
   b. The importance of semantics (slang, colloquialisms, "trigger words," etc.)
   c. Developing the ability to listen and comprehend, and to speak and be understood.
   d. The need to explain (not defend) changes in enforcement policies and actions.
C. Community Relations Programs as a Vehicle for Prevention
   1. The term "Police-Community Relations" too often is defined in narrow terms. It would appear more appropriate to refer to *all* relationships between the police and the community rather than in terms of relationships with racial minority groups. The

emphasis should be on special group problems within the larger community, regardless of their nature. It would be advisable to maintain contact with *all* groups, regardless of whether or not their viewpoints are compatible with those of the department.

2. Specialization in community relations offers advantages in all but the smallest department. Ideally a specialized unit would deal with all relations with all the community. Its secondary purpose would be to deal with special groups within the community.

3. Important to the formation of such a unit would be the criteria for selecting its staff. There should be assurance that those selected:

    a. Possess a sound background in general law enforcement, with a demonstrated record of good conduct, and stability.

    b. Have a record of having made *good* arrests, resulting in a high rate of convictions, with a minimum of resisting arrest charges involved.

    c. Have a suitable academic background.

    d. Have a substantiated reputation for fairness, good judgment, and an absence of any crippling bias or prejudice.

4. The head of the community relations unit would report directly to the department head and would act in a staff capacity to the rest of the organization. At the same time it would be important to stress that members of the unit must not discard their identity and responsibilities as policemen. Regardless of how deeply involved they become in their assignment, their primary responsibilities are still to the department. There must be a correlation between their goals and objectives, and that of the agency they serve.

5. A continuous and effective liaison should be maintained between this unit and special-interest community groups, and the human relations commission. This bond between the police and the community can be formed by:

    a. Making good community relations the responsibility of *everyone* in the department, from the patrolman to the chief.

    b. Actively seeking out and making the acquaintance of individuals and associations, not waiting for them to "make the first move."

c. Keeping the public fully informed.

d. Demonstrating a continuing interest in community problems; seeking citizen reaction and advice.

e. Being willing to listen to citizen complaints about the community, the police, the city government. Be willing to make referrals, or institute a police follow-up when appropriate.

f. Frankly stating the police position (when there is one) on community issues, and being willing to change positions that experience and common sense indicate need modification.

6. Press relations and publicity efforts of this unit should be within the framework of departmental policy. Major releases should always be cleared with the chief of police in advance. It would be ideal to use a professional public relations man in this unit, but in any event it would be desirable to utilize a staff member with special training in journalistic and public relations techniques.

7. Program goals of the community relations unit should be the result of extensive planning, and receive department head approval before attempts are made to implement them. Generally the program goals will be to bring about better understanding and mutual trust between the community and the police. Such programs are:

a. Those aimed at the entire community.

b. Those designed to reach children and teenagers, in and out of school.

c. Those designed to deal with problems presented by special groups.

D. Complaint Procedures

1. The organizational structure should be geared to accommodate the processing and disposition of citizen complaints. One satisfactory method is to:

a. Set up specific channels and procedures.

b. Supplement this with means of disseminating knowledge of this system to the public and members of the department.

c. Receive complaints made about departmental policies and/or procedures, as well as against individuals.

d. Establish procedures to insure prompt followup, and feed-back to the complainant.

e. Have a policy to issue public statements regarding false reports that have been maliciously and intentionally filed against an officer.

2. Establish channels to receive *complaints by police officers re the public*. Make it a policy to bring these complaints to the attention of the appropriate community group and the press to generate some responsible action on their part. Complaints by officers might include:

   a. Assaults on police officers.
   b. Verbal abuse, provocation, "baiting."
   c. Defiance of authority, interference with arrests and other police action.
   d. Lack of respect for constituted authority.
   e. False accusations.
   f. Preferential treatment for minorities.
   g. Apathy, lack of support for law and order.
   h. Untrue and/or unfair treatment of police by news media.

E. Some Consequences of Poor Police-Community Relations

1. There is reduced morale, efficiency, and attention to duty in the police department. Consequently there will probably be higher crime rates and detrimental effects on crime and delinquency generally.

2. There is reluctance on the part of the community to participate or assume responsibility in the process of law enforcement. This will result in less success in preventative and investigative police work.

3. There is an increased likelihood of abuse and injury to policemen in the field.

4. There is increasing likelihood of abuse, injury, and infringement of the rights and liberties of citizens.

5. The potential for large-scale violence between the police and segments of the community is greatly increased.

APPENDIX D
Law Enforcement
and Community Service Programs*

It has been said that, for America's poor and those in trouble, the police department is most often the first port of call in times of personal crisis.

Most of these cases involve problems of a noncriminal nature. With relatively few exceptions, the citizen with personal problems is left unaided or, at best, he is offered directions to the nearest social service agency. More often than not, this referral is inept or will prove to be of no benefit to the citizen. This occurs because he has been referred to the wrong agency or because the social service agency is ineffective and does not live up to its own sugarcoated advertising.

A fundamental premise involved here is that the police have a dual obligation as a public service unit in our society. The first is to regulate antisocial behavior by those methods that are legalistic and traditional. Secondly, the police have an obligation to help every indivdual who brings his problem to the attention of the police. These latter problems are mostly those of a noncriminal nature. Therefore, the police perform as controlling agents and as support agents. This dual role is performed one at a time, or simultaneously, and the role is interchanged as circumstances dictate.

It is a paradox that 99 percent of a law enforcement officer's training is devoted to the police control function, when 50 percent to 90 percent of a patrolman's time involves matters of a nonpolice nature. A number of

*J. E. Whitehouse, "Law Enforcement and Community Service Programs," *Journal of California Law Enforcement*, 8, No. 1 (July 1973), 28–39. By permission of the publisher (footnotes deleted).

studies have been made which indicate the volume of noncriminal business handled by police departments. The study by Cumming showed that 49.6 percent of incoming calls to a large metropolitan police department had to do with personal problems of a noncriminal nature. G. Douglas Gourley has written that, "It has been estimated that at least 90 percent of all police business is not of a strictly criminal nature." A survey by Dr. Richard Hoffman found that patrol and field officers in a large midwestern city spend 70 percent of their time on miscellaneous public services and only 10 percent to 15 percent of their time on criminal matters.

The police have rarely been trained to make referrals for people with problems. Recently, this fact was forcibly brought home when the writer attended a graduate seminar. The class was composed of experienced police officers. When it was explained to the class that Los Angeles County had approximately 1,500 social service agencies within its boundaries and Orange County approximately 700, shock and amazement were expressed by the students. A supervisory officer in Orange County knew of only one referral agency. A middle-management level officer, employed by one of the largest police departments in Los Angeles County, used a small referral list that he had found in an "underground" newspaper. None of the students were aware of the existence of standard directories of health, welfare, and recreational services which are found in every city. If supervisory and middle-management police officers working for graduate level university degrees are so uninformed about community service agencies, what does the man-on-the-beat know?

There is no suggestion anywhere in this paper which indicates that the police should abandon or even diminish current law enforcement functions. Throughout history no society has been able to survive without some method of enforcing mores, customs, taboos, or laws. Most certainly, no society in the modern world could long survive without some form of police system.

Suggestions made in this paper are limited to the narrow premise that the police should become more deeply involved in community service programs such as the one advocated here. This is to be accomplished in conjunction with the continued use of traditional law enforcement methods. Community service programs should be considered as a secondary support function of the police control role.

Compiling the Directory

It is evident that those involved in law enforcement are uninformed about the existence of referral directories. However, compiling a directory or referral handbook for use by field officers is not an insurmountable task. Several cities, including Washington, D.C., have compiled such handbooks for use by their patrolmen. *Every* police department can compile their own community service referral directory. It need not be extensive, and only those agencies which, in fact, help people should be listed.

Police departments in large cities will find directories of health, welfare, and vocational services already in existence. However, these directories rarely are complete. Consequently, an additional search for suitable agencies will have to be made. Various sources of information can be found under *Specific Sources* and *General Sources* listed below.

In smaller communities where no directories have been published the police must start from scratch. Those compiling directories in communities such as these will probably find the listings under *General Sources* most helpful.

Sample Entries

In compiling a referral directory great care should be used in selecting those agencies to be included. Many public and private service agencies possess an exaggerated opinion of what they do to help people in distress. It is recommended that personal contact be made with the director or immediate subordinate of each agency in order to obtain a firm understanding of the kind and extent of services provided. Unquestionably, the referral directory would have to be revised at regular intervals. It does no good to send a person in need of help to an agency which does nothing to alleviate the problem.

Each entry should contain the following information: correct title; AKA, if known; address; telephone numbers; hours open; after hours phone number, if any; accessibility to public transportation (bus route number); and a simple explanation of the services rendered, including "sometimes" services. Wherever applicable, the name of the person to contact within the agency should be listed, the area served by the agency, and the fees, if any. Examples of entry:

MILLER PSYCHIATRIC AND COMMUNITY MENTAL HEALTH CENTER

8572 Indian Hill Road, Claremount, Calif. 91711

Telephone: (714) 625-3327 or 625-3328

Hours: Monday–Friday, 9:00 A.M. to 5:30 P.M.; Emergency consultation services—24 hours; Telephone—625-5223

Director: Robert C. Miller, M.D.

Program: Out-patient clinic only—psychiatric evaluation and psychological testing; crisis therapy—group therapy, drug clinic.

Application Procedure: Call admitting desk.

Fees: Sliding scale according to ability to pay.

Area Served: San Gabriel Valley

Bus Route: 31 G

LEGAL AID FOUNDATION OF LONG BEACH
236 East Third Street
Long Beach, Calif. 90812
Telephone: (213) 437-0901
Hours: Monday–Friday, 9:00 A.M. to 5:00 P.M.
Program: Provides legal assistance in civil matters to persons unable to pay for a private attorney.
Application Procedure: Personal interview.
Fees: $2.00 registration.
Area Served: Long Beach and harbor health districts.
Bus Route: 14A

Sample Table of Contents

The outline listed below is not all-inclusive and is meant to be merely a guide. Each entry should be included under the type of service needed. For example, the Salvation Army programs might be listed under "Emergency Housing," "Alcoholism," "Family Services," "Missing Persons," or "Financial Assistance."

AGED:
 Housing
 Medical Care
 Protective Care

ALCOHOLISM:
 Counseling
 Family Services
 Hospital Car
 Mental Health
  Programs

ARMED FORCES:
 Counseling
 Financial Aid
 Housing
 Meals
 Police

BUSINESS MATTERS:
 Consumer Complaints
 Insurance Matters
 Legal Assistance

CHILDREN:
 Adoption
 Counseling
 Day Care
 Housing
 Medical Care

Mental Health
 Support

COMPLAINTS–PUBLIC
SERVICES:
 District, City,
  State Attorneys
 Legal
 Ombudsman
 Police Malpractice

DISCRIMINATION:
 Employment
 Housing
 Legal Assistance
 Public Services
 Voting Rights

EMPLOYMENT:
 Counseling
 Job Placement
 Pre-vocational
  Training
 Testing
 Unemployment
 Vocational
  Training

ENVIRONMENT:
 Smog Control

Water Pollution
Conservation

ETHNIC GROUPS:
American Indian
Black American
Mexican-American
Refugees
Others

FINANCIAL AID:
Counseling
Emergency
Assistance

HANDICAPPED:
Counseling
Employment
Home Care Services
Job Training
Medical Assistance

HEALTH:
Dental Problems
Family Planning
Free Clinics
Health Departments
Immunization
Nutrition Services
Public Health
Nursing Services
Unplanned
Pregnancies
Venereal Diseases

HOUSING:
Children
Families
Men
Women

LEGAL ASSISTANCE:
Legal Service
Centers
Legal Service
Societies
Public Defender

MENTAL HEALTH:
Family Counseling
Family Crises
Marital Counseling
Psychiatric Aid
Suicide Prevention

MISCELLANEOUS:
Bail
Homemaking
Planned
Parenthood
Social Security
Veterans' Affairs
Workman's
Compensation

NARCOTICS:
Complaints
Family Counseling
Information and
Counseling
Treatment

PAROLEES:
Case Work
Counseling
Employment

PUBLIC SERVICES:
Courts
Fire Department
Libraries
Police
Schools
Welfare Services

TRANSIENT:
Emergency Welfare
Assistance
Traveler's Aid

UTILITIES:
Electric
Gas
Telephone
Trash Removal
Water

YOUTH:
Athletic Teams
Big Brothers
Big Sisters
Boys' Clubs
Day Camps
Playgrounds
Summer Camps
Tutorial Services
Work Permits
Youth Corps
Youth Hostels

Sources of Information

The sources listed in this section contain some of the data that can be used to compile a referral diectory. Wherever possible, addresses are given. By necessity, some of the references pertain only to the Southern California area. However, these were included to give examples of where facts can be obtained; e.g. several entries came from the Sunday supplements of local newspapers. Many listings are from national directories which are useful in obtaining information in particular areas. Most of the agencies are very cooperative to those seeking information.

Specific Sources

Alcoholics Anonymous Publishing, Inc., Box 459, Grand Central Post Office, New York, New York, 10017

All-Nations Foundation
Goal is to alleviate governmental malpractice problems. They know of and work with various community coordinating councils.

American Friends Service Committee.
The material aids program for this group provides clothing, medical supplies, and other items.

ANNAND, DOUGLAS R.—*The Wheelchair Traveler*, 1972 Edition
Write to: "The Wheelchair Traveler," P.O. Box 169, Woodland Hills, California, 91364
The purpose of *The Wheelchair Traveler* is to bring under one cover as much information as possible specifically for the travel enjoyment of the handicapped traveler. It will be printed and available about March 1 of each year.

Around the Town With Ease, Junior League of Los Angeles, 1968.
A guide to the Southern California area for families, children, and visitors, with special added information for those with physical limitations.

ARTHUR, JULIETTA K.—*Employment for the Handicapped*, Nashville Abdingdon Press, 1967.
This book is a guide for the handicapped, their families and counselors. Contains wealth of information on services to the disabled. Contains addresses of state divisions of vocational rehabilitation and state agencies for the blind, United States Civil Service Commission local addresses, local addresses of small business associations, and local addresses of Veteran Administration field offices. Highly recommended.

Association of Rehabilitation Centers, Inc., 628 Davis Street Evanston, Illinois
Publishes a directory of rehabilitation facilities in America. This directory has appeared in the May–June, 1964, issue of *Journal of Rehabilitation.*

BLIED, DIANE–"Help!", *California Living*, March 7,1971, p. 10
Lists the Los Angeles County area hospitals which offer 24-hour emergency service.

Catalog of Federal Domestic Assistance, Washington, D.C., Government Printing Office, 1969. Explains purpose and nature of programs. Specifies major eligibility requirements and where to apply. Also, lists printed materials available. Twelve pages of Tables of Contents.

Child Welfare League of America, 44 East 23rd Street, New York, New York, 10010
Publishes directory of member agencies.

Civic and Business Directory, published by the Artesia Chamber of Commerce, November, 1970.
A convenient guide to the cities of Artesia, Cerritos, Hawaiian Gardens, and East Lakewood. Good example of local directory which lists names and addresses of public utilities, clubs, organizations, meeting halls, political information, schools, etc.

Directory of Agencies Serving Blind Persons in the United States, American Foundation for the Blind, Inc., 15 West 16th Street, New York, New York, 10011, 352 pages, 1969.

Directory of Correctional Institutions and Agencies of the United States of America, Canada, and Great Britain, approximately 100 pages, American Correctional Association Woodridge Station, P.O. Box 10176, Washington, D.C., 20018 (August Annually).

Directory of Health, Welfare, and Recreational Services in Long Beach–Lakewood–Signal Hill–Bellflower–Carson–Paramount–Artesia–Hawaiian Gardens–Cerritos, Community Planning Council, Long Beach Arena, 3515 Linden Avenue, Long Beach, California, 90807

Directory of Health, Welfare, Vocational and Recreational Services in Los Angeles County, Los Angeles, Welfare Information Service, Inc. 1969

Directory of Homemaker-Home Health Aide Service, 1966–67, National Council for Homemaker Services, Inc., 1740 Broadway, New York, New York, 10019, 181 pages.

Directory of Maternity Homes and Residential Facilities for the Unmarried Mother, 108 pages, 1966, National Council on Illegitimacy, 44 East 23rd Street, New York, New York, 10010

Directory of Member Agencies, 1969, 75 pages, 1969, Family Service Association of America, 44 East 23rd Street, New York, New York, 10010

Directory of Member Agencies and Associates, 108 pages, 1969, Child Welfare League of America, 44 East 23rd Street, New York, New York, 10010

Directory of National Associations Relating to the Education of Crippled and/or Other Health Impaired, compiled by the Office of Education, Department of Health and Welfare (no dates). Copies available from Unit Coordinator, Educational Programs for Crippled and Other Health Impaired, Washington, D.C., 10101

Directory of Organizations Interested in the Handicapped, no date. Committee for the Handicapped, the People-to-People Program, 1218 New Hampshire Avenue, N.W., Washington, D.C., 20036

Directory of Rehabilitation Facilities, Association of Rehabilitation Centers, Inc., 7979 Old Georgetown Road, Washington, D.C., 20014, 1968.
Listing of facilities in the United States and Canada.

Directory of United Funds, Community Chests, Community Health and Welfare Councils, 137 pages, (July Annually). United Community Funds and Councils of America, Inc., 345 East 46th Street, New York, New York, 10017

Directory of Vocational Counseling Services, American Personnel Guidance Association, 1605 New Hampshire Avenue, N.W., Washington, D.C., 20009
Lists pertinent information about 177 agencies approved by the American Board on Counseling Services.

"Drug Abuse: Where to Find the Facts," *Today's Health,* March, 1971, pp. 57–8.
Directory of free and inexpensive information for parents and teachers. Free copies available: Drug Facts, Singer—S.U.E., 1345 Diversey, Chicago, Illinois, 60614, (Send stamped self-addressed business envelope.)

Encyclopedia of Social Work, Fifteenth Issue, 1965, pp. 903–1022 and pp. 1025–26. Harry L. Lurie, Editor, National Association of Social Workers, 2 Park Avenue, New York, New York, 10016
2 Park Avenue, New York, New York, 10016
Contains extensive list of international, national, private, and governmental social service agencies. Also, contains list of periodicals pertaining to social work.

Facts, undated pamphlet.
Outlines functions of American Red Cross. 23rd Street, New York,

New York, 10010 Family Service Association of America, 44 East 23rd Street, New York, New York, 10010

Financial Assistance Programs for the Handicapped, Health, Education and Welfare, Government Printing Office, Washington, D.C., 20402, 1968.

Home Care Services for the Chronically Ill and Aged: An Annotated Bibliography, June, 1967. Institute of Gerontology, University of Iowa, Iowa City, Iowa, 52240

International Social Service, American Branch, Inc., 345 East 46th Street, New York, New York, 10017
I.S.S. is an international case work organization. The American Branch accepts referrals where intercountry case work service is needed to serve clients. I.S.S. assists in cases of adoption, child care, reunion of families, and other personal problems. All correspondence should be sent in triplicate.

LOVEJOY, CLARENCE E.—*Vocational School Guide,* New York, Simon and Schuster. Brought up to date every two or three years.
Lists vocational training sources both public and private in the United States.

National Association of Shelter Workshops and Homebound Programs, 1522 K Street, N.W., Washington, D.C., 20006
Association has up-to-date information about existing and proposed programs in given communities.

National Association of Social Workers, 2 Park Avenue, New York, New York, 10016
Publishes *Encyclopedia of Social Services.*

National Council on Alcoholism, 2 Park Avenue, New York, New York, 10016

National Directory of Private Social Agencies, Social Service Publications, 211-03 Jamaica Avenue, Queen's Village, New York, 11428

National Information Bureau, 205 East 42nd Street, New York, New York, 10017
Publishes bulletins on giving to charities.

The People Book, 1969: Directory of Health, Welfare, Education, Recreational and Vocational Services in Orange County, Community Referral Information Service, P.O. Box 355, Santa Ana, California, 92702

Probation and Parole Directory, United States and Canada, 1971 edition in preparation. National Council on Crime and Delinquency, 44 East 23rd Street, New York, New York, 10010

The Public Welfare Directory, 1969, American Public Welfare Association, 1313 East 60th Street, Chicago, Illinois, 60637
Directory contains lists of state welfare, mental health, and child welfare agencies, federal service agencies and Canadian agencies.

Red Cross Services and Programs, A.R.C. pamphlet No. 565, October, 1968.

Service Directory of the National Organizations Affiliated and Associated with the Assembly, Social Welfare Assembly, Inc., 345 East 46th Street, New York, New York, 10017
Contains information on approximately 500 Health and Welfare member organizations.

Service Directory of National Organizations—Welfare, Health, Recreation, National Assembly for Social Policy Development, Inc., 345 East 46th Street, New York, New York, 10017, (Biennial).

State Welfare Agencies
These agencies can be contacted and will supply information on a number of items such as mental health programs, child protective service, homes for the aged, and other community service information. The address of each state agency can be found in *The Public Welfare Directory, 1969*, cited above.

Travelers' Aid Society, located in most cities.
Will provide information on local case work services, emergency housing, and community resources.

"Treatment Services for Persons Suffering from Drug Problems," *California's One-Ten System Service*, Vo. II, No. 3, February 15, 1971, pp. 4–5.
County by county directory of community services for drug abusers in California.

United Community Funds and Councils of America, 345 East 46th Street, New York, New York, 10017
Publishes *Directory of Community Chests, Funds, and Councils*.

United States Bureau of Family Services, Washington, D.C.
Will provide information on government efforts to improve the conditions of the poor in America.

United States Government Organization Manual, Washington, D.C., Superintendent of Documents, Government Printing Office, April, 1969.

WEAVER, JOHN D.—"Help!", *West* Magazine, *Los Angeles Times*, August 2, 1970, p. 14.
Contains extensive list—name, address, phone number—of help agencies in Los Angeles County. Exhaustive number of categories.

General Sources

Archdiocese
Will frequently publish Catholic directory on community services and activities.

Assistance League of (Community Name).
Activities include family/marital counseling, parent/child relationships, social adjustment counseling, counseling on unplanned pregnancies and offers consultation services regarding community resources.

(Name of State) Association for Health and Welfare
Statewide membership group whose function is to bring together individuals and organizations interested in improving health and welfare. Membership list is excellent source.

Boys' Club
Activities include guidance, hobbies, athletics, and long and short camping trips. Directors are aware of community resources.

Chambers of Commerce and Junior Chambers
Will often publish directory of members which frequently include public and private social service agencies. They will generally know what service projects member organizations are involved in.

Community Coordinating Councils
These groups provide a cross section of organizations whose interests and activities are devoted to local needs.

Community Planning Councils
Will maintain liaison with area-wide social, civic, economic, and planning organizations.

Community Volunteer Offices
Generally, these groups are acquainted with a wide range of community clubs, agencies, and organizations.

Directories
Local welfare directories listing community services are published by different agencies. These are frequently entitled Community Referral Information Service, Community Planning Councils, Local Welfare Offices, Community Welfare Council, and the like.

Economic Developments or Opportunity Agencies
Will have information on employment opportunities, vocational training, and adult education programs.

Ecumenical Councils

These organizations can be found in most communities and they sometimes publish directories of members, community services, and activities.

Family Crisis Prevention Centers

Will have information on a wide variety of mental health resources.

Family Service Departments

Will have information on case work services to families and individuals, financial assistance, services to individuals in correctional institutions, missing persons, and emergency housing.

Free Clinics

Every urban area has a number of free clinics. These centers offer a variety of services to needy people. Their clientele, however, is composed largely of young people in their teens and twenties. The services offered at these clinics can include psychological counseling, medical and dental help, group therapy, advice on problem pregnancies, legal assistance, birth control and family planning, help with drug withdrawal, employment, public assistance, emergency food, clothing, shelter, and transportation services, runaway intervention service, and 24-hour crisis intervention service. In addition, many clinics have a speaker's bureau whereby the goals, functions, and services of the clinic can be explained in detail.

Local Health Departments

Clinics will either offer direct help or make referrals. They will offer wide range of physical and mental health services. Good source of information.

Midnight Mission

Director will generally know of employment opportunities, health and mental health clinics, and other sources.

Psychiatric Associations

Will publish directory of members.

Religious Denominations

Different religions will frequently publish a list of churches in given areas.

State Departments of Corrections

Under various titles, they generally will publish a *Directory of Correctional Services* in their states.

State Departments of Mental Hygiene

Will publish list of local clinics and services performed.

State Departments of Public Health
Will publish list of hospitals, homes, child care and related facilities.

State Departments of Rehabilitation
Will publish directory of services.

State Printing Offices
Generally will publish laws and codes relating to welfare in each state.

State Private Institution Bureau
Generally state licensing agency which issues licenses for private agencies handling mental illness, mental retardation, disturbed children, alcoholism, etc.

State Welfare Agencies
Generally will publish information on maternity homes, retirement homes, child placement agencies, mental health agencies, laws regarding child welfare, child adoption, publishers lists of licensed public and private institutions for the aged.

Suicide Prevention Centers
Will have information on a wide variety of mental health resources.

Underground Press
This faction of the news media publishes a wide variety of newspapers and magazines. Most of them will publish lists of places to go for emergency help. For example, the Los Angeles *Free Press* publishes a list each week containing information on where to go for legal help, ecology groups, abortions, free clinics, gay liberation, public assistance offices, mental health hotlines, hitchhikers international, poverty centers, rumor control offices, LSD rescue centers, free stores, and employment opportunities.

INDEX